"Len Sperry's second edition of *Family Assessment: Contemporary and Cutting-Edge Strategies* is the only student-, counselor-, and therapist-friendly book on the market today. In addition to being the most comprehensive text on systemic approaches, the organization of the later chapters will perfectly facilitate the development of a large repertoire of assessment options. There is simply no other book better suited to the teaching and learning of family assessment."

—James Robert Bitter, EdD, professor of counseling at East Tennessee State University and author of *Theory and Practice of Family Therapy and Counseling*

"Assessment is no longer a choice, nor is it a component separate from diagnostic and treatment procedures. In this valuable book, Dr. Sperry and his excellent selection of contributors provide a comprehensive focus on what clinicians need to conduct an evaluation and develop on-going treatment plans for couples and families. The evidence-based approaches to measurement—quantitative, qualitative, observational and/or self- report, among others—offer the necessary challenge to the standard protocols and help clinicians be effective throughout the treatment process."

—S. Richard Sauber, PhD, editor of *The American Journal of Family Therapy* and former professor of psychology at Brown University, Columbia University, and the University of Pennsylvania

"In this comprehensive volume, Sperry brings together many of the leaders in the realm of family assessment. *Family Assessment* is an important book for all who believe effective treatment is based on sound assessment and diagnosis."

—Florence Kaslow, PhD, editor of the *Handbook of Relational Diagnosis and Dysfunctional Family Patterns*

"Sperry's work is a lucid gateway to a myriad of assessment strategies and inventories. It is a work that is exceptional in depth, breadth, and practical utility. A unique and important contribution to the field! I recommend it highly."

—Craig S. Cashwell, PhD, professor in the department of counseling and educational development at the University of North Carolina-Greensboro and coeditor of *Integrating Spirituality and Religion into Counseling: A Guide to Competent Practice*

"In this thorough and accessible text, Sperry and his associates provide comprehensive coverage and explanation of family-assessment methods. Although the book as a whole is well done, the case examples that accompany the various assessment tools are particularly valuable. Both clinici ing and seasoned practitioners will experience this book as a use for understanding and applying assessment strategies in clinical p families, couples, and children."

—Richard E. Watts, PhD, LPC-S, University Distinguished Professor tor of the Center for Research and Doctoral Studies in Counselor Ec Sam Houston State University

"Clear, purposeful, and targeted assessment when working with families is what makes or breaks successful treatment. Len Sperry's most recent gem, *Family Assessment: Contemporary and Cutting-Edge Strategies*, is both the foundation and details of this critical element of family work. This volume is a must for practitioners, researchers, and students alike."

—Bret A. Moore, PsyD, editor of *Handbook of Counseling Military Couples* and author of *Wheels Down: Adjusting to Life After Deployment*

"*Family Assessment: Contemporary and Cutting-Edge strategies* is an ideal desk reference for family clinicians and clinical researchers, as this compendium offers a wealth of information about state-of-the-art quantitative and qualitative approaches to assessing families across the family-life cycle with myriad presenting problems. It also will appeal to teachers and students of interventions with both couples and families, as the distinguished authors detail over 130 assessment tools, documenting their psychometric properties and clinical and research utility. The richness and diversity of the clinical material provided makes family-assessment processes come alive."

— Nadine J. Kaslow, PhD, professor and vice chair in the department of psychiatry and behavioral sciences at Emory University School of Medicine

"Assessment is one of the most crucial aspects of conducting effective family therapy. This book is an outstanding resource that provides both a general and specific array of empirically grounded techniques for clinicians and researchers. It is written in clear and concise language and provides excellent examples that serve as a guideline for readers. This text should be a part of every family therapist's library. I also highly recommend its use for classroom adoption."

—Frank M. Dattilio, PhD, clinical instructor in psychiatry at the Harvard Medical School and author of *Cognitive-Behavioral Therapy with Couples and Families: A Comprehensive Guide for Clinicians*

Family Assessment

THE FAMILY THERAPY AND COUNSELING SERIES

Series Editor
Jon Carlson, Psy.D., Ed.D.

Kit S. Ng
Global Perspectives in Family Therapy: Development, Practice, Trends

Phyllis Erdman and Tom Caffery
Attachment and Family Systems: Conceptual, Empirical, and Therapeutic Relatedness

Wes Crenshaw
Treating Families and Children in the Child Protective System

Len Sperry
Assessment of Couples and Families: Contemporary and Cutting-Edge Strategies

Robert L. Smith and R. Esteban Montilla
Counseling and Family Therapy with Latino Populations: Strategies that Work

Catherine Ford Sori
Engaging Children in Family Therapy: Creative Approaches to Integrating Theory and Research in Clinical Practice

Paul R. Peluso
Infidelity: A Practitioner's Guide to Working with Couples in Crisis

Jill D. Onedera
The Role of Religion in Marriage and Family Counseling

Christine Kerr, Janice Hoshino, Judith Sutherland, Sharyl Parashak, and Linda McCarley
Family Art Therapy

Debra D. Castaldo
Divorced Without Children: Solution Focused Therapy with Women at Midlife

Phyllis Erdman and Kok-Mun Ng
Attachment: Expanding the Cultural Connections

Jon Carlson and Len Sperry
Recovering Intimacy in Love Relationships: A Clinician's Guide

Adam Zagelbaum and Jon Carlson
Working with Immigrant Families: A Practical Guide for Counselors

David K. Carson and Montserrat Casado-Kehoe
Case Studies in Couples Therapy: Theory-Based Approaches

Shea M. Dunham, Shannon B. Dermer, and Jon Carlson
Poisonous Parenting: Toxic Relationships Between Parents and Their Adult Children

Bret A. Moore
Handbook of Counseling Military Couples

Len Sperry
Family Assessment: Contemporary and Cutting-Edge Strategies, 2nd ed.

Family Assessment

Contemporary and Cutting-Edge Strategies

SECOND EDITION

Edited by Len Sperry

Routledge
Taylor & Francis Group
New York   London

This book is part of the Family Therapy and Counseling Series, edited by Jon Carlson.

Routledge
Taylor & Francis Group
711 Third Avenue
New York, NY 10017

Routledge
Taylor & Francis Group
27 Church Road
Hove, East Sussex BN3 2FA

© 2012 by Taylor & Francis Group, LLC
Routledge is an imprint of Taylor & Francis Group, an Informa business

Version Date: 20110831

International Standard Book Number: 978-0-415-89406-7 (Hardback) 978-0-415-89407-4 (Paperback)

Library of Congress Cataloging-in-Publication Data

Family assessment : contemporary and cutting-edge strategies / [edited by] Len Sperry. -- 2nd ed.
p. cm. -- (Family therapy and counseling)
Rev. ed of: Assessment of couples and families. 2004.
Summary: "In an era that demands ever-increasing levels of accountability and documentation, Family Assessment is a vital tool for clinicians. It covers more than one hundred assessment methods--both the most widely used strategies as well as those that are more specialized and issue specific. Techniques and instruments for assessments are summarized concisely in tables and discussed in depth in the chapters, often by the experts who developed the approaches they describe. Each chapter is also supplemented by recommended strategies for utilizing the assessment tools, as well as by case studies and observational method matrices. Readers will find the second edition of Family Assessment to provide the same comprehensive evaluation and thorough analysis as the first edition but with a fully updated focus that will invigorate the work of researchers, educators, and clinicians"-- Provided by publisher.
Includes bibliographical references and index.
ISBN 978-0-415-89406-7 (hardback) -- ISBN 978-0-415-89407-4 (paperback)
1. Family assessment. 2. Marital psychotherapy. 3. Family psychotherapy. 4. Couples--Psychology. I. Sperry, Len. II. Assessment of couples and families.

RC488.53.A875 2011
616.89'1562--dc23
2011029454

Visit the Taylor & Francis Web site at
http://www.taylorandfrancis.com

and the Routledge Web site at
http://www.routledgementalhealth.com

This book is again dedicated to the memory of the late Kenneth I. Howard, Ph.D., a cherished mentor, colleague, and friend, and a major figure in psychological evaluation and clinical outcomes research.

Contents

Series Editor's Foreword

"For every complex question there is a
simple answer—and it is wrong"

H.L. Mencken

Effective assessment allows the clinician to understand the presenting problem as well as to assess the effectiveness of treatment. Additionally, it is well accepted that inaccurate assessment leads to treatment failure as well as continuation of ineffective treatment practice. Partly for this reason, the first edition of this book has been one of the most popular in the Family Therapy and Counseling Series.

The changing population demographics make effective assessment strategies essential. The traditional couple or family with two opposite gender parents and two children accounts for only 25 percent of the population. Singles, same-sex couples, grandparents living with children are examples of the changing landscape. The instruments provided in this book allow the clinician to quickly assess and document family factors and dynamics.

This book (like the first edition) provides strategies for how to use assessment methods and measures with a wide range of issues that face children, adolescents, couples and families. Chapters include qualitative assessment, standardized assessment, observational assessment, and ongoing assessment. Additional chapters focus on assessing couples, child and adolescent strategies, parent-child strategies, child custody and divorce assessment, and child abuse inventories. The second edition also provides an easy to use matrix that summarizes the important information on each of the 130 instruments.

I again thank Len Sperry and his collaborators for this updated volume that provides the information that has been missing in our professional training.

Jon Carlson, PsyD, EdD
Distinguished Professor
Governors State University

Foreword

The field of couple and family therapy began with two broad foci: the building of a systemic theory applicable to families and the creation of innovative family-centered methods of intervention. This earliest era in family therapy was a time of "big" ideas (e.g., epistemology, systems theory, and cybernetics) that challenged the individual-centered paradigm that prevailed at the time. In this context, the systemic paradigm was presented as the explanation for all psychopathology (and for that matter for most human behavior) and family intervention was seen as the antidote for all human problems.

Although the positive impact of the systemic revolution cannot be overstated (having changed the fundamental way most mental health professionals view the social context in relation to individual behavior), it is striking that this early work in family systems theory and family intervention occurred devoid of the development of any technology for measuring couple or family process. Without such a technology, those interested in understanding the processes within couples and families were left to rely completely on their own observational skills and those of their colleagues for data testing their hypotheses. Given this, it is not surprising that, despite the considerable time and energy devoted to efforts to observe families in that era, family process remained very much in the eye of the beholder, subject to the idiosyncrasies of individual observation and construction. And many alternative strong arguments emerged about how these "data" from families provided evidence in support of various theoretical vantage points about what was essential to "healthy" family process, leading to widely disparate viewpoints about what was crucial in the lives of these families. Using these "data," proponents of each approach could look at families through their particular lens, and present convincing arguments for the accuracy of their particular vantage point.

The hindsight of history indicates that this state of affairs allowed for the emergence and development of many vital core insights, such as the importance of the social system on individual functioning and of circular arcs of causality. But it also led to the promulgation and wide dissemination of several regrettable errors, such as claims that double binds by mothers caused schizophrenia and the vision of a mutually shared co-creation of family violence. For all of the dramatic and important insights of the first generation of family therapists, the emergence of a true science of family relationships required the development of a body of methods for assessing couples and families.

Such instruments are core elements for building both a science of family process and science based clinical practice. Without measures, we are left without the means to operationalize key independent and dependent variables in research and, thus, to test hypotheses. Clinical practice is no less limited without instrumentation, lacking in methods of assessment to enable case formulation and to track treatment progress.

Unfortunately, the technology of instrumentation evolves slowly. Instruments first need to go through a stage of development to tap the core constructs within a domain, then need to be shown to be reliable and valid, and then must be normed on a large enough and sufficiently diverse sample, and finally to be marketed in a form that allows for dissemination. A good instrument often takes a decade to develop; some of the best in this volume have evolved over decades.

Furthermore, the technology of instrumentation requires a diversity of instruments. Self-report measures and those completed by raters serve different purposes and typically show less than perfect convergence, so that both types of measures are needed. There also are needs for brief measures and longer ones to serve different purposes, for measures of general couple and family functioning and for measures that are targeted to more specific aspects of family life (e.g., domestic violence), and for measures that easily translate into scale scores and for other measures that provide a wider range of qualitative information in the way of open-ended responses.

Family Assessment: Contemporary and Cutting-Edge Strategies, second edition, marks the progress that has been made in instrumentation for assessing couples and families. Its publication points to the emergence of a body of high-quality measures and methods for assessment that are now in an advanced stage of development in what has become a mature field. Bringing together experts in different areas of family assessment, this volume covers the breadth of methods for assessing couples and families. It includes a thorough consideration of both observational and self-report measures, quantitative and qualitative measures, and single time and progress research usage of measures. Several chapters cover measures specifically constructed for assessing couples and families, while other chapters provide a guide to applying measures developed to assess individual functioning in children and adults in the context of looking at couple and family functioning. Specific chapters summarize assessment in the frequently encountered contexts of divorce and child custody, child abuse, parent-child relationships, couple relationships, and problems in children and adolescents. Each chapter provides guidelines for how to employ the measures described, thorough information about the assessment method, and an illuminating clinical example of how assessment is applied in the particular domain.

The large number of sophisticated and well-constructed measures and methods described in this volume speak to the advance of measurement assessing couples and families. This advance runs parallel to and merges with the greater sophistication of the newest generation of couple and family therapies and of the most recent research on couple and family process. The measures and methods surveyed in this volume now can serve admirably to anchor research focused on couples and families and in the clinical assessment and in the ongoing tracking of progress in treatment. These measures and methods can also be used as the foundation for the kind of sophisticated assessment that can provide the basis for the development of the relational diagnoses of the future.

This important book will surely become, like the first edition, a core resource for students, practicing clinicians, and family researchers. Family Assessment: Contemporary and Cutting-Edge Strategies in its second edition marks the now highly evolved state of the art and science of methods and instrumentation for assessing couples and families.

Jay Lebow, PhD, ABPP
Evanston, IL
September 2011

Preface*

The field of family, child, and couples assessment continues to evolve and change since the first edition of this book appeared in 2004. This edition is a thoroughly revised and updated resource for anyone working with children, adolescents, couples, and families. It provides an in-depth description of an even larger number of sophisticated assessment tools and methods, including issue-specific tools, self-report inventories, standardized inventories, qualitative measures, and observational methods. Like the first edition, it provides strategies for systematically utilizing these various assessment methods and measures with a wide range of family dynamics that influence couples and families. These include couples conflict, divorce, separation, mediation, premarital decisions, parenting conflicts, child abuse, family violence, and custody evaluation. A new chapter has been added, which addresses various child and adolescent conditions (depression, anxiety, conduct disorder, bipolar disorder, obsessive compulsive disorder, autism, Asperger's syndrome, and learning disorders) that can significantly influence family dynamics.

This second edition brings together in a single publication the most common and important assessment tools and strategies for addressing problematic clinical issues related to working with families, couples, and children. Chapters 2 through 10 include a matrix that summarizes pertinent information on all instruments reviewed in that chapter. This feature allows the readers to instantly compare more than 130 assessment devices. Finally, it provides extensive clinical case material that illustrates the use of these various assessment tools and strategies in a wide array of clinical situations. In short, *Family Assessment: Contemporary and Cutting-Edge Strategies* (2nd ed.) will be useful to both trainees and practitioners as a ready reference on assessment measures and strategies for working with families, couples, and children.

---

* The use of most of the inventories featured in this book are well within the scope of practice of licensed marriage and family therapists, mental health counselors, and other professional clinicians. However, there are a few standardized psychological instruments such as the MMPI-2, MCMI-III, and the Rorschach that, while they can be of immense clinical value, do require formal training and licensure as a psychologist, in most states, to legally and ethically administer, score, and interpret them.

Contributors

Dennis A. Bagarozzi, Sr., PhD, Private Practice, St. Simons Island, Georgia

W. Robert Beavers, MD, Director Emeritus, Family Studies Center, University of Texas Southwestern Medical Center, Dallas, Texas

Ronald J. Chenail, PhD, Professor of Family Therapy, Nova Southeastern University, Fort Lauderdale, Florida

Lisa Connelly, MA, CCRP, Senior Clinical Research Coordinator, Mayerson Center for Safe & Healthy Children, Cincinnati Children's Hospital Medical Center, Cincinnati, Ohio

Alexandra Cunningham, M Ed, LMHC, Assistant Director of the Florida Atlantic University Center for Autism and Related Disabilities, Boca Raton, Florida

Maureen Duffy, PhD, Family Therapist, Consultant, and President of the International Institute for Human Understanding

M. Sylvia Fernandez, PhD, Professor & Chair, Counseling Department, Barry University, Miami Shores, Florida

Robert B. Hampson, PhD, Associate Professor of Psychology, Southern Methodist University Dallas, Texas

Luciano L'Abate, PhD, Professor Emeritus of Psychology at Georgia State University, Atlanta, Georgia

A. Rodney Nurse, PhD, ABPP, Psychologist, US Coast Guard Training Base, Petaluma, California

Erna Olafson, PhD, PsyD, Associate Professor of Clinical Psychiatry and Pediatrics, Cincinnati Children's Hospital Medical Center and the University of Cincinnati College of Medicine

Jack Scott, Ph.D., BCBA-D, Executive Director of the Florida Atlantic University Center for Autism and Related Disabilities, Boca Raton, Florida

Sloane E. Veshinski, MS, Clinical Director, The Sloane Center, Inc., Hollywood, Florida

Lynelle C. Yingling, PhD, Owner, J&L Human Systems Development

CHAPTER 1

Family Assessment
An Overview

Len Sperry

THE REALITY OF CLINICAL PRACTICE TODAY

Today, many clinicians are increasingly being referred for or called on to deal with critical clinical treatment issues that require a working knowledge of couple and family assessment resources. These referrals may involve various challenges such as suitability for marriage, marital separation, divorce, mediation, family violence, and child custody for which couple and family assessment data and/or methods and strategies would be useful or essential. Unfortunately, graduate education in clinical psychology and counseling primarily trains clinicians to work with individual clients and conceptualize cases in terms of individual personality dynamics rather than in terms of systemic or couple and family dynamics. Accordingly, many have not had formal coursework, training, or supervised experience in couple and family assessment. Even those who have completed degrees in marital and family therapy may not have received much in the way of formal training and supervised experience in formally assessing couples and families. Thus, the discussion in this and subsequent chapters can be helpful in addressing such clinical considerations as marital issues, family violence, or child custody.

This book provides a general framework for couple and family assessment and an overview of various types of general and specific strategies for systematically and effectively collecting and coordinating interview data, self-report inventories, observational methods, collateral information, and so forth, into the process of treatment planning and intervention. This chapter introduces the topic of couple and family assessment as an extension of individual assessment. It notes the diversity of views about assessment among the various family therapy approaches and considers whether formal family assessment is basically incompat-ible with such contemporary family approaches as narrative therapy and related social constructionist systems. It then provides a map of subse-quent chapters by providing an overview of the issues and assessment methods and strategies that clinicians need to work effectively with indi-viduals, couples, and families, emphasizing the psychometric properties of reliability and validity.

FROM INDIVIDUAL ASSESSMENT TO FAMILY ASSESSMENT

Why should a clinician be concerned with assessing family factors and dynamics, particularly if he or she is working primarily or entirely with individuals? A related question is whether family assessment (and, for that matter, couples assessment) is only of value to those conducting family therapy. This book endeavors to describe and illustrate the value of utilizing couple and family assessment for those who practice indi-vidual therapy as well as those who work therapeutically with couples and families.

The past few decades have witnessed a major shift in clinical assess-ment—from an exclusive focus on assessing personal attributes and indi-vidual pathology (i.e., symptoms and impaired functioning) to a greater awareness of the value of considering how family attributes, relationship patterns, systemic distress, and impaired functioning affect an individ-ual's attitudes, behaviors, distress, and level of functioning. The reasons for this shift in thinking are many, although a principal reason is the recognition that an individual is inseparable from the system, which is the site of pathology.

Diagnosis means "to know," and understanding a problem situation can be called diagnosing. The process of diagnosing starts with observ-ing data, forming concepts about the situation, and finally arranging the information in a particular way. All therapists have an epistemologi-cal base, and clinicians will diagnose differently according to this base (L'Abate, Ganahl, & Hansen, 1986, p. 34).

A traditional, nonsystemic epistemology, which is the basis of the medical model, focuses on combining discrete clinician observations and individual dynamics; a systemic epistemology, which is the basis of fam-ily systems thinking, focuses on the whole system, including relational dynamics. In systemic assessment, diagnosis depends on the clinician's observation and elicitation of relational functioning, patterns, and styles rather than simply on the diagnostic criteria and individual symptoms and impairment characteristic of DSM-IV-TR diagnostic thinking. "By bringing more people into therapy who are involved in the relational field of the identified patient, family therapy and diagnosis has moved more to the idea that the person within the system is part of the relationship system" (L'Abate et al., 1986, p. 34). In short, from a systemic perspective, an adequate assessment and diagnosis of an individual must necessarily involve the entire family system.

DIFFERING VIEWS OF COUPLE AND FAMILY ASSESSMENT

Even though a systemic epistemology informs assessment and diagnosis in family therapy, it cannot be concluded that those who practice family therapy have reached a consensus about what constitutes appropriate and effective couple and family assessment. Nor does a consensus exist on training therapists in family assessment. Although some training programs in marital and family therapy provide students and trainees with formal instruction and supervision in using formal assessment methods with couples and families, others do not. This is not to say that assessment is less important in some approaches but rather that it is different. Why is this? Some insight into this query comes about by examining and comparing the place of assessment in the major approaches to family therapy. In a comparison of seven such approaches (behavioral, structural, strategic, Bowenian, experiential, solution focused, and collaborative), Yingling, Miller, McDonald, and Galwaler (1998) noted that each of these diverse approaches adopts a uniquely different theoretical perspective that "determines" which factors and variables are indicative of functionality or dysfunctionality; therefore, it should not be too surprising that what is assessed and how and when it is assessed in the course of treatment varies considerably from approach to approach. For example, formal assessment and history taking are essential in behavioral family therapy, but neither is typically a part of experiential family therapy. Nevertheless, assessment "is a natural part of the (experiential family) therapy process. It is accomplished through information given by the family as the therapist becomes acquainted with them as a group and individually" (L'Abate et al., 1986, p. 38). Furthermore, although goals and clinical outcomes are specified in terms of changes in family structure and boundaries in structural family therapy, outcomes that evaluate the efficacy of the relationship of family and therapists are more important in collaborative approaches. The question becomes, Is an integrative approach to couple and family assessment possible? Many believe that such an approach will be possible to the extent that a set of common factors and dynamics involved in relational functioning is forthcoming.

Two encouraging developments in this regard are efforts to create a uniform system of relational diagnosis, the so-called Classification of Relational Disorders (CORD) that originated in the GAP Committee on the Family (Kaslow, 1996), and the introduction of the Global Assessment of Relational Functioning (GARF) into DSM-IV (1994) and DSM-IV-TR (2000).

Family Assessment and Narrative and Social Constructionist Therapies

Striking at the very heart of family assessment is the concern that formal family assessment is incompatible with narrative and social constructionist therapies. Some would agree, claiming that formal assessment is a modernist convention focused on objective "truth" and as such is incompatible with a social constructivist, postmodern view. Some family assessment models, that is, the Beavers family systems model and its assessment methods, the Beavers Interactional Scales, and the Self-Report Family Inventory (SFI), have much in common with structural family therapy and related approaches; however, the traditional use of these models and related assessment methods appear to have little in common with narrative and other constructivist approaches. Nevertheless, Carr (2000) would contend that family assessment models like the Beavers model can easily be viewed as social constructions. Assessment models and methods that "have been found to be useful for solving problems, the hallmark of a valid social construction" (Carr, 2000, p. 127), can be compatible with social constructivism, depending on how they are utilized.

For example, scores on the SFI can be used, not as global knowledge of a family's or family member's cohesiveness or conflict but rather as specific, local knowledge and insights that a particular client might consider. Thus, it is one thing for a therapist to share assessment feedback and indicate that coaching, problem solving, and communication skills might reduce the sense of distress and help solve presenting concerns more efficiently. It is another to imply or state the truth that the client is a poor communicator or poor problem solver. Finally, Carr notes that a commitment to social constructionism as a framework for clinical practice does not preclude a commitment to quantitative research grounded in empirical models of family functioning.

RECENT DEVELOPMENTS IN FAMILY ASSESSMENT

Since the publication of the first edition of this book, there have been a few noteworthy developments in the assessment of families. Perhaps the most obvious is the increasing number of assessment devices aimed at children, adolescents, and parent–child relations. There have been increases in the number of instruments on children and adolescent functioning (in several areas including academic achievement, psychopathology, personality, and social relations) as well as parenting that are available in the public domain and without cost. These are mostly in journal articles or researcher websites. However, an even larger number of these assessment devices are proprietary and involve a fee for its use. Assessment devices that have national norms are in high demand today. While academic researchers have and continue to produce useful instruments, they seldom have the financial resources to develop such norms. Because test publishers have such resources they have been able to develop such norms. As a result, they are cashing in on the need for standardized instruments on various considerations of children and adolescents as well as child–parent relations. School counselors, school psychologists, forensic psychologists, and other clinicians have become ready consumers for instruments that have solid national norms, are culturally sensitive, and are acceptable in juvenile and family courts.

INDICATIONS FOR UTILIZING ASSESSMENT WITH COUPLES AND FAMILIES

Providing treatment or recommendations without adequate assessment can be problematic. Clinicians need to know where the couple or family has been, is now, and what direction they want to go. By understanding couples and families and their concerns, clinicians are more likely to intervene in helpful ways. In other words, assessment is both an event and a process. Couples and family assessment can be done for general or specific indications.

As a general indication, assessment is a guide and rationale for couple or family treatment, and it can become an intervention in and of itself. Assessment can clarify issues, specify symptomatic distress, identify level of impairment, and identify the goals and focus of treatment. As an intervention, clinicians can use assessment to support and validate couples and families as well as encourage their involvement in the treatment process. Accordingly, clinicians use assessment to welcome families into the treatment process and join with them, to give them feedback, to validate their concerns, and to engender hope. By asking questions, clinicians intervene by prompting couples and family members to think about issues and relationships in different ways. Finally, clinicians can use assessment techniques to track ongoing progress, re-evaluate goals, and stay in touch with the couple's or family's changing context and self-evaluation.

Specifically, assessment is used to address particular questions. These include the following: Has child abuse or domestic abuse occurred and what are the effects? Is divorce inevitable or can couples therapy help? Is divorce mediation indicated? What is the most appropriate custody arrangement when children are involved? Chapters 6 through 9 address such indications and considerations.

TYPES OF MEASURES

Five broad types of measures are described and illustrated in this book. These are qualitative assessment, standardized assessment, observational assessment, ongoing assessment, and self-report assessment. This section briefly describes each.

Qualitative Assessment

Qualitative assessment is a type of evaluation that yields subjective data and narratives derived from unstructured methods of data collection, naturalistic observation, and existing records. In contrast to quantitative assessment, its methods tend to be holistic and integrated. Compared with standardized tests, qualitative assessment offers a more active role for clients, a more intimate connection between assessment and the treatment process, and greater adaptability to ethnic, cultural, age, gender, and other individual differences (Goldman, 1992). Qualitative methods are well suited for use with couples and families as they can foster mutuality, participation, and commitment and support communication and understanding in the treatment process. Examples of qualitative assessment range from unstructured interviewing and role playing to genograms and other graphic methods, such as photographs and collages. Chapter 2 provides a detailed discussion and illustration of qualitative assessment with families and couples.

Standardized Assessment

Standardized assessment is distinguished from other assessment types by the objectivity with which data are collected and analyzed and by its validity, reliability, and norms based on a large representative sample of the population. For many, the mention of standardized assessment brings to mind intelligence tests, such as the Wechsler Adult Intelligence Scale

(WAIS), and personality inventories, such as the Minnesota Multiphasic Personality Inventory (MMPI), the Millon Clinical Multiaxial Inventory (MCMI), and the Millon Adolescent Clinical Inventory (MACI). However, there are several other instruments that are standardized or normed on large populations. These include the Rorschach, particularly the Exner-based system, and drawing tests, such as the Draw-A-Person test and Kinetic Family Drawing. While such instruments are considered devices for assessing individuals, they are also used in specific family situations, particularly child custody evaluations. A common assessment battery in child custody situations includes the MMPI-2, the MCMI-III, the Rorschach, and the Kinetic Family Drawing test. Chapter 3 provides a detailed discussion and illustration of the use of standardized assessment with families and couples.

Observational Assessment

Observational assessment is a type of evaluation in which observers are trained to watch and record individual, couple, or family behavior with accuracy and precision but without personal bias or interpretation. To facilitate comparisons between families, it is common to establish a specific task to be performed by each family. The form of the task chosen should reflect common problematic situations in average family life (e.g., discussing how to solve a discipline problem with a child or adolescent). Video recording, tape recorders, one-way mirrors, and other devices may be used to increase accuracy. The McMaster Clinical Rating Scale is one such observational rating instrument that is based on the McMaster Model of Family Functioning (Epstein et al., 2003). Chapter 4 provides a detailed discussion and illustration of the use of observational assessment methods with families and couples.

Ongoing Assessment

Ongoing assessment is a type of evaluation in which assessment is viewed as a continuous process throughout treatment rather than as a single or pre–post measure of individual, couple, or family functioning. Also called continuous assessment, treatment monitoring, and serial clinical outcomes assessment (Sperry, 2010), ongoing assessment influences the direction of treatment in two ways. First, goals identified during the initial assessment may need to be modified to meet the changing needs of the client system. Second, ongoing assessment assists in increasing treatment efficacy and efficiency by providing the clinician immediate feedback, which can alter the focus on direction of interventions. Using such feedback to refocus and modify treatment actually increases treatment outcomes and reduces premature termination (Lambert, 2010). The Self-Report Family Inventory (SFI) and the Dyadic Adjustment Scale are two commonly used instruments for continuous assessment of families and couples. Chapter 5 provides a detailed discussion and illustration of ongoing assessment with families and couples.

Self-Report Assessment

Self-report measures are the most common means of assessing couple and family factors. Self-report measures include perceptions of the family by individual family members, ratings by family members of other family members' behavior or relationships, and self-reports of affect and emotions while engaging in certain behaviors. The value of self-report measures over other types of assessment is the ease with which ratings of partners or individual family members can be compared to ratings of the other partner or other family members regarding treatment issues. In the past decade, rapid assessment instruments were increasingly being utilized by clinicians.

Rapid Assessment Instruments. In this age of accountability, clinicians face increased demands to demonstrate the effectiveness of their evaluations and interventions. This can be accomplished with the use of rapid assessment instruments to measure a client's attitudes, beliefs, or level of functioning so that any subsequent change in functioning can be accurately detected over time. Rapid assessment instruments are typically short, self-report inventories for collecting information from couples or family members. These instruments are primarily in paper and pencil format and are usually quite easy and fast to administer and to score. The greater majority of measures described in Chapters 6 through 10 are of this type.

THE STRUCTURE OF SUBSEQUENT CHAPTERS

There is a common structure underlying Chapters 6 through 10. It addresses both an assessment strategy for a particular area of family assessment, for example, child custody and divorce, as well as the use of specific methods and inventories. The purpose of the assessment strategy is to provide the reader with a specific plan and protocol for planning and implementing the assessment of a specific family or couple issue. This seven- to eight-step strategy reflects the way experts in the field think about the process of assessment from deciding on assessment methods and inventories to making recommendations and providing feedback to clients. It is then illustrated with an extended case example. A selection of the most useful and available assessment methods and inventories is provided with an outline common in each of these chapters. The outline is the following:

Instrument Name
Type of Instrument
Use-Target Audience
Multicultural/Translations
Ease and Time of Administration
Scoring Procedure
Reliability
Validity
Availability and Source
Comment

The purpose of this reader-friendly outline is to facilitate a rapid comparison of instruments from section to section and chapter to chapter. The following five-point structure (I through V) incorporates both the assessment strategy and specific inventories in Chapters 6 through 10.

I. *Issues and Challenges of Assessment.* This section describes and briefly illustrates the specific clinical, legal, and ethical (if relevant) issues and challenges associated with the chapter focus. Typically, the need for assessment of couple and/or family dynamics and functioning is described along with various technical and practical issues relevant to the topic.

II. *Instruments.* This section provides a brief, clinically relevant description of a number of common inventories used by clinicians and family researchers. These instruments have been chosen because of their psychometric characteristics (i.e., reliability and validity), availability, and ease of administration. For the most part, each instrument or assessment method follows a common format. Table 1.1 summarizes this format.

III. *Strategy for Utilizing Assessment Results.* This section provides a step-by-step strategy for assessing a particular issue such as marital conflict, child custody, and so forth. For example, the assessment strategy might be (a) interview the clients, (b) administer specific inventories, (c) collect collateral data (school records, other interview data), (d) review and analyze the assessment data and various reports, (e) conceptualize the case based on the review and analysis, and

TABLE 1.1   Format for Instrument Description

Name of assessment	Indicates the authors or developers and date of publication and instrument or method revisions, if any, of the instrument or method.
Type of instrument	Indicates type and form of the instrument or method, e.g., self-report, observational, clinician-rated, standard psychological instrument, outcome measure, etc.
Use—target audience	Specifies main use and targeted client, i.e., couple, family, parent–child, child custody, etc.
Multicultural	Indicates cultural applicability of the method; specifies other available language versions besides English that are available.
Ease and time of	Characterize the ease of administration for the instrument of method, administration, i.e., easy, complicated, etc.; provides number of items and average time needed to complete the instrument; indicates if a manual is available.
Scoring procedure	Specifies the (a) method, i.e., paper and pencil, etc.; and (b) average time to score the instrument; if electronic or alternative form of administration or a computer scoring option is available, that information is indicated.
Reliability	Specifies types of reported reliability coefficients, such as test retest, internal consistency, i.e., Cronbach's alpha, and inter-rater (or scorer) reliability if applicable; also gives overall assessment: high, moderate, average, or below average reliability; if none reported, say: "no published or reported reliability data."
Validity	Specifies the types of reported validity, i.e., construct related, criterion related; if none reported, say: "no published or reported validity data."
Availability and source	Provides information on availability and source of the instrument or method; if journal article provides assessment device, then journal reference is indicated; when only commercially available, name and/or address/phone number of supplier is indicated.
Comment	Provides chapter authors with opportunity to share professional evaluations of clinical utility and value of this instrument or method.

(f) plan treatment and interventions based on these data and the conceptualization.

IV. *Case Example.* This section illustrates the use of specific instruments as well as the assessment strategy. The case material demonstrates how one or more of the specific inventories are incorporated as part of the preceding step.

V. *Inventory Matrix.* Finally, this very brief section summarizes pertinent information on all the instruments, inventories, or methods in the chapter in the form of a matrix or chart. The matrix provides the reader with a concise side-by-side comparison of each instrument.

Finally, Chapter 11 provides a critique of current family assessment methods and provides a glimpse at the future of assessment involving families and couples.

RELIABILITY AND VALIDITY: A BRIEF OVERVIEW

As just noted, the technical description of each assessment instrument or method includes data on two key psychometric properties: *reliability* and *validity*. Because major clinical recommendations such as child custody are often based on clinical assessment, it is essential that the assessment instruments and methods on which these recommended courses of action are made are highly reliable and valid. It is also necessary that the clinician be sufficiently apprised of the appropriate use and limitations of such devices.

Even though this is a text on assessment, it cannot be assumed that all readers will be sufficiently familiar with these two key psychometric properties to appreciate the technical discussion on the various inventories and assessment methods adequately. Graduate training programs in clinical psychology, counseling psychology, and family psychology are likely to require formal instruction and experience in assessment that addresses psychometric issues. However, other graduate programs, such as marital and family therapy training programs, are less likely to emphasize these concepts. Accordingly, a brief overview of the concepts of reliability will be given as well as descriptions and illustrations of various types of each.

Reliability

Reliability is the extent to which a test or any assessment procedure yields the same result when repeated. In other words, reliability is the consistency of a measurement, or the degree to which an instrument or assessment device measures the same way each time it is used under the same condition with the same individual. A measure is considered reliable if an individual's scores on the same test given twice are similar. Technically speaking, reliability is not measured but is estimated and represented as a correlation coefficient. The higher the reliability coefficient is, the more confidence one can have in the score. Reliability coefficients at or above .70 are considered adequate; those at or above .80 are considered good; those at .90 or above are considered excellent (Hambleton & Zaal, 1991). Three types of reliability can be described: test–retest, internal consistency, and interrater reliability.

- *Test–retest reliability*—the agreement of assessment measures over time. To determine it, a measure or test is repeated on the same individuals at a future date. Results are compared and correlated with the initial test to give a measure of stability. The Spearman–Brown formula is used for calculating this estimate of reliability.
- *Internal consistency*—the extent to which tests or procedures assess the same characteristic, skill, or quality. It is a measure of the precision between the observers or of the measuring instruments used in a study. This type of reliability often helps clinicians and researchers interpret data and predict the value of scores and the limits of the relationship among variables. For example, the McMaster Family Assessment Device (FAD) is a questionnaire to evaluate families in terms of seven functions including communication patterns. Analyzing the internal consistency of the FAD items on the Communications subscale reveals the extent to which items on this family assessment device actually reflect communication patterns among family members. The internal consistency of a test can be computed in different ways.
- *Split-half reliability*—a measure of internal consistency derived by correlating responses on half the test with responses to the other half.
- *Cronbach's alpha*—another, more sophisticated method. This method divides items on an instrument or measure and computes correlation values for them. Cronbach's alpha is a correlation coefficient, and the closer it is to one, the higher the reliability estimate of the assessment device.
- *Kuder-Richardson coefficient*—another means of estimating internal consistency. It is used for instruments or measures that involve dichotomous responses or items, such as yes/no, while Cronbach's alpha is used with Likert scale types of responses or items. Finally, it should be noted that the primary difference between test–retest and internal consistency estimates of reliability is that test–retest involves two administrations of the measure or instrument, whereas internal consistency methods involve only a single administration of the instrument.

- *Inter-rater reliability*—the extent to which two or more individuals (raters) agree. Inter-rater reliability addresses the consistency of the implementation of a rating system. For example, inter-rater reliability can be established in the following scenario: Two clinical supervisors are observing the same family being treated by a counseling intern through a two-way mirror. As part of the observation, each supervisor independently rates the family's functioning on the GARF Scale. One supervisor rates the family at 62 and the other at 64 (on the 1- to 100-point scale). Because inter-rater reliability is dependent on the ability of two or more observers to be consistent, it could be said that inter-rater reliability is very high in this instance.

Validity

Validity refers to the ability of an assessment device or method to measure what it is intended to measure. Whereas reliability is concerned with the accuracy of the assessment device or procedure, validity is concerned with the study's success at measuring what the researchers set out to measure. Five types of validity can be described:

- *Face validity*—concerned with how a measure or procedure appears. Does it seem like a reasonable way to gain the information? Does it seem to be well designed? Does it seem as though it will work reliably? Unlike content validity, face validity does not depend on established theories for support (Fink, 1995).
- *Criterion-related validity*, or criterion-referenced validity—used to demonstrate the accuracy of a measure or procedure by comparing it with another measure or procedure previously demonstrated to be valid. For example, a paper-and-pencil test of family functioning, the SFI, appears to measure the same family dynamics and functioning as does a related observational assessment, the Beavers Interactional Scales. By comparing the scores of family members' self-report of family functioning with the therapist's observational ratings of family functioning, the SFI was validated by using a criterion-related strategy in which self-report scores were compared to the Beavers Interactional Scales ratings.
- *Construct validity*—seeks agreement between a theoretical concept and a specific measuring device or procedure. For example, a family researcher developing a new inventory for assessing marital intimacy might spend considerable time specifying the

theoretical boundaries of the term *intimacy* and then operation-
ally defining it with specific test items or a rating schema to
achieve an acceptable level of construct validity.

- *Convergent validity* and *discriminate validity*—two subcat-
egories of construct validity. Convergent validity is the actual
general agreement among ratings, gathered independently of
one another, whereas measures should be theoretically related.
Discriminate validity is the lack of a relationship among measures
that theoretically should not be related. To understand whether
an assessment device has construct validity, three steps are followed. First, the theoretical relationships are specified. Next, the
empirical relationships between the measures of the concepts are
examined. Finally, the empirical evidence is interpreted in terms
of how it clarifies the construct validity of the particular measure
being tested (Carmines & Zeller, 1991, p. 23).

- *Content validity*—based on the extent to which a measurement
reflects the specific intended domain of content (Carmines &
Zeller, 1991, p. 20). Content validity can be illustrated using the
following example: Family researchers attempting to measure a
family structural dimension, such as adaptability, must decide
what constitutes a relevant domain of content for that dimension. They may look for commonalities among several definitions of adaptability or use the Delphi technique or a similar
strategy so that a consensus opinion or conceptualization of
family adaptability from a group of recognized experts on the
topic can be reached.

Correlation coefficients can be derived for criterion-related and
construct validity. Validity coefficients for assessment devices tend to
be much lower than reliability coefficients. For example, validity coefficients for the MMPI-2 are about .30.

CONCLUDING NOTE

This chapter has begun the discussion of couple and family assessment.
We have described the shift that has occurred, and is still occurring,
from individual assessment to family assessment. We have also noted
that, owing to the diversity of viewpoints on the content and process
of assessment, no single or integrative approach to family assessment
currently exists. In addition, a basic incompatibility appears to exist
between formal family assessment and the newer social constructivist
approaches; however, assessment methods are actually quite compatible

with such approaches, depending on the manner in which assessment information is framed with clients and families. Finally, the common structure of subsequent chapters was briefly introduced, and because of the diversity of graduate training in assessment theory, two key psychometric properties, reliability and validity, were described and illustrated.

REFERENCES

Bray, J., & Stanton, M. (Eds.). (2010). *The Wiley-Blackwell handbook of family psychology*. Oxford, UK: Blackwell.

Carr, A. (2000). Editorial: Empirical approaches to family assessment. *Journal of Family Therapy, 22,* 121–127.

Epstein, N. B., Ryan, C. E., Bishop, D. S., Miller, I. W. & Keitner, G. I. (2003). The McMaster model: A view of healthy family functioning. In F. Walsh (Ed.), *Normal family processes* (3rd ed., pp. 581–607). New York: Guilford Press.

Fink, A. (1995). *The survey handbook*. Thousand Oaks, CA: Sage Publications.

Goldman, L. (1992). Qualitative assessment: An approach for counselors. *Journal of Counseling & Development, 70,* 616–621.

Kaslow, F. (Ed.). (1996). *Handbook of relational diagnosis and dysfunctional family patterns*. New York: Wiley.

L'Abate, L., Ganahl, G., & Hansen, J. (1986). *Methods of family therapy*. Englewood Cliffs, NJ: Prentice Hall.

Lambert, M. (2010). *Prevention of treatment failure: The use of measuring, monitoring, and feedback in clinical practice*. Washington, DC: American Psychological Association.

Sperry, L. (2010). *Core competencies in counseling and psychotherapy: Becoming a highly competent and effective therapist*. New York: Routledge.

Yingling, L., Miller, W., McDonald, A., & Galwaler, S. (1998). *GARF assessment sourcebook: Using the DSM-IV global assessment of relational functioning*. Washington, DC: Brunner/Mazel.

ANNOTATED BIBLIOGRAPHY

American Psychological Association (1999). *Standards for educational and psychological testing*. Washington, DC: Author. This revision of the 1985 standards emphasizes psychometrics and the standards needed by clinicians and researchers for the proficient and ethical use and interpretation of tests.

Carmines, E. G., & Zeller, R. A. (1991). *Reliability and validity assessment.* Newbury Park, CA: Sage. An introduction to research methodology that includes classical test theory, validity, and methods of assessing reliability.

Epstein, N. B., Ryan, C. E., Bishop, D. S., Miller, I. W. & Keitner, G. I. (2003). The McMaster model: A view of healthy family functioning. In F. Walsh (Ed.), *Normal family processes* (3rd ed., pp. 581–607). New York: Guilford Press.

Fink, A. (1995). *The survey handbook.* Thousand Oaks, CA: Sage Publications.

Goldman, L. (1992). Qualitative assessment: An approach for counselors. *Journal of Counseling & Development, 70,* 616–621.

Hambleton, R. K., & Zaal, J. N. (Eds.). (1991). *Advances in educational and psychological testing.* Boston: Kluwer Academic.

Information on the concepts of reliability and validity in psychology and education and techniques in statistical analysis for social scientists are addressed.

CHAPTER 2

Qualitative Assessment

Maureen Duffy and Ronald J. Chenail

The most significant development in the past 10 years affecting couples and family therapists, and health care in general, has been the rapidly growing momentum of the evidence-based practice movement. Interestingly, the rise of evidence-based practice has happened at the same time as the traditional hierarchical relationships between health care providers and patients have yielded to more collaborative relationships and during the same time that health care providers, including couples and family therapists, have found themselves increasingly accountable to administrative requirements to demonstrate that their practice is evidence based (Gabbay & Le May, 2011).

The influence of the evidence-based practice movement has generated professional and policy discussions that have focused on questions of meaning within the movement and that have challenged narrow understandings of evidence-based practice as representing only the results of formal scientific research, in particular, randomized controlled trials. As a result of these conversations, a fuller understanding of evidence-based practice now includes not only formal scientific research evidence but also the evidence gleaned from clinical practice, with both kinds of evidence being subjected to ongoing individual and community professional conversation and evaluation (Gabbay & Le May, 2011; Lemieux-Charles & Champagne, 2008). Both low context scientific evidence and high context practice evidence are needed to provide quality care.

Evidence-based practice, which includes practice-based evidence, is about generating, making sense of, and utilizing knowledge that is of high quality and that has the greatest likelihood of helping consumers to obtain positive, desired outcomes for their routine and crisis health care needs. The couples and family assessments that are detailed in this chapter outline ways that skilled and conscientious couples and family therapists can utilize qualitative assessments to generate and apply high context evidence needed to gather critical information about their clients, make sense of that information in collaboration with their clients, and use the information to develop effective collaborative interventions grounded in practice-based evidence.

Use of qualitative assessments in couples and family therapy provides many of the same advantages that qualitative research provides in human science inquiry. Qualitative strategies are flexible and nonreductionist, focused on meaning and on understanding and interpretation of experience and relationships. The complexity and multiple perspectives present in couples and family therapy provide rich opportunities for the clinician interested in qualitative assessment to represent family members' thoughts, actions, interactions, conversations, realities, motivations, beliefs, and lives in terms of words, figures, pictures, diagrams, matrices, drawings, observations, and stories. Qualitative assessment strategies span the continuum from noninterventive, observational strategies to interventive, prescribed activities and tasks. The clinician can make qualitative diagnostic assessments single-handedly or, more commonly, can include the couple or family in a collaborative process of assessment (Jordan & Franklin, 2011). This chapter will present a number of clinically useful qualitative assessment methods. It provides detailed descriptions of each method and clear procedures for its use, interpretation, and evaluation. Then is described a strategy for utilizing qualitative assessments in clinical practice with families. Finally, it illustrates the strategy in an extended case example.

OBSERVATIONAL METHODS

Observing Structure, Hierarchy, and Interactions

Qualitative assessment name. Observing structure, hierarchy, and interactions is grounded in the work of Salvador Minuchin, who developed the structural model of family therapy, and Jay Haley, who developed the strategic model of family therapy. Minuchin and Haley are considered founders of family therapy and began to publish their work in the 1960s and 1970s.

Type of assessment. This is an observational assessment of family structure and organization, hierarchy, family subsystems, boundaries, coalitions, and alliances.

Use and target audience. This strategy is particularly suitable for family groups, including multigenerational families; it may also be used with couples and parts or subsystems of families.

Multicultural. Observation of structural, hierarchical, and interactional patterns of particular couples and families encourages therapist attention to the culturally specific and unique aspects of each couple and family.

Ease and time of administration. This strategy requires therapist understanding of the theoretical concepts underlying the observation; observation is continuous over the course of treatment. The therapist need not identify primarily as a structural or strategic family therapist to find these observations useful.

Scoring procedure. Scoring comprises clinical judgment and decisions based on observations.

Reliability/validity. Trustworthiness of structural and strategic model-based observations has been established by use over time. Outcome effectiveness has been scientifically validated by National Institute on Drug Abuse (NIDA) grant-supported work of Jose Szapocznik (Szapocznik & Coatsworth, 1999) and Howard Liddle (Liddle & Dakoff, 1995) at the University of Miami with drug-abusing adolescents.

Availability and source. For detailed information, see the works of Minuchin, Haley, Charles Fishman, Harry Aponte, Cloe Madanes, and James Keim. Selected references include Aponte, 1994; Haley, 1991; Madanes, Keim, and Smessler, 1995; Minuchin and Fishman, 1981; Minuchin, Lee, and Simon, 1996.

Comment. One of the significant contributions of the structural and strategic models is the emphasis on observation and assessment of truly interactional sequences and phenomena as opposed to the observation and assessment of individual affect and behavior. Assessments, interventions, and outcomes based on the structural and strategic models are among the most widely researched of the systemic approaches.

Conducting and Utilizing Observational Assessment of Structure, Hierarchy, and Interactions

Assessment of family or couple structure, hierarchy, and interactions is begun at the initial clinical interview and continues throughout therapy. This form of assessment is used to conceptualize the case, to develop appropriate interventions, and, during the termination phase of therapy, to evaluate clinical outcome and effectiveness. Assessment of structure, hierarchy, and interactions is integrated within the therapeutic process. No formal and separate assessment phase is used in this method. Much of the structure, hierarchy, and interactional patterns can be observed from how family members respond to clinical questions and interact together during the session. The therapist may also need to ask the couple or family particular questions related to the following indicators if additional information is required to make a fuller assessment.

The structure of a family refers to the members of the couple or family, including extended family members, and their patterns of inter-action, closeness, distance, conflict, conflict management, expressions of affect, problem-solving style, and rules and regulations (whether covert or overt) that govern their ways of relating to one another. The therapist assesses the family's structure by observing and assessing the following indicators:

- Who sits close to whom and who sits farthest away from whom
- Who initiates conversation about key family issues and who remains quiet
- Who speaks spontaneously and who speaks only when spoken to
- Who identifies the problem or goals for the therapy
- Who agrees and who disagrees with the identified problem or goals
- What topics are permitted to be spoken about, and who is allowed to talk about or comment on them; what topics seem to be off limits for family members to discuss
- Who can interrupt or disagree and who cannot
- How emotion is expressed and responded to by various family members
- Whose opinion counts most and whose does not; who attempts to solve problems and who is less involved
- Who is effective and competent at handling particular family tasks and who seems less effective
- Who teams up with whom to get something done or to take a position

Carefully observing and assessing these indicators will provide the couple and family therapist with a wealth of interactional information about the family's structure and boundaries between individual members as well as subsystems within the family. This information can then be uti-lized to develop appropriate systemic interventions and treatment plans.

Hierarchy is a concept related to the concept of family structure, but it is important to consider and observe specifically because of its connec-tion to issues of power, decision making, and roles within a couple or family. The therapist assesses hierarchy and other interactional patterns within the family by carefully attending to the following:

- Who is in charge of which activities and functions within the couple or family
- Who is in charge of discipline, and who is in charge of fun

- Who can make independent decisions, and who must be consulted
- Who has veto power over important decisions
- How family roles are tied to traditional gender roles
- Who gets nurtured and by whom; who gets less nurturing from other family members

Case Example

Janice and Tom were parents of two small children, a 4-year-old boy, Billy, and an 8-month-old girl who had just started sleeping through the night. Janice and Tom complained of being chronically exhausted and frazzled. They were up most nights because Billy would not stay in his bedroom at night and routinely came into their room, fidgeting and crying, shortly after they attempted to go to bed. During the initial family therapy session, the therapist observed the parents' weak and ineffectual attempts to manage Billy's demands for attention. Billy repeatedly interrupted conversation between the therapist and Billy's parents by whining or by persistently asking them to play with the toys he had brought with him to the session. Billy's parents tried to pacify him without clearly telling him to be quiet and entertain himself. In the same way, Billy's parents felt powerless and expressed disagreement over how to handle the increasingly intolerable nighttime situation. Their only point of agreement was that they disagreed with their pediatrician's suggestion to lock Billy in his room at night.

The therapist was able to support Billy's parents in their efforts to take charge of the situation and clearly enforce the "must stay in your own bed rule." The therapist also encouraged Janice and Tom to develop a variety of ways of taking charge—learning how to take charge by being firm and consistent and also learning how to take charge by being playful and comforting.

Summary

Since the development of the structural and strategic models of family therapy, multiple new theories and models of couple and family therapy have been developed. However, the relational assessment of a couple or family's structure, hierarchy, and patterns of interaction remains a cornerstone of sound systemic work and can enhance case conceptualization and treatment planning by therapists practicing from many different systemic models. It is significant that clinical research has established the success of structural and strategic assessments and interventions with adolescent drug abusers—a large population that is difficult to treat.

INTERVIEWING

Diagnostic Interviewing

Qualitative assessment name. Diagnostic interviewing refers to the general method of interviewing clients within a framework of pre-existing criteria that will then be used to make clinical assessments. In individual therapy, interviewing from within the framework of the DSM-IV-TR to arrive at a clinical diagnosis is an example of diagnostic interviewing. In couples and family therapy, diagnostic interviewing is used to identify areas that couples or family members experience as problematic and as sources of strength. Identifying psychopathology of an individual member of the couple or family may be a part of the diagnostic interviewing process, if, in the judgment of the clinician, the presence of individual psychopathology is compounding the relational problems.

Type of assessment. This interview format is open ended. In diagnostic interviewing for couples, the following interpersonal domains are explored to arrive at a clinical diagnosis of the relational problems: commitment to the relationship, emotional expressiveness, sexual functioning, development of shared goals and aspirations, gender roles and/or role functioning, communication skills and styles, perceptions of intimacy, and conflict management. In diagnostic interviewing for families, these domains are explored: goal setting, hierarchy and distribution of power, boundaries, problem-solving skills, role functioning, emotional expressiveness and responsiveness, communications skills and styles, social support, and conflict management. It is important to remember that diagnostic interviewing should focus primarily on process rather than on content areas. The specific questions chosen are inevitably tied to the theory and/or model that the therapist is utilizing.

Use and target audience. Couples and families are the target audience.

Multicultural. The therapist bears the responsibility for ensuring that the interview is conducted in a multiculturally sensitive way. Diagnostic interviewing should specifically take into account and include a focus on cultural factors unique to the couple or family.

Ease and time of administration. In most couples and family therapy, initial diagnostic interviews take between 1 and 2 hours. Additional sessions are scheduled as needed. Keep in mind that many family therapists purposefully do not make a clear distinction between "diagnosis" and "intervention."

Scoring procedure. Responses to the interview questions are compared to the criteria used by the therapist and a qualitative clinical assessment is then made. The assessment may be in the form of a problem description, a resource or strength description, and/or a score on the

Global Assessment of Relational Functioning (GARF) Scale (American Psychiatric Association, 2000).

Reliability/validity. The particular diagnostic framework used by the clinician determines these. The diagnostic interviewing work with couples of John Gottman (1999a, 1999b), for example, is based on rigorous empirical study and has resulted in a reliable model identifying couple behaviors predictive of marriages that fail or those that succeed.

Availability and source. Resources for diagnostic interviewing are ordinarily found in the theoretical literature describing a particular family therapy approach. Additional excellent resources to enhance diagnostic interviewing are also available, among them the work of Atkinson (1999), Carlson and Sperry (1997), and Gottman (1999a, 1999b).

Comment. Diagnostic interviewing requires the therapist to clearly think through and articulate the theoretical framework within which he or she is working.

Utilizing Diagnostic Interviewing With Couples

The sample interview questions included here are based on the work of Gottman (1999a) and Atkinson (1999). The first set of questions is designed to assess the commitment of each partner to the marriage and the strength of the marital bond. The second set is designed to assess the couple's management of conflict and the presence of behaviors predictive of marital failure. These samples are broad-based general questions that, in practice, would need to be broken down into smaller questions focusing on particular aspects of the general theme. These questions should be asked in a conjoint session.

Commitment and strength of marital bond questions are as follows:

- Does your partner know what your hopes and dreams are for your marriage?
- Do you have a shared set of hopes and dreams that you can talk about, or do you think that your hopes and dreams for your relationship are different from one another's?
- Do you know your partner's pet peeves, current interests and hobbies, and likes and dislikes?
- Does your partner know what you are most worried about now?
- Does your partner know how things are going for you at work and what challenges you experience there?
- What memories from the past and experiences from the present do you have that are closest to your image of what being together in a good way is like?
- When your partner wants to make you happy or laugh, what kinds of things is he or she likely to do?

These questions are important because they provide information about the commitment to the relationship, each partner's level of awareness of the other's internal world, and whether the couple has a shared vision for who they are together and for their future. Shared vision, friendship and reliance on the other, and awareness of the other's thoughts and feelings are predictive of marital success.

Conflict management questions are as follows:

- Can you describe what happens (what you say and do and how you feel) when you get into a disagreement?
- What do you see your partner saying and doing, and how do you imagine he or she is feeling?
- How do you try to resolve arguments or problems once they have come up?
- What behaviors (include verbal and physical behaviors) of your partner hurt or upset you most?
- Do both of you try to resolve problems once they have come up, or does one of you wind up doing more than the other to fix things?
- Do you feel that your partner values your opinions about things?
- If you have an idea about solving a problem or doing something differently in your relationship, is your partner open to hearing and trying out your suggestion or advice?

These questions are also important because they reveal how a couple fights and makes efforts to repair the relationship after the fight. They also reveal the presence of what Gottman (1999a, 1999b) calls the "four horsemen of the apocalypse," namely, *criticism, defensiveness, contempt*, and *stonewalling*. Contempt is the behavior in marriage most definitively predictive of marital failure, and Gottman clearly identifies it as a form of abuse that must not be empathized with but that must be named as abusive and stopped. Contempt takes the form of belittling, mocking, put-downs (especially in front of others), and other forms of scorn and derision that come from one person assuming a superior position in relationship to the other.

Case Example

Wanda wanted the racy new Infiniti FX 35 that she was crazy about. She loved it and knew that a lot of people called it the sexiest car on the face of the earth. Craig was very uncomfortable with the idea, complaining that they did not have $40,000 to spend on a car, and repeatedly asked her in a mocking kind of way who she was trying to impress and attract. Wanda countered that "you only live once" and they would manage to pay for the car somehow. She was outgoing, a little flamboyant, and loved beautiful clothes, furnishings, and cars that were a little out of reach financially. Craig grew up with the injunction not to "make a show of yourself or stand out." Wanda's desire for the car was highly symbolic for Craig in terms of their sexual functioning, financial goals, and as a challenge to the values of his family of origin.

In this case, the therapist could actively help each partner to understand the internal world of the other around the issue of the car by asking each to reflect on and share what meanings buying that car would hold for each, including exploring Craig's fears and insecurities and Wanda's needs and desires that she was seeing the car as fulfilling. This kind of therapeutic conversation would address what is at stake for each partner in the marriage in this situation and help unfold the maps of each one's internal world thus making these maps more available to the other. Additionally, the therapist would directly address Craig's derisive behavior by naming it as contempt, explain the research findings on contempt, and strongly suggest that Craig discontinue any practices of contempt. The therapist would point out that Craig had already expressed his admiration for Wanda in many ways to which he could reconnect and would also help Craig learn ways of clearly expressing a different point of view without resorting to insults.

Summary

Diagnostic interviewing is a theoretically driven method of obtaining information from client couples and families to arrive at a clinical description of the client's problems and strengths. This information forms the basis for developing targeted interventions that use the client's resources to manage problems differently in a more effective and satisfying way.

Interventive Interviewing

Qualitative assessment name. Interventive interviewing is based on the idea that any relationship or involvement is interventive in that it changes the system. Interventive interviewing refers to the use of a variety of categories of questions designed not only to obtain information for assessment but also to initiate therapeutic change simultaneously. The categories of questions include circular questions (Fleuridas, Nelson, & Rosenthal, 1986); reflexive questions (Tomm, 1987a, 1987b, 1988); solution-focused questions (Berg & De Jong, 1996; de Shazer, 1988); and narrative questions (White & Epston, 1990). The Milan Group introduced the idea of circular questioning, and Tomm introduced the phrase "interventive interviewing."

Type of assessment. The interview format is open ended.

Use and target audience. Individuals, couples, and families are the target audience.

Multicultural. Interventive interviewing is multiculturally respectful because it elicits information unique to the client's culture and world-view and makes no normative presuppositions.

Ease and time of administration. This interviewing method requires theoretical understanding of interventive interviewing and skill in question construction.

Scoring procedure. No formal scoring is done; "scores" are clients' responses to interventive questions that trigger changes in perception and/or behavior.

Reliability/validity. These are determined by trustworthiness demonstrated pragmatically through clinical effectiveness of technique over time.

Availability and source. An excellent "primer" on the use of circular questioning is the article by Fleuridas et al. (1986). Tomm's (1987a, 1987b, 1988) *Family Process* series on interventive interviewing is the landmark articulation of the method and rationale.

Comment. Interventive interviewing has changed the landscape of family therapy by operationalizing the second-order cybernetics view (von Foerster, 1981), namely, that one is part of the system that one observes or "assesses" and changes the system by virtue of doing so.

Utilizing Interventive Interviewing With Couples and Families

Interventive interviewing with couples and families is marked by the therapist's reliance on the question rather than on the statement, on the interrogative form rather than on the declarative form. Statements communicate the worldview and preferences of the therapist, but questions invite clients to reflect on their experiences and to communicate their worldviews. Questions are seen as having the potential for triggering client change by inviting clients to see things differently within the context of the interaction between therapist and client. Interventive questions are nonblaming questions that invite clients to reflect on their beliefs, feelings, and behaviors thus freeing them to think about themselves and their relationships with others in less defensive, more exploratory ways. Interventive questions avoid or remove the negative connotations usually associated with conversations about problems and stuck patterns of living.

Questions, framed nonjudgmentally, also have the potential for increasing clients' awareness of and concern for the other. Thus, questions are not considered neutral tools for obtaining information and assessment but rather are interventive by their very nature, inviting change that can occur rapidly. The major categories of interventive questions are circular questions, reflexive questions, solution-focused questions, and narrative questions. To facilitate demonstration of the variety of interventive questions, examples of each will be included within the description for clinical use and not as a separate "case example" category.

Circular questions. In contrast to linear questions, circular questions focus on the relationships among persons and among the beliefs and views held by an individual person. Linear questions assume a sequence of action, such as cause and effect. The question, Why are you so angry? is a good example of a linear question because it presumes that there is a knowable cause for the anger that the cause precedes in time. Examples of circular questions are as follows:

How does your partner begin to reconnect with you when you have been arguing with each other? or When you get upset and raise your voice, which of your children seems to be most concerned and which seems to be least concerned? or How do they know that you have cooled down? Circular questions invite clients to reflect on the relational effects of their thinking and acting. Such questions shift the client's view from that I actor to that of observer, from first or second person ("I" or "you") to third person ("he," "she," or "they"), bringing the presence of the other into much greater focus.

Reflexive questions. Reflexivity refers to a blurring between subject and object, self and other. It is the presence of the observer in all description. For example, assigning a DSM-IV diagnosis results in a particular description of a client, but it also reveals that the diagnostician has some alignment with the assumptions and theories supporting the DSM-IV. Likewise, the nightly news presents information about current events, but the order of the news items reveals editorial values about what is most significant. Reflexive questions invite clients to think about how they experience and describe themselves, how they present themselves to others, how others perceive them, what a change would mean to their lives and relationships, and how that change might be accomplished. Because reflexive questions are relational, they are also circular, but Tomm (1987b) distinguishes reflexive questions from circular questions by suggesting that "reflexive questioning focuses more heavily on an explicit recognition of the autonomy of the family in determining the outcome" (p. 182).

Examples of reflexive questions are as follows: In the midst of the monumental job of caring for your dying adult son, how are you maintaining your own sense of balance so that you can continue to be there for him? and, In that so much of what you are saying to your son is said by your being there for him now, what things would upset you if you did not get to say them to him in words before he died? and, Even if it never happens, what conversation do you imagine would be most helpful for your son's father to have now so that after your son's death, his father would be less angry and less hurt? These questions are gently suggestive of possible alternatives for action and reflection for the family to consider.

Solution-focused questions. Solution-focused questions play to the strength and resilience side of the court and are grounded in the postmodern constructivist view of knowledge. This view holds that individuals bring forth knowledge by their language practices and that Western language practices are predominantly problem focused. As a result of problem-saturated talk, the strengths and solutions to problems that people utilize in their daily lives go unnoticed and are not brought forth in language to the same extent that problems are. Solution-focused questions are designed to bring forth exceptions to problem saturation and to emphasize competence, resilience, and strength.

Several categories of solution-focused questions exist:

- *Presession change questions*—ask what differences occurred between the time the appointment was set and the first session, capitalizing on the hope and positive change that often occur before the first session.
- *Exception questions*—ask about when the problem is less intense or less of a concern for the client or when it could have occurred but did not.
- *Miracle questions*—ask clients to describe how they would know the problem was not there anymore if they went to sleep and a miracle happened, and the problem went away—but they did not know that the miracle had happened because they were sleeping. This question encourages clients to focus, in a detailed and specific way, on how life would be different in the absence of the problem and how they would be feeling and living differently.
- *Scaling questions*—ask clients to consider how they would know they had made some progress from baseline toward their goals and what they would need to do to move another point or half point forward. The scaling question breaks goals down into manageable, realistic steps.
- *Coping questions*—ask how clients have been able to do what they have done, emphasizing the strength and dignity in surviving and managing life's hardships and obstacles.

Examples of solution-focused questions are, When were there times that your toddler son might have had a tantrum but did not? Instead of having a tantrum, what did he do? What was different about how you were responding to him?

Narrative questions. Narrative questions are rooted in the metaphor of the story and are designed to help clients represent their lives, relationships, and life experiences as part of an expanding and richer narrative or story line. The work of White and Epston (1990) has been pivotal in providing family therapists with a theoretical framework and question construction guidelines from which to develop narrative practices. White and Epston drew from French philosopher Michel Foucault's analysis of knowledge in which persons were seen as being recruited into particular ways of thinking about the world and themselves and then measuring themselves and their lives against this dominant view. An example of a dominant discourse is the contemporary Western representation of female beauty as young, thin, and unblemished. This dominant discourse provides an unyielding and agonizing standard against which young girls and women measure themselves and find themselves wanting.

Narrative questions help clients to reflect on their unwitting participation in this dominant discourse and to separate themselves from it. Clients are encouraged, through narrative questions, to think about their lives and relationships differently and to develop their own preferred stories and accounts of their life and relationships. Dominant narratives box people in. Narrative questions can be seen as a form of protest against the anonymous but powerful requirements of collective social knowledge and as an opportunity for clients to free themselves from the restrictions of such knowledge. Examples of narrative questions are, What does being a "good enough" mother as opposed to a "perfect" mother mean for you? How would a good enough mother think about the problems your teenage daughter is having? What would a good enough mother tell a perfect mother about being gentler on oneself?

Summary

Understanding the systemic and nonnormative, nonpathologizing nature of circular, reflexive, solution-focused, and narrative questions and practicing of question construction are the key skills required for effective interventive interviewing. Interventive interviewing involves therapist and client in a process of ongoing collaborative assessment and change.

Adult Attachment Interview

Qualitative assessment name. The Adult Attachment Interview (AAI) was developed by George, Kaplan, and Main through the Department of Psychology at the University of California, Berkeley, in 1985; the third edition was developed in 1996 (George, Kaplan, & Main, 1985, 1996). Both are unpublished manuscripts.

Type of assessment. The AAI is a semi-structured interview designed to identify attachment representations in adults by examining narrative accounts of adults' early childhood experiences with parents or other primary caregivers for coherence, quality of presentation, and level of remembered detail.

Use and target audience. The AAI is intended for use with adults. Because early key attachment experiences are conceptualized as influencing emotion and behavior in later significant relationships, the AAI is particularly useful in couples work.

Multicultural. Emerging research (Rodrigues, Wais, Zevallos, & Rodrigues, 2001) is suggesting the universality of attachment scripts across cultures and therefore supports the use of the AAI with diverse populations.

Ease and time of administration. The AAI takes between 45 minutes and an hour and a half to complete. It consists of 20 open-ended questions, many requiring clarifying and/or probing follow-up questions. Administering the AAI requires specific training in the method and general skill in interviewing.

Scoring procedure. Scoring of the AAI is a complex process and requires completion of a 2-week intensive training course in the scoring and coding procedures developed by Main and Goldwyn. Each interview is transcribed verbatim and is rated on 14 nine-point scales. Certification in the administration and scoring of the AAI requires an additional 18 months, consisting of three tests taken at 6-month intervals. Each test requires the trainee to code a set of approximately 10 AAI transcripts.

Reliability/validity. Test–retest reliabilities of 78% (Bakermans-Kranenburg & Van IJzendoorn, 1993) and 90% (Benoit & Parker, 1994) have been reported.

Availability and source. The AAI protocol is available on the Internet at www.psychology.sunysb.edu/attachment/measures/content/aai_interview.pdf. It is made available on the Internet only to provide context and access to the interview questions for those interested in the AAI and research surrounding it. The scoring manual is available only to those who have completed the specialized AAI training.

Comment. Data from this assessment interview are now being linked to developments in neuroscience (Cozolino, 2002; Siegel, 2007). The quality of brain integration of neural networks is hypothesized to be linked to the quality of early attachment relationships with parents or primary caregivers—the more secure the attachment, the better the integration of neural networks. This is a fascinating frontier at the intersection of neuroscience, attachment theory, and clinical family therapy practice.

Utilizing the Adult Attachment Interview in Couples and Family Therapy

The AAI is a semi-structured interview in which the interviewer asks the respondent a series of questions primarily focused on recollections of the relationship with his mother and father. The bulk of the interview concentrates on the respondent's memories of early childhood and adolescent experiences and whether he experienced a parent as threatening or coercive. The interview includes specific questions about whether the respondent feels that any early childhood experience was negative or served as an impediment in life. For example, Question 8 of the AAI is *"Did you ever feel rejected as a young child? Of course, looking back on it now, you may realize it wasn't really rejection, but what I'm trying to ask about here is whether you remember ever having been rejected in childhood."* The interview shifts to the present when the interviewer asks how the respondent thinks his childhood experiences have affected the development of his personality in general, what the quality of the respondent's current relationship with his parents is like, and how the respondent feels when he is separated from his children now. For example, Question 10 reads, *"In general, how do you think your overall experiences with your parents have affected your adult personality?"* The interview also includes questions about loss of a loved one or other traumas and invites the respondent to speculate on why her or his parents acted as they did when the respondent was a child. The interview ends with a future focus in which the respondent is asked questions about her or his hopes and wishes for her or his children. The interview is taped and a verbatim transcript is made.

The respondent's answers to the questions compose a narrative of understanding and meaning or lack of it and of coherence or confusion about childhood experiences. Persons specifically trained in the coding of the AAI code the transcript according to the conventions of qualitative discourse analysis. The results of the coding are classified into one of four categories:

(F) Secure—freely autonomous when the transcript narratives are internally coherent and consistent. Those with traumatic childhoods as well as those with stable, loving childhoods may be classified as secure because the criteria for classification are about narrative coherence not the nature of the childhood experiences.

(D) Insecure—dismissing when the narratives give evidence of minimization or denial of the significance of early childhood experiences and of relationships with parents or show idealization of parents.

(E) Insecure—preoccupied when the narratives show confusion and inconsistency about early childhood relationships, experiences, and their meaning. The transcripts also give evidence of preoccupation with parents and/or current relationships with parents characterized by anger or by efforts to please.

(U) Unresolved—narrative disorganization about a loss or trauma within the context of a narrative that meets the criteria for one of the three preceding categories and would be so classified if it were not for the evidence of intense mourning, guilt, or irrational beliefs surrounding a loss or trauma.

The quality of early attachment experiences is increasingly being linked to brain development and neural integration (Schore, 2003). Narrative coherence and therefore secure attachment as scored on the AAI are hypothesized as reflecting better integration of neural networks in the brain (Cozolino, 2002; Siegel, 2007).

Case Example

A mother whose AAI score is (E) insecure–preoccupied may oscillate between anger at her parents and attempts to please them, thus, preoccupying herself so that she has difficulty identifying and responding to the emotional needs of her young child. Her attachment template oscillates between overvaluation and derogation of her parents, negatively affecting her ability to think clearly and making her vulnerable to emotional overreactions to her child's behavior.

Summary

The AAI is an instrument that has been widely used and researched by developmental psychologists and is gaining wider attention as neuroscience links early attachment experiences to brain development and integration. For family therapists, the attachment profiles obtained from the AAI provide information about the primary attachment pattern influencing a parent or spouse. For those who are insecurely attached, interventions can be appropriately targeted to help dismissive clients identify and respond to the emotional needs of others, to help preoccupied clients individuate and react less intensely to the behaviors of others, and to help those with unresolved trauma make sense and construct meaning around their experience of loss or abuse.

GRAPHIC METHODS

Genogram

Qualitative assessment name. The conceptual foundation for the use of genograms was advanced by Murray Bowen. The graphic and interpretive techniques for constructing and using genograms were developed and elaborated by McGoldrick and colleagues at the Multicultural Family Institute of New Jersey.

Type of assessment. A genogram is a graphic representation of a person's family, interpersonal relationships among family members, and family history over multiple generations. The genogram is typically co-constructed by the therapist and client and represents key life-cycle events (e.g., birth, marriage, divorce, death) as well as the nature and intensity of relationships among family members. For example, it can be used in family assessment from a normative and a nonnormative clinical standpoint. Used by Bowenian therapists, the genogram can be used to track family patterns of enmeshment and disengagement—concepts that are normative within Bowen family systems theory. On the other hand, the genogram can also be used in a nonnormative way by solution-focused therapists to identify family patterns of strength, resilience, and problem-solving skill.

Use and target audience. The genogram can be used in couples and family therapy to represent family relationships visually and to identify or construct patterns of relationship, feeling, and behaving across a number of generations. In couples therapy, genograms can be constructed for each partner; major family patterns and themes can then be compared and discussed. For therapists working with individual clients who wish to introduce a family perspective, the use of a genogram can be particularly helpful in invoking the wider influence of family and context. In addition to the uses of genograms described elsewhere in this section, genograms have been used and recommended for understanding couples and family spirituality (Hodge, 2005), for use in addressing trauma and trauma-inscribed memories (Jordan, 2006), and very recently for use with military families (Weiss, Coll, Gerbauer, Smiley, & Carillo, 2010). Genograms have been utilized in solution-focused work (Weiss et al., 2010) and in collaborative, narrative, and social constructionist-informed practices (Dunn & Levitt, 2000; Milewski-Hertlein, 2001; Rigazio-DiGilio, Ivey, Kunkler-Peck, & Grady, 2005) as well as in their classic use in Bowen family systems work (Kerr & Bowen, 1988).

Multicultural. The genogram is a culturally sensitive and culturally specific assessment tool. The cultural genogram and cultural context of the family and of individual family members is considered a fundamental part of using and interpreting the genogram (Hardy & Laszloffy, 1995; Shellenberger et al., 2007).

Ease and time of administration. This is a simple method requiring that the therapist use pencil and paper and have a basic knowledge of the symbols and conventions used in genogram construction. A basic genogram can be developed in only several minutes; adding detail and complexity may require that the therapist encourage the client to gather more information about family history. The genogram can be enlarged and refined over time as more information about family history becomes available.

Scoring procedure. Representing and interpreting family history and family patterns of feeling and behaving is a process of co-construction between the client and therapist. Factual information about marriages, significant relationships, births, divorces, deaths, and so forth, is obtained from the client and represented graphically. As information about individual members of the client's extended family is gathered, patterns of feeling and behaving may become evident and may be identified or suggested by the client or the therapist. The process of interpretation is akin to thematic analysis in qualitative research in which recurring and dominant themes are identified.

Reliability/validity. The trustworthiness of the genogram is demonstrated by its consistent use over time by family therapists to identify family patterns and themes and the consistently perceived usefulness of the tool by therapists and clients. The use of the genogram has expanded to include a focus on strengths, resilience, culture, spirituality, and problem-solving skills, as well as its traditional use to identify pathology and family emotional themes. Reliability and validity issues do emerge with respect to the role of memory and the accuracy of retrieved family history data.

Availability and source. McGoldrick's books on genograms (McGoldrick et al., 2008; McGoldrick et al., 1999) are basic references for developing skills in the construction and use of the genogram in therapy. Various computer software programs to facilitate production of professional quality genograms are available.

Comment. Irrespective of preferred family therapy modality, a focus on a client's family history through the use of the genogram immediately expands the frame to include larger cultural themes and context.

Utilizing the Genogram in Couples and Family Therapy

Constructing a genogram is similar to building a family tree. The first step in developing a genogram is to identify the index person. The index person is typically the identified patient in family therapy or each partner in couples therapy. Squares are used to identify males and circles to identify females. Birth and death dates are written above the symbol on the left and right, respectively. An "X" inside the symbol indicates the family member is dead. Marriage is indicated by a solid horizontal line connecting the symbols for male and female; living together is indicated by a dotted horizontal line connecting the symbols for the partners. Lesbian couples in a committed relationship are indicated by two circles with inverted triangles inside them connected by both solid and dotted horizontal lines. Gay couples in committed relationships are indicated by two squares with inverted triangles inside them connected by both solid and dotted horizontal lines. The solid and dotted horizontal lines used together represent unmarried committed relationships. Where gay or lesbian couples are legally married, the horizontal line between the symbols for the individuals should be solid as in heterosexual marriages. Divorce is indicated by a double hash mark on the horizontal line connecting the couple, with the dates of the marriage and divorce next to it. Children are listed from oldest to the youngest, from left to right, with the symbols for male or female on vertical lines descending from the horizontal line between the couple. A solid vertical line indicates a biological child; a dotted vertical line indicates a foster child; and a dual solid and dotted vertical line indicates an adopted child. Other symbols indicate pregnancy, miscarriage, stillbirth, and identical or fraternal twins. Substance abuse is indicated by a horizontal line bisecting the symbol for male or female with the bottom half of the symbol shaded in. A significant mental or physical problem is indicated by a vertical line bisecting the symbol for male or female and the left side of the symbol shaded in. (See Figure 2.1.)

In the genogram, the index person is indicated by a double circle or square and marriage or living together is then indicated as described earlier, with any children also symbolized. Parents and siblings of the index person are then symbolized, as are grandparents, aunts, uncles, and cousins as the family history becomes known. Each generation occupies its own line or latitude on the genogram, similar to a family tree, with the older generations (great grandparents, grandparents) on the upper part of the genogram and the children and subsequent generations on the lower part.

Relationships within a generation (for example, between siblings) or across generations, (for example, between a grandmother and granddaughter) are also indicated by specific symbols: Two solid lines between two people on the genogram indicate a close relationship; a dotted line indicates a distant relationship; a zigzag line indicates a conflicted or hostile relationship; and two solid lines with a zigzag line between them indicate a close, conflicted relationship.

A basic genogram can be constructed within a single therapy session using the knowledge of family history that the client brings with him or her. The therapist may ask the client to interview various family members to find out more information about family members, particularly in preceding generations. As the client brings in more information about his or her family, the genogram can be enhanced. A sufficiently detailed genogram will immediately reveal patterns of marriage and divorce, family size, multiple marriages or relationships, separation and divorce, and substance abuse or physical illness. The therapist will then use the genogram to help the client develop an enhanced understanding of larger family patterns. These patterns would include family vulnerabilities such as

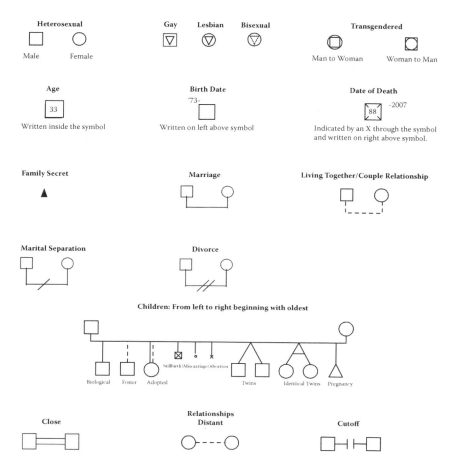

FIGURE 2.1   Basic genogram symbols. (Based on McGoldrick, Gerson, & Petry (2008).)

addiction or depression, losses, and traumas, as well as family strengths, resources, and resiliencies, such as adapting and prospering as an immigrant family without the support of extended kin. Ideally, this increased awareness will allow the client to see his or her place in the family history with greater emotional distance and increased cognitive understanding.

Case Example

Eric and Joy had been married for 18 months when they sought therapy because of increasing arguments and tension over money and communication. Eric complained that Joy was not as warm and close as she once was and that she did not pay attention to the cost of things; Joy complained that Eric wanted to spend too much time at home and was becoming boring. Eric was building his own spin-off business, with his father's help, from his father's successful insurance agency. Joy had a degree in advertising and was signed up with a professional temp agency. She worked 3 or 4 days most weeks. When she did not feel like working, she turned down the temporary jobs.

Eric's Genogram   Eric was the older of two boys. His mother and father had been married for 31 years; in the early years of their marriage, Eric's mom worked in the insurance agency that her husband had started. Gradually, as the business became more successful, she turned her attention to the children and their school and extracurricular activities. Eric's dad was very focused on doing the right thing, working hard, being a good provider, and living by the book. His father was a career military officer who bred this sense of duty and consistency into him. Eric was protected by his mother and tried very hard to receive approval from his father, who was not emotionally expressive.

Joy's Genogram   Joy was the third child of five, with one older brother and sister and one younger brother and sister. Joy's mother and grandmother worked as professionals—her grandmother as a physician and her mother as a pharmacist. Joy's father was an investigative journalist for the leading newspaper in their city. Family life was rough and tumble with boisterous dinner conversations and a steady stream of friends and her father's talkative newspaper colleagues throughout the house. Joy's mother participated in rock climbing, sailing, and white-water rafting whenever she could. Joy was interested in everything but had a hard time focusing on anything in particular. She worshipped her father and had little time for her mother, whom she saw as self-centered and aloof.

Interpretation and Therapeutic Use   Eric valued the pattern of hard work, commitment, and loyalty that he saw in his family when considering his genogram. He also saw the multigenerational father–son pattern of seeking approval and lack of emotional expressiveness. Joy relished the intellectual vigor that characterized her multigenerational family. In thinking about her genogram, Joy also began to see the women in her family in a new light. Although she had always valued her father's curiosity, love of life, and brashness, she began to appreciate her mother and grandmother as trailblazers and independent spirits in their own, more quiet ways.

In discussing Joy's genogram, Eric was vividly reminded of how Joy's own free-spirited ways were what had attracted him to her in the first place. Eric also recognized that he did not want to spend the rest of his life waiting for his father's approval and began to see himself as a "good enough" son already. In so doing, he moved closer to Joy and began to accept her invitations to have more fun and play in their relationship. For her part, Joy began to see herself as a strong woman in a line of strong women, although not as quiet or solitary as her mother, and started to focus on her career aspirations, which pleased Eric. Joy also began to see Eric's steadiness and loyalty as a reflection of his commitment to her rather than as a boring and plodding personality trait. She saw that, in overvaluing her father's unpredictable hours and activities, she had undervalued Eric's reliable presence and pleasure in the ordinary things of domestic life.

Summary

The genogram is a basic family therapy assessment tool that has numerous applications in clinical practice. The genogram enables therapist and client to identify family patterns of strength and deficit quickly and to locate an individual's life within the multigenerational family and wider community and culture.

DISCURSIVE METHODS

Recursive Frame Analysis

Qualitative assessment name. Recursive Frame Analysis (RFA), developed by Bradford Keeney in 1987 (Keeney, 1991), is a qualitative tool designed to assess the flow of communication in couple and family members' interactions. RFA was originally created as a real-time coding system to help couple and family therapists track clinical conversations and has been developed into a micro and macro qualitative assessment system (Chenail, 1991; Rambo, Heath, & Chenail, 1993).

Type of assessment. RFA is used to conduct three separate but connected types of discursive analyses: semantic, sequential, and pragmatic (Chenail & Duffy, 2011; Cotton, 2010). In the semantic assessment, the analyst listens to conversations and/or reads the transcript and notes how the individual speakers contribute to the creation of meaning. This is done by noting small units of meaning, known as frames, and then grouping frames of semantically similar meaning into larger semantic groupings known as galleries. Galleries can be grouped into larger semantically similar groupings known as wings, which in turn can be grouped into still larger collections known as museums. In the semantic analysis, the analyst makes note of which family members contribute frames to which galleries and which family members do not. In the sequential assessment, the analyst listens to conversations and/or reads the transcript and notes when the individual family members shift the conversational flow from one frame or gallery to another new or old frame or gallery. These shifts are noted as openings from one frame or gallery to another frame or gallery. In the pragmatic analysis, the analyst makes note of how family members (a) maintain conversational presence in a particular frame or gallery, (b) generate an opening to a new frame or gallery, (c) connect one gallery or frame to another frame or gallery, or (d) reverse the relationship between a gallery and its frames.

Use and target audience. RFA can be used to assess individual, couple, family, and group conversations.

Multicultural. RFA can be used with individuals, couples, and families from all cultures.

Ease and time of administration. RFA used as a conversational scoring method to assess semantic and sequential flows can be done in real time by a trained analyst. To conduct more micro-analyses, it may take the analyst 1 to 2 weeks to produce a detailed assessment of the semantic, sequential, and pragmatic patterns in a 1-hour conversation.

Scoring procedure. Conversations are coded in terms of (a) frames, galleries, wings, and museums for semantic analyses; (b) openings, frame-to-frame, frame-to-gallery, and gallery-to-gallery for sequential analyses; and (c) conversational moves or speech acts for pragmatic analyses. These renderings can be conducted and presented in textual presentations: Gallery 1: Frame 1a, Frame 1b; or they can be presented in graphical displays:

Graphical Display

Gallery 1: Problems With Son Frame 1a: Son doesn't clean room Frame 1b: Son doesn't obey father	Opening 1: Exceptions ⟹	Gallery 2: Son's Good Acts Frame 3a: Son helps set the table Frame 3b: Son looks after little sister

With either the textual or graphical approach, the analyst could include excerpts from the conversation to support the frame and gallery constructions (Chenail & Duffy, 2011).

Reliability/validity. RFA employs a number of techniques to increase the rigor of its analysis: (1) incorporation of the constant comparative method of analysis from grounded theory that requires individuals conducting the analysis to return continuously to the transcript to validate the coding process (Corbin & Strauss, 2007), (2) utilization of multiple analysts to conduct the RFAs and multiple judges to assess the individual RFAs to produce consensual RFAs (Hill et al., 2005), and (3) use of member checking by presenting the RFAs to the clients for their validation of the results (Patton, 2002).

Availability and source. Information on RFA can be located at the Recursive Frame Analysis home page (http://www.nova.edu/~ron/rfa.html).

Comment. RFA has been used to analyze a variety of clinical discourse including family therapy sessions (Cotton, 2010) and written clinical discourse (Chenail, Somers, & Benjamin, 2009).

Utilizing Recursive Frame Analysis in Couples and Family Therapy

Whether utilizing RFA in real-time conversational scoring or in its more macro-analytical forms, the analyst can write observations on a piece of paper or use software applications, such as Microsoft Word or PowerPoint, to record the RFA (Chenail & Duffy, 2011). Whether by pencil or keyboard, the analyst starts by listening or reading what each family member says. As the first family member speaks, the analyst makes a determination as to the meaning of the words being spoken. Similar to open coding in grounded theory (Corbin & Strauss, 2007), the analyst attempts to keep an open mind as each word is spoken until a declaration of meaning can be assigned to the words, or in RFA, a frame is created (Chenail & Duffy, 2011). From that initial framing of the family member's word, the analyst continues to track the conversation so that what family members are saying from point to point in the talk can be noted as words that convey something similar in meaning to what had been previously uttered (e.g., talk continuing in the same frame) or something different in meaning to what had been prior to that time (e.g., a new frame or a return to a previous frame).

For example, on hearing the following words from a mother, "I am worried that our daughter Ellen is having trouble at school. She is not getting good grades. Her teacher says she doesn't pay attention in class. And we have noticed some changes with her at home too," the analyst could create these frames: Frame 1: Mother worries about daughter's (Ellen) trouble at school; Frame 2: Ellen not getting good grades; Frame 3: Teacher says Ellen doesn't pay attention in class; and Frame 4: Mother (and father) notice changes with Ellen at home. As these frames are generated, the analyst can group frames with similar meanings into galleries. In the case of these four frames, the analyst could group Frames 1, 2, and 3 into one gallery: Gallery 1: Ellen's School Problems; then, the analyst could create a second gallery for Frame 2: Gallery 2: Ellen's Problems at Home. The analyst could decide to group both Gallery 1 and Gallery 2 into one Wing called Wing 1: Mom's Worries About Ellen.

As the father joins the conversation, the analyst notes how this parent joins in with the mother's talk or possibly speaks differently about Ellen. For example, the father may report, "Yes, I have heard what Ellen's teacher has said, but I'm not sure if I agree. I think Ellen is just going through a phase." From an RFA perspective, the father's opening frame appears to be spoken within the context of Gallery 1: Ellen's School Problems. But as the talk continues ("but I'm not sure if I agree"), his talk suggests that the focus of the conversation is shifting from Ellen's School Problems (Gallery 1) to a new gallery: Gallery 3: Fathers Disagrees About Ellen Having School Problems. As the father continues to speak, the analyst can note the conversation seems to be leaving Wing 1: Mom's Worries About Ellen, and entering a new Wing, Wing 2: Father Sees Ellen Going Through a Phase.

Besides noting these semantic frames in relationship to each other, the analyst can focus on how the speakers maintain conversation within one gallery or shift the talk to new ones. For example, the father's use of a "Yes, but" way of speaking can be noted as a speech act known as an *opening up closing* (Chenail & Duffy, 2011) by which a speaker can speak initially within one topic or gallery (e.g., Gallery 1: Ellen's School Problems) but then close down that part of the conversation while opening up a new flow to the talk (e.g., Gallery 3: Father Disagrees About Ellen Having School Problems). Over the course of the conversation, the analyst continues to frame the meaning of speakers' words, to frame the meaning of frames into galleries, to frame the meaning of galleries into wings, and to frame the meaning of wings into museums while also noting how the conversation opens into new frames and returns to existing ones.

Summary

RFA can be used to assess the flow of family members' conversations in real time and to conduct more micro-analyses of semantic, sequential, and pragmatic patterns of communicative interactions. It can be used with naturally occurring family conversations, with therapy sessions, and with scenarios or role playing. RFA has significant clinical utility in that it provides the basis for understanding what themes family members are focusing on and repeating, what themes family members have variant perspectives about, and to what degree themes and perspectives about couples and family life are held either rigidly or flexibly by particular family members.

STRATEGY FOR UTILIZING QUALITATIVE ASSESSMENT

The following protocol provides summative guidelines for using the preceding qualitative assessment strategies with couples and families.

1. Select qualitative assessment strategies appropriate for the couple or family and their presenting problem(s). Considerations are noted: Are the strategies selected compatible with the therapist's theoretical framework and clinical operating assumptions?

2. Determine whether the assessment strategies to be used will be diagnostic only or iterative (diagnostic and interventive). Considerations are noted: Will the selected strategies be used at intake only or throughout therapy on an ongoing basis? Diagnostic interviewing and the AAI should be used primarily during intake and as part of a formal assessment process. Observing structure, hierarchy, and interactions; interventive interviewing; genograms; and RFA are typically used iteratively.

3. Implement the selected qualitative strategy.
   1. Collect data. (Observe, and/or interview, and/or develop the genogram, and/or conduct the RFA.)
   2. Analyze and interpret the data. (Ensure that data analysis and interpretation methods are appropriate for the selected strategy.)

4. Collect additional collateral information about the couple or family, as needed. Possible collateral information could include review of clinical records; interviews with significant others in the client's relational system (e.g., teacher, physician, probation officer, family member, or friend); and results of other clinical or psychological assessments (e.g., inventories of personality, family, self-report, family violence or child abuse, or divorce or child custody). Collecting data from several sources (e.g., multiple family members, other assessments, clinical records, etc.) is a process called *triangulation* in qualitative research and is a method of confirming and verifying results.

5. Review the preceding information and develop an initial qualitative report for the couple or family assessed. The report may summarize the couple or family system from a relational perspective only, or it may additionally provide assessment information about each individual member of the couple or family. Individual family member reports should be akin to *within-case* analyses in qualitative research and relational or systemic reports akin to *cross-case* analyses. Some reports include within-case and cross-case analyses, whereas others include the cross-case or relational perspective only. The clinician determines the most appropriate report form based on the clinical purpose for the report.

   Reports can be oral, written, and/or graphic in format. Reports based on observing structure, hierarchy, and interactions are often oral. Reports based on diagnostic interviewing and the AAI are typically written. Reports based on interventive interviewing may be oral or written; if written, such reports may be in the form of letters to the client and may include reflections of the therapist about the client's new understandings or positive life changes. Reports based on the genogram should include a graphic component, and reports using RFA may include both a narrative and graphic component.

6. Present preliminary assessment results or reports to the couple or family before revising the qualitative report. Use of qualitative assessment strategies involves a collaborative process of verification of results. What this means is that the clinician presents preliminary results and interpretations to the couple or family for their comments and feedback prior to revising or summarizing the results. In qualitative research, this process is called *member checking*. The revised report incorporates the results of this member checking process.

For the preliminary and the revised reports, qualitative assessments about parental or couple functioning should never be provided to parents in the presence of children. Qualitative reports about children's functioning should be provided to parents and may be provided to the children in an age-appropriate way. Qualitative assessments of adolescent functioning should be given to an adolescent and to the adolescent's parents within a context of respect and sensitivity for the adolescent's growing autonomy.

7. Review preliminary report and feedback from member checking and develop a revised report. This can be an iterative report reflecting the interactional effect between the therapist's use of the qualitative strategies and movement in the couple or family since the beginning of the clinical assessment process, or it can be a summative report more reflective of the clinician's diagnostic impressions.

EXTENDED CASE EXAMPLE

Background Information and Presenting Problem

Elaine, a 43-year-old paralegal, and her 45-year-old husband Sam, the owner–operator of a small house-repairs business, came to therapy requesting help for their 14-year-old son, Brian, who expressed fear and resentment about transferring to a new middle school. The family had recently moved to a new neighborhood because they wanted Brian and his 10-year-old sister, Danielle, to benefit from the better schools in this new location. The parents described Brian as quiet and "into himself," but they said they had never thought much of it and were happy that he had not been a behavioral problem at school or home. Brian's academic performance at his previous middle school was average. The family moved to their new neighborhood about 6 weeks before the start of the school year. During the first 3 weeks of school, Brian attended school for only 7 full days. On the other days, Brian came home sick or did not go to school in the first place because of stomach pain and headaches. The school's attendance office had contacted the parents about Brian's situation; his parents had taken him to their primary care doctor who could not find anything wrong with him and referred him for therapy.

Based on the presenting problem and on the therapist's systemic theoretical framework, the therapist decided to utilize the following qualitative assessment strategies: observation of structure, hierarchy, and family interactions; interventive interviewing; construction of a genogram; and conduction of an ongoing RFA to note the shifts in family-therapist discourse throughout the therapy encounter (Step 1). She elected to use the strategies iteratively (diagnostically and interventively) with the goal of facilitating rapid change (Step 2).

During the initial 90-minute session, the therapist observed the family's structure, hierarchy, and interactions. In her RFA of the session, the therapist created a "Brian's School Difficulties" gallery and filled it with the frames shared by the parents. Although the parents expressed concern for Brian and his obvious difficulty in going to school, they were not emotionally expressive with each other or toward Brian. They easily lapsed into a pattern of bewildered silence, shrugging their shoulders and waiting for the therapist to say something. When Brian's parents asked him if there were any problems at school, Brian said that he did not know, and the family lapsed into silence again. The therapist observed that the "Brian's School Difficulties" gallery lacked any frames contributed by Brian himself and that the individual family members had not added new frames to build on previously generated frames by the other family members in the session. The therapist quickly concluded that the parents had limited skill in providing emotional support to each other or to their introverted 14-year-old son and that the family was floundering in the domain of emotional expressiveness. Family members were having difficulties providing support to one another. The therapist utilized interventive interviewing to help the family members give voice to their unexpressed feelings and worries and lived experiences within their family. In her RFA, the therapist noted a new opening as she asked each family member to describe what he or she imagined the other family members were most worried about as they sat in the room finding it hard to say anything. The therapist added family member frames, which she placed into the new gallery and titled, "Other Family Members' Worries" (Step 3).

In addition, the therapist recorded another opening in the RFA as she asked the parents about their fondest hopes for Brian and what they imagined he had been going through since the move and transfer to the new middle school. The therapist recorded the parents' hopeful talk in a "Mom and Dad's Hopes for Brian" gallery. In a series of openings to new galleries, the therapist asked the parents to think back to their early teenage years and to describe a time when an older person had given them some encouragement or helped out and what that had meant to them. She also asked the parents to share their perspectives on how being a teenager today is different from being a teenager when they were growing up. The frames and galleries the therapist noted from the family through the process of interventive interviewing provided the basis for her further assessment of Brian's and his parents' worries and fears and also began to open up space for connection between them through sharing of meanings and reflections about adolescence and getting support from adults. To make these connections, the therapist drew a side-by-side rendering of the problem wing populated by galleries, such as "Brian's School Difficulties," on one side of her paper and a hopeful wing with galleries, such as "Family Members' Shared Adolescent" on the other side of the page (Step 4).

Building on the emerging themes of isolation versus mutual support and bewilderment versus active encouragement and emotional expressiveness as noted across the "Brian's School Difficulties" and "Family Members' Shared Adolescent" galleries, the therapist helped the family to construct their genogram and locate themselves within the wider context of their larger family and cultural history, at least as much of it as they were able to pull together. Brian's parents were second-generation Irish immigrants and were part of the Irish diaspora, with close relatives whom they had never met in Australia, England, and other parts of the United States. As they constructed their genogram, the family members began to see that their enduring work ethic and "suffer in silence" style made sense given the challenges and lack of support that their grandparents and great-grandparents contended with as immigrants to the southern United States without extended family or an Irish exile community to depend on. Brian began to express an interest in his cultural history, and his parents began to reflect on how difficult it had been for their families without active support from other relatives or a community. As the therapist charted these new frames, she collected them in a gallery she titled, "Family's Shared History."

The qualitative assessments that the therapist had selected worked synergistically and helped the family to reflect on themes of isolation, support, encouragement, and expressiveness. From within these "problem" galleries, the therapist began to construct new, more solution-focused frames as Brian's parents began thinking about and commenting on their cultural heritage of suffer in silence and were questioning how they could change that history for Brian and Danielle. A fuller assessment of Brian's particular fears about school and his relationships was critical. The therapist decided to involve the family fully in that assessment because the context had now been set for greater reflection and sharing with one another through use of the other qualitative assessments described.

The therapist used oral and written reports to Brian and his family in an iterative process throughout therapy and worked collaboratively with the family to develop graphic assessments through the use of the genogram (Step 5 and Step 6). The oral reports consisted of summarizing and commenting on the wings, galleries, and frames derived from the qualitative assessment data—namely, isolation versus mutual support and bewilderment versus active encouragement and emotional expressiveness. The therapist invited Brian and his parents to reflect on these themes and to add their own comments and meanings to them in an ongoing collaborative and iterative process. The therapist added these new frames to her RFA of the case.

The therapist developed written reports in the form of letters to Brian and his parents after each session. In the letters, the therapist would include her RFA drawings and reflect on the most recent therapy session by posing interventive questions to each family member related to the major theme discussed in the session. In this way, more data for ongoing iterative assessment and intervention were collected. Through building a genogram, the family created a more coherent and articulated history than they had constructed previously, and they were able to stand back from that history and see themselves and their own challenges within it. Through the RFA scoring of their session, the therapist was able to show the family how their work in therapy allowed them to present the important problems they were facing individually and collectively while also identifying some hopeful and solution-focused directions they could take together (Step 7).

CONCLUDING NOTE

The qualitative assessment methods included in this chapter consist of classic assessments, such as the genogram, and structural and strategic observations and innovative methods, such as RFA. The postmodern perspective on interpersonal assessment is represented in the section on interventive interviewing. Additionally, an overlooked resource, the AAI, has been included for family therapists interested in using this assessment to guide therapy toward repair of insecure attachments in the service of brain integration, consistent with the latest findings in

TABLE 2.1 Matrix: Qualitative Assessment Strategies With Couples and Families

Assessment Instrument	Specific Couple and Family Applications	Cultural/ Language	Instructions/Use: T = Time to Take S = Time to Score I = Items (# of)	Computerized: (a) Scoring (b) Report	Reliability (R) Validity (V)	Availability
Observing Structure, Hierarchy, & Interactions	Parents, partners, or children; provides visual & language-based profile of relational patterns	Administer in any language	T = 60–120 min S = 60–120 min I = N/A	a = No b = No	Triangulation	Books, journal articles
Diagnostic Interviewing	Parents, partners, or children; provides visual & language-based profile of relational patterns	Administer in any language	T = 60–120 min S = 60–120 min I = Responses to questions	a = No b = No	Triangulation, member checks	Books, journal articles
Adult Attachment Inventory (AAI)	Parents or partners; provides narrative accounts of relational patterns	Administer in any language	T = 45–90 min S = Several hours I = 20	a = No b = No	Test–retest reliability = .70–90	AAI workshops, AAI websites
Interventive Interviewing *Circular Reflexive Solution-Focused Narrative*	Parents, partners, or children; language-based; used to identify and change relational patterns	Administer in any language	T = 60–120 min S = 60–120 min I = responses to questions	a = No b = No	Triangulation, member checks	Books, journal articles
Genogram	Parents, partners, or children; provides graphic of multigenerational relationships and family themes	Administer in any language	T = 10–30 min S = 20–60 min I = N/A	a = No b = Yes	Triangulation, member checks	Books, journal articles, computer software
Recursive Frame Analysis (RFA)	Parents, partners, or children; provides semantic, sequential, and pragmatic discourse analysis of conversations, interviews, scenarios, or role-playing sessions	Administer in any language	T = Real-time conversational scoring S = Several hours for micro-analysis I = N/A	a = No b = No	Consensual, member checks, constant-comparative method	Books, chapters, journal articles, www.nova. edu/~ron/rfa. html

neuroscience. Use of RFA can help the therapist to identify the most promising areas for intervention by tracking conversational themes and shifts in themes. RFA provides the therapist with a map of family members' conversations so that the easy to overlook openings to new and more desirable ways of thinking and acting can then be amplified. When using RFA, it is more difficult for the therapist to miss the nuanced and subtle possibilities for positive difference that can easily get lost in large chunks of conversation about problems.

The role of theory in assessment selection has been emphasized and assessment techniques representing multiple philosophical paradigms have been presented. Qualitative assessments in couples and family therapy are the cornerstone of the work of practicing family therapists; in fact, some therapists also suggest that the use of qualitative approaches can have therapeutic benefits for clients (e.g., Gale, 1992). In addition, the qualitative assessments described in detail above provide a highly legitimated avenue for developing high context, rapidly usable practice-based evidence. It is hoped that this chapter has been a review of methods with which the reader is already familiar as well as an invitation to explore some new ones.

REFERENCES

American Psychiatric Association. (2000). *Diagnostic and statistical manual of mental disorders* (4th ed., text revision). Washington, DC: Author.

Aponte, H. J. (1994). *Bread and spirit: Therapy with the new poor: Diversity of race, culture, and values.* New York: Norton.

Atkinson, B. (1999, July/August). Brainstorms: Rewiring the neural circuitry of family conflict. *Family Therapy Networker*, 23–33.

Bakermans-Kranenburg, M. J., & Van IJzendoorn, M. H. (1993). A psychometric study of the adult attachment interview: Reliability and discriminant validity. *Developmental Psychology, 29,* 870–880.

Benoit, D., & Parker, K. C. H. (1994). Stability and transmission of attachment across three generations. *Child Development, 65,* 1444–1456.

Berg, I. K., & De Jong, P. (1996). Solution-building conversations: Co-constructing a sense of competence with clients. *Families in Society,* 77(6), 376–391.

Carlson, J., & Sperry, L. (Eds.). (1997). *The disordered couple.* New York: Taylor & Francis.

Chenail, R. J. (1991). *Medical discourse and systemic frames of comprehension.* Norwood, NJ: Ablex.

Chenail, R. J., & Duffy, M. (2011). Utilizing Microsoft Office to produce and present recursive frame analysis findings. *The Qualitative Report, 16*(1), 292–307. Available at http://www.nova.edu/ssss/QR/QR16-1/rfa.pdf

Chenail, R. J., Somers, C. V., & Benjamin, J. D. (2009). A recursive frame qualitative analysis of MFT progress note tipping points. *Contemporary Family Therapy, 31*(2), 87–99. doi:10.1007/s10591-009-9085-7

Corbin, J., & Strauss, A. (2007). *Basics of qualitative research: Techniques and procedures for developing grounded theory* (3rd ed.). Thousand Oaks, CA: Sage.

Cotton, J. (2010). Question utilization in solution-focused brief therapy: A recursive frame analysis of Insoo Kim Berg's solution talk. *Qualitative Report, 15*(1), 18–36. Available at http://www.nova.edu/ssss/QR/QR15-1/cotton.pdf

Cozolino, L. (2002). *The neuroscience of psychiatry: Building and rebuilding the human brain.* New York: Norton.

de Shazer, S. (1988). *Clues: Investigating solutions in brief therapy.* New York: Norton.

Dunn, A. B., & Levitt, M. M. (2000). The genogram: From diagnostics to mutual collaboration. *Family Journal, 8*(3), 236–244.

Fleuridas, C., Nelson, T. S., & Rosenthal, D. M. (1986). The evolution of circular questions: Training family therapists. *Journal of Marital and Family Therapy, 12*, 113–127.

Gabbay, J., & Le May, A. (2011). *Practice-based evidence for healthcare: Clinical mindlines.* London: Routledge.

Gale, J. (1992). When research interviews are more therapeutic than therapy interviews. *The Qualitative Report, 1*(4). Available at http://www.nova.edu/ssss/QR/QR1-4/gale.html

George, C., Kaplan, N., & Main, M. (1985). *The attachment interview for adults.* Unpublished manuscript, University of California, Berkeley.

George, C., Kaplan, N., & Main, M. (1996). *Adult attachment interview.* Unpublished manuscript (3rd ed.), Department of Psychology, University of California, Berkeley.

Gottman. J. M. (1999a). *The marriage clinic: A scientifically based marital therapy.* New York: Norton.

Gottman, J. M. (1999b). *The seven principles for making marriage work.* New York: Crown.

Haley, J. (1991). *Problem-solving therapy* (2nd ed.). San Francisco: Jossey-Bass.

Hardy, K. V., & Laszloffy, T. A. (1995). The cultural genogram: Key to training culturally competent family therapists. *Journal of Marital and Family Therapy, 21*, 227–237.

Hill, C. E., Knox, S., Thompson, B. J., Williams, E. N., Hess, S. A., & Ladany, N. (2005). Consensual qualitative research: An update. *Journal of Counseling Psychology, 52*(2), 196–205.

Hodge, D. R. (2005). Spiritual assessment in marital and family therapy: A methodological framework for selecting between six qualitative assessment tools. *Journal of Marital and Family Therapy, 31*(4), 341–356.

Jordan, K. (2006). The scripto-trauma genogram: An innovative technique for working with trauma survivors' intrusive memories. *Brief treatment and crisis intervention, 6*(1), 36–51.

Jordan, C., & Franklin, C. (2011). *Clinical assessment: Quantitative and qualitative methods* (3rd ed.). Chicago: Lyceum Books.

Keeney, B. P. (1991). *Improvisational therapy: A practical guide for creative clinical strategies*. New York: Guilford Press.

Kerr, M. E., & Bowen, M. (1988). *Family evaluation*. New York: Norton.

Lemieux-Charles, L., & Champagne, F. (2008). *Using knowledge and evidence in healthcare: Multidisciplinary perspectives*. Toronto: University of Toronto Press.

Liddle, H. A., & Dakoff, G. A. (1995). Family-based treatment for adolescent drug use: State of the science. In E. Rahdert & D. Czechowicz (Eds.), *Adolescent drug abuse: Clinical assessment and therapeutic interventions* (National Institute on Drug Abuse Research Monograph No. 156, NIH Publication No. 95-3908, pp. 218–254). Rockville, MD: National Institute on Drug Abuse.

Madanes, C., Keim, J., & Smessler, D. (1995). *The violence of men: A therapy of social action*. San Francisco: Jossey-Bass.

McGoldrick, M., Gerson, R., & Petry, S. S. (2008). *Genograms: Assessment and intervention* (3rd ed.). New York: Norton.

McGoldrick, M., Gerson, R., & Shellenberger, S. (1999). *Genograms: Assessment and intervention* (2nd ed.). New York: Norton.

Milewski-Hertlein, K. (2001). The use of a socially constructed genogram in clinical practice. *American Journal of Family Therapy, 29*(1), 23–38.

Minuchin, S., & Fishman, H. C. (1981). *Family therapy techniques*. Cambridge, MA: Harvard University Press.

Minuchin, S., Lee, W-Y., & Simon, G. M. (1996). *Mastering family therapy: Journeys of growth and transformation*. New York: Wiley.

Patton, M. Q. (2002). *Qualitative research & evaluation methods* (3rd ed.). Thousand Oaks, CA: Sage.

Rambo, A. H., Heath, A. W., & Chenail, R. J. (1993). *Practicing therapy: Exercises for growing therapists*. New York: Norton.

Rigazio-DiGilio, S. A., Ivey, A. E., Kunkler-Peck, K. P., & Grady, L. T. (2005). *Community genograms: Using individual, family and cultural narratives with clients*. New York: Teachers College Press.

Rodrigues, L. M., Wais, D. P., Zevallos, A., & Rodrigues, R. R. (2001, April). *Attachment scripts across cultures: Evidence for a universal script*. Poster session presented at Society for Research in Child Development, Minneapolis, MN.

Shellenberger, S., Dent, M. M., Davis-Smith, M., Seale, J., Weintraut, R., & Wright, T. (2007). Cultural genogram: A tool for teaching and practice. *Families, Systems, and Health, 25*(4), 367–381. doi:10.1037/1091-7527.25.4.367

Schore, A. N. (2003). *Affect dysregulation and disorders of the self*. New York: Norton.

Siegel, D. (2007). *The mindful brain: Reflection and attunement in the cultivation of well-being*. New York: Norton.

Szapocznik, J., & Coatsworth, J. D. (1999). An ecodevelopmental framework for organizing risk and protection for drug abuse: A developmental model of risk and protection. In M. Glantz & C. R. Hartel (Eds.), *Drug abuse: Origins and interventions* (pp. 331–366). Washington, DC: American Psychological Association.

Tomm, K. (1987a). Interventive interviewing: Part I. Strategizing as a fourth guideline for the therapist. *Family Process, 26*, 3–13.

Tomm, K. (1987b). Interventive interviewing: Part II. Reflexive questioning as a means to enable self-healing. *Family Process, 26*, 167–183.

Tomm, K. (1988). Interventive interviewing: Part III. Intending to ask lineal, circular, strategic, or reflexive questions? *Family Process, 27*, 1–15.

von Foerster, H. (1981). *Observing systems*. Seaside, CA: Intersystems.

Weiss, E. L., Coll. J. E., Gerbauer, J., Smiley, K., & Carillo, E. (2010). The military genogram: A solution-focused approach for resiliency building in service members and their families. *Family Journal, 18*(4), 395–406. doi:10.1177/1066480710378479

White, M., & Epston, D. (1990). *Narrative means to therapeutic ends*. New York: Norton.

CHAPTER 3

Standardized Assessment*

A. Rodney Nurse and Len Sperry

INTRODUCTION

When a family assessment includes a standardized test battery, the assessment applies scientifically sound psychological instruments that have stood the test of time with practicing clinicians. Although most of these tests were originally developed to evaluate individuals, the instruments discussed in this chapter have considerable value with couples and families. This chapter will describe four well-known and highly regarded instruments for the process of couple and family evaluation. These tests are the Minnesota Multiphasic Personality Inventory-2, the Millon Clinical Multiaxial Inventory-III, the Rorschach Inkblot Test, and the Kinetic Family Drawing Test. Then, it describes a seven-step clinical strategy for effectively utilizing these instruments in the process of assessing couples and families. Finally, it provides a detailed case example that illustrates the tests and the clinical protocol. This chapter reflects the basic orientation of A. Rodney Nurse's *Family Assessment: Effective Uses of Personality Tests With Couples and Families* (1999).

The focus, however, in this revised chapter shifts away from the use of full test batteries and toward increased use of computerized, assessment instruments, conserving professional time and reflecting the economic realities of this past decade.

---

* The results of standardized psychological instruments such as the MMPI-2, MCMI-III, and the Rorschach can be of immense clinical value. However, these instruments do require formal training and licensure as a psychologist, in most states, to legally and ethically administer, score, and interpret them.

INSTRUMENTS

MMPI-2: Assessing Symptoms, Moods, and Couple Types

Instrument name. The Minnesota Multiphasic Personality Inventory (MMPI) is the most widely used clinical testing instrument in the United States. It was developed by Starke Hathaway and Charnley McKinley, named after the University of Minnesota, and first published in 1943. A revised version, MMPI-2, was published in 1989. For clinical pattern interpretation purposes, both versions of the test are sufficiently similar to justify applying the couple pattern research drawn from the original MMPI to MMPI-2 clinical patterns. This application is particularly appropriate with well-defined, high two-point clinical scores above *T* of 70, or close (Butcher, 1990, 2002; Greene, 2000). Recently the MMPI-2 normative sample was updated psychometrically, major scales restructured, the number of items reduced to 338, and other changes made to capitalize on the strength of the instrument. Additionally, some wordings were normalized. Pending results of additional independent research and accrual of clinical experience with the revision, named the MMPI-2-RF, we continue to recommend using the MMPI-2, for which extensive research and clinical literature exists.

Type of instrument. MMPI-2 is a standardized personality inventory providing, at its original core, a quantitative measure of psychological symptoms, emotional adjustment indications, and psychopathological patterns: 1-Hypochondrisais, 2-Depression, 3-Hysteria, 4-Psychopathic Deviate, 5-Masculinity/Femininity, 6-Paranoia, 7-Psychasthenia, 8-Schizophrenia, 9-Hypomania, 10-Social Introversion. Because these names are either obsolete or convey distorted meanings of the present understandings of these dimensions, these scales are ordinarily referred to by numbers.

Use and target audience. The MMPI-2 is intended as a personality screening tool for individuals 18 and older. A related instrument, the Minnesota Multiphasic Personality Inventory–Adolescent (MMPI-A), is designed for use with 14- to 18-year-olds and is useful with parents or partners for a variety of purposes. Five common couple clusters have been articulated and are described in this chapter.

Multicultural. The MMPI-2 is available in English, Spanish, Hmong, French, Chinese, Hebrew, Korean, and Italian. Computer-generated interpretive reports are available only in English.

Ease and time of administration. An easy-to-administer inventory, the MMPI-2 calls for the client to respond "true" or "false" to 567 items and takes 60 to 90 minutes to complete. The MMPI-2 may be taken in paper-and-pencil format, audiocassette, or in a computer format and requires a sixth- to eighth-grade reading level.

Scoring procedure. The MMPI-2 is always scored on at least 10 scales measuring various clinical or personality dimensions and 3 scales related to validity and test-taking attitude. Ordinarily, 4 additional validity scales are scored together with more than 80 additional clinical scales, including 2 germane to marital and family issues. It may take 15 to 20 minutes to hand-score and chart the basic clinical profile. Computerized scoring, however, is typically the standard, not only because it easily scores the large number of additional scales, but also because accuracy is guaranteed, additional hypotheses are generated, and basic research-grounded interpretive statements may be provided.

Reliability. As indicated in the MMPI-2 manual, moderate test–retest reliabilities are reported, ranging from .67 to .92. Split-half reliabilities are also moderate median correlations of .70 (Groth-Marnat, 2003).

Validity. An unweighted mean validity coefficient of .30 is reported (Weiner, Spielberger, & Abeles, 2002).

Availability and source. Several scoring and interpretive computer programs are available, including the version generated by the developers of the MMPI-2 distributed by Pearson Assessments (formerly National Computer Systems) to qualified professionals. Pearson sells the test manual (Butcher, Dahlstrom, Graham, Tellegen, & Kaemmer, 2001). Although basic interpretive hypotheses are provided in addition to scoring, clinicians interested in an in-depth, research-grounded dynamic interpretive report may utilize the Alex Caldwell report system (2001).

Comment. This is the most widely used standardized psychological test and has considerable value with couples and families, as noted in the following sections.

Using the MMPI-2 With Couples

Because work with couples typically focuses first on dysfunctional relationships, the MMPI-2—which measures behavioral symptoms and mood states that may have an impact on a partner, stem from a partner's impact, or both—has considerable usefulness as an initial assessment device. Two new scales have been developed that have particular relevance to family and couple assessment:

- *Family Problems Scale* (FAM). Families with high scores on this content scale are described as lacking in love and being quarrelsome and unpleasant. Their childhoods may be portrayed as abusive and their marriages seen as unhappy and lacking in intimacy and affection. FAM is a gross measure reflecting problems, past and present, in the family as a whole. It is useful in initial screening to ascertain the degree of seriousness of family problems.

• *Marital Distress Scale* (MDS). This scale has the advantage of focusing on measuring distress or discord in close relationships, rather than measuring more global family problems as with the FAM. The MDS is described as an efficient discrimination of maladjustment in marriages at a *T* score of 60 or above.

Five-Cluster Classification of Couples Seeking Therapy

Research on the original MMPI cited by Nurse (1999) suggests that as many as 50% of couples with marital problems fall into one of five recognized MMPI clusters. Renaming them slightly from the original research, Nurse labels these clusters as openly warring couples; unhappy, problem-focused couples; husband-blaming couples; psychologically disordered couples; and distant, calm couples. Each of these couples and MMPI codes is briefly described in terms of interactional dynamics and unique treatment issues. Wives codes are presented first, husbands second, in the parentheses next to the name of the couple pattern.

Openly Warring Couples (4-3/4-9 Codes) Warring wives present with poorly controlled anger and hostility that is expressed in a cyclical fashion, as reflected in their 4-3 high-point code. Following a submissive, suppressive phase, a build-up of tension can result in a loss of control seen in angry, aggressive acting-out. This may be triggered as much by internal stimuli as by externally based stress. Between stormy bouts of anger expressions, they are models of (older generational culturally stereotyped) "femininity," displaying passivity and submissiveness (but demonstrating periodically complaining behavior) as they defer overtly to their husbands. Not surprisingly, this submissive behavior adds to suppressed resentment that, in time, erupts.

Warring husbands act regularly on their impulses and are frequently rebellious against the restraints of authority and usual socially accepted standards. This reflects their high Scale 4. Integral to this personality style is a high level of energy, indicated by Scale 9, which serves to provide fuel to the acting-out. Because of their freedom from anxiety, worry, and guilt, these husbands often make a comfortable, smoother, and socially facile appearance initially. At the same time, they are impatient with anything deeper than a superficial relationship consistent with their craving for action and excitement. A seemingly submissive wife, who follows the husband's lead uncritically and without question, as well as satisfying needs for attention and sex, fits the husband's comfort with someone to cater to his impulses and action orientation. Therapy with this couple tends to be volatile, and the therapist's challenge is to join with their fighting style and help them learn to fight fairly or to identify this overall repetitive conflict pattern and work with conflict resolution skills. However, this is not typically a couple that excels at communicating verbally or reasons well with problems. Instead, this is an action-oriented couple that, if they can fight fairly to resolve conflicts, may be able to reach reasonable solutions to their problems, despite their overall pattern, and may stay together satisfactorily.

Unhappy, Problem-Focused Couples (2-1-3/2-7 Codes) This couple is seen quite commonly in couples therapy, often presenting with unhappiness or depressive features and high levels of marital dissatisfaction. They typically present with a problem-solving orientation and an openness to self-appraisal. Unhappy, problem-focused husbands tend to have 2-7 codes and present with unhappiness, worry, and tension. They blame themselves; easily feel inadequate despite their achievements; and, interestingly, have the capacity for satisfying and rewarding interpersonal relationships because they are turned in on themselves. They seek advice and help from therapists and are likely to follow therapeutic suggestions. Unhappy, problem-focused wives tend to have major symptoms of depression. Their overall code is often 2-1-3, which is known as the neurotic triad configuration. Like their husbands, they are anxious and self-doubting and tend to be dependent and immature. They seem capable of maintaining a long-suffering, unhappy role in the relationship; consequently, their motivation for change may be less than optimal. Not only will a worsening of the relationship present a crisis, but positive change can also upset the couple or family homoeostatic balance. In couples therapy, therapists may find that intimacy is the core issue for these couples and that they deal with intimacy issues by maintaining some degree of disengagement. Thus, efforts to increase their interaction and intimacy may increase conflict and their perception that therapy "makes things worse." Accordingly, the strategy is to focus gently on the dynamics of interaction, without blaming, and concentrate on the couple's ability to work on practical solutions to identified problems. Such couples do maintain long-standing marriages, solving problems somehow with avoidance and yet resolving them nevertheless. If therapy goes even reasonably well, these couples have the potential to move past their avoidant pattern, interact more directly, and evolve into a positive, growing marriage relationship.

Husband-Blaming Couples (4-6/2-4 Codes) In these couples, angry husband blaming (4-6) by the wives is linked to apologetic, although sometimes resentful, acceptance of blame by the husbands (2-4). These women attempt to present themselves as psychologically healthy yet are guarded, as reflected in L and K scores elevated above the F score. They tend to see the world in right–wrong, black–white terms and are reluctant to engage in self-criticism, which is consistent with the 4-6 code. When Scale 1 is also elevated, "whining somatization" can be noted. A blaming woman is also wary and suspicious; if there is verified reason for this suspiciousness and no history of delinquency or past major difficulty in social relations, it may well be that she is reacting to the present couple dispute instead of this being a characterological problem.

The striking feature of the husbands' typical profile (2-4) is depression; these men are suffering from a generally unhappy, dysphoric mood accompanied by feelings of inadequacy, lack of self-confidence, self-depreciation, and strong guilt feelings. For the husbands, their wives' blaming and perceived nagging may provide justification for their resentfulness and self-destructive behavior (e.g., alcohol abuse and suicidal ideation). Therapy needs to focus on both partners learning to take responsibility for themselves, avoiding blaming, and understanding more of their own psychological make-up. Therapy can help them learn to be more empathic with their partners. To this end, a couples group could prove useful. If the husband's depression continues, a medication evaluation should be considered. For wives, a group separate from their husbands could also provide a place to learn to modify the extreme black-and-white thinking and to learn how to shoulder more responsibility without blaming.

Psychologically Disordered Couples (1-2-3/2-4-6-8 Codes) These couples have the greatest conflict potential of all five couple clusters. Psychologically disordered husbands are clearly seeking help and may even be exaggerating symptoms to attract attention. However, they appear to be seeking help for good psychological reasons. Their clinical scale profile is a saw-toothed pattern in which Scales 2, 4, 6, and 8 are significantly elevated above the other scales. These husbands are depressed, angry, and distrustful as well as feeling alienated from others; others view them as moody and unpredictable. They are likely to be ruminative, preoccupied, and inflexible in problem solving. In contrast to the overly acute nature of their husbands' presentation, psychologically disordered wives are attempting to avoid, deny, and generally not deal with unacceptable feelings and impulses. However, despite this effort, they appear to have a chronic neurotic condition and are usually diagnosed with somatoform disorders, anxiety disorders, depressive disorders, or all of these. They are unsure, rather inept females who may have grown accustomed to a high level of unhappiness and considerable discomfort. When in therapy, these wives are seldom highly motivated for treatment because of their melancholy adjustment to a chronic condition and their pattern of denial, which contrasts with their husbands actively seeking help. However, because of the unstableness of their condition, the husbands may have difficulty in persevering in treatment. Unlike couples in the four other clusters, these couples may need intensive individual psychological evaluation, including a psychological testing battery, and they may require collateral psychiatric evaluation for medication.

When therapy is undertaken, the therapeutic plan, including goals, objectives, and intermediate tactics, must be thoroughly delineated with as much collateral help as appropriate (e.g., psychiatry, support groups, and provisions for emergencies). If these couples make changes, the changes will be even more threatening than for many couples with other dysfunctional patterns. If the disordered husband behaves in a more sane way, he must take more responsibility for his actions. At the same time, the disordered wife must tolerate the anxiety of looking at herself psychologically and assuming more responsibility for herself without focusing as much on her husband. Not surprisingly, psychophysiological stress reactions are to be expected.

Distant, Calm Couples (Within Normal Limits 4-8/8 Spike Codes) Typically, the MMPI profiles for these couples fall within normal limits. Compared to other couple clusters, these couples are relatively satisfied with their marriages. They tend to be older and have been married longer than other couple clusters. These distant, calm husbands are likely to think somewhat differently from others (mild 8). This may reflect their creativity, avant-garde attitude, or schizoid or avoidant personality structure. They tend to avoid reality through daydreaming and fantasy. Their distant, calm wives also have some sense of differentness and avoidance, yet they may be more genuinely concerned about social problems and issues. The couple's distancing pattern may reflect their response to situational conflicts, or it may reflect their habitual level of social and interpersonal related-ness. Their apparent lack of acute distress does not mean that they are not silently suffering the angst of emptiness, separation, deprivation, and lack of meaning associated with their high Scale 8 scores. Nevertheless, therapists who come across such seemingly normal MMPI profiles, suggesting the couple is without symptoms and is not demonstrating any obvious psychopathology, might look to other instruments such as the MCMI-III or the Millon Index of Personality Styles (MIPS; Millon, 1994) for further diagnostic understanding and for treatment planning. Among MMPI-2 interpreters, such "normal" profiles can sometimes mean that the couple has become adjusted to their chronically ingrained problems and issues.

Interpreting Couple MMPI-2s Not in the Five Clusters

Some of the MMPI-2 couple patterns falling outside the five groupings will have one partner who does fit a pattern in one of the five groups. The reader is referred to descriptions of other code types in Greene (2000) and Groth-Marnat (2003). The evaluating therapist should also be cognizant of certain red flag warnings about potentially dangerous problems. These include high elevations on Scale 9 (Mania), which can indicate narcissistic, grandiose, and overly active (hypomanic) behavior, and high elevations on Scale 6 (Paranoid) that could indicate suspicious hostility, blaming, or projection of negative feelings onto others. See Nurse (1999) for a discussion of other red flags and interview suggestions related to following up on them. Nurse (1999) also discusses gender issues related to two MMPI-2 scales, as well as scale indicators of spousal dominance and submission issues.

Summary

This section presented an approach for interpreting couple MMPI-2s based on an elaboration of probable interactional dynamics of an MMPI-2 typology of five types of couples originally identified in MMPI research. Because up to 50% of couples with marital problems fall into this typology, therapists would do well to become familiar with these types and their therapeutic implications for couples treatment. Suggestions were also made for considering other patterns and the clinical utility of other specialized and content scales relevant to working with couples.

MCMI-III: Assessing Personality Styles or Disorders of Marital Partners

Instrument name. The Millon Clinical Multiaxial Inventory (MCMI-III), in its third edition, was developed by Theodore Millon (1977, 1996, 1997a, 2008).

Type of instrument. The MCMI-III is a standardized personality inventory that includes 24 clinical scales and 4 scales concerning reliability and validity, on which every test taker is scored. Eleven clinical scales measure clinical personality patterns and three indicate severe personality patterns, with very high scores similar to DSM-IV-TR personality disorders. Moderate clinical personality pattern scores reflect personality traits, while a slightly elevated score represents personality features. Seven scales assess DSM-IV-TR, Axis I, clinical syndromes (i.e., anxiety, somatoform, bipolar, dysthymia, alcohol dependence, drug dependence, and posttraumatic stress disorder) and three reflect serious clinical syndromes (i.e., thought disorder, major depression, and delusional disorder). In addition, the Grossman Facet scales identify personality processes that underlie overall scale elevations on the 14 Personality Pattern Scales but are activated only when a Personality Pattern Score reaches a significantly high level.

Use and target audience. This instrument is used for assessing and making treatment decisions in adults (18 years and older), focusing on personality style and disorders, and is unique among tests. An adolescent version, the Millon Adolescent Clinical Inventory (MACI), is available and has been normed on 13- to 19-year-olds.

Multicultural. English and Spanish versions are available. Computer-generated interpretive reports are available only in English.

Ease and time of administration. The inventory consists of 175 statements about personality and behavior to which the individual responds "true" or "false" as applied to him or her. It can be completed in 20 to 30 minutes and may be taken directly on a computer or in paper format. An eighth-grade reading level is specified.

Scoring procedure. Computer scoring takes only a few minutes to provide a simple profile with minimal interpretive comments or a full interpretive report.

Reliability. Moderate levels of reliability have been noted. Test–retest reliabilities have been reported in a range from .67–.91 to .67–.69 for 1 year as well as an internal consistency of .80 (Groth-Marnat, 2003).

Validity. Although the positive predictive power of the MCMI-II ranged between .30 and .80, predictive values for the MCMI-III were not reported in the test manual (Millon, 1997a).

Availability and source. This inventory can be obtained from Pearson Assessments (formerly National Computer Systems, Inc.).

Comment. The MCMI-III, developed empirically from a theoretical base, has accrued over 600 references, including a number of books. Over the course of a quarter of a century, it has reached an established place among clinicians, including those working with couples in whom DSM-IV Axis I and II issues are suspected in one or both partners.

Using the MCMI-III With Couples

At the present time, the MCMI-III is the only major and widely used psychological inventory that assesses qualities of personality styles and personality disorders within the context of an empirically derived theory consistent with DSM-IV-TR. This makes it a core instrument for a comprehensive assessment battery. Even used alone for screening, the inventory is extremely useful in arriving at hypotheses about the personality structure and interactive pattern of the underlying immediate conflicts, overt anxiety, and depressive, or acting-out, features that partners present with in couples therapy.

The Process of Couple MCMI-III Analysis

1. Check for satisfactory validity and response style scores.
2. Next, note significant scores on the profile of each spouse so that indications of personality disorders or styles (traits or disorders indicated by elevated scores falling at a level below

disorders) and any clinical syndromes are compared with other information collected, such as the clinical interview and previous records or collateral data. Beyond comparing family history of psychiatric and substance dependence, information on the partners' family-of-origin histories, attraction to each other, and courting history can be usefully compared with their scores on the 14 personality style/disorders scales.

3. After completing this overall analysis, an in-depth analysis of the personalities and interaction patterns needs to be undertaken. This can be done with the help of Millon's *MCMI-III Manual* (1997a) or, in greater depth, Millon's *Disorders of Personality* (1996). The most recent comprehensive MCMI-III reference material may be found in Millon's second edition of *The Millon Inventories* (2008). Consistent with the purposes of this writing, we recommend the chapter in that book by Nurse and Stanton.

Using the MCMI in Treating Couples

With couple interpretations, it is particularly important to look at the behavioral level, that is, expressive behavior and interpersonal behavior. From this level, inferences can be systematically drawn about linkages with features or domains falling at other levels. These levels include the polarities of *pleasure–pain, active–passive,* and *self–other.* Identifying where couples fall with reference to these polarities (especially self–other) and their personality styles/disorders can be most clinically useful in understanding the homeostatic function of these balances. This is because the couple or family system tends to make adjustments to maintain the status quo, thereby preserving the relationships between individuals that meet some individual needs. This analysis permits a more detailed description of the interactive pattern of the personality expressions of the couple and provides the basis for planning and therapeutic treatment, which can be sharpened by reference to personality-guided therapy (Millon, 1999). A detailed example of this analysis process applied to the dependent/narcissistic couple may be found in Nurse's (1997) chapter in *The Disordered Couple* (Carlson & Sperry, 1997). See also the Nurse and Stanton chapter in *The Millon Inventories* (Millon, 2nd ed., 2008), and the Stanton and Nurse chapter in *The Handbook of Family Psychology* (Bray & Stanton, 2009), which provide illustrations of the process.

Prototypic MCMI-III Couple Relational Patterns

This section briefly describes six MCMI-III couple relationship patterns commonly seen in outpatient treatment settings.

Narcissistic Male/Histrionic Female   Males with a very high score on the Narcissistic scale (5) may act in an arrogant fashion with a tendency irresponsibly to ignore social norms and standards. They may show little empathy and act in an interpersonally exploitive manner, seemingly unaware of the negative impact on others. These males may have self-glorifying fantasies of success, yet may move from job to job always looking for employment that meets how they think they should be treated. Yet, narcissistic males maintain a cool aura, seemingly not shaken by anything. However, it is particularly important on this scale to determine whether a high score represents a style or a disorder (Craig, 1999). With a narcissistic style, subtle attitudes may be reflective in a moderate way of these characteristics, except under pressure when the attitudes and behaviors can become significantly more pronounced. Females in this relational pattern often show a marked peak on the Histrionic scale (4). They convey an engaging, fleeting, and often theatrical attitude, conveying a high level of excitement and activity. Histrionics seek to be the center of attention, developing ways of being socially stimulating, but they avoid reflecting on even fleeting unwanted emotions, seeking to deny contradictory feelings as they are constantly in action. At the trait level, they may be dramatic and energetic but can enter more into relationships with some success. Given the frequent lack of any symptoms evident on the MCMI clinical syndrome scale scores, some with slight scale elevations appear to have simply histrionic features and are upbeat and free from indications of maladjustment. If an elevation on the Compulsive scale (7) occurs, their general emotional style is likely to be balanced by some capacity to be organized, thorough, and conscientious while remaining expressive and outgoing, as reflected in a moderately elevated Histrionic scale score. This pattern suggests a person functioning relatively effectively.

In the couple relationship, the truly histrionic female will likely be attracted to the narcissistic male because of his sureness, command, and seeming interest in her. He is likely to be attracted to her, however, because of her apparent attraction to him and his own fantasies of how enhanced his life would be and how others will see him with her on his arm. They are likely to become disillusioned, periodically fight, and sometimes even triangulate a child or other individual in a struggle to gain power and make up for what they do not have with each other. Because these patterns represent some gender stereotypes, it may be useful for the couple to be seen by a male–female co-therapy team. Each therapist in individual sessions prior to some of the couple sessions could prepare his or her same-gendered client by acknowledging strengths and achievements coupled with setting structured goals. For the female, these sessions could include practicing on channeling of controlling feeling expressions; for the male, they could focus on empathy practice (with the therapist avoiding mirroring, which serves to reinforce narcissism). For the more moderate, normal-appearing histrionic/narcissistic couple, it may be that that couple's difficulties lie more in relationship communication problems than in the personality structure of either.

Compulsive Female/Dependent–Avoidant Male   Females with a high elevation on the Compulsive scale (7) appear excessively disciplined and maintain a highly structured, organized life. They see themselves as conscientious, devoted to thoroughness, and fearful of not doing things in the best possible way. They maintain an inner world that is cognitively constricted (i.e., narrow and rule bound, anticipating that others will behave similarly). Sometimes using reaction formation as a major defense, they appear super-reasonable, not dealing with contrary feelings, and fearful of underlying feelings such as anger. Although their lives may be full of tension and tight control of emotions, research suggests that an elevated compulsive score may indicate more conscientiousness than compulsivity (Craig, 1999), an effective and rewarded style in many environments. Males with an elevation on the Dependent (3) and Avoidant (2A) scales have a need for close relationships but hesitate about approaching others out of a fear of rejection. Their style is interpersonally submissive but not expressive. They may be seen as cognitively naive, avoiding confrontation; sometimes they experience themselves as weak and alienated. They may feel a need to become involved with, if not devoted to, others; they introject others' views and maintain relationships through the use of fantasy in order to avoid significant anxiety. At a level of personality style, moderate-level scores point to a person with a significant emotional neediness who, because of the importance of relationships, is hesitant to take action without being sure of acceptance.

Couples therapy with couples demonstrating more pronounced score patterns needs to proceed slowly and may benefit from accompanying individual sessions. Conjoint sessions must appeal to the female's need to do the right thing and the male's need for a close relationship with reassurance of acceptance. In couple sessions the goal is for the male to become more assertive and capitalize on his abilities developed outside the home and to become more active in the home. The goal for the female is modify her sometimes too conscientious pattern so as to be in more control of it, thus turning it to positive use and being less constricted by it, and to move from being passive and only (restrictively) nurturing others to paying increased attention to her own needs as well as those of others.

Narcissistic Male/Narcissistic Female   As noted earlier, males with a marked peak on the Narcissistic scale (5) may act in an arrogant, condescending fashion with a tendency to irresponsibly ignore social norms and standards. They likely possess an interpersonally exploitive manner, seemingly unaware of the negative impact on others. They tend to view themselves as special and have fantasies of love and success that drive them to high levels of achievement, yet they may repress and/or reshape affect and distort facts to maintain their self-illusions in the face of failures. Typically, they maintain a cool aura of self-possessed optimism unless their confidence is shaken. Females with very high elevations on the Narcissistic scale (5) may present much as narcissistic males. They are interested in others in large part for what they can gain from them in terms of their own self-esteem, and thus they can behave amorously. Nevertheless, they tend to be self-deceptive, self-centered, and rationalize; until their confidence is shaken, they present with a cool, imperturbable demeanor.

As a couple, narcissistic males and females tend to have similar blind spots: repressing and denying the same negative aspects of their personalities. This means that they cannot easily confront each other without being aware of similar self-aggrandizing traits in themselves. Although they believed earlier in their relationship that they were "made for each other" (because they reflected each other), with the arrival of a child or other shifts in their interpersonal balance, each misses the other's focused attention. Their intense attachment can switch from positive to negative, blaming each other and pointing out the negative parts of the other's personality, and thereby warding off confronting themselves with their own experiences of deprivation and recognition of their shortcomings. By recognizing the couple's interlocking narcissistic styles, a couples therapist can more easily avoid responding negatively to these individuals' self-focused approaches to life and instead can support their effectiveness while gently helping them gain more empathy with each other. A couple demonstrating narcissistic traits (rather than disorders) may have developed a broader base and a better interpersonal connection, giving the therapist a platform to assist them in building a sounder marriage relationship despite the arrival of a child, loss of a job, illness, or other unbalancing occurrence.

Histrionic–Narcissistic Female/Compulsive Male In this profile, the Histrionic pattern (Scale 4), mixed with Narcissistic features (Scale 5) of superiority and entitlement, increases the possibility of irresponsible, acting-out behavior considerably beyond that of the prototypical histrionic personality disorder in females. These individuals tend to be attracted to Compulsive (Scale 7), that is, conscientious, males whom they view as stable, goal oriented, and secure. However, with time they experience such men as boring and rigid. These females may have sought out other types of relationships but, after being wounded, may have retreated to safe kinds of husband–father relationships with a compulsive male in order to lick their wounds.

Males with a compulsive or conscientious personality (Scale 7) are likely to have been excited and attracted to these affectively dominated females, whom they typically view as intriguing, colorful, and vivacious. Yet, with the passage of time and relational demands, these males become disconcerted with their partners, whom they now view as flighty, irresponsible, and supremely selfish and vain. Relationally, these females will be the source of feeling expressiveness in the relationship, while these males will be the voice of reason. Couples therapy stressing improved communication could focus on having these couples get to know each other as specific, unique individuals. Unfortunately, without the benefit of couples therapy or other corrective experiences, neither partner is likely to move beyond these limiting roles without expressing his or her humanity.

Antisocial Female/Antisocial–Narcissistic Male Clinicians inexperienced with the MCMI-III may improperly conclude that both partners are antisocial or psychopathic personalities because of elevated 6A Scales. In keeping with Millon's clinical formulation of this scale as primarily a measure of aggression, such scale elevations (particularly at a moderate level) reflect the competitive, aggressive attitude and style associated with successful entrepreneurs. These are the "antisocial" style individuals who are likely to come in for couples therapy. It would be surprising if true psychopaths, who comprise only a minority of antisocial personality disorders, came for therapy.

Couples with this pattern who show up for therapy typically take risks, exploit (usually within the limits of the law), and shade the truth to meet their own needs. Yet, they view themselves as law-abiding individuals. When they become involved in close romantic relationships, they can carry some of these antisocial qualities into that relationship. Thus, they can be competitive and can view their relationship as a game in which they match wits with each other. They may admire each other's ability to succeed in business; however, they can be tough, argumentative, and insensitive to each other's feelings. With this couple, an imbalance can be anticipated because of the male's narcissistic (Scale 5) entitlement. His partner will become incensed at his self-centeredness. When she finds ways to puncture his confident front, he may respond with hurt, rage, and vindictiveness. Their motivation for coming for couples therapy is probably so that each can gain an advantage over the other. When the therapist does not express judgment of who is right, they can impatiently join in turning on the therapist, only to seek a new one. Therapists need to be aware that this therapy could be the first stage in a long divorce battle in which neither gives because winning is everything for them.

Dependent Male/Dependent Female Dependent partners (Scale 3) tend to be so "nice" to each other that they inevitably tread lightly in their relationship. Unfortunately, treading lightly allows little opportunity for openly dealing with their problems. Consequently, problem solving only appears to occur when one partner quickly acquiesces in order to avoid being criticized. At some level, each partner may be looking for a good parent and thus may develop considerable resentment, although each tends to squelch this; if irritation comes out unexpectedly, that partner may hurriedly apologize. Each partner has the capacity to be kind, loving, and caring with each other. If they begin to develop personally outside the relationship—through work experiences, for instance—and maintain their same way of couple relating, this dissonance in their lives may bring them to couples therapy. By helping each recognize his or her growing resentment and assisting each in learning to communicate feelings more directly, the therapist can help these needy people experience developing together. When dependent style couples seek help, the therapist needs to discover what has unbalanced their relationship, for example, the personal growth of one more than the other, a new child, a promotion, a relationship external to the marriage, and so forth.

Summary

The MCMI-III uniquely provides informational, descriptive hypotheses about personality structure as well as syndromal indications. The MCMI-III profile helps the couples therapist draw understandable hypotheses about the couple relationship and interactive pattern in guiding planning for interventions.

The Rorschach: Application to Families

Format of the Rorschach

Instrument name. The Rorschach Inkblot Test, usually called the Rorschach, was named after the Swiss psychiatrist who developed and first published it in 1921.

Type of instrument. It is a projective test consisting of 10 inkblots.

Use and target audience. This test is used with all ages (except the youngest of children) for gathering information describing personality as reflected in the perceptual processes of the person and the associational dynamics related to content. It is particularly valuable for in-depth personality evaluations of parents or partners with issues involving child custody, child abuse, and divorce, as well as in planning psychotherapy with adults, adolescents, and children.

Multicultural. This instrument can be administered in any language. A Spanish language manual is available from the publisher of Exner's

Comprehensive System for the Rorschach; however, computer-generated interpretive reports based on Exner's system are available only in English.

Ease and time of administration. In administering the Rorschach using Exner's *Comprehensive System* (Exner, 1993, 2001; the most extensively used system), the examiner sits side by side with the examinee, thus avoiding distractions or unconscious shaping of responses caused by an examiner's inadvertent changes of facial expression or body posture. The examiner presents each blot with the instructions to respond to the question: "What might this be?" A follow-up inquiry using carefully delineated questioning helps the examiner to be clear about the location of the response, what went into making the response, and a sense of the nature of the content of the response. Worthy of note is that a new Rorschach close to publication is designed "to reflect evolution change in Rorschach research" and to supersede the Rorschach Comprehensive System (CS)." The new system is designated as the Rorschach Performance System (R-PAS; Meyer et al., 2011).

Scoring procedure. Using the *Comprehensive System*, responses are categorized by using scoring procedures painstakingly developed to maximize consistency of assessor scoring. Entered into a computer, these resulting scores are combined based on research-derived procedures. A computer program provides not only the combinations of scores but also a lengthy narrative of research and clinically based hypotheses for the assessor to use as an interpretive base (Exner et al., 2003).

Reliability. Test–retest reliabilities are reported in the range of .75 to .85, while intercoder agreement is in the range of .79 to .88 (Groth-Marnat, 2003).

Validity. An unweighted mean validity coefficient of .29 is reported in more than 2,200 Rorschach protocols. This suggests that the Rorschach "is generally as valid as the MMPI" (Weiner, Spielberger, & Abeles, 2002, p. 9).

Availability and source. Materials for the comprehensive system are distributed by Psychological Assessment Resources, Inc., to qualified professionals.

Comment. Despite this empirically based comprehensive system protocol, crafting a clinical report requires intensive instruction and supervision. It also requires extensive experience with the Rorschach, coupled with interview data about the examinee, typically complemented by the results of other psychological tests and inventories.

Using the Rorschach With Families

The Rorschach has a unique, significant, and often essential place in family treatment situations in which a thorough, in-depth understanding of personality is required on which to base decisions with far-reaching effects on the lives of family members, particularly children. For example, when an appraisal is sought about the mental state of parents and children in a heated, drawn-out, child custody dispute, the Rorschach can be a crucial source of uniquely salient information. It can also be helpful in complicated family situations when a puzzling child problem presents. Notably, the Rorschach findings in these situations may uncover processes not readily apparent, such as a thought disorder, the discovery of depression and its depth, or the dynamics of acting-out problem behavior.

Response styles (Exner, 1993) have particular relevance for understanding family behavior because they consistently influence or provide direction for various and sometimes diverse personality features manifest in family interaction. As such, they form major anchoring points for the therapist in searching for family system patterns. At the same time, the therapist must pay attention to consistent, pervasive behaviors on the part of each individual. These dominant Rorschach features are the Lambda Index, Experience Balance, Reflections, the Passive/Active Relationship, and the Hypervigilance Index. Nurse (1999) provides a cogent description of each of these dominant Rorschach features and suggests how each may have an impact on the family process and the strategy of the family therapist.

In considering the interpersonal, family-related implications of Rorschach findings, Exner's handbook on interpretation can serve as a primary reference (Exner, 2001). Research has resulted in identifying 11 key variable or clusters that provide substantial core information on the individual's personality and point the way toward organizing the remaining Rorschach data. Nurse (1999) offers a clinically useful discussion of these key variables.

Summary

The Rorschach is particularly applicable in situations requiring in-depth personality evaluations because at that time a family is facing situations that have far-reaching effects on its members, especially those involving children. In addition to diagnostic assessment and treatment planning, these issues include separation, divorce, abuse, and identifying psychosis and clinical depression. This section focused on the dominant interpersonal style and key characteristics of the Rorschach and their implications for understanding family interaction and for developing targets for therapeutic change.

The Kinetic Family Drawing Test: Clues to Family Relationships

Instrument name. The Kinetic Family Drawing Test (KFD) follows in the tradition of other family drawing tests described since 1950. Robert Burns

and S. Harvard Kaufman are credited with adding the highly important "kinetic" conception to the family drawing test (Burns & Kaufman,
1970). By adding the word *kinetic* to the test-taking instructions, they
"force" the test taker to draw an action picture of relationships among all
family members. Alternatively, the family members may be asked to draw
one KFD representing the entire family. Either way, useful hypotheses
about the family system can be generated in the process of discussions
with the family. Understanding the family system is fundamental to the
work of the family practitioner. By contrast, neither the Draw-A-Person
(DAP) nor the House Tree Person (HTP) has this focus.

Type of instrument. This test is a projective drawing measure of
family dynamics.

Use and target audience. The KFD is utilized with children, adolescents, and adults individually to ascertain an individual's view of his
or her family system. A second purpose is to obtain a family drawing as
drawn together by the entire family.

Multicultural. Owing to the unique instructions for administration,
this test can be administered in any language.

Ease and time of administration. The KFD is easy to administer:
Simply provide the family member with a plain sheet of ordinary size
white paper and a number-2 pencil and say, "Draw a picture of everyone in your family, including you, doing something. Try to draw whole
people, not cartoons or stick people. Remember, make everyone doing
something—some kind of action" (Burns & Kaufman, 1970, pp. 19–30).
When asking the entire family to complete one drawing, it is best to provide one large sheet of art paper with pencils or crayons, paraphrasing the
instructions to fit the family context (Thompson & Nurse, 1999, p. 127).
As noted, the instruction to have everyone "doing something" added to
instructions to draw a family has turned out to be a very important contribution. The testing procedure usually takes 20 to 30 minutes.

Scoring procedure. There is no generally accepted scoring procedure even though a formal scoring system that focuses on actions, styles,
and symbols has been proposed (Burns & Kaufman, 1972; Handler &
Habenicht, 1994). Some contend that the proposed scoring system has not
proven particularly useful and a more integrative, holistic approach has
been offered instead (Thompson & Nurse, 1999). One holistic approach
is for the therapist/evaluator, after the drawing system, to try to duplicate
physically the actual postures and imagine the actions indicated on the
KFD. These kinesthetic experiences can trigger feelings and thoughts for
the therapist/evaluator that may be akin to the client's. For instance, acting out a child's smile with arms out toward family members, compared
with duplicating a scowling, hiding child crouching in a corner, would
certainly elicit different feelings and thoughts for the clinicians.

Reliability. Test–retest reliabilities have been low, which is not surprising because this instrument is often scored or interpreted qualitatively. However, when quantitative scoring was used, interscorer agreement is reported in the range of .87 to .95 (Groth-Marnat, 2003).

Validity. Overall validity has been rather low and variable (Groth-Marnat, 2003).

Availability and source. The KFD and the Kinetic School Drawing (KSD; Knoff, 1985), comprising the Kinetic Drawing Systems (KDS; Knoff & Prout, 1985), are distributed by Western Psychological Services, Inc. Of course, it is possible to follow the instructions provided here if no scoring system is desired.

Comment. Although it lacks the extensive empirical and experimental data that would provide it the validity of such clinical instruments as the MMPI-2, the MCMI-III, or the Rorschach, the KFD is included in this chapter because it is the only widely used drawing method that attempts to elicit responses pertaining directly to understanding the family system from the perception of the person drawing. It has been noted that the KFD is considered a pictorial analog of "family sculpting" as described by Satir (1967).

Using the KFD With Families

The KFD can be utilized with families in various ways. The standard way is to collect and analyze the KFD from the child or children at the onset of treatment and use it in conceptualization of, and treatment planning for, the case. Thompson and Nurse (1999) suggest some other uses of this assessment tool. One is to have everyone in a family session do a KFD by him- or herself, then have the family discuss the different drawing perceptions of the family members with the guidance of the therapists. Such discussion of similarities and differences can stimulate talk about affectionate family bonds and significant differences among family members.

Alternatively, the therapist may have family members work together to draw one KFD on a large sheet of art paper with crayons rather than on a regular sheet of paper with a pencil. The instructions are the same except that family members are asked to decide together what each member is to draw and where on the large sheet of paper each member will accomplish the drawing task. This step is particularly important because it gives the observer examples of family interaction. The therapist–observer pays attention to such questions as who leads, who has the final say, and how the drawing is executed by those involved. These observations can be shared in subsequent discussions with the family to ascertain if these family patterns are representative outside the consulting room and, if they are, what the implications of these patterns might be. Or, the therapist can request the family to complete one KFD as a family and simply observe how the family goes about doing the task and, afterward, question them. An additional approach is for the family to act out the actions depicted in the family KFD. Finally, the KFD can serve as a starting point for a general family discussion, with the drawer or drawers of the picture alone or involving the entire family.

Summary

KFD is a useful method for family therapists. Although it currently lacks the impressive psychometric properties of other standard assessment measures, the KFD is the only drawing method that appears to tap consistently into family interrelationships. Because it can provide clues about family relationships, it is particularly helpful as one instrument in a battery of tests, although it can be used by itself. Given its simplicity of administration, it will probably continue to be used worldwide.

STRATEGY FOR USING STANDARDIZED TESTS WITH COUPLES AND FAMILIES

The following protocol can be useful when utilizing the MMPI/MMPI-2, MCMI-III, KFD, and the Rorschach with couples and families.

1. Select psychological tests that are appropriate to the questions raised that call for the psychological assessment, and are appropriate for the couple or family.
2. Administer and score the tests.
3. Collect additional information on the couple or family through interview, observation, clinical records, collateral information, or other self-report measures.
4. Review and develop an initial test report for each partner or each family member tested.
5. Review and develop a final test report with a focus on the couple and/or family relationships.
6. Feed data back to the couple or family as appropriate.

It is useful to keep in mind that, when developing an initial test report (Step 4) involving the MMPI/MMPI-2, MCMI-III, KFD, and Rorschach, a concurrence of results on these instruments may or may not occur. Differences may reflect the need to over-report symptoms to gain some advantage or to under-report symptoms to put the best foot forward (e.g., the parent seeking child custody in a divorce proceeding). Finn

(1996) and Nurse (1999) have offered some clinically useful guidelines for reviewing such test results. A modified version of these guidelines is presented here. When disturbance is present on the MMPI/MMPI-2 and the Rorschach, most probably the client is aware of difficulties in coping on a day-to-day basis and ordinarily has a history of confirming that difficulty. When the MMPI/MMPI-2 clinical scale scores fall within the normal range while the Rorschach shows significant disturbances, the clinician needs to consider the possible uses of the test as viewed by the client carefully. For example, if the client has something to gain by appearing "normal," his MMPI scores may simply mean under-reporting. If it appears that nothing is to be gained for under-reporting, it is likely that psychological disturbances appear under stressful, unfamiliar circumstances despite ordinarily maintaining an adequate adjustment in familiar surroundings, or there may be a conscious denial of disturbance by the family member.

When the disturbance is high on the MMPI/MMPI-2 and low on the Rorschach, two possibilities exist. The client may be over-reporting on the MMPI/MMPI-2, which may reflect malingering or a call for help, probably for assistance with an immediate situation. Alternatively, if the Rorschach is defensive, constricted, and generally shut down, it may be that the client can respond accurately on the impersonal MMPI/MMPI-2, while needing to be protective in the interpersonal, emotionally arousing context of the Rorschach. In this instance, high MMPI/MMPI-2 scores do not necessarily represent over-reporting, particularly if the situation involves no anticipated gain for expressing psychopathology.

Very rarely, low disturbances are noted on the MMPI/MMPI-2 and on the Rorschach. Although this is not common in clinical settings, it does occur occasionally in marital evaluations. For example, both partners may have little in the way of psychological disturbance yet may need to enhance their relationship, or they may be so ill-matched that they need to find a more effective way of relating, coexisting, or divorcing.

When data on the MMPI/MMPI-2 and the Rorschach diverge, a review of the MCMI-III may clarify matters. For example, the narcissistic person may have great difficulty consciously describing himself in other than self-aggrandizing terms on the MMPI/MMPI-2 with accompanying minimizing awareness of psychological problems. In contrast to this under-reporting, the Rorschach may pick up considerable psychological disturbance. Similarly, the identification of a dependent personality on the MCMI-III may indicate a propensity to over-report symptoms on the MMPI/MMPI-2 to establish a therapeutic relationship. The anticipation of the dependent personality may be that appearing needy is necessary to be cared for and loved; however, the Rorschach may indicate relatively little disturbance.

In the process of developing a final test report on the couple or the family (Step 5), individual test reports are reviewed along with interview, observational, and other sources of data. This information is then synthesized and integrated and forms the basis for feedback and possible modification of the original treatment plan.

Providing feedback to the couple or family is an important part of the assessment process (Step 6). Under the ethics code of the American Psychological Association, a clinician or evaluator who is a psychologist would have an obligation to discuss test findings with clients. Typically, the clinician or evaluator meets with individual partners or parents to discuss their own results.

Reviewing results individually with the clinician and without the presence of the other partner or parent provides an environment more conducive to exploratory discussion, including considering the implications for the couple relationship or family. A joint meeting with partners or parents and the clinician follows. At that meeting, each partner or parent is encouraged to share as much about his own test feedback, as he is willing. The clinician then focuses on key couple or family dynamics that have emerged from the evaluation and discusses relevant treatment or decisional implications and recommendations.

If a family evaluation is involved and the child tested is below the age of 13, feedback on the child's testing would be provided primarily to the parents. However, if the individual is an adolescent, feedback would be provided first through a private discussion with him or her. Then the adolescent would be helped in a joint session with the therapist and parents to tell the parents what he or she considered most important about the test results. The therapist would support the adolescent and fill in important gaps in feedback for the parents.

CASE EXAMPLE

The following case report, involving issues of divorce and child custody, delineates the use of traditional psychological assessment methods with a family in counseling. The case illustrates the protocol for using tests with couples and families wherein each step is noted in parentheses.

Background Information and Reason for Testing

Jack S., a 31-year-old engineering technician, and Jill S., his 30-year-old wife who works in a clerical managing position, are separated and have initiated divorce proceedings. Both have begun new live-in relationships.

Their 9-year-old daughter, Mary, has witnessed many of the couple's fights over the years. Her teacher has raised concern that she is functioning below her intellectual potential and does not relate well to her classmates. As part of the child custody evaluation, each family member is given a battery of tests (Step 1 and Step 2), and additional information is gathered from a number of sources, including their new partners; interviews, home visits, discussions with collaterals, letters, legal documents, and other data sources (Step 3). Jack is requesting primary custody of Mary and is open to liberal visitation by the child's mother.

Individual and Family Testing Summary

MMPI-2 and Rorschach results for Jack suggest a test pattern (Step 4) of low disturbance levels on both, while his MCMI-III profile indicates little if any disturbance and is consistent with an overall controlled, organized, and constricted person. His style is to sidestep dealing with his feelings by pushing them away or avoiding any awareness of them. Complementing this conscientious/avoidant style is a perceptual processing style in which he narrows and simplifies information as it comes to him; thus he can maintain an appearance of composure, work efficiency, and conventionality in his behaviors. Nevertheless, this suppressive defensive process feeds underlying resentment that can periodically break through. There is also some indication that he is ruminating about some self-perceived negative features in his personality and behavior. The testing also suggests that he has some positive parenting skills and attitudes.

MMPI-2 results for Jill indicate low disturbance, whereas the Rorschach points to a significant level of disturbance. Her MCMI-III also indicates psychological disturbance characteristic of individuals with anxiety disorders in the context of a histrionic personality disorder. Despite the appearance of putting up a good front, indications are that she is grief stricken about an emotional loss. Testing reveals a personality style that has important implications for her parenting (Step 4). She behaves socially in an often charming and effective way consistent with her histrionic and (mildly) narcissistic style. Unfortunately, this appearance of focusing on others seems motivated less by her interests in them than in what they can do for her. She is fearful of rejection and needs constant reassurance that she is the superior, effective person she strives to be. This self-focus may be so strong that it can interfere with her ability to extend herself toward her daughter as her daughter evolves into an increasingly independent person. Furthermore, her readiness for underlying hostility to break through would be expected to stimulate at least uneasiness and a readiness to be annoyed with other household

members. The potential violence of her verbal and possibly physical outbursts is at a level to be potentially damaging for a child. The ubiquity
of her underlying hostility means that her relationships with adults and
children are likely to be more superficial, and she is likely to put others
off. Finally, she has not developed a workable problem-solving style in
that, faced with a problem, she vacillates and is unsure about which
choice is better for her. She reverses decisions, thus having a hard time
depending on herself; others also find it difficult to depend on her.

On the KFD Mary identifies her family as her father, stepmother
(father's new partner), her aunt and uncle (who are temporarily stay-
ing with her father), and their son. Strikingly, Mary does not include
her mother in her drawing. Based on all information gathered, Mary is
a very angry girl. As reflected by her anger, her distress is marked. Its
power and its pervasiveness are such that it impairs her ability to think
things through without internal disruptions. Her inconsistent decision-
making patterns create an unsettled state, and she suffers from poor
reality testing accompanied by distortions in her ways of thinking about
the world. Perhaps it is this internal disorganization that makes her feel
so vulnerable, resulting in hypervigilance. Mary clearly needs help in
dealing with her anger and to alleviate negative feelings about herself.
Testing reveals that her sense of personal worth is very poor and her
need for safety is significant. A concern that needs to be addressed is that
her mother views Mary as very disturbed, seeing her as acting-out and
acting-in, with depression and probably high anxiety. This relationship
between mother and daughter is reinforced by the fact that Mary does
not include her mother in her family drawing. Interestingly, her father
does not see a disturbance in Mary. Their different views of Mary may
reflect their different relationships with her. That is, mother–daughter
relationships may reflect conflict and difficulty, whereas the relationship
with her father may be relatively free of problems.

Based on these test interpretations, which primarily reflect individual
dynamics, an integrative, synthesis interpretation of family dynamics and
relationships can be articulated (Step 5). The over-riding feature of this family grouping is that of angry expression. The mother, Jill, has not only a tem-
per but also a ubiquitous angry quality underlying her relationships, despite
an overt orientation to charming others. This readiness to break through
her social, other-oriented exterior is made worse by her inadequate controls
over expression of feelings, particularly anger. Her anger seems matched
by her daughter's marked hostility, also characterized by lack of adequate
controls, even in comparison with other 9-year-olds. Collateral information
confirms a long history of flare-ups between mother and daughter that have
become increasingly frequent since the parental break-up.

It is likely that Mary's fear of abandonment, stimulated when the mother left, significantly fuels these flare-ups, even though the mother has returned to visit regularly. Despite Jill's action in leaving the family home, her sense of loss and accompanying loneliness are probably related to her frayed connection to her daughter. She cannot acknowledge her ambivalence at not having more contact with her daughter and thus fights in a custody "battle" for her, precipitating this evaluation. Were she not to fight so strongly, she would need to confront her ambivalence about her daughter, manage her anxiety, and deal with the guilt for, in many ways, rejecting her daughter. Jack, as father, does not have the same problem of ubiquitous anger that his wife displays. Rather, he holds in all feelings, including anger, until, rarely, the provocation is strong enough that he can explode. He can pick Jill's most extreme behavior to righteously express his own and thereby not need to look at his own role in the family conflict. The mix of anger between them has developed and serves to maintain a cyclical fight dynamic.

Mary was traumatized and responded with her fearfulness by identifying with her aggressive mother even while being very angry with her. Mary's anger overwhelms her, disrupting her thinking process, particularly when confronted with her mother's anger or in the wake of it. Mary's reaction generalizes to others. She is hyperalert, wary, and mistrustful, and does not easily mix with other children. This standoffish attitude means that she cannot benefit from the day-to-day feedback from peers so necessary for adequate development. Thus, her personality development is faltering at the present time.

Treatment and Custody Recommendations

Based on these findings, Mary needs some individual play therapy to handle her built-up trauma. Jill, her mother, likewise needs individual therapy to learn to manage her anger and find more constructive ways to respond under pressure. The two of them need sessions with a family therapist to work on their relationship. A final healing process is for mother, daughter, and father to meet with the family therapist to rework the child's trauma with them and establish a working co-parenting relationship. In the meantime, the recommendation is for the father to continue to have primary physical custody and the parents to have joint legal custody. Relatively short, 2- to 4-hour mother–daughter visits are recommended, perhaps 3 times per week. Jill can utilize long-term therapy to help her modify her histrionic style and narcissistic traits.

TABLE 3.1　Matrix: Four Standard Psychological Tests With Families and Couples

Assessment Instrument	Specific Couple and Family Applications	Cultural/Language	Instructions/Use: T = Time to Take S = Time to Score I = Items (# of)	Computerized: (a) Scoring (b) Report	Reliability (R) Validity (V)	Availability
Minnesota Multiphasic Personality Inventory (MMPI-2)	Parents or partners/adolescent version; provides symptoms & mood states; five common couple clusters are described	English, Spanish, Hmong, French	T = 60–90 min S = 2–3 min I = 567	a = Yes b = Yes	R = .70 split-half R = .67–.92 test–retest V = .30	National Computer Systems, Inc.
Millon Clinical Multiaxial Inventory (MCMI-III)	Parents or partners; provides personality style/syndromal data; six common couple relational patterns	English, Spanish (interpretive reports only in English)	T = 20–30 min S = A few min I = 175	a = Yes b = Yes	R = .67–.91 test–retest R = .80 internal consistency V = Low to .30	National Computer Systems, Inc.
Rorschach (Comprehensive System Version)	Parents or partners; for in-depth personality evaluations, e.g., child custody, abuse, divorce, etc.	Administer in any language; (interpretive reports only in English)	T = 45–60 min, including inquiry S = Variable I = 10 inkblots	a = Yes, with clinician input b = Yes	R = .75–.85 test–retest R = .79–.88 intercoder agreement V = .29	Psychological Assessment Resources, Inc.
Kinetic Family Drawing (KFD) Test	Children, adolescents, or whole family to assess family relationships and interaction	Administer in any language	T = 20 min S = Variable I = N/A	a = No b = No	R = .87–.95 interscorer agreement V = Low and variable	Journal article; Western Psychological Services, Inc.

Feedback of Results

The clinician/assessor provided feedback to the parents (Step 7). The evaluator first met individually with Jack, and then with Jill, to review their individual results, but each parent's individual results were not discussed with the other parent. However, in a joint session with the evaluator, each parent was encouraged to share as much as he or she was willing with the other. With the parents together, the circular problem of the anger dynamic with the three of them and the mother–daughter conflict was discussed, and feedback to the parents about Mary's testing was provided. Mary's results were not discussed with her because of her age.

CONCLUDING NOTE

This chapter has described the use of standard psychological tests in the process of evaluating couples and families. Four such tests were discussed: MMPI-2, MCMI-III, Rorschach, and KFD, as well as a protocol for utilizing these instruments in clinical practice. The instruments and the protocol were illustrated in a detailed case example, suggesting how therapists might use such instruments, as long as their use is within their scope of practice, or the alternative of referring to a family-experienced, systemically oriented psychologist for such an evaluation. Finally, the previous matrix, Table 3.1, summarizes key attributes of these instruments.

REFERENCES

Burns, R., & Kaufman, S. (1970). *Kinetic Family Drawing (KFD)*. New York: Brunner/Mazel.

Burns, R., & Kaufman, S. (1972). *Actions, styles, and symbols in kinetic family drawings (KFD)*. New York: Brunner/Mazel.

Butcher, J. (1990). *MMPI-2 in psychological treatment*. New York: Oxford University Press.

Butcher, J. (2002). *Clinical personality assessment* (2nd ed.). New York: Oxford University Press.

Butcher, J., Dahlstrom, G., Graham, J., Tellegen, A., & Kaemmer, B. (2001). *MMPI-2: Manual for administration and scoring*. Minneapolis: University of Minnesota Press.

Caldwell, A. (2001). *Caldwell MMPI-2 report*. Los Angeles: Author.

Carlson, J., & Sperry, L. (Eds.). (1997). *The disordered couple.* New York: Brunner/Mazel.

Craig, R. (1999). Overview and current status of the Millon Clinical Axial Inventory. *Journal of Personality Assessment, 72*(3), 390–406.

Exner, J. (1993). *The Rorschach: A comprehensive system. Basic foundations.* (Vol. 1, 3rd ed.). New York: Wiley.

Exner, J. (2001). *A Rorschach workbook for the comprehensive system.* Asheville, NC: Rorschach Workshops.

Exner, J., et al. (2003). *Rorschach interpretation assistance program: Version 4 plus for Windows.* Odessa, FL: Psychological Assessment Resources.

Exner, J., Weiner, I., & PAR Staff (2011). *RIAP5: Scoring Program (RIAP5:S).*

Finn, S. (1996). Assessment feedback integrating MMPI-2 and Rorschach findings. *Journal of Personality Assessment, 67*(3), 543–557.

Greene, R. (2000). *The MMPI/MMPI-2: An interpretive manual* (2nd ed.). Boston: Allyn & Bacon.

Groth-Marnat, G. (2003). *Handbook of psychological assessment* (3rd ed.). New York: Wiley.

Handler, L., & Habenicht, D. (1994). The kinetic family drawing technique: A review of the literature. *Journal of Personality Assessment, 63*(3), 440–464.

Knoff, H. (1985). *Kinetic drawing system for family and school: Scoring booklet.* Los Angeles: Western Psychological Services.

Knoff, H., & Prout, T. (1985). *Kinetic drawing system for family and school: A handbook.* Los Angeles, CA: Western Psychological Services.

Meyer, G. J., et al. (2011). *Understanding the new Performance Assessment System (R-PAS) as applied to a case.* Paper delivered at the Society for Personality Assessment annual symposium, Boston, MA.

Millon, T. (1977). *Manual for the Millon Multiaxial Inventory (MCMI).* Minneapolis, MN: National Computers Services.

Millon, T. (1994) *Millon index of personality styles.* New York: Psychological Corporation.

Millon, T. (1996). *Disorders of personality: DSM-IV and beyond.* New York: Wiley.

Millon, T. (1997a). *Manual for the Millon Multiaxial Inventory-III (MCMI-III).* Minneapolis, MN: National Computers Services.

Millon, T. (1999). *Personality-guided couple therapy.* New York: Wiley.

Millon, T. (2008). *The Millon inventories* (2nd ed.). New York: Guilford Press.

Nurse, A. (1997). The dependent/narcissistic couple. In J. Carlson & L. Sperry (Eds.), *The disordered couple* (pp. 315–332). New York: Brunner/Mazel.

Nurse, A. (1999). *Family assessment: Effective uses of personality tests with couples and families*. New York: Wiley.

Nurse, A., & Stanton, M. (2008). Using the MCMI in treating couples. In T. Millon & C. Bloom (Eds.), *The Millon Instrument* (pp. 347–368). New York: Guilford Press.

Satir, V. (1967). *Peoplemaking*. Palo Alto, CA: Science and Behavior Books.

Stanton, M., & Nurse, A. R. (2009). Personality-guided couples psychology. In J. H. Bray & M. Stanton (Eds.), *The Wiley-Blackwell handbook of family psychology* (pp. 258–271). New York: Wiley-Blackwell.

Thompson, P., & Nurse, R. (1999). The KFD Test: Clues to family relationships. In A. Nurse, *Family assessment: Effective uses of personality tests with couples and families* (pp. 124–134). New York: Wiley.

Weiner, I., Spielberger, C., & Abeles, N. (2002). Scientific psychology and the Rorschach inkblot method. *Clinical Psychologist, 55*(4), 7–12.

CHAPTER 4

Observational Assessment

Robert B. Hampson and W. Robert Beavers

> Not wrung from speculations and subtleties,
> but from common sense and observation.
>
> —Sir Thomas Browne

> He is a great observer, and he looks
> quite through the deeds of men.
>
> —Shakespeare

> Observations always involve theory.
>
> —Edwin Hubble

Learning about people by watching them behave is perhaps the oldest assessment tool in evaluating human behavior. Direct observation of humans in context allows an undiluted behavior sample untainted by verbiage, self-report social desirability, or purposeful distortions. However, as will be demonstrated, the behavior must be interpreted and rated within a context and within the theoretical bounds of an assessment model. The observer is provided a conceptual framework, and specific behaviors, to observe and rate. Hence, the observational rating is a product of the tool, so understanding the model and tool is a necessary step in choosing and using an assessment model.

In the past decade since the first edition of this chapter was written, most of the major models presented at that time have remained on the forefront of clinical and research utility as measures of whole-family functioning. In terms of newer instruments, the tendency is toward briefer and more specific observational assessments, such as assessing marital instability, couples' intimate behavior, and parenting behaviors. Many of these more specific measures are attempts to measure and predict response to treatment, need for intervention, and improvements through the course of treatment. It should also be noted that there are available self-report scales for most of the major general family models, including the Beavers, Circumplex, and McMaster models.

This chapter will describe several well-known and frequently used clinical rating scales and observational assessment tools designed for the overall evaluation of couples and families. The instruments and underlying models will first be discussed. Then a strategy for utilizing these instruments in everyday clinical practice will be briefly described. Next, two detailed case examples illustrate how observational assessment can be incorporated in clinical practice with families.

INSTRUMENTS

Beavers Interactional Scales: Competence and Style

Instrument name. The Beavers Interactional Competence Scale and the Beavers Interactional Style Scale were derived originally from the Beavers-Timberlawn Scale (Beavers, 1977). These scales were refined and standardized by W. Robert Beavers and Robert B. Hampson (Beavers & Hampson, 1990).

Type of instrument. These scales are presented as Likert-type ratings. Subscales are rated from 1 to 5, and the global competence rating is a 1 to 10 scale. The ratings are based on family interaction observed over a 10-minute period.

Use and target audience. The intended target group is a two (or more) generational family system, usually parent(s) and child(ren). The scales can and have been used for couples, but several of the subscales do not apply to single-generational systems.

Multicultural. The scales have been used (and norms published) on various ethnic groups in the United States (Hampson, Beavers, & Hulgus, 1990). The scales have also been used in Finland, Sweden, Denmark, Italy, France, Germany, Mexico, and Japan. The accompanying self-report scale (Self-Report Family Inventory) is also available in several foreign languages. This instrument has been studied and used with clinical and nonclinical families.

Ease and time of administration. Once a rater has been trained to reliability, the actual time of administration is 10 minutes. Prior to an initial session, the family is instructed to "Discuss together what you would like to see changed in your family," while the interviewer leaves the room. Ten-minute segments are usually videotaped. Rater teams (for research) or the therapist view the tape or the live interaction, and the ratings are done immediately following the 10-minute interaction.

Scoring procedure. The interactional scales are hand-scored imme-diately after the 10-minute observation.

Reliability. Inter-rater reliability coefficients of .85 or above have been noted for global ratings of competence and style. Reliability of indi-vidual Likert subscales range from .74 to .93.

Validity. The Beavers Interactional Competence Scale correlates +.72 (canonical correlation) with the self-report scale (Self-Report Family Inventory [SFI]). The Competence scale also correlates favorably with other measures of family functioning (e.g., the McMaster model; Beavers & Hampson, 1990).

Availability and source. These rating scales have been made readily available through the authors' book, *Successful Families: Assessment and Intervention* (1990).

They can also be ordered from Dr. Hampson directly: Psychology Department, P.O. Box 0442, Southern Methodist University, Dallas, TX 75275-0442 (rhampson@smu.edu). There is no charge for the use of the observational scales or the accompanying Self-Report Family Inventory (SFI). The authors request final results from studies using the scales.

Comment. The Beavers Interactional Scales have evolved over 45 years of observation of clinical and nonclinical families of a wide variety of structure, ethnicity, and nationality. The scales are based on the Beavers Systems Model, which has studied family competence as well as family dysfunction. The model also can be used to identify family system lacks and needs at different levels of disturbance and suggest strength-building procedures and guidelines for therapy at different levels. The Style scale, unique to this model, provides a rating of Centripetal (internalizing) and Centrifugal (externalizing) forces, which is also useful in therapy planning.

The Beavers Systems Model

The dimensions of competence and style provide a useful map for identifying levels of family health and dysfunction. Figure 4.1 illustrates this model.

Family competence ranges from Optimal to Severely Dysfunctional and is plotted along the horizontal axis. From left to right, the contin-uum of family competence ranges from extreme rigidity (chaotic, non-interactive), through marked dominance-submission patterns, to greater capacity for egalitarian and more successful transactions.

The vertical axis represents family Style, a dimension unique to the Beavers model. It ranges from highly Centripetal (internalizing, lower end) to highly Centrifugal (externalizing, upper end). The representa-tion is intended to depict more rigid and extreme styles to be found in more dysfunctional families and a more blended and flexible style in the more competent families. The resultant arrow shape shows the clinical

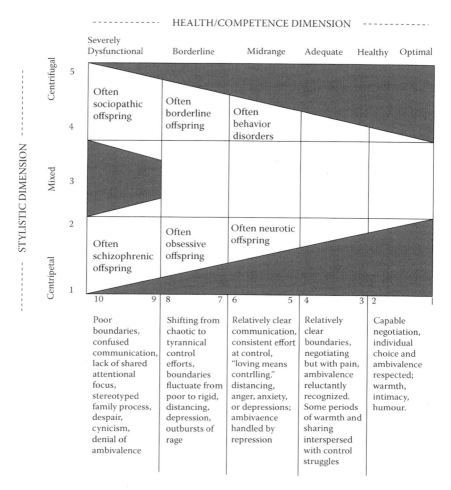

FIGURE 4.1   Beavers Systems model.

and empirical findings that healthy families show a flexible and blended family style, such that they can adapt stylistic behavior as developmental, individual, and family needs change over time. At the most dysfunctional end of the competence dimension are the most rigid and extreme family styles; these families' extreme rigidity and limited coping skills disallow variation in interactional behavior. The V-shaped "notch" on the left represents the finding that severely disturbed families show more extreme and rigid styles, with no moderation or blending of stylistic behavior.

The Rating Scales

The Competence Scale has a global rating, which is based on the ratings on 12 subscales. These are (with inter-rater reliabilities in parentheses) the following:

1. Structure of the Family
   Overt Power: chaotic to egalitarian (.83)
   Parental Coalition: parent–child to strong parental bond (.85)
   Closeness: indistinct boundaries to close, distinct boundaries (.72)
2. Mythology: reality perception: incongruent to congruent/realistic (.86)
3. Goal-Directed Negotiation: inefficient to efficient problem solving (.83)
4. Autonomy:
   Clarity of Expression: indirect to direct expression of feelings/ thoughts (.82)
   Responsibility: disowning versus owning responsibility for personal issues (.86)
   Permeability: open versus unreceptive to other members (.86)
5. Family Affect:
   Range of Feelings: taboos to wide range of feeling expressed (.84)
   Mood and Tone: open/optimistic to cynical/pessimistic (.89)
   Unresolvable Conflict: chronic unresolved to ability to resolve (.77)
   Empathy: empathic versus inappropriate responses (.88)
6. Global Health/Pathology: optimal to dysfunctional (.85)

The Beavers Interactional Style Scale has a global rating, as well as seven subscales. Middle ratings on each scale are representative of mixed/blended style in more competent families, while extremes of style are more characteristic of the rigid (either/or) styles found in more dysfunctional families.

1. Dependency Needs: encouraged (CP) to discouraged (CF) (.81)
2. Adult Conflict: covert/hidden (CP) to open/direct (CF) (.74)
3. Physical Proximity: very closely spaced (CP) to distant (CF) (.83)
4. Social Presentation: overly concerned (CP) versus unconcerned (CF) about their impression (.74)
5. Expression of Closeness: high (CP) versus denial (CF) of closeness (.77)
6. Aggressive/Hostile Expression: discouraging (CP) versus solicitation/encouragement (CF) (.81)
7. Types of Feelings: warm/positive (CP) versus angry/hostile (CF) (.83)

Global CP/CF Rating: Extreme CP to Mixed to Extreme CF (.80)

Using the Beavers Scales With Families and Couples

The 10-minute observation usually precedes the first therapy session, after which the therapist trained in the use of the Beavers system begins to work with the family. The Beavers model offers specific guidance for developing a therapy plan for the family, based on the observational assessment. The assessment of family competence and style provides for seven different clinically useful groupings of families, which have been described in detail elsewhere (Beavers & Hampson, 2003); each requires a somewhat different therapeutic stance (Hampson & Beavers, 1996a, 1996b). A brief summary of family types typically encountered in a clinic setting follows.

Midrange families are the most frequently occurring families in the general population and represent a substantial number of families seeking clinical help. They are of quite traditional structure and are invested in maintaining a consistent rule structure ("loving means controlling"). Cultural stereotyping of sex roles is predominant in these families.

Midrange Centripetal families are characterized by concern for rules and authority; no overt defiance is expected. They expect control efforts to be successful. Family members keep their anger and dissension in check; there is no allowance for expression of overt disagreement or hostility. Hence, internalizing and repression will manifest as anxiety and depression. Only modest levels of spontaneity are seen, and sex role stereotyping is rigid and traditional. These families need therapists who will join them, model straightforward expression and negotiation of differences, encourage clarity and honesty, and promote nonverbal awareness of affect. Paradoxical techniques often backfire, because trust is so vital to these families. If there is a clinical patient, most likely that individual will be the symptom bearer and manifest an internalizing disorder.

Midrange Mixed and Midrange Centrifugal families also attempt to control by authority, but that control is less effective in producing consistent and internalized behavior control. To deal with behavioral transgressions, these families use criticism, blame, and anger expressed overtly. In these families, no one person is to blame, and everyone feels the brunt of power and control struggles. Adults spend little time together, and satisfaction is sought outside the family. Individual manifestations of psychiatric disturbance are manifest as acting-out disorders. Centrifugal families rarely present voluntarily for treatment, because they have more reliance on action than words as a means of dealing with human distress. They require therapists who can maintain some control over conflict situations and help the family verbalize conflict issues. Eventually, the therapist helps the family redefine bad behavior as needy and conflict as desire for nurturance. These therapists cannot "join" the family as "warm and fuzzy"; they need to exert more structuring and control.

Borderline-level families are more concerned about control issues than are midrange families, to the near exclusion of concerns for happiness, intimacy, or satisfaction. Individual family members find little emotional support in these rigid and fluctuating systems, yet separation and individuation issues are often unresolved.

Borderline Centripetal families are control-oriented systems that are often rigidly organized. They alternate between rigid control efforts to stem chaos and chaotic interaction. Offspring are typically rigidly obsessive or compulsive (including anorexic), which mimics the family pattern of little joy and an illusory level of control over self and the world. Observers of these families will see fluctuations between effective domination and disintegration into chaos. Scapegoats in these families are often symptom bearers of the system itself (rigid control). Others are rebels from the tight reins and are the "fallen saints" of the system. Hence, some acting-out behavior may be seen in some of these families. This is why therapists for this family group need to maintain a power differential with the family and physically set boundaries against intrusions. They need to focus on satisfaction and possibilities, including the possibility of satisfaction and enjoyment in relating. Paradoxical procedures can be useful in interrupting vicious cycles of behavior (and this is perhaps the only clinical group where this is effective).

Borderline Centrifugal families are much more open in the direct expression of anger and hostility; there is frequent leave-taking. Control themes are overt blaming and direct emotional assaults; the cyclical chaos is more overt than covert. Nurturance is not available to parents or children, and satisfaction is sought outside the family. Each person is on his or her own to try to get whatever is needed. In these families there is no single "fallen saint"; multiple members act out à la a "pack of like sinners." Psychiatric disorders typically include externalizing disorders (conduct, substance abuse) and cyclical disorders that reflect the rigid-to-chaos fluctuations (Borderline Personality Disorders are common among members of these families). They need therapists who can maintain effective control, limit the number of members attending therapy sessions, focus on the basics, help the family organize simple actions and activities, organize generational boundaries, and help members take risks with neediness and emotional pain.

Severely Dysfunctional families are the most limited in making adjustments for developmental needs of offspring in negotiation and basic communication skills, and in clarity and contextual coherence. Boundaries are vague and amorphous, and parent–child coalitions may supplant adult coalitions in these families. Expressions of coherent affective tone are missing, and family members typically look bewildered and feel considerable despair. As a result of the limited degree of autonomy and differentiation (indeed, these were the families Murray Bowen described in his work), people cannot resolve conflict or offer intimacy. These systems flounder like a ship without a rudder.

Severely Dysfunctional Centripetal families are vague and indistinct structures wherein verbal incoherence and chaos predominate. There is little if any sense of individuation; members frequently speak for each other; children do not progress through normal patterns of separation and autonomy. Crises and losses are not handled through sharing; emotional isolation and taboos about dealing with crisis issues are firmly felt. Children in these families are inhibited and overcontrolled; some of these families have schizophrenic offspring (obviously with strong biological loadings). The adult coalition is nearly nonexistent, and often there are covert parent–child alliances. Therapists who work with these families must structure and organize; promoting contextual and communicational clarity is job number one. Through every session, the therapist must facilitate encounters, demand coherence, promote clarity, block intrusions, and reinforce collaboration among family members.

Severely Dysfunctional Centrifugal families are characterized by chaos of a different sort; their boundary with the outside world is diffuse (the definition of who constitutes the family is often ambiguous), and the internal chaos is more behavioral than verbal. Family interaction is characterized by negative exchanges: disrespect, name-calling, put-downs, and overt hostility. Leave-taking is frequent, and when satisfaction (which is sought away from home) is not attained, family members may return home even more cynical than when they left. There is no nurturance provided for offspring, and they develop a hostile attitude toward others, often manifested as sociopathy or extreme aggression. Family members spread out across the room, keeping both physical and emotional distance. Hopelessness pervades these families. These families seldom come to therapy on their own; for those that do, or are court ordered to attend therapy, they need a therapist who can keep firm control of the session, including seating arrangements and determining who shall attend. Eventually, the therapist has to help family members pair words with behavior, coordinate basic activities, and emphasize risk taking with positive feelings.

Using the Beavers model observational rating scales can provide a useful roadmap, not only for the classification of families but in anticipating a given family's basic lacks and needs. An appropriate "match" of therapist orientation with the competence and style level of the family (Hampson & Beavers, 1996a) or couple (Hampson, Prince, & Beavers, 1999) can facilitate greater gains in therapy than an apparent mismatch. Family competence is a much stronger predictor of therapy outcome

(Hampson & Beavers, 1996b) or dropout status (a study currently in progress) than any other factor, including family structure, income and socioeconomic status, and ethnicity. Family competence has also been related to health outcomes; a recent study using the Beavers scales found that obese adolescents in the most competent families were able (with family support) to lose the most weight while participating in a family-based weight loss and nutrition program (Kitzman et al., 2009).

We also use the scales to monitor a family's progress. For example, on the "Closeness" dimension, a Severely Dysfunctional Centripetal family will be seen as having "Amorphous, vague and indistinct boundaries among members." If a family is making progress, we will see the next higher level, as the family members show "Isolation and distancing." This is therapeutic progress, even though family members fear being lost to each other.

The observational scales can be used in conjunction with the self-report instrument from the Beavers model, the Self-Report Family Inventory (SFI). This is a brief (36 items) and reliable instrument that measures family Competence, Style (Cohesion), and three additional scales: Conflict, Leadership, and Emotional Expressiveness. It is often informative to see which family members view the family as more or less competent in planning therapeutic goals and strategies. The SFI also shows a high level of convergence with the observational scales in a clinical sample (Hampson, Beavers, & Hulgus, 1989).

The McMaster Model Clinical Rating Scale

Instrument name. The McMaster Clinical Rating Scale is an observational rating scale based on the McMaster Model of Family Functioning (Epstein, Ryan, Bishop, Miller, & Keitner, 2003). The original model was developed by Epstein while at McMaster University. More recently, the clinical rating scale, its sibling self-report scale (Family Assessment Device [FAD]) and structured interview (McMaster Structured Interview for Family Functioning [McSIFF]; Bishop et al., 2000) have been studied by the Brown University group (Miller, Ryan, Keitner, Bishop, & Epstein, 2000).

Type of instrument. The McMaster CRS is a Likert-type rating scale designed to measure overall Family Functioning (a global rating). There are also six subscales, each rated from 1 (very disturbed) to 7 (superior): Problem-Solving, Communication, Roles, Affective Responsiveness, Affective Involvement, and Behavior Control. The rating is based on observation (or conducting a detailed family interview).

Use and target audience. The McMaster CRS is designed to be used on whole families, following a detailed clinical interview.

Multicultural. The self-report FAD has been translated into 14 different languages and has been used on a wide variety of ethnic and socioeconomic groups in North America. The CRS, however, has been studied primarily with clinical and nonclinical families, mostly of middle-class status (Miller et al., 2000).

Ease and time of administration. The CRS can be completed by trained raters in a matter of minutes. However, because it is based on the observation of a detailed clinical interview, that time must be factored into the total administration. The McSIFF and its precursor, the McMaster Model Structured Interview (Bishop, Epstein, Keitner, Miller, & Zlotnick, 1987), can take 90 minutes to administer. These authors indicate that individuals at various levels of training can become reliable on the CRS, but the interview needs to be conducted by a more experienced clinician.

Scoring procedure. Each scale is rated from 1 (very disturbed) to 7 (superior). A manual describes concise anchor descriptions for points 1, 5 (nonclinical range), and 7 on each scale.

Reliability. Miller et al. (1994) report acceptable test–retest reliabilities (.81–.87) across subscales and good inter-rater reliabilities (.68–.87).

Validity. The CRS has shown adequate correspondence with the self-report FAD scales for a variety of clinical groups (Miller et al., 1994). In one study of discriminative validity, the CRS scores were significantly more disturbed for patients' families during the acute phase of depression than at post-acute follow-up.

Availability and source. The McMaster CRS is $15, and the McSIFF interview protocol is $40. The scales are available from Christine Ryan, Ph.D. or Ivan Miller, Ph.D., Brown University Family Research Program, Rhode Island Hospital—Potter 3, 593 Eddy Street, Providence, RI 02903 (phone: (401) 444-3534; FAX: (401) 444-3298).

Comment. The McMaster CRS is based on 30 years of clinical observation and research. Descriptors of disturbed families are based firmly upon collective observations in clinical settings. The scale does not attempt to measure all aspects of family life—only the dimensions deemed to be most predictive of disturbance versus competence in families in clinic settings.

Using the McMaster Clinical Rating Scale

Following the detailed clinical interview (McSIFF), the McMaster CRS ratings quantify and summarize the major findings that were probed during the interview. The questions in the interview deal with family functioning by asking the family members directly a question about how they operate. For example, under the domain of family roles, the interviewer asks directly who is involved in grocery shopping, laundry, repairs, and so on. The clinical interview takes from 90 to 120 minutes.

The CRS has six family functioning domains and a summary Overall Family Functioning. By providing summary ratings from 1 (very disturbed) to 7 (superior), a profile of family strengths and needs is constructed, which then allows the therapist to construct goals.

Problem Solving is the first dimension rated. Effective problem solving refers to family behavior that resolves problems to a degree that the family can move along effectively. The most effective families do not have fewer problems but are able to solve them readily. The McMaster model offers seven steps in effective problem solving (Epstein et al., 2003). More disturbed families are less able to resolve differences or solve problems effectively, so there are more unresolved problems.

Communication refers to the exchange of verbal information within the family. Communication within families is subdivided into instrumental (task) and affective areas. More competent families utilize clear (coherent) and direct (spoken to the intended recipient) verbal messages. At lower levels of competence, the communication becomes more masked (unclear) and indirect (deflected or diverted to or through someone else).

Role Functioning has to do with consistent role maintenance within the family. This dimension addresses the assignment of roles in the family (allocation) and the ability to maintain stable role performance over time (accountability). More competent families have more stable, predictable performance and maintenance of key family functions, while more disturbed families show more fluctuation and less accountability in performance of key family functions.

Affective Responsiveness has to do with the range and appropriateness of family members' emotional interaction. Healthy families are able to experience and respond to a full range of human emotions, in a context appropriate to that emotion, while more disturbed families show limitation on the range and type of feelings expressed, as well as some inappropriate emotional responses (e.g., laughing at someone's sorrow).

Affective Involvement refers to the level and type of dyadic relationships within the family structure. This addresses the manner in which family members show interest and investment in each other. The model presents six types of involvement, ranging from lack of involvement to symbiotic involvement, with "empathic involvement" in the middle as a descriptor of the more competent families. The extremes of involvement represent the relationships in more disturbed families.

Behavior Control refers to the family's means of shaping and directing members' behavior in three major domains: dangerous situations, development of socialization skills, and satisfying or regulating biological needs and drives. Families differ in the way in which they are consistent, direct, and fair. More competent families employ "flexible behavior control," which represents reasonable and negotiable methods of discipline. More disturbed families are of two extremes: "rigid behavior control" (narrow, rigid, non-negotiable) and "laissez-faire behavior control" (lax, no standards, no a priori rules).

Identifying a family's strengths and weaknesses can alert a therapist what problem areas are most pressing as therapy begins. Therapists derive a family profile of strengths and needs, and then follow the McMaster model's treatment approach, as described in the Problem Centered Systems Therapy of the Family (PCSTF; Epstein & Bishop, 1981). Subsequent evaluations can be used in research studies evaluating the effectiveness of family therapy, or they can be used individually to monitor the progress of a given case.

Circumplex Model Clinical Rating Scale

Instrument name. Clinical Rating Scale for the Circumplex Model of Marital and Family Systems (Olson & Killorin, 1988) is an observational rating scale based on the major theoretical dimensions of the Circumplex model (Olson & Gorall, 2003). It was initially developed in 1980 and has evolved over several modifications of the Circumplex model, with revisions in 1983, 1985, and 1988.

Type of instrument. The CRS is a checklist-type rating scale, with descriptors for each dimension at each rating point. It is to be used following observation or direction of a semi-structured family interview.

Use and target audience. The Circumplex CRS is designed to be used by trained raters for observing couples and families.

Multicultural. The scales of the Circumplex model, including the self-report Family Adaptability and Cohesion Evaluation Scales (FACES I, II, III, and IV), have been used in many foreign countries and have been translated into several languages. The CRS is less widely used than the FACES.

Ease and time of administration. The completion of the rating scale itself takes only a few minutes for trained raters. The clinical interview on which the ratings are based is of an unspecified length. Olson and Killorin (1988) indicate that the clinical interview can be semi-structured, yet should cover the basic dimensions of the model (Cohesion, Flexibility, and Communication). It is also important for the family to dialogue with each other; for example, the interviewer might ask them to describe what a typical week is like and how they handle their daily routines.

Scoring procedure. Each of the three major theoretical dimensions of the Circumplex model, and composite subscales, are rated by the observer following the interview. The scales and their composites will be described below. Cohesion dimensions are rated from 1-2 (disconnected) through 5-6 (connected) to 9-10 (enmeshed). Flexibility dimensions are rated from 1-2 (inflexible-rigid) through 5-6 (flexible) to 9-10 (overly flexible–chaotic). Communication dimensions are rated from 1-2 (low) through 3-4 (facilitating) through 5-6 (high). The first two scales are based on a curvilinear distribution, where competence is theoretically in the middle; communication is a unidimensional scale, from low to high.

Reliability. The Circumplex CRS has good internal and inter-rater reliability. Alpha coefficients for the three dimensions include .95 for Cohesion, .94 for Adaptability (flexibility), and .97 for Communication (Thomas & Olson, 1993). Test–retest reliabilities have also been reported: .83 for Cohesion, .75 for Adaptability (flexibility) and .86 for Communication.

Validity. Support for the Curvilinear distribution of Circumplex rating scale scores has been demonstrated via regression analysis. Both Cohesion and Flexibility have been curvilinearly related to family communication and family satisfaction (both linear). Hence, the CRS more closely fits the circumplex theory than do the self-report FACES instruments.

Availability and source. The Circumplex CRS is available for $30 from Life Innovations, 2660 Arthur Street, Roseville, MN 55113 (http://www.facesiv.com/studies/family_scales.html). There is also a Circumplex Training Package, containing a training manual, training video, and the CRS; it costs $50.

Comment. The CRS is a less widely used instrument than the Circumplex model self-report scale, the FACES. There have been challenges in the past regarding the curvilinear nature of some of the scales, especially the Flexibility scale (and its predecessor, "Adaptability"). Other models (Beavers & Voeller, 1983; Lee, 1988) state that Chaos and Rigidity are closely related in evolution of system development, rather than polar opposites.

Using the Circumplex CRS With Couples and Families

Following an interview or detailed discussion task, raters (or therapists) rate the family on specific dimensions of each of the subscales of the major dimensions of Cohesion, Flexibility, and Communication. The Cohesion subscales, which range from Disconnected (1-2) to Overly Connected/ Enmeshed (9-10), include dimensions of Emotional Bonding, Family Involvement, Marital Relationship, and Parent–Child Relationships. The Cohesion dimension also provides ratings for Internal Boundaries (time, space, decision making) and External Boundaries (friends, interests, and activities). Descriptive rating points for each level of cohesion are provided.

The Flexibility scales, representing a curvilinear distribution from Inflexible (rigid) through Flexible to Overly Flexible/Chaotic, provide the following subscales: leadership (authoritarian to limited leadership), discipline (autocratic to laissez-faire), negotiation (imposed decisions to impulsive decisions), roles (rigid to shifting roles), and rules (inflexible to changing rule structure).

The Communication scale is a directional, linear rating from Low to High levels of communication skills. The dimensions rated include listeners' skills empathy, attentive listening), speakers' skills (speaking for oneself, speaking for others), self-disclosure, clarity, continuity, and respect and regard. Olson's view of communication is that it is a facilitating dimension within the various family types as described by the Flexibility and Cohesion dimensions. Communication is also an important part of the PREPARE/ENRICH assessment for premarital and married couples.

Global Assessment of Relational Functioning (GARF) Scale

Instrument name. The Global Assessment of Relational Functioning (GARF) scale is an appendix in the current DSM-IV and DSM-IV-TR, to assist clinicians in their evaluation and diagnosis of individual patients by emphasizing their relational context. The current instrument evolved through multi-organization collaboration. Spearheaded by a critique, by Lyman Wynne, of the DSM system's lacking a family or relational axis, the GAP Committee on the Family began developing such a rating scale. In 1989, after key DSM-IV chairpersons endorsed the development of such a scale, a multi-organization task force was convened by Robert Beavers (then president of AAMFT, on the GAP Committee, and on the board of AFTA). The result was the Coalition on Family Diagnosis, co-chaired by Florence Kaslow and Herta Guttman; that coalition, with participation from 12 different organizations, developed the GARF (Yingling, Miller, McDonald, & Galewater, 1998).

Type of instrument. The GARF is a dimensional rating scale analogous to the Global Assessment of Functioning (GAF) Axis in DSM-IV. Ratings are based on a scale from 1 to 99. The most satisfactory family ratings are 81 to 99; less satisfactory, 61 to 80; predominantly unsatisfactory, 41 to 60; rarely satisfactory, 21 to 40; and chaotic, 1 to 20. These ratings are done for the global family or couple interaction. Separate subratings of the family or couple's Problem Solving, Organization, and Emotional Climate can also be made using the same number line.

Use and target audience. The GARF is intended to be used for rating the contextual relationship for a given patient or client, regardless of the formal definition of that relationship. This includes couples and families but can also include life partners, key friendships, and support networks for single or unattached people.

Multicultural. Most of the published reports regarding the GARF are set in clinical settings, primarily with English-speaking clients.

Ease and time of administration. The GARF can be completed in a matter of minutes by trained clinicians. The rating most typically follows the completion of a family or couple therapy session, although less formal interactions can be rated. It is even possible to rate a family on the basis of a client's *report* of the relational system.

Scoring procedure. Following the session or interaction observed, the rater completes a GARF rating scale for Global Functioning, as well as the subscales addressed above. A single number is assigned to each dimension.

Reliability. Reliability analysis of the GARF has shown a fairly broad spectrum of inter-rater reliability scores. Because the GARF presents a 20-point range within each of the five levels of functioning, exact-number reliability between pairs of raters has ranged from .34 to .75 (Gordon, 1997). However, when the range of ratings was broadened to within 5 rating points *within the same level*, the reliability estimates (*kappa* coefficients) were consistently higher: Global +.79; Problem Solving +.73; Organization +.86; Emotional Climate +.83 (Gordon, 1997). There is evidence that raters with higher levels of training in family systems theory and therapy have higher agreement and generalizability ratings (Mottarella, Philpot, & Fritzsche, 2001).

Validity. The relationship between GARF ratings and other ratings of family or couple functioning indicate generally adequate construct and clinical validity. For example, GARF and Beavers Interactional Competence were correlated –.69 (different directions of scores) at the initial session, and –.54 with mother's Self-Report Family Inventory competence (Henney, 1994). GARF change scores (pre–post GARF ratings across therapy) have correlated well with therapists' ratings of change (.47), and clients' report of change (.36). Also initial GARF ratings have been associated with severity ratings of the client at intake (–.52; Ross & Doherty, 2001).

Availability and source. The GARF is printed in the DSM-IV and DSM-IV-TR as an Axis Provided for Further Study. A good resource is *GARF Assessment Sourcebook: Using the DSM-IV Global Assessment of Relational Functioning,* 1998, by Yingling and her co-authors (Brunner/Mazel).

Comment. The GARF is a brief and fairly simple instrument that can be used by therapists and researchers. It can be used on a session-by-session basis to track progress in relational functioning. It addresses only the "competence" dimension of family and couple functioning.

Using the GARF With Couples and Families

GARF ratings may be performed by therapists or nonparticipating raters. Although the particular interaction task or setting is not specified, it is typical that the raters provide global and subscale ratings following the first therapy session, rather than after a specified interaction sequence. Yingling et al. (1998) provide several excellent examples of the use of the GARF to monitor session-by-session progress in family therapy cases. It is important that the rater be the same person every session, as between-rater variance for exact-point numerical ratings can be rather large (Henney & Hampson, 1994). Recent validation research has shown the GARF to have adequate inter-rater reliability (Denton, Nakonezny, & Burwell, 2010).

The functioning categories and ranges of scores help classify families from dysfunctional to satisfactory. Based on the history of the couple or family, it is often useful to classify not just current relational functioning but also past relational functioning. The GARF authors recommend rating the highest level of functioning and the lowest level of functioning within the past year, much like the GAF rating in the DSM-IV.

Ratings are performed for the overall level of family functioning. The GARF developers also recommend subscale ratings for more specific behaviors. *Problem Solving* refers to the relational unit's ability to negotiate rules and differences, adapt to and cope with stressful events, provide clear and direct communication, and resolve conflict. *Organization* refers to the clarity and ongoing distinctness of roles and interpersonal boundaries, power distribution and hierarchical functioning, behavioral control, and personal responsibility for actions. *Emotional climate* represents the family's overall mood and tone; quality of caring, attachment, and empathy; respect and valuing; and quality of sexual relating. While it is true that there are not going to be large differences among these ratings (Beavers & Hampson, 1990), these ratings can be useful in determining specific family or couple lacks and needs.

The highest level of functioning, satisfactory relational functioning (81–100), describes a relational context that is structured and predictable yet flexible in the face of the need to adapt. Conflicts are typically resolved successfully. Each member is unique, and the power distribution is shared. These relational units appear satisfied and optimistic, and therefore can display a wide range of feelings as the situation dictates.

Somewhat unsatisfactory relational units (61–80) demonstrate adequate, mostly normal patterns of relating, but with more pain and struggle than the satisfactory group. Some conflicts are not resolved. Although decision making is competent, there may be control struggles that interfere with egalitarian relationships. There is a masking of some feelings; warmth and caring are present but not as unconditional as in the satisfactory units. Parenting is adequate but less spontaneous than in the former group.

Predominantly unsatisfactory couples and families (41–60) demonstrate more difficulty with clarity, problem solving, and transitory adaptations to change. Control themes predominate, and an emphasis on rules is common. Decision making is intermittently effective; these families are either rigid or lack sufficient structure to enforce rules (see Beavers' Style dimension). Different feelings are disallowed; pain and anger are typically not handled well. Although there is some warmth and support, it is often contingent and unequally distributed.

Rarely satisfactory units (21–40) provide relatively low levels of support. Expectations for behavior are rigidly and obsessionally held to, or they are largely ignored. These units do not handle change and transition well. Obvious emotional distancing or physical leave-taking and hostility prevent smooth communication and negotiation. The emotional climate is barren or openly hostile. Alternations between attempts at rigid control and chaotic functioning disallow continuity in these families.

Chaotic relational units (1–20) lack coherence and continuity. Day-to-day routines are negligible and communication is indirect and incoherent. Relationships are overly dependent (cf. "Centripetal") or overly distant and hostile (cf. "Centrifugal"). Relational boundaries fluctuate, and no one knows where he or she stands with other family members. Despair, cynicism, and lack of hope predominate, so there is little emotional nurturance provided.

By rating a family or couple on global functioning and the individual subscales, a profile of family strengths and needs can be mapped (Yingling et al., 1998).

Marital Instability Index

Instrument name. Marital Instability Index (MII) measures proneness to divorce by taking cognitions as well as behaviors into account.

Type of instrument. The MII makes use of a 14-item dichotomous scale in Part I. It also has five Likert-scale questions in Part II, which measures other risk factors and adds to the accuracy of this assessment. It is most useful the more recently it is administered in relation to specified cognitions and behaviors. It holds promise for predicting, with greater accuracy, the outcome of marital relationships.

Ease and time of administration. It can be easily administered by an interviewer.

Scoring procedure. The number of divorce-prone answers are summed and recorded at the bottom of the measure where a corresponding "chance of divorce" figure is presented. Part II is scored by adding or subtracting a given number of points to the "divorce proneness" score based on the answers to questions in Part II.

Reliability. The MII has excellent internal consistency with an alpha of .93.

Validity. The MII has good predictive validity. Only 3% of people who showed no signs of marital instability divorced 3 years later compared to 27% of those who scored at the other extreme. It also has good construct validity, correlating positively with measures of marital problems and marital "disagrees."

Availability and source. The MII is available by journal article and was written by John N. Edwards, David R. Johnson, and Alan Booth: Coming Apart: A Prognostic Instrument of Marital Breakup, *Family Relations, 36,* 168–170.

Comments. There are no norms or demographic data reported for this instrument. However, this instrument is valuable because it is short, so it would be good for a retest during follow-up. Also, 2,034 people were included in the sample, but because we do not know the demographics, one must be careful when interpreting results with various populations.

Environmental Assessment Index

Instrument name. Environmental Assessment Index (EAI) assesses the educational and developmental quality of children's home environment.

Type of instrument. The EAI is a 44-item instrument (22 items in the short version), used in homes of children ages 3 to 11.

Ease and time of administration. The EAI is relatively easy to administer. How long it takes to administer this scale will be determined by whether the observer answers questions by direct observation, which will take longer than just asking the mother.

Scoring procedure. Score "yes" or "no" for each item based on direct observation or information from the mother. Each "yes" is scored 2, and each "no" receives a score of 1. The total score is the sum of all items. The scores on the long form range from 44 to 88 and from 24 to 48 on the short form.

Reliability. The Cronbach alpha is .84 for the long form and .82 for the short form, suggesting good internal consistency. The correlation between the long and short form is .93, which suggests alternate form reliability. Test–retest reliability ranged from .67 to .96.

Validity. The EAI has good concurrent and predictive validity with significant correlations between the scale and intellectual functioning.

Availability and source. The EAI was written by Robert H. Poresky and is available by journal article: Environmental Assessment

Index Reliability, Stability and Validity of the Long and Short Forms, *Educational and Psychological Measurements, 47, 969–975.*

Comments. The EAI is viewed as being useful in assisting with child placements, assessing the effectiveness of home interventions, and understanding the home environment's influence on children's development. It was normed with nonurban, two-parent, Midwest families; therefore, its use may be limited in metropolitan areas like South Florida. Also, some items referred to in the questionnaire, such as "Record player and at least five records appropriate to the child's age," need to be updated.

Couples' Intimate Behavior Rating System

Instrument name. The Couples' Intimate Behavior (CIB) Rating System assesses the depth of factual, emotional, and cognitive self-disclosure of the speaker and the understanding, validation, and caring expressed by the listener in each interaction.

Type of instrument. The Couples' Intimate Behavior Rating System is a global system in which ratings of each type and class of behavior are made on a 5-point Likert scale.

Ease and time of administration. This system is somewhat time consuming due to the fact the rater must watch a video of a couple's discussion two times. However, the segments rated are each only 5 minutes long (A. Mitchell, personal communication, 2011).

Scoring procedure. Raters look at video recordings twice to rate, first, the speaker on factual, emotional, and cognitive disclosure. Then raters watch it again to rate the listener's understanding, validation, and caring. Higher ratings reflect greater depth of disclosure.

Reliability. Inter-rater reliability ranged from .79 to .92.

Validity. Unavailable.

Availability and source. Mitchell, Alexandra E., Castellani, Angela M., Herrington, Rachael L., Joseph, Jana I., Doss, Brian D., Snyder, Douglas K., Predictors of intimacy in couples' discussions of relationship injuries: An observational study. *Journal of Family Psychology, 22*(1), 2008, 21–29.

Comments. This rater system has not been normed and was developed for the primary purpose of researching couple intimacy.

Child and Adult Relational Experimental Index

Instrument name. Child and Adult Relational Experimental Index (CARE-Index) is an observational measure of parenting behavior (Crittenden, 1988).

Type of instrument. This measure was specifically designed to distinguish at-risk from adequate parenting behavior. Mothers' ratings on the measure also were associated with children's interactive behavior and with an estimation of risk based on a multifaceted, comprehensive assessment. The measure's relation to estimation of risk remained significant when two other predictors of risk, maternal caregiving attitudes and insight into mental illness, were considered. Taken together, the findings suggest that the measure can provide reliable, valid, and independent information on parenting behavior that could inform comprehensive, multifaceted assessments of parenting risk.

Ease and time of administration. Easy to administer and can be used in different settings.

Scoring procedure. Raters weighed the various risk and protective factors, assigning each parent into a high- (3), moderate- (2), or low- (1) risk category. Higher risk scores were given when the evidence indicated that even if a mother was offered interventions, the prognosis for her being able to provide adequate parenting to her child in a reasonable time frame was poor. A lower risk score meant that there was a reasonable likelihood that the mother could successfully parent her child effectively if specific interventions were offered and accepted.

Reliability. Independent and trained raters achieved a high level of reliability on the measure. Inter-rater reliability was high ($\kappa = .95$).

Validity. Mothers' scores on the CARE-Index were associated in meaningful ways with children's behavior. Maternal sensitivity was linked to cooperative child behavior. Maternal hostility/intrusiveness was linked to difficult child behavior in children up to 18 months of age and only to compulsive compliant child behavior in children ages 18 months and older. Unresponsive maternal behavior was associated with passive child behavior, and was not linked to compulsive/compliant or difficult child behavior. Unresponsive maternal behavior also predicted adult attachment problems 20 years later in a longitudinal study (Zayas, Mischel, Shoda, & Aber, 2010).

Availability and source. See Crittendon (1988).

Comments. As mental illness is becoming more common and children in general, even outside of mental illness, are being maltreated, this instrument can become more and more useful. As it is used more, norms will be developed.

STRATEGY FOR UTILIZING OBSERVATIONAL ASSESSMENTS

The following protocol can be useful when utilizing any of the whole-family assessment rating scales addressed in this chapter. Some require more time and detail in terms of administration, and some require a videotaped assessment segment.

1. Obtain written consent for the observational procedure and consent for videotaping (when used). Assure the family that no one outside the clinic supervisors and direct therapists will be viewing the videotape.

2. Select an assessment tool that fits the needs of the clinic or practice that is using the instrument. For example, the Beavers model rating scales can be used within a rather brief time period at the beginning of the first session. The McMaster model provides much more overt detail (McSIFF interview), which is then summarized through the rating scales.

3. An interviewer or therapist introduces the discussion task. For the Beavers scales, the introduction is "For the next 10 minutes, I would like you to discuss together what you would like to see changed in your family," while the interviewer leaves the room. For the McMaster model, the detailed clinical interview (McSIFF) is used, conducted by an experienced clinician. For the Circumplex model, there is no one specific task, but the family is asked to engage in interactive dialogue, such as describing their typical week. No set procedure or task is specified for the GARF.

4. Rate the family, based on the observed interactional sequences. Raters typically are trained and well versed in the particular model they are using. For example, it takes approximately 15 hours of rater training to reach inter-rater reliabilities of +.90 using the Beavers scales.

5. When possible, use the self-report version of the model with individuals, to compare each member's perception of the family with the overall ratings. These are the SFI (Beavers), FAD (McMaster), and FACES III or IV (Circumplex).

6. Use the family ratings to help set therapeutic goals. The identification of specific lacks and needs of the family helps provide an operational list of what tasks need to be accomplished. The identification of family competence and style (Beavers) also helps therapists tailor their approach to each family, in terms of control (power differential), partnership, and disclosure of strategy with the family.

7. Re-rate the family at several points along the therapy timeline, to monitor progress and check on the therapeutic alliance. In our clinical setting, families are re-rated at the sixth session, and even six sessions thereafter. In several studies using the GARF, these ratings are provided after every session (Yingling et al., 1998).

8. Provide feedback to the family about the assessment, for example, telling them where they appear to be having problems and that certain goals can be established right there in the initial session.

Whenever rating scales are used, there may be a certain degree of subjectivity, so the decision about who will perform the rating is important. In our studies, the therapist is always one of the family's raters, because it is done at the outset of the first session. We also have neutral research rating teams view the tapes during the week, and these ratings are added to the case files prior to the second session. Interestingly, and much like the findings of Kolevzon, Green, Fortune, and Vosler (1988), we have found that therapists tend to rate the families they are beginning to treat as slightly more dysfunctional than the neutral raters in the beginning. Family members' ratings (on the SFI) tend to line up more with those of the neutral raters. At the close of therapy, the therapists' ratings put the family in a more competent direction than do the neutral raters, and line up more with the family members' views.

It is also informative to see which family member's or members' rating on the SFI rates the family as more or less disturbed than the outside raters. Our studies have found that adolescents in general, and acting-out adolescents in particular, rate their families as more disturbed than do the raters. However, in certain internalizing (CP) patterns, it is not uncommon for the symptomatic adolescent (e.g., anorexic adolescents) to paint a picture of perfection in their families. These varying perspectives can provide a therapist some important insights into family dynamics.

CASE EXAMPLE: A CENTRIFUGAL FAMILY

The school district referred this family because Jose, age 12, was disruptive in class and was not making adequate progress in any subject. In previous years Jose had done grade-appropriate work and had not demonstrated behavioral problems.

This family, of Hispanic origin, consisted of Jose, his mother Rosa, age 35, and an older sister Lupe, age 17, who was not is school; in addition, there was the father, Miguel, age 37, who had lived elsewhere for the last year in another household that included his 22-year-old girlfriend. Jose had had frequent verbal conflicts with Rosa and in one instance was stopped by Lupe from physically hurting his mother. The onset of Jose's defiant behavior coincided with Miguel's departure.

Miguel came frequently into the home and brought groceries and gave money to Rosa at irregular intervals. He worked as an auto mechanic and was hard pressed to keep two families going. He would not come to evaluation or treatment, so the family that appeared (Step 1: Obtain informed consent for evaluation) consisted of Jose, Rosa, and Lupe. The family discussion task ("What would you like to see changed in your family?"), based on the Beavers Interactional Scales (Step 2: Choose an appropriate instrument and model; Step 3: Introduce the discussion task), was punctuated by uncomfortable silence and distancing. When the family members spoke, it was about blaming Jose for not being more compliant and respectful of his mother. Lupe and Rosa had a tentative coalition, mostly against Jose, but also in their unlikely wish to have Miguel reintegrated into the family. The family fluctuated between chaotic outbursts and attempts at rigid control; they had poor negotiation skills. Each member tended to blame someone else for his or her frustrations. The family affect was rather hopeless and cynical, and unresolved conflict abounded. The family was rated at "Borderline" in competence on the Beavers Interactional Competence Scale (Step 4: Rate the family's interaction).

In terms of stylistic behavior (also Step 4: Rate the family's interaction), there were consistent indicators of Centrifugal family behavior: open conflicts, more open hostility, and discouraged dependency needs in the offspring. The family also spaced themselves physically apart, especially Jose, who was all the way across the room from his mother and sister. They also appeared unconcerned about their social presentation to outsiders. The family was rated "Borderline Centrifugal," which, according to the Beavers model, is open in the direct expression of anger and hostility and in which there is frequent leave-taking. Control themes are overt blaming and direct emotional assaults; the cyclical chaos is more overt than covert. Nurturance is not available to parents or children, and satisfaction is sought outside the family. Psychiatric disorders typically include externalizing disorders (conduct, substance abuse) and cyclical disorders that reflect the rigid-to-chaos fluctuations (Borderline Personality Disorder is often present among members of these families). They need therapists who can maintain effective control, limit the number of members attending, focus on the basics, help the family organize simple actions and activities, organize generational boundaries, and help members take risks with neediness and emotional pain.

On the SFI, taken by all three members of this family (Step 5: Use self-report scales related to the observational model), there were similar results except that Jose graded the family somewhat lower in competence than his sister and mother. All three rated the family Style ("Cohesion" factor) as disengaged/Centrifugal. Jose's lower Competence rating is characteristic of the "symptom bearer," indicating lower levels of family satisfaction and higher levels of unresolved conflict, as well as greater emotional distance from the rest of the family.

The combined results placed the family in the borderline CF group. In the six sessions we had with this family, it was necessary to focus on reasonable goals (Step 6: Set reasonable goals based on the assessment). It was established that Rosa did not expect Miguel to ever return to her home and that Jose's acting out was coincidental with his father's moving out and taking up with another woman. Rosa was unemployed and had a sixth-grade education, and Lupe was poorly equipped for the working world because she had left school after the 10th grade.

Task 1 was to help Rosa to become empowered to become the head of the family. With help, she was able to tell Miguel that she needed and appreciated his help but that he was confusing and damaging his son with his intermittent appearances in which he behaved as the authoritarian father. This confused Jose and undermined Rosa's authority, which was necessary to develop some kind of structure that could be relied on. Rosa was able to tap into Miguel's real love for Jose, and Miguel became more clearly an adjunct to Rosa's running the house rather than trying to run her as well.

Task 2 (Task 1 attended to makes this goal easier to accomplish) was to reduce or eliminate Jose's disruptive behavior and get him back on track in school. As he was helped to see his mother as a dedicated parent who loved him, he was also allowed to vent his anger and sadness that Miguel was not going to return to the home and be a real father. Less confusion meant less despairing anger, and he began to focus on his schoolwork again and accept the loss of this father.

Task 3, Lupe was encouraged to study for a G.E.D., which would assist her in getting her high school diploma so that she could get a job. She was an intelligent young woman who needed some direct encouragement in growing up and being helpful to herself and to her family.

The Borderline CF style dictated the necessity for a more directive approach to help the family clear up confusion and focus on the "do-able."

The grief over the loss of a father was brought out and reduced the overt hostility always seen in Borderline CF families.

Because our Family Studies Center contracts for a six-session family model with our grantors, the SFI is a better instrument for evaluating results than is the GARF. The SFI reflects changes more rapidly (Step 7: Re-evaluate the family periodically). Our use of the GARF is limited to longer-term treatment. In both of these case histories, there was significant increase in reported family competence, though the style did not change with the CP family and only modestly with the CF family. The use of the SFI with schoolchildren and school reports of behavior and functioning offer better and quicker evidence of improvement (Step 8: Share the results to help the family plan future goals).

CASE EXAMPLE: A CENTRIPETAL FAMILY

The Lee family referred themselves to the sliding fee clinic as a result of acting-out behavior in their younger daughter, Michelle, who was 18 and a senior in high school. The family consisted of the father, Benny; his wife, Grace; their older daughter, Rosa (22); and Michelle. The family was Filipino; they moved from the Philippines when Rosa was a baby; Michelle was born in the United States. Mr. Lee was an educated professional. Mrs. Lee held a college degree but did not work outside the home.

Mr. Lee had gotten fed up with Michelle's increasing tendency to defy her parents. His blood pressure was up and tension headaches were common; he had three auto accidents in the past 2 months. Some of her behaviors involved sneaking out in the middle of the night, taking the car without permission, and running up charge cards to the maximum. Michelle constantly complained that her parents were too strict, and she had to sneak out and defy in order to have a halfway "normal" life. The Lees referred to their expectation of compliance as "the Filipino way" and thought Michelle was entirely "too American."

The entire family presented for the initial family assessment. Mr. Lee had trouble with the fact that a videotape was being made of the family's interaction. He consented (Step 1) to participate only if the therapist remained in the room (she said that she would, but she would not talk), and he remained off camera. The family discussion task (again, "What would you like to see changed in your family?," Steps 2 and 3) revealed a number of key interactions. First, Mr. Lee controlled every exchange in the family, from directing who was to talk to correcting the perspective of individuals who had a divergent view. His wife, no patsy, would occasionally redirect or contradict his comments. However, these exchanges were all done with little emotion, in a very mechanical tone. When Michelle disagreed or tried to defend her behavior as "normal," he would lecture on about how she was threatening to blow the family apart by not following the Filipino way. The older daughter, Rosa, was a passive, sad, and ineffectual person who deferred to her parents. She also had a negative relationship with Michelle, who referred to Rosa as "the narc." There was a tone of invasiveness on both parents' part, who labeled the behaviors of their daughters as "American" and "little mama." It was clear, however, that the scapegoat in this system was Michelle. While many CP families have individuals with only internalizing disorders, this "fallen saint" pattern is another variation on the scapegoating theme.

From the observation of the family, and their description of the circular nature of the interaction (act out, ground her, more acting-out, etc.), that the control themes in the family were quite rigid, and that rigid control gave way to chaos as the effectiveness of parental control was defied. The family was stuck. The operating themes within the family were expectations for perfect behavior, condemnation for not following the "correct" culture, and dominance/submission. This family was rated as "Borderline" in competence on the Beavers Competence Scale (Step 4), and as Centripetal in Style (Step 4 also), given the emphasis on compliant and "correct" behavior, and the suppression of the expression of negative feelings. Michelle was clearly the "fallen saint" in this system.

The Borderline Centripetal family system, according to the Beavers model, is a control-oriented structure that lacks intimacy and spontaneity. They are stuck in control efforts. When these families seek help, it is to help further control the fallen saint, not to relinquish control. Any effort on the therapists' part to increase the control (shape the offender) or challenge the control of the tyrant is doomed to failure. The former solidifies the cyclical control themes, and the latter will result in the controlling member pulling the family out of treatment. Instead, the therapist needs to go below the control issues, to the underlying feelings of the family members. They are upset, disappointed, and probably very lonely. Hence, getting family members to address what they miss and long for can be a powerful tool.

Second, there will be strong attempts of different factions to pull the therapist toward their side of the struggle. The therapist needs to steer clear of judgments and side-taking. As the focus on relationships and lost hopes and dreams progresses, it becomes clear that there is not a specifically defined villain and victim. They are all hurting. It is a good idea to cater to the emotional needs of the most powerful person in the family initially, so he or she feels understood. This can go a long way to preventing the powerful member from pulling the family out of therapy. The SFI (Step 5) was not administered to the Lees.

For the Lee family, the therapeutic goals were several (Step 6). One was to develop a focus on the feeling level, especially with family members asking for more of what they liked, rather than on the rigid rule structures. A second was to shift the "blame" for behavior from the clash of cultures to the individual level. A third was for the parents to learn cooperation and negotiation skills, so they could share parenting roles and duties. A related theme had to do with helping Rosa develop some sense of autonomy, in that the parents would view her strivings to be more independent as a sign of individual competence and not defiance. Finally, Michelle would learn that as control themes softened, she needed to rely less on rebellious tactics to get what she wanted. When the family began dealing with Task 1, it became clear that each member was feeling isolated and lonely. The guilt-inducing and controlling exchanges that characterized the family began to be interspersed with questions such as "Well, what would you like to see more of?" It was much harder for Mr. Lee than the others to address the feeling level. He also had more difficulty with the second task, that of personalizing rather than culturalizing the deviant behavior. However, there was an important breakthrough when the parental dyad began addressing working as a team (Task 3). The more Mr. Lee observed that his wife was reasonably competent in talking with the girls, and even soliciting cooperation from them, the more he felt that he could back off. In fact, he soon "allowed" his wife and daughters to continue counseling without him, a major step in altering his rigid control efforts.

Once this step had been reached, the three women were able to negotiate on some key matters, including a more modest social schedule for Michelle and some independent maneuvering for Rosa. Rosa began taking some classes at the community college and joined several activity groups at the church. The three women (the family subset) attended a total of 15 sessions and reported a much higher degree of satisfaction. From their reports, Mr. Lee was also happier and was significantly less stressed out at home.

Re-evaluation (Step 7) at the 12th session involved only Mrs. Lee, Rosa, and Michelle. The discussion was productive and respectful. It was clear that there was less testy behavior on Michelle's part, and the respect for each other was higher. However, because Mr. Lee was not present, it was not possible to tell whether this same interaction would have occurred had he been there. By their reports, however, negotiation and overall interaction were much smoother at home, especially because Mr. Lee had decided that he did not need to control everyone and everything. The rating at the 12th session found this family at the higher Midrange level of competence, still with a modestly Centripetal style, so there was a noticeable improvement in their functioning level.

CONCLUDING NOTE

The various family observational assessment systems in this chapter focus on the "macro" level of assessment, examining the "big picture" of family functioning. As mentioned earlier, there is a wide variety of more "micro" assessment procedures that measure highly specific behaviors within family interaction sequences, but these may be less amenable to therapy planning and intervention than the models presented here.

There are probably more similarities than differences across the global assessment models presented in this chapter. The Beavers model addresses family competence, which refers to structure, autonomy, communication clarity, and boundaries. In a similar vein, the McMaster

TABLE 4.1   Matrix: Observational Family Ratings

Assessment Instrument	Specific Couple and Family Applications	Cultural/ Language	Instruction/Use: T = Time to Take S = Time to Score I = Items (# of)	Computerized: (a) Scoring (b) Report	Reliability (R) Validity (V)	Availability
Beavers Interactional Competence and Beavers Interactional Style; SFI	Whole families; classifies family competence and behavioral style, and suggestions for appropriate therapy	English, Spanish, Italian, Portuguese, Greek, Chinese, Japanese, German, French	T = 10 min S = 10 min I = 12 Competence 8 Style	a = No b = No	R = .85 (inter-rater) R = .88 (alpha) V = .72 (canonical)	Directly from Dr. Hampson (Dallas, TX) rhampson@smu.edu
McMaster Clinical Rating Scale	Whole families; classifies families on general functioning and composite behaviors	English, French, 12 other languages	T = 90 min, with interview S = 10 min I = 7 scales McSIFF interview has 35 pages of questions	a = No b = No	R = .68–.87 (inter-rater) R = .81–.87 (test-retest) V = Good clinical validity	Brown University Family Research Program
Circumplex Clinical Rating Scale	Whole families; couples. Measures Cohesion, Change (Adaptability), and Communication	English, Spanish, several other languages	T = 45–60 min S = 10–15 min I = 3 global scales, 13 subscales	a = No b = No	R = .95–.97 (alphas) R =.75–.86 (test-retest) V = Good support for circumplex theory	Life Innovations, Inc., Minneapolis, MN www.lifeinnivations.org
GARF	Any relational unit: family, couple, partner, support system	English	T = 15–60 min S = 10 min I = 4 global ratings	a = No b = No	R =.73–.86 (inter-rater) V = .69 (with Beavers Competence)	American Psychological Association (DSM-IV-TR)

Measure	Description	Language	Time/Subscales/Items	Scoring	Reliability/Validity	Source
Marital Instability Index (MII)	Measures marital instability	English; no demographics reported	T = Short S = Short I = 14	Easy hand-scoring	R = .93 (internal consistency) V = Good predictive validity (3% break-up among those w/ no signs of break-up; 27% break-up at other end of spectrum)	Journal article
Environmental Assessment Index (EAI)	Measures quality of family's home environment for children	English	T = Not given S = Not given I = 44 (22 in short form)	Hand-scoring	R = Cronbach .84 (.82 short form) V = Good predictive & concurrent validity	Journal article
Couples' Intimate Behavior Rating System	Assesses the depth of factual, emotional, and cognitive self-disclosure of the speaker and understanding, validation, and caring expressed by listener in each interaction	English		Hand-scoring	R = .79–.82 V = Not specified	Journal article
Child and Adult Relational Experimental Index (CARE-Index)	Measure of parenting behavior	English	T = 90 min	Hand-scoring	R = Inter-rater reliability was high ($\kappa = .95$) V = Passed several tests of validity	Journal article

model addresses overall family functioning, which is also a linear, more-is-better dimension consisting of important family tasks and communication skills. The GARF is also a linear rating scale, comprised of dimensions of emotional climate, problem solving, and organization. The Circumplex Communication rating is also a linear scale, ranging from low to high. However, the Flexibility dimension is a curvilinear scale, ranging from polar opposites of Rigid to Chaotic; these dimensions are close kin in the Beavers model, representing dysfunctional to borderline levels of competence.

The Style dimension of the Beavers model describes the behavioral climate of the family and is highly associated with the nature of behavior disorders in family members. This is more of a curvilinear dimension, in that middle levels of style are associated with healthy family functioning, and extremes are found in more disturbed families. This maps on to the Circumplex model's Cohesion factor, where extremes of Disengaged and Enmeshed are associated with family disturbance. This dimension is addressed on the Affective Involvement rating on the McMaster model, where "empathic involvement" is optimal, and the extremes of "lack of involvement" and "symbiotic involvement" are more pathological. This dimension is not addressed directly on the GARF.

The major models and their instruments are described in Table 4.1.

REFERENCES

Beavers, W. R. (1977). *Psychotherapy and growth: A family systems perspective.* New York: Brunner/Mazel.

Beavers, W. R., & Hampson, R. B. (1990). *Successful families: Assessment and intervention.* New York: W. W. Norton.

Beavers, W. R., & Hampson, R. B. (2003). Measuring family competence: The Beavers Systems Model. In F. Walsh (Ed.), *Normal family processes* (3rd ed., pp. 549–580). New York: Guilford Press.

Beavers, W. R., & Voeller, M. N. (1983). Family models: Comparing the Olson Circumplex Model with the Beavers Systems Model. *Family Process, 22,* 85–98.

Bishop, D. S., Epstein, N. B., Keitner, G. I., Miller, I. W., & Zlotnick, C. (1987). *McMaster Structured Interview of Family Functioning (McSIFF).* Providence, RI: Brown University Family Research Program.

Bishop, D. S., Epstein, N. B., Keitner, G. I., Miller, I. W., Zlotnick, C., & Ryan, C. E. (2000). *McMaster Structured Interview of Family Functioning (McSIFF).* Providence, RI: Brown University Family Research Program.

Crittenden, P. (1988). Relationships at risk. In J. Belsky & T. Nezworski (Eds.), *Clinical implications of attachment* (pp. 136–174). Hillsdale, NJ: Lawrence Erlbaum.

Denton, W. H., Nakonezny, P. A., & Burwell, S. R. (2010). Reliability and validity of the Global Assessment of Relational Functioning (GARF) in a psychiatric family therapy clinic. *Journal of Marital and Family Therapy, 36,* 376–387.

Epstein, N. B., & Bishop, D. S. (1981). Problem centered systems therapy of the family. In A. S. Gurman & D. P. Kniskern (Eds.), *Handbook of family therapy* (pp. 444–482). New York: Brunner/Mazel.

Epstein, N. B., Ryan, C. E., Bishop, D. S., Miller, I. W. & Keitner, G. I. (2003). The McMaster model: A view of healthy family functioning. In F. Walsh (Ed.), *Normal family processes* (3rd ed., pp. 581–607). New York: Guilford Press.

Gordon, E. D. (1997). *The Global Assessment of Relational Functioning (GARF): Reliability and validity.* Unpublished master's thesis, Southern Methodist University.

Green, R. G., Kolevzon, M. S., & Vosler, N. R. (1985). The Beavers-Timberlawn Model of Family Competence and the Circumplex Model of Family Adaptability and Cohesion: Separate, but equal? *Family Process, 24,* 385–398.

Hampson, R. B. & Beavers, W. R. (1996a). Family therapy and outcome: Relationships between therapist and family styles. *Contemporary Family Therapy, 18,* 345–369.

Hampson, R. B., & Beavers, W. R. (1996b). Measuring family therapy outcome in a clinical setting: Families that do better or worse in therapy. *Family Process, 35,* 347–361.

Hampson, R. B., Beavers, W. R., & Hulgus, Y. F. (1989). Insiders' and outsiders' views of family: The assessment of family competence and style. *Journal of Family Psychology, 3,* 118–136.

Hampson, R. N., Beavers, W. R., & Hulgus, Y. F. (1990). Cross-ethnic family differences: Interactional assessment of White, Black, and Mexican-American families. *Journal of Marital and Family Therapy, 16,* 307–319.

Hampson, R. B., Prince, C. C., & Beavers, W. R. (1999). Marital therapy: Qualities of couples who fare better or worse in treatment. *Journal of Marital and Family Therapy, 25,* 411–424.

Henney, S. M. (1994). *Relational diagnosis and assessment in family therapy.* Unpublished master's thesis, Southern Methodist University.

Henney, S. M., & Hampson, R. B. (1994). *Social desirability effects on family self-report ratings.* Presented at the American Psychological Association Convention, Los Angeles.

Kitzman, H., Hampson, R. B., Wilson, D., Presnell, K., Brown, A., & O'Boyle, M. (2009). An adolescent weight-loss program integrating family variables reduces energy intake. *Journal of the American Dietetic Association, 109,* 491–496.

Kolevzon, M. S., Green, R. G., Fortune, A. E., & Vosler, N. R. (1988). Evaluating family therapy: Divergent methods, divergent findings. *Journal of Marital & Family Therapy, 14*(3), 277–286.

Lee, C. (1988). Theories of family adaptability: Toward a synthesis of Olson's Circumplex and the Beavers Systems Models. *Family Process, 27,* 73–85.

Miller, I. W., Kabacoff, R. I., Epstein, N. B., Bishop, D. S., Keitner, G.I., Baldwin, L. M., & van der Spuy, H. I. J. (1994). The development of a clinical rating scale for the McMaster Model of Family Functioning. *Family Process, 33,* 53–69.

Miller, I. W., Ryan, C. E., Keitner, G. I., Bishop, D. S., & Epstein, N. B. (2000). The McMaster approach to families: Theory, assessment, treatment, research. *Journal of Family Therapy, 22,* 168–189.

Motarella, K. E., Philpot, C. I., & Fritzsche, B. A. (2001). Don't take out this appendix! Generalizability of the Global Assessment of Relational Functioning Scale. *American Journal of Family Therapy, 29,* 271–278.

Olson, D. H., & Gorall, D. M. (2003). Circumplex Model of Marital and Family Systems. In F. Walsh (Ed.), *Normal family processes* (3rd ed.). New York: Guilford Press.

Olson, D. H., & Killorin, E. (1983). *Clinical Rating Scale for the Circumplex Model of Marital and Family Systems.* Minneapolis: University of Minnesota, Department of Family Social Science.

Olson, D. H., & Killorin, E. (1988). *Clinical Rating Scale for the Circumplex Model of Marital and Family Systems.* Minneapolis: University of Minnesota, Department of Family Social Science.

Ross, N. M., & Doherty, W. J. (2001). Validity of the Global Assessment of Relational Functioning (GARF) when used by community-based therapists. *American Journal of Family Therapy, 29,* 239–253.

Thomas, V., & Olson, D. H. (1993). Problem families and the Circumplex model: Observational assessment using the clinical rating scale. *Journal of Marital and Family Therapy, 19,* 159–175.

Yingling, L. C., Miller, W. E., McDonald, A. L., & Galewater, S. T. (1998). *GARF Assessment sourcebook: Using the DSM-IV Global Assessment of Relational Functioning.* New York: Brunner/Mazel.

Zayas, V., Mischel, W., Shoda, Y., & Aber, J. L. (2010). Roots of adult attachment: Maternal caregiving at 18 months predicts adult peer and partner attachment. *Social Psychological and Personality Science.* Advance online publication. doi:10.1177/1948550610389822

CHAPTER 5

Ongoing Assessment of Couples and Families

Len Sperry

The practice of behavioral health at the onset of the 21st century is increasingly different from practice during most of the 20th century. This is largely due to the paradigm shift in behavioral health practice that has been under way since the late 1980s. This shift involves every facet of behavioral health practice, including the role of the clinician and the nature of the relationship between clinician and client, as well as clinical practice patterns. This shift has already resulted in the demystification of some basic tenets and "sacred cows" of clinical lore. Central to this paradigm shift is the increasing emphasis on quality and accountability of clinical services provided. Accordingly, quality indicators and cost effectiveness have become primary considerations in behavioral health today. Not surprisingly, clinical outcomes data, a key marker of quality and of accountability, have recently become the norm for the provision of behavioral health services.

This chapter introduces the concept of *clinical outcomes assessment* with couples and families. It begins with a description of the emergence of the concept of *accountability* and the so-called outcomes revolution and its impact on clinical practice. It then has a description of the various types and levels of outcomes assessment and its clinical implications, particularly the practice of family therapy. *Therapeutic effectiveness*, *efficacy*, and *efficiency* are defined, and the point is made that outcomes monitoring fosters the most important of the three concepts: therapeutic efficacy. Next is a discussion of recent developments in outcomes measurement and monitoring with couples and families, and then a description of the use of five specific measurement tools. Finally, a protocol for utilizing these tools in measuring and monitoring outcomes with couples and families is provided and illustrated with a couple therapy case example.

CLINICIANS, FAMILY THERAPY, AND
OUTCOMES MEASUREMENT

Clinical outcomes data and the associated outcomes revolution (Sperry, 1997) reflect a norm radically different from that in which most clinicians were trained. In the past, clinical practice was characterized by independence of clinical judgment, practice constraints, emphasis on therapeutic process, and subjective assessment of clinical progress. The recent shift in focus to an emphasis on accountability, that is, outcomes instead of process and objective assessment of clinical progress, has resulted in many clinicians' confusion and concern about the meaning and implications of this paradigm shift imposed on the profession. Some view this emphasis on accountability and quality as an intrusion into their practice style or as actually or potentially unethical. Some have embraced this norm wholeheartedly, while others have come to accept it as inevitable (Sperry, Brill, Grisson, & Marion, 1997). Whatever their perspective, clinicians must contend with the reality that therapeutic accountability and clinical outcomes assessment in particular have become a core feature of clinical practice today and will be in the future.

In short, clinical outcomes assessment has been regarded as a necessary but unwelcome task by clinicians, particularly those conducting family therapy who are process oriented. "A focus on results rather than process has been anathema to family therapists" (Yingling, Miller, McDonald, & Galwaler, 1998, p. 49). Can this process versus outcome dilemma be resolved? Wynne (1988) suggested a potential solution, which is to "recommend that two primary baselines be given priority in family therapy research: (a) the multiple versions of the family members' 'initial' presenting problem, and (b) the problem identified by consensus of family and therapist" (p. 253). Yingling and colleagues (1998) contend that using data from self-report measures of family members along with data from therapist ratings or observations (i.e., the Global Assessment of Relational Functioning [GARF]) can provide data relevant to process and outcome assessment. They also note that "discussing GARF parameters and charting progress with the client can enhance the therapeutic process ... [and] the GARF can also be used as a process research tool when combined with case notes that include therapeutic interventions and reflections" (Yingling et al., 1998, p. 49).

RECENT DEVELOPMENTS IN ONGOING
ASSESSMENT OF COUPLES AND FAMILIES

Since the publication of the first edition of this book, there have been a few noteworthy developments in clinical outcomes assessment in general, and with couples in particular. Most obvious is that clinical outcomes assessment has become increasingly mainstream. This reflects the "culture of accountability" in which we live and the expectation that clinicians will utilize evidence-based treatment and demonstrate the effectiveness of the therapy they provide. A related development is that a number of new instruments and assessment devices have become available and are increasingly being utilized not only to address specific assessment questions but also to monitor progress and evaluation treatment outcomes. It is noteworthy that clinicians and researchers are effectively responding to the phenomenon of high rates of premature termination (40%–70%) by advocating the use of measuring and monitoring key therapeutic factors with brief assessment instruments (Lambert, 2010).

Particularly notable are the following developments. First is the introduction of shorter and *ultra-brief* instruments (often 3 or 4 items) taking only 1 to 2 minutes to complete. This contrasts with the 150 items of the Marital Satisfaction Inventory, Revised (MSI-R), which takes about 25 to 30 minutes to complete. Second, because of the limited administration time, such as for the Outcome Rating Scale, it is possible and preferable to monitor client or family progress at each session. This contrasts with the necessity to limit monitoring of progress to every fourth session or so or, more commonly, before the first and after the last treatment sessions (the pre–post model of evaluation). Third, because of increasing use of these brief instruments (completed immediately before a session begins), it is now possible for client ratings to be discussed in that session. This "continuous progress feedback" strategy (Miller, Duncan, Brown, Sorrell, & Chalk, 2006) provides immediate client feedback, which facilitates the modification of the treatment process. This feedback process has been shown not only to increase treatment outcomes appreciably but also to reduce the likelihood of premature termination (Lambert, 2010).

TYPES OF OUTCOMES SYSTEMS AND THEIR CLINICAL VALUE

Most clinicians are likely to have had some experience with at least one type of outcomes system. The most common, and often the only, assessment of treatment outcomes that may be required is a simple measure of client satisfaction. Usually, client satisfaction is assessed by a short paper-and-pencil questionnaire that includes such items as how well the client thought he was treated by the therapist and how much he thought he improved during therapy. Although client satisfaction is important, it has not been shown to be an accurate assessment of treatment outcomes; in fact, it is actually a poor measure of clinical improvement. For example, Atkisson and Zwick (1982) showed that symptom improvement explains only 10% of the variance in client satisfaction, while the relationship between clinical improvement and reported satisfaction is not statistically significant for clients still in treatment or for those who have completed treatment.

On the other hand, other outcomes measures have shown clinical utility and value. Outcomes measures and outcomes measurement systems can yield three types of benefits, one of which is its capacity to identify effective treatments. This requires pretreatment and post-treatment assessment of a client's status to determine changes that occurred as a result of treatment. Aggregation of these data across all clients who received a specific treatment is the basis for this first benefit. A second benefit is immediate feedback to clinicians and case managers. This feedback will enable clinicians to identify clients who are improving adequately, those who have improved to a point at which treatment may no longer be necessary, and those whose lack of progress or determination suggests that their treatment should be changed. The third benefit is the ability to identify the specific changes most likely to move the unimproved client onto a more positive growth path—that is, to determine whether involvement of a spouse or family in treatment, transfer to a different therapist and different type of therapy, referral for a medication evaluation, or some other alteration in treatment is most likely to get the client well.

By incorporating feedback from an outcomes system into ongoing clinical cases, clinicians effectively supplement or support a clinician's intuition about treatment decisions. Serial data on changes in symptoms and functioning can be utilized in modifying the course and duration of treatment in terms of focus, modality, and intervention strategies with individuals, couples, or families.

Essentially, three levels of outcomes assessment exist (Sperry, 1997):

> *Outcomes measurement*—quantification or measurement of clinical and functional outcomes during a specific time period. Outcomes measures have traditionally been collected at the beginning and end of treatment. However, serial or concurrent assessment is becoming more common. Measures often include change in symptoms, well-being, functioning, and even patient satisfaction.
>
> *Outcomes monitoring*—serial or concurrent use of outcomes measures during the course of treatment. The goal of outcomes monitoring is comparison against a standard of expected results to monitor progress or lack of progress over the course of treatment. Monitoring can be done after each session, every third session, or on some other scheduled basis. The data are then used to alter treatment when it is off course or stagnating. They

can also be used to follow progress in a single case or summed and adjusted for risk to compare several patients or programs. Outcomes monitoring can only be accomplished with repeated or concurrent measures, and the information must be available during the treatment.

Outcomes management—ultimate utilization of monitored data in a way that allows individuals and health care systems to learn from experience. Usually, this results in reshaping or improving the overall administrative and clinical processes of services provided. Patient profiling, provider profiling, and site profiling are three common aspects of an outcomes management system.

In a sense, these three levels are developmental levels or stages, with each level a prerequisite for the next. Currently, the majority of outcomes assessment activity is occurring at the outcomes measurement and the outcomes monitoring levels. It is useful to distinguish therapeutic effectiveness and efficacy from therapeutic efficiency. *Therapeutic effectiveness* is the determination that a treatment has a beneficial effect and is the expected outcome for a typical client treated in common practice settings by a typical clinician. On the other hand, *therapeutic efficacy* is the expected outcome for clients treated under optimal conditions by highly qualified clinicians. In short, efficacy defines optimal clinical practice, while effectiveness compares actual with optimal practice (Sperry, Brill, Howard, & Grissom, 1996).

In contrast, *therapeutic efficiency* refers to highly beneficial treatment tailored to the unique needs of a specific client (individual, couple, or family) as they are noted—or measured—over the course of treatment. Therapeutic effectiveness and efficacy answer the question, which treatment or approach is better or best? Therapeutic efficiency answers the question, which is the best treatment for this client and how can it be optimally provided? Accordingly, ongoing monitoring of clinical treatment outcomes fosters therapeutic efficiency.

CLINICAL OUTCOMES WITH INDIVIDUALS, COUPLES, AND FAMILIES

The earliest outcomes measurement efforts were primarily focused on psychotherapy with individuals, largely because a principal focus of psychotherapy research was on treatment outcomes. In the late 1980s, two instruments for outcomes assessment with individuals, COMPASS-OP and the Outcomes Questionnaire 45.2 (OQ-45), were widely utilized in clinical practice to measure pre–post-treatment outcomes, rather than monitor clinical outcomes on an ongoing basis. It is true that the Dyadic Adjustment Scale (DAS) was utilized as a pre–post-treatment measure of therapeutic effectiveness in a handful of research studies over the years.

However, only recently has the use of such inventories and scales as the DAS and the MSI-R (Marital Satisfaction Inventory, Revised) been advocated for monitoring clinical outcomes of couples therapy (Jacobson, 1984; Jacobson & Follette, 1985; Latham, 1990; Prouty, Markowski, & Barnes, 2000; Snyder & Aikman, 1999).

In terms of treatment outcome measures with families, the Self-Report Family Inventory (SFI), GARF Scale, and the Systematic Assessment of Family Environment (SAFE) Scale have all been utilized as pre–post-treatment measures in clinical research studies (Hampson & Beavers, 1996a; Hampson, Prince, & Beavers, 1999; Yingling, 1996; Yingling, Miller, McDonald, & Galwaler, 1994a). As clinicians become more familiar with the GARF Scale, it has tremendous potential for monitoring clinical outcomes on a session-by-session basis with families (Yingling et al., 1998).

The next section of this chapter is a description of the use of five inventories and scales for clinical outcomes measurement and for the ongoing monitoring of clinical outcomes with couples and families: GARF, SFI, SAFE, DAS, and MSI-R.

OUTCOME MEASURES PRIMARILY FOR FAMILIES

This section includes three well-regarded instruments with considerable potential in clinical outcomes measurement and monitoring: the Global Assessment of Relationship Functioning, the Systematic Assessment of Family Environment, the Self-Report Family Inventory, as well as a new and promising instrument, the Systemic Clinical Outcomes and Routine Evaluation.

Global Assessment of Relational Functioning (GARF)

Brief description of the GARF. The GARF is a therapist-rated device for indicating functioning or a family or other ongoing relationship on a continuum ranging from a low of 1 to a high of 100. The continuum is divided into five categories: 1 to 20 = chaotic; 21 to 40 = rarely satis-factory; 41 to 60 = predominantly unsatisfactory; 61 to 80 = somewhat unsatisfactory; and 81 to 100 = satisfactory. It is the only family-oriented measure included in the pages of the DSM-IV/DSM-IV-TR and is located in Appendix B (American Psychiatric Association, 2000). GARF is analogous to Global Assessment of Functioning Scale (GAF), which is a measure of individual symptomatic distress and functioning; both are coded on Axis V. When assessing or rating a relationship, the clinician is asked to consider three dimensions of relational functioning: problem solving, organization, and emotional climate. Recent reliability and validly data on the GARF support it as a reliable and valid measure of relational functioning whose ratings can be made quickly and reliably, particularly among clinicians and supervisors with clinical experience, and are related to depression (Denton, Nakonezny, & Burwell, 2010).

Yingling and colleagues (1998) have slightly modified the dimensions Interactional, Problem Solving, Organization, and Emotional Climate, making them subscales that are scored separately, along with an overall GARF score. The psychometric properties and additional information about GARF are discussed in Chapter 6.

The GARF as an outcomes measure. Considerable published research and clinical reports are available in which GARF is utilized as an outcomes measure. Most of these reports involve GARF in pretreatment and post-treatment measurement (Hampson & Beavers, 1996b; Ross & Doherty, 2001; Yingling et al., 1994a, 1994b, 1998). With regard to ongoing assessment of outcomes, Yingling and colleagues (1998) discuss five case examples of the use of GARF as a treatment outcomes monitoring measure. These couple and family cases provide session-by-session ratings of overall GARF scores and subscale ratings for therapy lasting from 7 to 10 sessions. These case discussions are particularly valuable because data from the ongoing monitoring are utilized by the therapists to modify treatment focus and interventions.

Systematic Assessment of Family Environment (SAFE)

Brief description of the SAFE. The Systematic Assessment of Family Environment (SAFE) was developed by Yingling in 1991 along with field testing of the GARF (cf. Chapter 8 for an extended discussion of this instrument). It is a 21-item global assessment instrument for measuring three relational subsystem levels of the family system using two functioning factors for each subsystem level. The three subsystems are dyadic marital–executive subsystem, parent–child subsystem, and extended family subsystem. Organizational Structure and Interactional Processes are the two factors assessed for each subsystem. Scoring yields ranges for four family types: competent, discordant, disoriented, or chaotic (Yingling, 1996). SAFE is user friendly and available in a Spanish version as well as a cartoon version for use with children under the age of 10 (Yingling et al., 1998). Validity is reported as .74 and .82 (Yingling et al., 1998).

The SAFE as an outcomes measure. The SAFE provides information that can easily be incorporated into a treatment plan. Relatively little has been published about using SAFE for pre–post-treatment evaluation of change or ongoing monitoring of family therapy. Nevertheless, Yingling and colleagues (1998) report collecting serial data on GARF and SAFE for monitoring treatment outcomes. The ease of administration makes this instrument a valuable outcomes measure with families.

Self-Report Family Inventory (SFI)

Brief description of the SFI. The Self-Report Family Inventory (SFI) is a 36-item self-report family instrument developed by Beavers and Hampson (1990) and is based on the Beavers Systems Model of Family Functioning. It measures five family domains: health and competence, conflict resolution, cohesion, leadership, and emotional expressiveness. The SFI correlates highly with two well regarded therapist observational rating scales: the Beavers Interactional Competence Scale and the Beavers Interactional Styles Scale. Spanish and Chinese versions are also available. The psychometric properties and additional information about SFI are discussed in Chapter 5.

The SFI as an outcomes measure. Some research in which the SFI has been utilized as an outcomes measure has been published. These reports involve the SFI in pretreatment and post-treatment measurement (Hampson & Beavers, 1996a, 1996b; Hampson et al., 1999). Apparently, no research or other published reports describe the use of the SFI as an ongoing measure of clinical outcomes; however, the ease of administration and brevity of the instrument (only 36 items) make it particularly valuable for monitoring session-by-session outcomes.

SCORE 15

Brief description of the SCORE 15. The Systemic Clinical Outcome and Routine Evaluation (SCORE) was developed for the ongoing evaluation of clinical outcomes of families in therapy (Stratton, Bland, Janes, & Lask, 2010). It was originally a 40-item self-rating instrument. To make it more user friendly, it was reduced to 15 items, and factor analysis provided the basis for specifying three subscales: strengths and adaptability, overwhelmed by difficulties, and disrupted communication. The SCORE 15 as the short version is called has these reported psychometric properties:

Cronbach's alpha .89, split-half correlation .81; Guttman split-half coefficient .89. The extent to which the 15 items represent the original SCORE 40 items provided a multiple regression coefficient of .975.

The SCORE 15 as an outcomes measure. As a ongoing measure of clinical outcomes of families in therapy, the SCORE 15 is easily administered—about 2 to 4 minutes—and scored, about a minute or so. The instrument is currently available at the website of the Association for Family Therapy (www.aft.org.uk). It is in English, and it is reported that translation is underway in 12 European languages (Stratton et al., 2010).

OUTCOME MEASURES PRIMARILY FOR COUPLES

This section includes two well-regarded instruments with considerable potential in clinical outcomes measurement and monitoring: the Dyadic Adjustment Scale and the Marital Satisfaction Inventory, Revised, as well as a new and promising instrument, the Intersession Report.

Dyadic Adjustment Scale (DAS)

Brief description of the DAS. The Dyadic Adjustment Scale (DAS) is a 34-item self-report instrument for assessing dyadic or relationship adjustment. This instrument was developed by Spanier (1976) to measure the quality of adjustment of couples and other dyads. The DAS comprises four scales: Dyadic Satisfaction, Dyadic Cohesion, Dyadic Consensus, and Affectional Expression. It is one of the first and most extensively utilized relational instruments in clinical practice. A shorter, 14-item version is also available. The psychometric properties and additional information about DAS are discussed in Chapter 7. Spanier developed the instrument on the assumption that the quality of relational adjustment was the key indicator of the viability of a relationship. He defined marital quality as "how the marriage functions during its existence and how partners feel about and are influenced by such functioning" (Spanier, 1979, p. 290). The DAS has consistently distinguished couples with better adjustment from those who are more dissatisfied with their relationship, including couples with a greater likelihood of divorce (Prouty et al., 2000). Well over 1,000 research studies have been published involving the DAS. Although the instrument has evolved over the years, it remains one of the most commonly used measures of couples adjustment by researchers and clinicians.

The DAS as an outcomes measure. The DAS has a long history of use as an outcomes measure. Considerable research has been reported

on its use as a pre–post-treatment assessment tool in studies of therapeutic efficacy and effectiveness with couples (Adam & Gingras, 1982;
Brock & Joanning, 1983; Jacobson, 1984; Jacobson & Follette, 1985;
Latham, 1990; Prouty et al., 2000). Even though neither this research
nor other published reports describe the DAS as used as an ongoing measure of clinical outcomes, the brevity of the instrument—particularly the
14-item version—makes it an attractive choice for monitoring session-
by-session outcomes.

Marital Satisfaction Inventory, Revised (MSI-R)

Brief description of the MSI-R. The Marital Satisfaction Inventory,
Revised (MSI-R) is a 150-item self-report instrument developed by Snyder
(1997). The earlier version, MSI (Snyder, 1981), was well regarded and
one of the most often used relational inventories in research and clinical
practice. The MSI-R has 13 scales:

- Global Distress
- Affective Communication
- Problem-Solving Communication
- Aggression
- Time Together
- Disagreement About Finances
- Sexual Dissatisfaction
- Role Orientation
- Family History of Distress
- Dissatisfaction With Children
- Conflict Over Child Rearing
- Inconsistency (validity scale)
- Conventionalization (validity scale)

The MSI-R is useful as a diagnostic and a therapeutic tool, as well as
a screening instrument. Psychometric properties of and additional information about MSI-R are discussed in Chapter 7.

The MSI-R as an outcomes measure. The MSI-R is typically used
in the initial phase of therapy in discussing the couple's presenting
concerns and in formulating treatment goals. However, it can also be
utilized before and after therapy, in a pre–post-treatment fashion, to
evaluate overall treatment outcomes (Frank, Dixon, & Grosz, 1993;
Iverson & Baucom, 1988; Snyder & Berg, 1983; Snyder, Mangrum,
& Wills, 1993; Snyder, Wills, & Grady-Fletcher, 1991). Snyder and

Aikman (1999) also note the value of using MSI-R serially throughout the course of treatment in the evaluation of change and for revising treatment goals and interventions. The instrument "can be readministered at multiple points during treatment to evaluate and consolidate gains that the couple has made and to identify residual areas of distress for further work. This idiographic approach to outcome evaluation emphasizes within partner change across time" (Snyder & Aikman, 1999, p. 1198).

The Intersession Report

Brief description of the Intersession Report. The Intersession Report is a recently reported short and easily administered instrument for individuals and couples as well as families (Johnson, Ketring, & Anderson, 2010). It has nine items, the first eight of which are suitable for individual clients, while the ninth item—which rates the couple's relationship with the therapist—is added when working with couples. The Intersession Report assesses clients' level of functioning and symptomatic distress, as well as the therapeutic alliance. Accordingly, three subscales represent Functioning, Symptoms, and Alliance. Reported psychometric properties suggest the instrument is reasonably robust. Cronbach's alpha estimates range from .74 to .90. Convergent and discriminant validity was established by correlating it with the Outcome Questionnaire 45.2 (OQ-45.2), the Revised Dyadic Adjustment Scale (RDAS), the Experiences in Close Relationships (ECR), and the Couples Therapy Alliance Scale (CTAS). Results of exploratory factor analyses and low correlations among the three subscales of the Intersession Report suggest that the three subscales are distinct.

The Intersession Report as an outcomes measure. The instrument is administered at the beginning of each session. It takes about 2 to 3 minutes to complete and about 1 minute to review and score. The authors indicate that it provides useful ongoing feedback to the therapist. They also indicate that session-to-session use provides feedback that can decrease attrition and improve supervision (Johnson et al., 2010).

STRATEGY FOR ONGOING ASSESSMENT

The following six-step protocol can be useful in utilizing the GARF, SFI, SAFE, DAS, and MSI-R when measuring and monitoring clinical outcomes with couples and families.

1. Initially interview the couple or family.
2. Choose and administer specific inventories.
3. Collect collateral data (relevant work, school, medical records, etc.) and other interview data.
4. Review assessment data and plan treatment.
5. Monitor ongoing clinical outcomes and modify treatment accordingly.
6. Evaluate pretreatment and post-treatment outcomes, if feasible.

Well-executed interviews of the couple and family (Step 1 and Step 3) are essential in providing sufficient data and background information to develop and implement an effective treatment plan and intervention strategies. At the present time, the decision of which inventories and rating scales (Step 2) to use to measure and/or monitor clinical outcomes is much less complex than the protocols suggested by Bagarozzi (Chapter 6) or Yingling (Chapter 8). For example, Bagarozzi advocates a four-step funneling or filtering process that progresses from choosing global measures to focused measures. Because of the limited number of suitable potential inventories and scales (i.e., ease of administration and reasonable cost), the clinician might decide to utilize the SFI and GARF or the SAFE and GARF with families and use the GARF and DAS or MSI-R with couples.

Step 5 reflects the basic reason for monitoring outcomes, for example, session by session, every third session, and so forth. In this step, outcomes data transform into valuable feedback information that the clinician can utilize to modify the course and duration of treatment in terms of focus, modality, and intervention strategies. As a result of this feedback and subsequent treatment "course correction," couple or family therapy becomes more closely tailored to couple or family need and circumstance. Presumably, this should lead to more effective and efficient treatment. Finally, the clinical value of outcomes measurement can be evaluated in Step 6 by examining overall pre–post-treatment effects on the given outcome measures, inventories, and/or scales.

CASE STUDY

Jack and Nancy, both age 33, were referred to couples therapy by Nancy's gynecologist. During their first conjoint session (Step 1), the therapist learned that the couple had been married for 7 years and had a 2½-year-old daughter, Sybil. Sybil was their "wonder" child because she had been born after several years of unsuccessful efforts to conceive, including 2 years of painful fertility treatment. Jack had been an accountant at a low-tech manufacturing corporation until he was laid off some 3 months previously; Nancy had worked as a nurse at a local hospital for 3 or 4 years before she married Jack. Both had known each other since college but had never really seriously dated until after graduation.

The couple presented with increased argumentativeness, social and emotional withdrawal, and decreased sexual intimacy. These issues were relatively new in their relationship, apparently beginning soon after Sybil's birth. Nancy had been concerned about Jack's rigidity and seeming lack of emotional expressiveness since they had married and on more than one occasion had indicated her desire for them to seek couples therapy, but Jack was not interested in talking to anyone about himself or his marriage. In the time since he had been laid off, Jack had become increasingly sullen and emotionally distant; Nancy, who had been working part time at the hospital, now felt "forced" to go full time to cover their bills. She was particularly distraught about this because it meant she had less time to care for her daughter. During a recent appointment with her gynecologist, Nancy had begun sobbing when asked how she was doing. It was at this point that the gynecologist referred Nancy for conjoint couples therapy. Both partners acknowledged a moderate level of commitment to their marriage and an even deeper commitment to Sybil, who had become, for all practical purposes, the center of their lives.

The plan was to administer the MSI-R to the couple at the end of the first conjoint session and to interview Nancy and Jack individually in the following week. Then, during their second conjoint session, extensive feedback would be provided incorporating MSI-R, GARF, and interview material to formulate a tailored treatment plan collaboratively with the couple. GARF would be evaluated at each conjoint session, and the MSI-R was to be administered after every third session and after the last session (Step 2).

Individual interviewing provided a fuller understanding of each partner, their attraction to one another, and the nature of their marital relationship. Nancy's description of her family of origin suggested that she had experienced a warm and secure attachment style and that her early life experiences with parents, siblings, and peers were wholesome and supportive. Her parents were described as encouraging and believed in expressing affection openly. She was the oldest of three siblings and enjoyed helping her mother raise her younger sister and brother. Nancy was a very good student and a leader among her peers. Although Nancy's depression did not meet criteria for a major depressive episode, a diagnosis of adjustment disorder with depressed mood was noted. Although her current GAF was 54, her highest level of function in the past 12 months was judged to be about 85.

On the other hand, Jack's family of origin was less warm and less secure. His mother was described as emotionally unavailable, and his father was often critical and demanding. He was a second child and, although he was a competent student, he was no match for his older brother, who was an honor student and top athlete. Needless to say, his brother was his father's favorite child. Jack's fearful attachment style seemed to reflect a sense of personal unworthiness along with an expectation that others would be rejecting and untrustworthy. Jack's current GAF was 62, although his highest level in the past year, when he was still working and quite content with his professional and family life, was probably about 72.

Not surprisingly, Jack had been wary of intimacy and tended to be socially distant and even awkward. However, he felt and acted differently when he first met Nancy. Her energetic presence seemed to make him come alive and feel hopeful about himself and the future. For her part, Nancy was attracted to Jack's quiet, patient gentleness as well as his ruggedly handsome features. Nancy described Jack as a caring father who adored Sybil. She noted that he was certainly more patient as a parent than she and that she had no qualms about his ability to care for their daughter while she was working. Nevertheless, she was angry that she had to work full time and so could not spend much time nurturing her growing daughter. It appeared that this reasonably healthy couple's GARF might have been in the mid-70s during the best period of their relationship but had slipped considerably in the past several months (Step 3).

An initial MSI-R profile was derived. It was noteworthy that raw scores on Global Distress (GDS) and Affective Communication (AFC) and Problem-Solving Communication (PSC) were extremely high for Jack and Nancy (see CS-1 in Table 5.1). In line with interview data, Jack and Nancy reported considerable marital distress in their relationship (GDS) and acknowledged a high degree of dissatisfaction with the extent of affection shown each other (AFC). This was particularly evident for Nancy, which reflected Jack's emotional distancing and lack of warmth. Similarly, the profile for both suggested their difficulty in intimate sharing, which most likely was exacerbated by their difficulty in resolving problems and conflict (PSC).

A GARF score of 52 was assessed, using Yingling's profiling system for the GARF (1998). Subscores on Interactional (46), Organizational (56), and Emotional Climate (42), as well as an overall score of 52 were recorded (see Table 5.2). Similar to the MSI-R, their GARF profile suggested that communication was frequently inhibited by unresolved conflict, that ineffective anger and emotional deadness interfered with their

TABLE 5.1   MSI-R Subscale Score Monitoring per Specified Conjoint Session (CS) for Female (F) and Male (M) Partners

Subscale	Gender	CS-1	CS-3	CS-6	CS-9
Global Distress (GDS)	F	13	11	7	2
	M	12	9	6	3
Affective Communication (AFC)	F	12	8	5	2
	M	13	10	4	0
Problem-Solving Communication (PSC)	F	13	13	6	3
	M	12	11	5	2
Aggression (AGG)	F	2	1	0	0
	M	1	0	0	0
Time Together (TTO)	F	5	4	3	1
	M	4	4	3	2
Disagreement About Finances (FIN)	F	0	0	0	0
	M	0	0	0	0
Sexual Dissatisfaction (SEX)	F	7	7	5	2
	M	13	13	10	9
Role Orientation (ROR)	F	10	10	10	10
	M	10	10	10	10
Family History of Distress (FAM)	F	1	1	1	1
	M	4	4	5	5
Dissatisfaction With Children (DSC)	F	0	0	0	0
	M	0	0	0	0
Conflict Over Child Rearing (CCR)	F	0	0	0	0
	M	0	0	0	0

TABLE 5.2   GARF Scores and Subscore Monitoring per Conjoint Session (CS)

Subscale/global	CS-1	CS-2	CS-3	CS-4	CS-5	CS-6	CS-7	CS-8	CS-9
Interactional	46	46	62	66	70	71	78	80	83
Organizational	56	56	62	65	65	75	78	81	86
Emotional Climate	42	45	51	55	60	60	65	70	80
Global therapist GARF	52	52	58	63	68	70	75	80	83

relationship, and that their decision making was intermittently effective at best. In short, ineffective communication was inhibiting intimacy, problem resolution, and decision-making processes.

Based on these clinical data, a treatment focus, goals, and intervention strategies were planned and implemented. Because this was a reasonably healthy and functional couple facing a major stressor (i.e., job loss and its relational sequelae) and the couple appeared to have some relational skill deficits, skill-focused couples therapy seemed indicated. It is also noteworthy that this couple brought some important strengths to therapy: a relatively conflict-free 7-year marriage, their positive experience as parents, and Nancy's early secure attachment style, which implies that she possesses considerable emotional resilience. Accordingly, the goals of treatment were to increase communication and foster emotional intimacy and effective problem resolution and decision making (Step 4).

The first and second sessions initiated this emphasis on communication by focusing on increasing listening skills and learning to use the language of affect. Little change was noticed on GARF subscales after session two or on GDS, AFC, and PSC scores of the MSI-R. Accordingly, the treatment focus shifted in subsequent sessions to assertive communication and conflict resolution. For the next four sessions, the couple worked in sessions and between sessions on skill learning and practice in these two areas. Not surprisingly, Interactional, Organizational, and Emotional Climate subscales of the GARF improved (see Table 5.2), as did the AFC and PSC subscales of the MSI-R when they were assessed at the sixth session. Because overall marital distress and dissatisfaction with this couple seemed to be linked intimately to affective communication and problem-solving communication, the GDS was significantly lowered by the sixth session (see Table 5.1). Subsequent sessions—sixth through the ninth—focused even more on emotional intimacy as well as problem solving involving specific issues such as jobs and careers. Relationally, things had improved considerably, so treatment would terminate with the ninth session.

In session eight, Jack announced he had just been offered the position of comptroller for a mid-size service corporation. Although this was the next step in a senior accountant's career path, it was a step that Jack had avoided for the past few years, even though others had noted that he possessed the requisite skills and experience. Although he admitted to some feelings of uncertainty about whether he could handle the kinds of responsibilities associated with that position, he felt that with the recent upsurge in Nancy's support and encouragement, he would succeed (Step 5).

Pre–post-treatment outcomes reflected the significant degree of change and growth in this marital relationship. On the MSI-R, major pre–post-treatment changes were noted on the three subscales directly related to the couple's main concerns. On the GDS, the changes went from a 13 to a 2 for Nancy and a 12 to a 3 for Jack; with AFC, changes went from 12 to 2 for Nancy and 13 to 0 for Jack; and with PSC, changes went from 13 to 3 for Nancy and 12 to 2 for Jack. On these subscales, changes went from the highest, or most, problematic to the lowest, or least, problematic range (see Table 5.1). On the GARF, a noticeable shift in relational functioning was from occasionally unsatisfactory to highly satisfactory. More specifically, the following subscale changes were noted: Interactional subscale from 46 to 83, Organizational subscale from 56 to 86, Emotional Climate subscale from 42 to 80, and overall GARF from 52 to 83. In other words, now a greater degree of shared understanding and agreement about roles, tasks, and decision making; better problem-solving communication and negotiation; and a general atmosphere of warmth, caring, and sharing were present (Step 6; see Table 5.2).

CONCLUDING NOTE

Because the concepts covered in this chapter have only recently become a part of the conversation of assessment with couples and families, they are seldom discussed in texts on family therapy, much less books on family and couple assessment. Nevertheless, the paradigm shift in accountability in clinical practice has propelled clinical outcomes assessment to center stage. This chapter highlighted five inventories or scales that have been shown to have some clinical utility in measuring and monitoring outcomes in couples and family therapy. Presumably, other instruments exist that research and clinical practice will show have similar value (Table 5.3).

The future of ongoing assessment is bright with the promise of additional instruments. For example, the INTERSESSION STIC is a newly developed instrument for ongoing assessment of individuals, couples, and families. It is derived from the Systemic Therapy Inventory of Change (STIC) but is substantially shorter and designed to be administered to clients prior to each session following the first (Pinsof & Chambers, 2010). The psychometric properties of the STIC have already been published, with the psychometrics of INTERSESSION STIC following in a subsequent article (Pinsof et al., 2009).

TABLE 5.3   Matrix: Reference Guide to Clinical Outcomes Assessment Instruments With Families and Couples

Assessment Instrument	Type/ Use	Cultural/ Language	Instruction/Use: T = Time to Take S = Time to Score I = Items (# of)	Computerized: (a) Scoring (b) Report	Reliability (R) Validity (V)	Availability
Global Assessment of Relational Functioning (GARF)	Therapist rating/couples & families		5–10 min for inquiry/ scoring	None		Appendix B of DSM-IV-TR
Self-Report Family Inventory (SFI)	Self-report/families	Yes, Chinese	Easy to administer, 5–15 min (36 items)	None	R = Test–retest 0.30–0.87 V = Criterion-related	Journal article
Systematic Assessment of Family Environment (SAFE)	Self-report/families	Yes, Spanish	(21 items)	a = Yes		Yingling et al. (1998)
Marital Satisfaction Inventory, Revised (MSI-R)	Self-report/couples	Yes, Spanish	25 min to administer & score (150 items)	a = Yes b = Interpretive report	Factor analysis	Western Psychological Services, Inc.
Dyadic Adjustment Scale (DAS)	Self-report/couples	Yes, French, Chinese	5–10 min (34 items; also a 14-item version)	a = Yes	R = .86–96 V = .86–88	Journal article; Multi-Health Systems, Inc.
SCORE 15	Self-report/families	Translations under way	2–5 min to administer & score (15 items)	None	R = .89 alpha .88 split-half	Journal article; website
Intersession Scale	Self-report/individuals & couples		2–5 min to administer & score (9 items)	None	R = .74–.90. V = Convergent & discriminant	Journal article

REFERENCES

Adam, D., & Gingras, M. (1982). Short- and long-term effects of a marriage enrichment program upon couple functioning. *Journal of Sex and Marital Therapy, 8,* 97–118.

American Psychiatric Association. (2000). *Diagnostic and statistical manual of mental disorders* (4th ed., text revision [DSM-IV-TR]). Washington, DC: Author.

Atkisson, C., & Zwick, R. (1982). The clients' satisfaction questionnaire: Psychometric properties and correlations with service utilization. *Evaluation and Program Planning, 5,* 233–237.

Beavers, W. R., & Hampson, R. B. (1990). *Successful families: Assessment and intervention.* New York: Norton.

Brock, G., & Joanning, H. (1983). A comparison of the relationship enhancement program and the Minnesota Couples Communication Program. *Journal of Marital and Family Therapy, 9,* 295–305.

Denton, W., Nakonezny, P., & Burwell, S. (2010). Reliability and validity of the global assessment of relational functioning (GARF) in a psychiatric family therapy clinic. *Journal of Marital and Family Therapy, 36,* 376–387.

Frank, B., Dixon, D., & Grosz, H. (1993). Conjoint monitoring of symptoms of premenstrual syndrome: Impact on marital satisfaction. *Journal of Counseling Psychology, 40,* 109–114.

Hampson, R., & Beavers, W. (1996a). Family therapy and outcome: Relationships between therapist and family styles. *Contemporary Family Therapy, 13*(3), 345–370.

Hampson, R., & Beavers, W. (1996b). Measuring family therapy outcome in a clinical setting: Families that do better or do worse in therapy. *Family Process, 35,* 347–361.

Hampson, R., Prince, C., & Beavers, W. (1999). Marital therapy: Qualities of couples who fare better or worse in treatment. *Journal of Marital and Family Therapy, 25*(4), 411–424.

Iverson, A., & Baucom, D. (1988). Behavioral marital therapy outcomes: Alternative interpretation of the data. *Behavior Therapy, 21,* 129–138.

Jacobson, N. (1984). A component analysis of behavioral marital therapy: The relative effectiveness of behavior exchange and communication/problem-solving training. *Journal of Consulting and Clinical Psychology, 52,* 295–305.

Jacobson, N., & Follette, W. (1985). Clinical significance of improvement resulting from two behavioral marital therapy components. *Behavior Therapy, 16,* 249–264.

Johnson, L., Ketring, S., & Anderson, S. (2010). The Intersession Report: Development of a short questionnaire for couples therapy. *American Journal of Family Therapy, 38,* 266–276.

Lambert, M. (2010). *Prevention of treatment failure: The use of measuring, monitoring, and feedback in clinical practice.* Washington, DC: American Psychological Association.

Latham, J. (1990). Family-of-origin intervention: An intergenerational approach to enhancing marital adjustment. *Journal of Contemporary Psychotherapy, 20,* 211–222.

Miller, S., Duncan, B., Brown, J., Sorrell, R., & Chalk, M. (2006). Using outcome to inform and improved treatment outcomes: Making ongoing, real-time assessment feasible. *Journal of Brief Therapy, 5,* 5–23.

Pinsof, W., & Chambers, A. (2010). Empirically informed systemic psychotherapy: Tracking client change and therapist behavior during therapy. In J. Bray & M. Stanton (Eds.), *The Wiley-Blackwell handbook of family psychology* (pp. 431–446). Oxford, UK: Blackwell.

Pinsof, W., Zinbarg, R., Lebow, J., Knobloch-Fedders, L., Durbin, E., Chambers, A., et al. (2009). Laying the foundation for progress research in family, couple, and individual therapy: The development and psychometric features of the initial systemic therapy inventory of change. *Psychotherapy Research, 19,* 143–156.

Prouty, H., Markowski, E., & Barnes, H. (2000). Using the DAS in marital therapy: An exploratory study. *Family Journal: Therapy for Couples and Families, 8*(3), 250–257.

Ross, N., & Doherty, W. (2001). Validity of Global Assessment of Relational Functioning (GARF) when used by community-based therapists. *American Journal of Family Therapy, 29,* 239–253.

Snyder, D. (1981). *Marital Satisfaction Inventory (MSI) manual.* Los Angeles: Western Psychological Services.

Snyder, D. (1997). *Marital Satisfaction Inventory, revised (MSI-I) manual.* Los Angeles: Western Psychological Services.

Snyder, D., & Aikman, G. (1999). Marital Satisfaction Inventory, revised. In M. Maruish (Ed.), *Use of psychological testing for treatment planning and outcome assessment* (2nd ed. , pp. 1173–1210). Hillsdale, NJ: Erlbaum.

Snyder, D., & Berg, P. (1983). Predicting couples' response to brief directive sex therapy. *Journal of Sex and Marital Therapy, 9,* 114–120.

Snyder, D., Mangrum, L., & Wills, R. (1993). Predicting couples' response to marital therapy: A comparison of short- and long-term predictors. *Journal of Consulting and Clinical Psychology, 61,* 61–69.

Snyder, D., Wills, R., & Grady-Fletcher, A. (1991). Long-term effective-ness of behavioral versus insight-oriented marital therapy. *Journal of Consulting and Clinical Psychology, 59,* 138–141.

Spanier, G. (1976). Measuring dyadic adjustment: New scales for assess-ing the quality of marriage and similar dyads. *Journal of Marriage and the Family, 38,* 15–28.

Spanier, G. (1979). The measurement of marital quality. *Journal of Sex and Marital Therapy, 5,* 288–300.

Sperry, L. (1997). Treatment outcomes: An overview. *Psychiatric Annals, 27*(2), 95–99.

Sperry, L., Brill, P., Howard, K., & Grissom, G. (1996). *Treatment outcomes in psychotherapy and psychiatric interventions.* New York: Brunner/Mazel.

Sperry, L., Grissom, G., Brill, P., & Marion, D. (1997). Changing clini-cians' practice patterns and managed care culture with Outcomes systems. *Psychiatric Annals, 27*(2), 127–132.

Stratton, P., Bland, J., Janes, E., & Lask, J. (2010). Developing an indica-tor of family function and a practicable outcome measure for sys-temic family and couple therapy: The SCORE. *Journal of Family Therapy, 32,* 232–258.

Wynne, L. (1988). *The state of the art of family therapy research: Controversies and recommendations.* New York: Family Process Press.

Yingling, L. (1996). *A manual for the use of the Systematic Assessment of the Family Environment (SAFE): A self-report instrument for assessing multi-level family system functioning.* Rockwell, TX: J & L Human Systems Development.

Yingling, L., Miller, W., McDonald, A., & Galwaler, S. (1994a). *Verifying outcome: Paradigm for the therapist-researcher.* Paper presented at the meeting of the Texas Association for Marriage and Family Therapy, January, San Antonio, TX.

Yingling, L., Miller, W., McDonald, A., & Galwaler, S. (1994b). *Verifying outcome: Paradigm for the therapist-researcher.* Paper presented at the meeting of the American Association for Marriage and Family Therapy, November, Chicago, IL.

Yingling, L., Miller, W., McDonald, A., & Galwaler, S. (1998). *GARF assessment sourcebook: Using the DSM-IV global assessment of relational functioning.* Washington, DC: Brunner/Mazel.

CHAPTER 6

Couples Assessment Strategy and Inventories

Dennis A. Bagarozzi and Len Sperry

The use of empirically devised instruments and procedures to make pre-treatment assessments, monitor clinical progress, evaluate treatment outcomes, and conduct follow-up investigations is a sine qua non for evidence-based interventions (Bagarozzi, 1989; L'Abate and Bagarozzi, 1992). Unfortunately, such practices are rarely implemented outside academic settings and training institutions. Although the use of valid and reliable treatment tools and procedures is routine for most behaviorally oriented clinicians, it is less common for many clinicians following contemporary models of marital therapy (Gurman, 2008). For the most part, private practitioners and therapists who work in public agencies rarely have the time or the luxury to engage in such thorough and systematic endeavors. One way to encourage the increased use of assessment procedures by private practitioners and agency personnel is to provide them with assessment tools that are time sensitive and pragmatic. Taking this into consideration, we have decided to omit from our revision of this chapter a number of previously reviewed instruments that we consider to be too lengthy and time consuming for everyday use. The measures we have omitted are the Conflict Tactics Scales (Straus, 1979); the Marital Satisfaction Inventory (Snyder, 1979, 1981, 1997); ENRICH (Olson, Fournier, & Druckman, 1982); PREPARE, PREPARE-MC, PREPARE-CC, and MATE (Olson, 2002); and the Adult Attachment Interview (George, Kaplan, & Main, 1996). In their place, we have chosen to include some more recently developed instruments that are brief, concise, valid, and pragmatic measures that can be used in most clinical settings. We begin with a recapitulation of seven of the instruments that were originally cataloged. Next, a strategy for utilizing couples assessment instruments in clinical practice is outlined. Finally, a case example illustrates the use of this strategy with a couple.

COMMON SELF-REPORT MEASURES FOR COUPLES

Locke-Wallace Marital Adjustment Test

Type of instrument. The Locke-Wallace Marital Adjustment Test was developed in 1959 to provide a reliable and valid measure of marital adjustment. Using selected, nonduplicated, and statistically significant items from a variety of previously developed measures with high item discrimination, Harvey Locke and Carl Wallace (1959) composed a 15-item marital adjustment scale. *Marital adjustment* is defined by Locke and Wallace as an accommodation of partners to each other at a given time.

Use and target audience. The purpose of this brief instrument is to assess relational adjustment. The Locke-Wallace Marital Adjustment Test is used with married or cohabitating couples in clinical and in research settings.

Multicultural. This instrument is available only in an English version.

Ease and time of administration. The Locke-Wallace Marital Adjustment Test is a self-report instrument that is easy to administer and takes approximately 5 minutes to complete. It is available only in a paper-and-pencil format.

Scoring procedure. This instrument can be hand-scored in 5 minutes or less. No automated score system or computer-generated report is available.

Reliability. Reliability studies were initially conducted by Locke and Wallace (1959). Internal consistency was estimated by the Spearman–Brown formula and found to be a respectable .90 (Cross & Sharpley, 1981). Data on test–retest reliability are not available.

Validity. Known-groups validity of this instrument is high, with scores discriminating between adjusted and maladjusted couples. Hunt (1978) found the correlations between the Locke-Wallace Marital Adjustment Test and the Dyadic Adjustment Scale to be $r = .93$ for husbands and for wives. Discrimination, item, and factor analyses have been conducted by Cross and Sharpley (1981).

Availability and source. The scale is available in the original journal article (Locke & Wallace, 1959).

Comment. The Locke-Wallace Marital Adjustment Test has been used extensively since it first appeared in 1959. Because of its history and widespread use, it is used as a benchmark standard for assessing the degree of adjustment in marriage. When it was first introduced, it was one of the first short measures of marital adjustment, and it remains that today. Because the instrument is a global measure, it may not be useful in planning treatment when behavioral specificity is indicated.

Although this instrument can be completed in 5 minutes or less and scored in approximately the same amount of time, busy clinicians may wish to use two 10-point Likert-type questions to assess marital satisfaction and satisfaction with one's spouse:

1. In general, how satisfied are you with your marriage?

    1   2   3   4   5   6   7   8   9   10
    Not at all Satisfied   Extremely Satisfied

2. In general, how satisfied are you with your spouse?

    1   2   3   4   5   6   7   8   9   10
    Not at all Satisfied   Extremely Satisfied

One hundred and sixty-two respondents were asked to complete the Locke-Wallace Marital Adjustment Test (1959) and these two questions as part of a larger study (Bagarozzi, 1983). Both questions were found to correlate significantly with this scale—satisfaction with one's marriage $r = .73$, $p < .01$ and satisfaction with one's spouse $r = .71$, $p < .01$.

Dyadic Adjustment Scale

Type of instrument. Like the Locke-Wallace Marital Adjustment Test, the Dyadic Adjustment Scale (DAS) had its origin in family sociology. Developed by Graham Spanier, the Dyadic Adjustment Scale is a 32-item questionnaire that utilizes a Likert-type format. Because 11 of these items were taken directly from the Locke-Wallace Marital Adjustment Test, it is not surprising to find that the Dyadic Adjustment Scale correlates $r = .86$ with the Locke-Wallace Marital Adjustment Test.

Use and target audience. This instrument is designed to assess relational quality as perceived by couples. It can be used as a general measure of marital satisfaction by using total scores, or its subscales can be utilized to measure cohesion, consensus, satisfaction, or expression of affect. The instrument has also been adapted for interviewing couples.

Multicultural. In addition to an English-language version, French-Canadian and Chinese versions are available.

Ease and time of administration. This 32-item self-report instrument can be completed in 5 to 10 minutes. In addition, a briefer, 14-item version is available (Busby, Christiansen, Crane, & Larson, 1995; Crane, Middleton, & Bean, 2000).

Scoring procedure. The instrument can be hand-scored in 5 minutes or less. A Quik-Score ™ form and a DOS-based computing scoring are also available. Total score is the sum of all items, which range from 0 to 151.

Reliability. Cronbach's alpha for the overall scale is reported to be .96. For the Dyadic Consensus, Dyadic Satisfaction, Dyadic Cohesion, and Affectional Expression scales, the Cronbach's alpha scores are .90, .94, .86 and .73, respectively (Spanier & Thompson, 1982).

Validity. Criterion-related validity was established by comparing the responses of married and divorced individuals for each of the 32 items. The divorced sample differed significantly from the married sample at the $p < .001$ level for each item. T tests were used for making these comparisons. The mean total score for married individuals was 114.8; the mean score for divorced individuals was 70.7. Concurrent validity is evidenced by high correlations ($r = .86$) with the Locke-Wallace Marital Adjustment Test.

Availability and source. The scale is available in the original journal article (Spanier, 1976). It is also available from Multi-Health Systems, Inc., (800) 456-3003, including the Quik-Score form and DOS-based computing scoring.

Comment. The DAS is one of the oldest and most extensively used relational instruments in clinical practice today. Besides its value in clinical practice, the Dyadic Adjustment Scale continues to be used by researchers throughout the world. Because of its favorable psychometrics and ease of administration, it is commonly utilized in thesis and dissertation research.

Spousal Inventory of Desired Changes and Relationship Barriers (SIDCARB)

Type of instrument. Although the Locke-Wallace Marital Adjustment Test and the Dyadic Adjustment Scale have been used to represent marital satisfaction, neither actually asked respondents to rate satisfaction with their spouse or their marriage. Essentially, adjustment has been equated with satisfaction. However, stable marriages are not necessarily satisfying marriages, and spouses dissatisfied with their mates may simply have "adjusted" to their conjugal situation and lot in life. To assess the dynamics of marital satisfaction and its relationship to marital stability, Bagarozzi (1983) developed the Spousal Inventory of Desired Changes and Relationship Barriers (SIDCARB), based on the three major principles of social exchange theory as applied to marriage: (a) satisfaction with the exchange process, (b) availability of more satisfying alternative relationships, and (c) absence of prohibitive barriers to separation and divorce.

Use and target audience. This instrument is useful in assessing marital satisfaction and stability in couples undergoing couples therapy and in couples workshops.

Multicultural. This instrument is currently available in an English version only.

Ease and time of administration. SIDCARB is a 29-item self-report questionnaire that takes approximately 5 minutes to complete. Currently, it is in a paper version only.

Scoring procedure. The questionnaire is hand-scored, and it takes approximately 5 minutes to score each partner's questionnaire. No computer scoring or computer-generated report is available.

Reliability. Cronbach's alpha of reliability was computed for each subscale; the reliabilities were found to be .86, .74, and .80 for Factors I, II, and III, respectively.

Validity. Factor analysis revealed significant loadings on three factors: I = Dissatisfaction and Desire for Change in Spouse's Behavior; II = Willingness to Separate and Divorce, and Internal Psychological Barriers to Relationship Termination; and III = External Circumstantial Barriers to Relationship Termination (Bagarozzi & Pollane, 1983).

Availability and source. SIDCARB and scoring guidelines are reprinted in Appendix A of Bagarozzi (2001).

Comment. When the Locke-Wallace Marital Adjustment Test, Dyadic Adjustment Scale, and Spousal Inventory of Desired Changes and Relationship Barriers are used in concert, the therapist can gain a better understanding of the interplay among several factors that will have a bearing on therapeutic outcome, for example, Satisfaction, Adjustment, Stability, Level of Commitment, and Barriers to Separation and Divorce. Another important dimension to consider in marital assessment is the degree of emotional attachment that exists between the spouses. The presence of a positive emotional attachment (feelings of love, caring, closeness, and affection) between the partners often portends a successful therapeutic outcome. Conversely, the more distant, removed, estranged, and apathetic the spouses are, the less successful the therapy is likely to be. Therefore, this measure of positive emotional attachment can be a very helpful diagnostic tool.

Marital Disaffection Scale

Type of instrument. In 1993, Karen Kayser published the Marital Disaffection Scale (Kayser, 1993). She defined *disaffection* as the gradual loss of positive emotions—love, caring, affection, and closeness—that occurs between spouses over time, as dissatisfactions accumulate. Disaffection does not necessarily lead to relationship dissolution because a number of internal and external barriers may cause a couple to remain together in what appears to be a stable marriage, even when the emotional relationship is dead. The theoretical model of the disaffection process is based on the work of Snyder and Regts (1982) and Duck (1982).

Use and target audience. This instrument is a measure of the level of disaffection or loss of positive emotions toward one's spouse. Although it was designed primarily for use in couples therapy, it has been used in research studies in couples in clinical and nonclinical settings.

Multicultural. This instrument is currently available in an English version only.

Ease and time of administration. The Marital Disaffection Scale is a 21-item self-report inventory that takes approximately 3 to 5 minutes to complete. Currently, this inventory is available in a paper version only.

Scoring procedure. The range of scores for the Marital Disaffection Scale is 21 to 84. This instrument can be hand-scored in 3 to 5 minutes. No automated scoring or computer-generated report is currently available.

Reliability. Using Cronbach's alpha, internal consistency of the instrument is reported as .93 (Kayser, 1993). Kayser (1996) also presents data on inter-item reliability.

Validity. To determine construct validity, factor analysis was performed. Although three factors—Attachment, Emotional Estrangement, and Emotional Support—could be discerned, many of the items were found to cross load so that clear and distinct independent factors did not emerge. Therefore, Kayser (1993) considers the Marital Disaffection Scale to be unidimensional, suggesting that only the total, full scale score be used when measuring disaffection. Kayser's criterion-referenced study offered additional support for the scale's validity study. A comparison of recently divorced individuals with a random sample of married individuals from the general population showed means for these two groups were 70.8 and 33.7, respectively. Kayser (1996) presented additional data on criterion-related validity and discriminant validity.

Availability and source. The instrument and scoring instructions are included in *When Love Dies: The Process of Marital Disaffection* (Kayser, 1993).

Comment. Interestingly, scores on the Marital Disaffection Scale showed significant positive relationships ($r = .36$) with a spouse's problem drinking behavior and ($r = .48$) with workaholic behavior of a spouse. These results support the use of the Marital Disaffection Scale as a measure of emotional estrangement in marriage (Flowers, Robinson, & Carroll, 2000). Besides possessing good psychometric properties, this scale has been demonstrated to be easy to use for assessing spouses' feelings of affection/disaffection toward their partner and for planning appropriate interventions in conjoint therapy.

Areas of Change Questionnaire

Type of instrument. In the course of conducting research into marital conflict and behavioral marital therapy at the Oregon Research Institute, the Areas of Change Questionnaire was developed by Robert Weiss and colleagues (Weiss, Hops, & Patterson, 1973). The questionnaire has two parts: Part I includes the behaviors that the client would like the partner to do more, less, or not change; Part II addresses what each thinks the partner would like more of, less of, or not change. Thus, this inventory lends itself to the calculation of a number of scores: desired change, perceived change, perceptual accuracy, and total change. Another version of this instrument, the Comprehensive Areas of Change Questionnaire, is briefly described in the "Comments" section.

Use and target audience. The Areas of Change Questionnaire is a 34-item self-report inventory designed to assess the amount of change a couple desires for their relationship. Communication, Separation of Duties, and Sexual Activity are three areas.

Multicultural. This instrument is currently available in an English version only.

Ease and time of administration. The Areas of Change Questionnaire consists of 34 items with a 7-point Likert scale format. This inventory is available in a paper version as well as an MS-DOS computer version. It takes between 10 and 20 minutes to complete the inventory.

Scoring procedure. Hand-scoring of this inventory is initially cumbersome because the responses of both partners, on two separate scoring sheets, must be compared at the same time. The amount of scoring time depends on the number of items scored and the scorer's facility with the scoring process. Fortunately, a computerized scoring system is available.

Reliability. Split half reliability has been found to be .80; Cronbach's alpha is between .84 and .89; and test–retest reliabilities for husbands and wives are reported to be .96 and .74, respectively (Mead & Vatcher, 1985).

Validity. Discriminant validity has been demonstrated between distressed and nondistressed couples (Birchler & Webb, 1977). Pretreatment and post-treatment sensitivity to change has also been reported (Baucom, 1982).

Availability and source. The Areas of Change Questionnaire is available from Multi-Health Systems, Inc., (800) 456-3003, which distributes the computer version and scoring system.

Comment. Although the Areas of Change Questionnaire provided a global indexing of marital complaints, Mead and Vatcher (1985) found that only 45% (13 of 29 categories developed by a national sample of therapists) was accounted for by the inventory. Therefore, Mead and Vatcher set out to develop a questionnaire that would truly canvas the 29 areas of change; this required increasing the number of items that the questionnaire now comprises, including 24 of the original items from the Areas of Change Questionnaire. Scoring procedures and categories from the original scale were retained. Psychometric properties of the new instrument equal or exceed the reliability and validity indices of the Areas of Change Questionnaire (Roberts, 1988; Vatcher, 1988).

Intimacy Needs Survey

Type of instrument. Bagarozzi (1990, 2001) developed the Intimacy Needs Survey to help couples conceptualize their need for interpersonal closeness in a way that would make sense to them. This survey is a clinical tool that allows spouses to explore whether their needs for intimacy are being met in nine specific areas: Emotional, Psychological, Intellectual, Sexual, Physical (Nonsexual), Spiritual, Aesthetic, Social & Recreational, and Temporal. Intimacy is conceptualized as a basic human need that has its origins in, and develops out of, the more fundamental survival need for attachment. Intimacy differs from individual to individual, and the nine components of this more general need also vary in strength from person to person.

Use and target audience. The Intimacy Needs Survey is designed to assess couples' perceptions of their need for, and type of, intimacy. It allows the therapist to assess whether each spouse's intimacy needs are met satisfactorily by his or her partner. In addition to use in couples therapy, it can be used in couples enrichment workshops.

Multicultural. This instrument is currently available in an English version only.

Ease and time of administration. Administration of the Intimacy Needs Survey is simple and straightforward. This 44-item self-report questionnaire takes no more than 10 minutes to complete. It is currently available in a paper version only.

Scoring procedure. This instrument is hand-scored in approximately 15 minutes. For the first eight subcomponent needs, numerical scores are calculated. The ninth dimension, Temporal, is viewed qualitatively and is considered separately. Three scores are computed for each of the eight component needs examined in the questionnaire: component need strength, receptivity satisfaction, and reciprocity satisfaction. A total intimacy needs strength score is calculated simply by summing all eight component needs strength scores. No computer scoring or computer-generated report is currently available.

Reliability. The Intimacy Needs Survey is still in its experimental stages of development. Reliability has yet to be established.

Validity. The survey is still in its experimental stages of development. Validity has yet to be established. Nevertheless, four interrelated factors are evaluated by the Intimacy Needs Survey: Overall Intimacy Needs Strengths of Both Partners; the Strength of Each Component Need for Both Partners; Each Partner's Satisfaction With His or Her Spouse's Openness, Receptivity, Responsiveness, Willingness, and Ability to Meet and Satisfy Each Specific Component Need; and Each Partner's Satisfaction With His or Her Mate's Willingness and Ability to Reciprocate Similar-Depth Levels of Sharing, Openness, Self-Disclosure, Self-Revelation, and Personal Exchange.

Availability and source. The Intimacy Needs Survey is reprinted in Bagarozzi (2001).

Comment. This instrument assesses several components of intimacy that are not considered in other instruments. Among these are spiritual intimacy, aesthetic intimacy, and temporal intimacy. Because it is common for couples to complain that they have "intimacy problems," it is valuable to distinguish these various components to determine which areas are problematic.

Sexual Desire Inventory

Type of instrument. The Sexual Desire Inventory was initially developed by Spector (1992) and further refined by colleagues (Spector, Carey, & Steinberg, 1996). Items included in the scale were selected based on models of sexual desire and the researchers' clinical experience in assessing sexual desire disorders. The inventory consists of two factors: Dyadic Sexual Desire (interest in having sexual relations with a partner, not necessarily one's specific partner) and Solitary Sexual Desire (interest in behaving sexually by oneself).

Use and target audience. The Sexual Desire Inventory allows the therapist to assess whether each partner's sexual needs are being met satisfactorily by his or her partner. The primary use of this instrument is in sex therapy and in couples therapy.

Multicultural. This instrument is currently available in an English version only.

Ease and time of administration. This self-report instrument consists of 14 items and is easy to administer. It takes less than 5 minutes to complete.

Scoring procedure. The instrument is hand-scored in 5 minutes or less. No automated scoring system or computer-generated report is available.

Reliability. Samples used to assess psychometric properties of the scale include college students (N = 380), geriatric adults (N = 40), and couples (N = 40). Internal consistency using Cronbach's alpha coefficient was r = .86 for the Dyadic Sexual Desire subscale and r = .96 for the Solitary Sexual Desire subscale. Test–retest reliability is reported to be r = .76 over a 1-month period.

Validity. Factor validity, as well as concurrent and discriminant validity, is reported by Spector (1992). For females, Dyadic Sexual Desire was shown to be positively correlated with relationship adjustment, as measured by the Dyadic Adjustment Scale (Spanier, 1976); with sexual satisfaction, as measured by the Index of Sexual Satisfaction (Hudson, 1992); and with sexual arousal, as measured by the Sexual Arousal Inventory (Hoon, Hoon, & Wincz, 1976). For males, only Dyadic Sexual Desire was found to correlate with sexual satisfaction. Gender differences in responding to this scale have also been found; males were found to have significantly higher levels of dyadic and solitary desire than were females.

Availability and source. See the journal article for the inventory (Spector, Carey, & Steinberg, 1996).

Comment. The Sexual Desire Inventory is a self-report instrument that is quick and easy to administer and score. In addition to having credible psychometric properties, it has remarkable clinical utility. More specifically, discussing the results of the inventory provides therapists and couples an occasion for discussing the matter of dyadic as well as personal sexual desire, which can be a source of considerable embarrassment to many couples.

MORE RECENT INSTRUMENTS

Empirical investigations have shown that approximately 25% of men and 15% of women in the United States have become involved in an extramarital sexual relationship at some time during their marriage (Lauman, Gagnon, Michael, & Michaels, 1994). It has been estimated that about 30% of the couples who enter marital therapy do so to deal with the aftermath of an extramarital affair (Glass & Wright, 1988; Whisman, Dixon, & Johnson, 1997). The reasons for engaging in an extramarital sexual relationship are varied and often complex. Seven types of affairs have been identified (Bagarozzi, 2008). These include brief unplanned encounters, periodic premeditated sexual involvements, instrumental and utilitarian affairs, short-term sexual relationships that are triggered by developmental changes or changing life circumstances, paraphiliac affairs, unconsciously motivated cathartic affairs, and long-term sexual relationships. Understanding the factors that might have contributed to the development of marital infidelity is essential for helping couples work through this devastating and traumatic experience and for re-establishing trust in their relationship when reconciliation is the stated treatment goal.

To help the therapist focus the treatment, there are two measures that should be considered: the Justification for Extramarital Involvement Questionnaire (Glass, 2001) and the Trust Scale (Rempel, Holmes, & Zanna, 2001). These are discussed below.

Justification for Extramarital Involvement Questionnaire

Type of instrument. The Justification for Extramarital Involvement Questionnaire (Glass, 2001; Glass & Wright, 1997) is a 17-item self-report instrument that can help the therapist quickly identify and categorize a spouse's motives for engaging in an extramarital relationship. It uses a Likert-type format. Four response options are available: "I would feel completely justified," "I would feel partially justified," "I would feel not justified," and "I would feel completely unjustified."

The questionnaire given to respondents in titled "Attitudes About Extramarital Relationships." The respondent is asked to what extent each reason would serve as a justification for engaging in an emotional or sexual extramarital relationship.

Use and target audience. The Justification for Extramarital Involvements Questionnaire can be used in both clinical and research settings. Therapists will find that it can be a valuable adjunct to a clinical or problem-focused initial interview. When both spouses are asked to complete this questionnaire, their responses may offer the therapist some insights into the couple's nonverbalized, unconscious collusive agreements about extramarital relationships.

Multicultural. This questionnaire is available only in English.

Ease and time of administration. This instrument can be completed in a few minutes. Scores for the constituent four factors can be computed in less than 5 minutes.

Psychometric properties. The initial study used a sample of 303 Caucasian middle-class married individuals living in Maryland. The mean number of years married for the 148 male participants was 14.6. For the 155 female respondents, the mean was 13.1. The mean age for women who participated was 36.5 ($SD = 9.4$). For men, the average age was 40.4 ($SD = 9.4$). All subjects were married and not separated at the time of the study. Of the female respondents, 25% reported having had extra-marital sexual intercourse, compared to 44% of the male respondents. In addition, 47% of female respondents and 63% of male respondents reported either intercourse or emotional involvement and extramarital sexual experiences that did not culminate in sexual intercourse.

The 17 items of the Justification for Extramarital Involvement Questionnaire were subjected to a factor analysis. The result was a four-factor solution: Emotional Intensity, Extrinsic Motivation, Sexual Gratification, and Love. Reliability data are not reported.

Availability and source. The Justification for Extramarital Involvement Questionnaire is available in the *Handbook of Family Measurement Techniques* (Perlmutter, Touliatos, & Holden, 2001).

Comments. Spouses' responses to each of the questions contained in the Justification for Extramarital Involvement Questionnaire can be taken at face value, or they can be seen as defensive rationalizations. However, they also can be understood as surface manifestations of deeper personal and/or relationship difficulties. For example, the spouse who justified his or her infidelity to have fun or to have a novel, exciting, or new romantic experience (Questions 1, 2, 10, 13) may be exhibiting symptoms of a personality disorder. On the other hand, a spouse who has an affair to relieve sexual deprivation and frustration or to have an enjoyable sexual experience may be responding to serious sexual difficulties in his or her marriage (Questions 5 and 7). Engaging in an affair with someone with whom one can share thoughts and feelings and discuss problems (Questions 2, 6, 9) may be evidence of unmet intimacy needs.

One drawback for this instrument is that it cannot be used as a pre-treatment–post-treatment assessment tool. Its strength lies in its ability to quickly zero in on some of the major causes of marital infidelity.

Trust Scale

Type of instrument. The Trust Scale (Rempel, Holmes, & Zanna, 2001) measures three components of trust in marriage: Predictability, Dependability, and Faith. It is a 17-item questionnaire. The respondent is asked to circle one of seven possible responses ranging from Strongly Disagree −3 to Strongly Agree +3. A Neutral option, 0, serves as a median between the negative and positive poles.

Use and target audience. The Trust Scale is designed to measure three dimensions of trust in marriage and intimate relationships. It can be used to assess all aspects of the clinical process, that is, pretreatment, therapeutic progress, post-treatment, and follow-up evaluations.

Multicultural. This instrument is available only in English.

Ease and time of administration. This measure can be completed in 2 or 3 minutes.

Scoring procedure. The Trust Scale is hand-scored and takes only seconds to tally each subscale factor score.

Reliability. Item-total correlations for each subscale were found to range from .43 to .60 for Faith, .35 to .59 for Dependability, and .33 to .58 for Predictability in a number of studies.

Validity. Validity was assessed through an exploratory factor analysis. Initially, the questionnaire contained 26 items. Ten items were constructed to measure Faith, nine items were devised to measure Dependability, and seven items were designed to measure Predictability. The final three-factor subscales showed significant loadings for seven items on the Faith factor, five items for the Dependability factor, and five items for the Predictability factor. Factor loadings using an oblique rotation ranged from .43 to .84.

Availability and source. The Trust Scale is available in the *Handbook of Family Measurement Techniques* (Perlmutter, Touliatos, & Holden, 2001).

Comments. Even though the Justification for Extramarital Involvement Questionnaire and the Trust Scale have been available for use by social psychologists for more than 2 decades, these instruments have not been adopted by marriage therapists and clinical researchers. Given the fact that a high percentage of couples who enter marital therapy do so to deal with the traumatic effects of an extramarital affair, therapists should consider including the Justification of Extramarital Involvement Questionnaire in addition to clinical interviews and global measures of marital satisfaction, communication, commitment, and so on, which are routinely used by clinicians who specialize in the treatment of infidelity (Gordon, Baucom, Snyder, & Dixon, 2008). Similarly, since re-establishing trust is a central issue when infidelity is the presenting problem, it behooves the therapist to assess the degree to which trust has been regained and maintained once formal treatment has been concluded. The Trust Scale is ideal for this purpose.

Family Adaptability and Cohesion Evaluation Scale: FACES IV

Type of instrument. The Family Adaptability and Cohesion Evaluation Scale IV, made available in 2011, is the latest revision of a self-report assessment instrument designed to assess the two central dimensions of the Circumplex Model of Marital and Family Systems (Olson, Sprenkle, & Russell, 1979). More than 1,200 published articles and dissertations have used the various versions of this instrument since it was first developed. The Circumplex model is comprised of three key concepts for understanding and measuring marital and family functioning, that is, Cohesion, Flexibility, and Communication. The main hypothesis of the Circumplex model (which is based on family systems theory) is that balanced levels of cohesion and flexibility are most conducive to healthy marital and family functioning, and unbalanced levels of cohesion and flexibility are associated with problematic functioning.

Use and target audience. FACES IV can be used throughout the entire treatment process (i.e., pretreatment assessment, intersession monitoring, post-treatment evaluation, and follow-up investigations) and is appropriate for use with couples as well as entire family systems.

Multicultural. This version of FACES is available only in English and has not been used extensively with clinical samples and diverse populations as has been the case with FACES I, II, and III.

Ease and time of administration. This 42-item self-report measure can be completed in less than 5 minutes.

Scoring procedure. Each spouse's perception of his or her marriage or family system can be plotted on a 5 × 5 grid. Twenty-five combinations of cohesion and flexibility are possible. There are nine balanced types, which are located in the central area of the grid. Twelve mid-range types of relationships reflect imbalance in either cohesion or flexibility. The remaining four types of relationships are considered to be unbalanced. These reflect extreme scores for both cohesion and flexibility. A simple mathematical formula is used to calculate balanced and unbalanced scores for each dimension. These scores are then used to plot a spouse or family member's location on the Circumplex model.

Reliability. An alpha reliability analysis was used to examine internal consistency of the six factor analytically divined scales. These reliabilities are as follows: Enmeshed = .77, Disengaged = .87, Balanced Cohesion = .89, Chaotic = .86, Balanced Flexibility = .84, and Rigid = .82.

Validity. Factor validity, concurrent validity, and discriminant validity have been reported for FACES IV (Olson, 2011).

Availability and source. FACES IV, accompanying manual, and scoring procedures are available from David Olson at Life Innovations, Inc.

Comments. FACES has gone through a number of modifications since its introduction in 1979. It is one of the few theory-based and empirically validated measures available for both clinical and research purposes. Not only does it provide accurate pretreatment assessments, but it is very useful in helping couples and families formulate realistic treatment goals (e.g., to develop more or less structure in their relationships and to increase or decrease the degree of connectedness between spouses and family members), monitor progress toward these goals, and evaluate therapeutic outcome.

Intersession Report

Type of instrument. The Intersession Report is a short, nine-item questionnaire that clients complete at the beginning of each therapy session, which allows clinicians and researchers to assess clients' perceptions of improvement from session to session. The first seven Likert-type questions measure clients' subjective feelings about their personal and interpersonal functioning and progress toward therapeutic goals. The last two questions ask clients to rate their relationship with the therapist. Only the therapist's supervisor is privy to these responses.

Use and target audience. The Intersession Report has two general purposes, that is, to provide the clinician with periodic feedback about client progress and to offer supervisors clients' critical appraisal of the therapeutic relationship that supervisees have with individuals, couples, and families whom they are treating.

Scoring procedure. No scoring procedures are available at this time.

Reliability. For the three factor analytically derived subscales, Cronbach's alpha estimates ranged from .74 to .86 for Functioning, .77 to .90 for Symptoms, and .86 to .90 for Alliance.

Validity. A three-factor solution was used to establish validity. Factor I–Functioning was found to represent 31% of the variance. Factor II–Symptoms was found to represent 18% of the variance, and Factor III–Alliance made up 16.9% of the variance. These three factors explained 66.3% of the total variance. Both convergent validity and discriminant validity are also reported.

Availability and source. The Intersession Report appears in Johnson, L. N., Ketring, S. A., and Anderson, S. R. (2010). The Intersession Report: Development of a Short Questionnaire for Couples Therapy. *American Journal of Family Therapy, 38,* 266–276.

Comments. The Intersession Report can be a valuable tool for therapists and supervisors. It allows clinicians to monitor clinical progress and offers clinical trainers valuable insights into the therapeutic relationship/alliance. However, the effect of having clients rate the effectiveness of their therapy, on an ongoing basis, cannot be overlooked. Researchers have understood experimenter effects for decades. One should not lose sight of the fact that having clients evaluate their treatment is treatment. Similarly, having clients evaluate their therapists sets up a meta-therapeutic relationship between clients and supervisors. The possibility of client-supervisor-therapist triangulation becomes a reality that cannot be overlooked. Any research done with the Intersession Report in the future should address these issues.

STRATEGY FOR UTILIZING COUPLES ASSESSMENT INSTRUMENTS

The following simple, four-step process for selecting assessment instruments for use with couples should be helpful to therapists.

1. *Assess marital quality.*
   This process begins with the therapist selecting some tried and true, empirically tested measures of relationship quality to get a fairly accurate appraisal of the couple's level of distress and dissatisfaction. The instrument selected is administered again at the conclusion of treatment so that the success of therapy can be determined through pretreatment–post-treatment comparisons of global satisfaction/dissatisfaction scores for each spouse.

   Although such measures target some of the most salient domains of marital or couple dynamics that frequently are the source of conflict (e.g., finances, sexual relations, in-laws, children, friendships, recreation, expression of love and affection, conventionality, conflict resolution), they do not sample the broad range and scope of potential relationship conflicts and issues of concern necessary for advancement to the second step in the procedure. To do so, more comprehensive measures are necessary.

2. *Perform a comprehensive assessment.*
   The goal at this juncture of pretreatment assessment is to canvas as many areas of potential relationship conflict and dissatisfaction as possible. A number of instruments can be used for this purpose.

3. *Categorize areas of conflict and disagreement.*
   Once all areas of conflict, issues of disagreement, problems, and so on, in the marriage or relationship have been identified, they are categorized so that they can be dealt with more effectively. Categorization can be done in a variety of ways. For example, acts of aggression may constitute one category (verbal aggression, physical aggression, hostility, passive–aggressive behavior, etc.); trust may constitute another category (e.g., lying, deception, reliability, fidelity). Categorization may also be done according to couples' unmet expectations in specific areas of

their relationship (e.g., finances, sexual relations, marital roles and tasks, parenting). Another way to categorize issues of concern, problems, and conflicts is to assign them to theoretically meaningful categories, for example, couple cohesion, communication patterns, relationship structure, power, rules, hierarchies, and boundaries.

Once categories have been determined, they are hierarchically ordered and ranked according to their importance, severity, urgency, and so on, depending on the needs of a given couple and the nature of the presenting problem. The couple, in conjunction with the therapist, then agrees on a sequence in which these categories will be addressed in therapy.

4. *Assess specific areas of concern in a given category.*
The fourth and final step in this procedure is refinement. Specific instruments are selected that can be used for in-depth analysis and exploration of the problems, conflicts, and concerns included in a particular category. Depending on the breadth and scope of a given category, more than one measure may be required if coverage is to be adequate, if not comprehensive.

CASE EXAMPLE

Fred was a high-profile businessman and president of his church's parish council. He had been married to Julia, a high school art teacher, for 23 years. They had a 19-year-old son who was attending college in another state. Fred suspected that Julia was having an affair and confronted her. Julia admitted to having had a brief sexual encounter but gave no further details. She said that personal guilt would not allow her to continue the affair and that she had recently ended the relationship. The couple was referred for counseling by their parish priest. Their stated goal was reconciliation.

Assessment

All couples accepted for therapy are first seen for an initial interview. During this interview, the couple is asked to identify the presenting problem and to agree on a desired therapeutic outcome. The couple's ability to communicate functionally and resolve conflicts is also assessed. A treatment contract is then negotiated. Each spouse is seen for two separate, individual interviews during which personal histories and relationship histories are gathered. These interviews are also used to make individual diagnoses.

Assessment instruments are determined by the nature of the presenting problem. The following instruments were chosen for this couple:

1. Dyadic Adjustment Scale (DAS)
2. Spousal Inventory of Desired Changes and Relationship Barriers (SIDCARB)
3. Justification for Extramarital Involvement Questionnaire (JEIQ)
4. Trust Scale (TS)
5. Marital Disaffection Scale (MDS)
6. Intimacy Needs Survey (INS)

Assessment Findings and Interpretations

The first issue to consider when extramarital involvement is the presenting problem is to determine the nature of the extramarital relationship (Bagarozzi, 2008).

The second issue to consider is whether the offending spouse's behavior is symptomatic of an underlying personality disorder because personality factors will determine, to a large degree, the course of therapy and its probable success. The personality dynamics of the offended spouse must also be taken into account because these will influence that spouse's ability to reconcile and grant forgiveness.

Finally, how each spouse perceives the marriage will affect his or her willingness to put forth the effort necessary to resolve the infidelity. The following factors are relevant:

1. Each spouse's subjective feelings of satisfaction with the marriage prior to the infidelity.
2. Each spouse's subjective judgments and beliefs about the voluntary or nonvoluntary nature of the marriage for himself or herself and his or her partner.
3. Each spouse's commitment to his or her partner and the marriage and to resolving the infidelity.

Scores for the DAS that are below 100 are indicative of marital distress. Fred's DAS score was 82, and Julia's score was 79. After the couple had completed all questionnaires, both spouses were asked to retake the DAS. For the second administration, however, Fred and Julia were instructed to answer all questions as they would have responded to them at a time when they considered their marriage to have been the "most satisfying." These scores provided retrospective baseline data that could be used to gauge the degree of distress caused by the affair. They also

TABLE 6. 1   Fred and Julia's SIDCARB Profile

Factor	Fred	Julia
I	67	68
II	70	72
III	69	73

Note: Mean = 50; Standard Deviation = 10.

served as a criterion against which therapeutic progress could be measured. These "most satisfying" scores were 110 and 105 for Fred and
Julia, respectively. When these findings were discussed with the couple,
both spouses agreed that their relationship had never been an "extraordi-
narily passionate one." Commitment was considered to be a major factor
for both of them. This was reflected in their SIDCARB profile (Table 6.1).

For the first factor (Dissatisfaction With One's Spouse and Desire
for Behavior Change), both Fred and Julia scored slightly more than 1
standard deviation above the mean. Factors II and III represent two conceptually different types of commitments that also serve as barriers to
relationship termination. Factor II = Internal Psychological (Obligations
to Children, Commitment to Marriage Vows, Religious Beliefs, and
Concern for Relatives). Factor III = External Circumstantial (Concern of
Friends and Neighbors, Job Considerations, Legal Costs, and Financial
Circumstances). Factor II and Factor III scores for both Fred and Julia
clearly show that divorce was not an option for this couple.

Emphasizing the commitment dimension of Factors II and III and
de-emphasizing their barrier strength aspect was used as a positive con-
notation that offered hope and encouragement to the couple. It also provided an additional incentive for working toward reconciliation.

Julia's responses to the Justification for Extramarital Involvement
Questionnaire were instructive. She endorsed only 3 of the 17 possible
items as "partially" justifiable reasons for having an affair. These were
"For Companionship," "For Intellectual Sharing," and "For Someone
to Understand Problems and Feelings." Sex and romance were not identified as motivating factors for Julia. Fred, on the other hand, could not
justify an extramarital sexual relationship under any circumstances.
He said that he had had the opportunity to do so on several occasions,
but being unfaithful was not in his "nature." Nevertheless, he was willing to discuss the possible causes of Julia's behavior with her and to
explore how he might have contributed to the couple's problem.

Disaffection scores as measured by the MDS were surprisingly low
given the nature of the presenting problem, indicating that both spouses
were still emotionally invested in each other. Fred's score was 42. Julia's
score was 37. Not surprisingly, Trust Scale ratings of Julia's behavior

TABLE 6.2   Matrix: Self-Rating Scales for Couples

Assessment Instrument	Specific Couple Applications	Cultural/ Language	Instructions/Use: T = Time to Take S = Time to Score I = Items (# of)	Computerized: (a) Scoring (b) Report	Reliability (R) Validity (V)	Availability
Locke-Wallace Marital Adjustment Test	Assesses relationship adjustment, conflict resolution, cohesion, communication	English	T = 3–5 min S = 5 min I = 15	a = No b = No	R = .90 V = .63	Journal article
Dyadic Adjustment Scale	Assesses relationship adjustment and couples' satisfaction	English French Chinese	T = 5–15 min S = 5 min I = 34 (14 items)	a = Yes b = No	R = .86–.96 V = .86–.88	Journal article; Multi-Health Systems, Inc.
Areas of Change Questionnaire	Assesses the amount of change desired in relationship	English	T = 5 min S = 5 min I = 15	a = No b = No	R = .90 V = .63	Multi-Health Systems, Inc.
Intimacy Needs Survey	Assesses couples' perceptions of type and need of intimacy	English	T = 10 min S = 15 min I = 44	a = No b = No	R = No data V = No data	In *Enhancing Intimacy in Marriage: A Clinician's Guide* (2001)
Marital Disaffection Scale	Assesses level of disaffection or loss of positive emotions toward spouse	English	T = 3–5 min S = 3–5 min I = 21	a = No b = No	R = .93 V = Discriminant and criterion related	In *When Love Dies: The Process of Marital Disaffection* (1993)

Name	Description	Language	Time/Subscales/Items	a/b	Reliability/Validity	Source
SIDCARB	Assesses marital satisfaction and stability in couples	English	T = 5 min S = 10 min I = 26	a = No b = No	R = .74–.86 V = Factor analysis	Appendix A of *Enhancing Intimacy in Marriage: A Clinician's Guide* (2001)
Sexual Desire Inventory	Assesses sexual desire (dyadic and solitary) in couples	English	T = 5 min S = 5 min I = 14	a = No b = No	R = .76–.96 V = Factor analysis	Journal article
Justification for Extramarital Involvement Questionnaire	Assesses reasons for extramarital relationships	English	T = 2–3 min S = N/A I = 17	a = No b = No	R = N/A V = N/A	*Handbook of Family Measurement Techniques*
Trust Scale	Assesses trust in marital relationships	English	T = 2–3 min S = 2–3 min I = 17	a = No b = No	R = .35–.60 V = Factor analysis	*Handbook of Family Measurement Techniques*
FACES IV	Assesses adaptability and cohesion in marriage and family relationships	English	T = 4–5 min S = 4–5 min I = 42	a = Yes b = Yes	R = .77–.89 V = Factor concurrent discriminant	Journal article
Intersession Report	Assessment of clients' improvement and satisfaction with the therapist	English	T = 1–3 min S = N/A I = 9	a = N/A b = N/A	R = .74–.90 V = Factor analysis	Journal article

by Fred reflected his mistrust. All five items on the Dependability sub-scale and all five items that make up the Predictability subscale were rated negatively. Only two items out of the seven that make up the Faith subscale were identified as concerns. The only area where Fred was rated negatively by Julia was on the Faith subscale. Five of these seven items were identified as problematic by Julia. These five items are best described as dealing with intimate communication between the spouses.

Responses to the Intimacy Needs Survey provided an in-depth exploration of this dimension of the couple's relationship. Total Intimacy Needs Strength scores range from 10 to 800. Average scores for individuals seen in therapy are between 450 and 600. Fred's Total Intimacy Needs Strength score was 395, and Julia's was 465, placing both spouses at the low end of the continuum. Receptivity and Reciprocity Satisfaction scores were not considered to be problematic for Fred. However, Receptivity and Reciprocity scores for Psychological and Emotional Intimacy were identified as falling below acceptable levels for Julia.

When Julia was asked why she had chosen to become involved in an extramarital relationship at this point in the couple's relationship, she said that a void had been created in her life after her son left for college. Prior to his departure, he had been the one who had been able to satisfy her needs for psychological and emotional intimacy. Her affair was characterized as a desperate, stop-gap measure. The sexual aspect of this relationship was described as being "incidental" and had never been her central focus. The time Fred devoted to his business and his involvement in community affairs had never seemed to be a problem for her until her son left home. In retrospect, she said that she had probably become depressed when he finally did leave home.

The critical question for this couple was whether Fred would be willing and able to meet Julia's needs for psychological and emotional intimacy. Given the fact that both Fred and Julia did not have high needs for intimacy and both spouses desired to reconcile, helping them achieve a level of mutual satisfaction was seen as an achievable and realistic goal. To do so, however, a number of modifications in the couple's established patterns of relating would be required. Training in functional communication, empathic listening, and conflict negotiation was the first step in helping them move toward greater intimacy. Sometimes the acquisition of these basic skills is all that is needed to help a couple establish a new equilibrium, especially when commitment is high and divorce is not an acceptable option. Unfortunately, in some cases, barriers to relationship termination can have a very negative effect on a marriage and on the therapeutic process in relationships where anger, resentment, jealousy, and the desire to retaliate are present. Such feelings and motives make it difficult for the spouses to reconcile. This was not the case for Fred and Julia. Gradually, trust began to build and wounds began to heal. At the end of treatment, DAS scores for Fred and Julia were 105 and 102, respectively. Julia's needs for psychological and emotional intimacy were being met by Fred to some degree but still were not considered totally satisfying. However, the marriage was moving in a positive direction.

REFERENCES

Bagarozzi, D. A. (1983). Methodological developments in measuring social exchange perceptions in marital dyads (SIDCARB): A new tool for clinical intervention. In D. A. Bagarozzi, A. P. Jurich, & R. W. Jackson (Eds.), *New perspectives in marital and family therapy: Issues in theory, research and practice* (pp. 79–104). New York: Human Sciences Press.

Bagarozzi, D. A. (1989). Family diagnostic testing: A neglected area of expertise for the family psychologist. *American Journal of Family Therapy, 17*, 261–274.

Bagarozzi, D. A. (1990). *Intimacy needs questionnaire.* Unpublished instrument, Human Resources Consultants, Atlanta.

Bagarozzi, D. A. (2001). *Enhancing intimacy in marriage: A clinician's guide.* New York: Brunner-Routledge.

Bagarozzi, D. A. (2008). Understanding and treating marital infidelity: A multidimensional model. *American Journal of Family Therapy, 36*, 1–17.

Bagarozzi, D. A., & Pollane, L. (1983). A replication and validation of the Spousal Inventory of Desired Changes and Relationship Barriers (SIDCARB): Elaborations on diagnostic and clinical utilization. *Journal of Sex and Marital Therapy, 9*, 303–315.

Baucom, D. H. (1982). A comparison of behavioral contracting and problem solving/communications training in behavioral marital therapy. *Behavior Therapy, 13*, 162–174.

Birchler, G. R., & Webb, L. J. (1977). Discriminating interaction behaviors in happy and unhappy marriages. *Journal of Consulting and Clinical Psychology, 45*, 494–495.

Busby, D. M., Christensen, C., Crane, D. R., & Larson, J. H. (1995). A revision of the Dyadic Adjustment Scale for use with distressed and non-distressed couples: Construct hierarchy and multidimensional scales. *Journal of Marital and Family Therapy, 21*, 289–308.

Crane, D. R., Middleton, K. C., & Bean, R. A. (2000). Establishing criterion scores for the Kansas Marital Satisfaction Scale and the Revised Dyadic Adjustment Scale. *American Journal of Family Therapy, 28*, 53–60.

Cross, D. G., & Sharpley, C. F. (1981). The Locke-Wallace Marital Adjustment Test reconsidered: Some psychometric findings as regards it reliability and factorial validity. *Education and Psychological Measurements, 41*, 1303–1306.

Duck, S. (1982). A topography of relationship disengagement and dissolution. In S. Duck (Ed.), *Personal relationships IV: Dissolving personal relationships* (pp. 1–30). London: Academic Press.

Flowers, C., Robinson, B., & Carroll, J. (2000). Criterion-related validity of the marital disaffection scale as a measure of marital estrangement. *Psychological Reports, 86*, 1101–1104.

George, C., Kaplan, J., & Main, M. (1996). *Adult Attachment Interview protocol* (3rd ed.). Unpublished manuscript, University of California at Berkeley.

Glass, S. P. (2001). Justification of Extramarital Relationships Questionnaire. In J. Touliatos, B. F. Perlmutter, & G. H. Holden (Eds.), *Handbook of family measurement techniques* (pp. 100–101). Thousand Oaks, CA: Sage.

Glass, S. P., & Wright, T. L. (1988). Reconstructing marriage after the trauma of infidelity. In W. K. Halford & H. J. Markman (Eds.), *Clinical handbook of marriage and couples intervention* (pp. 471–473). Hoboken, NJ: Wiley.

Gordon, K. C., Baucom, D. H., & Snyder, D. K. (2008) In A. S. Gurman (Ed.), *Clinical handbook of couple therapy* (4th ed.) New York: Guilford Press.

Gurman, A. S. (Ed.). (2008). *Clinical handbook of couple therapy* (4th ed.). New York: Guilford Press.

Hoon, E. F., Hoon, P. W., & Wincze, J. P. (1976). The SAI: An inventory for the measurement of female sexual arousability. *Archives of Sexual Behavior, 5*, 291–300.

Hudson, W. (1992). *The WALMYR assessment scales scoring manual.* Tempe, AZ: WALMYR Publishers.

Hunt, R. A. (1978). The effect of item weighting on the Locke-Wallace Marital Adjustment Scale. *Journal of Marriage and the Family, 43*, 651–661.

Johnson, L. N., Ketring, S. A., & Anderson, S. R. (2010). The Intersession Report: Development of a short questionnaire for couple therapy. *American Journal of Family Therapy, 38*, 266–276.

Kayser, K. (1993). *When love dies: The process of marital disaffection.* New York: Guilford Press.

Kayser, K. (1996). The Marital Disaffection Scale: An inventory for assessing emotional estrangement in marriage. *American Journal of Family Therapy, 24*, 83–86.

L'Abate, L., & Bagarozzi, D. A. (1992). *Sourcebook of marriage and family evaluation*. New York: Brunner/Mazel.

Lauman, E. O., Gannon, J. H., Michael, R. T., & Michaels, S. (1994). *The social organization of sexuality: Sexual practices in the United States*. Chicago: University of Chicago Press.

Locke, H. J., & Wallace, K. M. (1959). Short marital adjustment and predictions test: Their reliability and validity. *Marriage and Family Living, 21*, 251–255.

Mead, D. E., & Vatcher, G. (1985). An empirical study of the range of marital complaints found in the Areas of Change Questionnaire. *Journal of Marital and Family Therapy, 11*, 421–422.

Olson, D. H. (2002). *PREPARE:ENRICH counselor's manual*. Minneapolis: Life Innovations, Inc.

Olson, D. H. (2011). FACES IV and the circumplex model: Validation study. *Journal of Marital and Family Therapy, 37*, 51–80.

Olson, D. H., Fournier, D. G., & Druckman, J. M. (1982). Counselor's manual for PREPARE/ENRICH (unpublished manuscript, University of Minnesota, Department of Family Social Science.

Olson, D. H., Sprenkle, D. H., & Russell, C. (1979). Circumplex model of marital and family systems: I. Cohesion and adaptability dimensions, family types and clinical applications. *Family Process, 18*, 3–28.

Perlmutter, B. F., Touliatos, J., & Straus, M. A. (Eds.). (2001). *Handbook of family measurement techniques* (3 vols). Thousand Oaks, CA: Sage.

Rempel, J. K., Holmes, J. G., & Zanna, M. P. (2001). The Trust Scale. In J. Touliatos, B. F. Perlmutter, & G. H. Holden (Eds.), *Handbook of family measurement techniques* (p. 111). Thousand Oaks, CA: Sage.

Roberts, S. (1988). *Test-retest reliability of the Comprehensive Areas of Change Questionnaire*. Unpublished master's thesis, Brigham Young University, Provo, UT.

Snyder, D. K. (1979). *Marital Satisfaction Inventory*. Los Angeles: Western Psychological Services.

Snyder, D. K. (1981). *Manual for the Marital Satisfaction Inventory*. Los Angeles: Western Psychological Services.

Snyder, D. K. (1997). *Marital Satisfaction Inventory–Revised*. Los Angeles: Western Psychological Services.

Snyder, D. K., & Regts, J. M. (1982). Factor scales for assessing marital disharmony and disaffection. *Journal of Consulting and Clinical Psychology, 50*, 736–743.

Spanier, G. (1976). Measuring dyadic adjustment: New scales for assessing the quality of marriage and similar dyads. *Journal of Marriage and the Family, 38*, 15–30.

Spanier, G. B., & Thompson, L. (1982). A confirmatory analysis of the Dyadic Adjustment Scale. *Journal of Marriage and the Family, 44*, 731–738.

Spector, I., Carey, M., & Steinberg, L. (1996). The Sexual Desire Inventory: Development, factor structure, and evidence of reliability. *Journal of Sex and Marital Therapy, 22*, 175–190.

Spector, I. P. (1992). *Development and psychometric evaluation of a measure of sexual desire*. Unpublished doctoral dissertation, Syracuse University, New York.

Straus, M. (1979). Measuring intrafamily conflict and violence: The Conflict Tactics (CT) Scales. *Journal of Marriage and the Family, 41*, 75–88.

Vatcher, G. (1988). *An empirical study of the Comprehensive Areas of Change Questionnaire*. Unpublished doctoral dissertation, Brigham Young University, Provo, UT.

Weiss, R. L., Hops, H., & Patterson, G. R. (1973). A framework for conceptualizing marital conflict, a technology for altering it, some data for evaluating it. In F. W. Clark & L. A. Hamerlynck (Eds.), *Critical issues in research and practice: Proceedings of the 4th Banff International Conference on Behavior Modification* (pp. 309–342). Champaign, IL: Research Press.

Whisman, M. A., Dixon, A. E., & Johnson, B. (1997). Therapists' perspectives of couple problems and treatment issues in couple therapy. *Journal of Family Psychology, 11*, 361–366.

CHAPTER 7

Child and Adolescent Assessment Strategy and Inventories

Alexandra Cunningham and Jack Scott

INTRODUCTION

Other chapters in this book address specific family dynamics (couples conflict, divorce, separation, parenting, family violence) that influence couples and families. By contrast, this chapter addresses various child and adolescent conditions that can greatly influence family dynamics. Not surprisingly, these conditions can and do significantly impact family functioning and well-being.

In recent years, there have been increased efforts made to appropriately diagnose and treat children with behaviors that disrupt family and school life. The National Institute of Mental Health (NIMH) and the Centers for Disease Control report that for school-age children, between the ages of 8 and 18 years old, between 13% and 21% have a diagnosable mental disorder (Merikangas et al., 2010). Based on these rates, it is evident that children with these special needs, and sometimes severe disorders, require effective treatment to be more successful in their environments. Included in these prevalent disorders are the diagnoses that will be discussed in this chapter: Attention Deficit and Hyperactivity Disorder (ADHD), Depression and Bipolar Disorder, Autism Spectrum Disorders (ASD), Obsessive-Compulsive Disorder, and Learning Disorders.

Differentiating among these diagnoses can prove difficult as many symptoms overlap, creating confusion about how to best treat these children. The educational system has done a lot of work to include these children at school, both academically and socially, with legislation through the 2004 Individuals with Disabilities Education Act. Mental health professionals are an integral part in facilitating this inclusion through effective assessments and proper treatment planning. This will be a comprehensive description of assessments that are being used as best practice when providing services to children with the aforementioned diagnoses.

Our focus is to present clinicians with the most accessible and evidence-based assessment tools available for each of the special needs populations addressed. All of the instruments presented are authorized for use by any b-level clinician* to assist with diagnosing and treatment planning. Before reviewing the assessment tools, we will provide a general discussion of the diagnoses.

SPECIAL NEEDS

Attention Deficit and Hyperactivity Disorder

Attention Deficit and Hyperactivity Disorder is the most prevalent diagnosis for children between the ages of 8 to 15, with an estimated 8.7% here in the United States (NIMH, 2009). Children who present with this diagnosis exhibit characteristics of being inattentive to details, easily distractible, fidgety, and impulsive. When a child is considered "disruptive" in school or at home, an assessment for ADHD is common in order to distinguish whether symptoms are clinically significant enough to warrant a diagnosis.

ADHD, by nature and clinical description, is a diagnosis that provides caregivers and professionals with many externalized behaviors that are easily identified through observation. Children and adolescents exhibiting such observable behaviors must be doing so for a period of 6 months or longer at a level that is inappropriate to their developmental level. Diagnosticians are asked to focus on three categories of behaviors, inattention, hyperactivity, and impulsivity, marked by examples of behaviors such as forgetfulness, excessive talking, and trouble waiting for one's turn.

Criteria within the diagnosis of ADHD provide clear examples, and therefore assessment tools have been created to which parents,

---

* Level b qualified clinicians have a master's degree in psychology, education, occupational therapy, speech-language pathology, social work, or in a field closely related to the intended use of the assessment, and have formal training in the ethical administration, scoring, and interpretation of clinical assessments.

teachers, and caregivers can easily relate and clearly identify with children. Although this diagnosis seems clearly delineated through external behavioral examples, there is a good deal of clinical judgment used in determining level of disruption and inappropriateness for developmental level (APA, 2000). Clinicians need to utilize assessment tools to help them make the distinction between a typical child's inattention, activity level, and impulsivity before diagnosing and treating, especially because many children who receive the diagnosis of ADHD utilize both psychotherapy and medication interventions (Sprafkin, Gadow, & Nolan, 2001). It is appropriate, if not recommended, for clinicians to provide information and referrals to professionals such as psychiatrists or neurologists, who can consult on the issues of medication management for children and adolescents with ADHD.

Depression and Bipolar Disorder

In the United States, 2% to 8% of children and adolescents experience symptoms of depression (Birmaher, Brent, & Benson, 1998). Unlike the externalized behaviors observable in ADHD, children with mood disorders such as Major Depressive Disorder often demonstrate internalized symptoms that are more difficult to identify. Some of the red flags to be aware of when assessing for depression with a child are refusal to participate in daily activities like school or play, clinging to a caregiver, getting into trouble, and displaying a negative or irritable attitude. It is important not to overlook some of these symptoms, as research shows that childhood depression can be a predictor of more severe illnesses in the future (Weissman et al., 1999).

Many children who suffer from depression go untreated because their behaviors are attributed to the move through different developmental stages. Before the age of 15, or puberty, the prevalence of depression in males and females is equal, but after this critical developmental stage, girls are twice as likely to be diagnosed with a major depressive episode. In working to help treat children and adolescents with depression, a combination of psychotherapy and medication has proven to have the most effective outcomes (March et al., 2004). Educating families about this is important, as are appropriate referrals and consultation with a physician.

Historically the diagnoses of Bipolar Disorders have been exclusive to adults, with an identified age of onset of 20 years old. In the most recent edition of the DSM, DSM-IV-TR, the only mention of children indicates that, "10-15% of adolescents with Major Depressive Episodes will develop Bipolar I Disorder" (APA, 2000, p. 385). Early-onset bipolar disorder, occurring in childhood or early adolescence, appears to be more severe than when it appears in older adolescence or adulthood. This is typically marked with more frequent mood swings, somatic symptoms, and manifestations of both manic and depressive (mixed) episodes (Birmaher et al., 2006).

One of the most dangerous aspects of bipolar disorders in children and teens is the threat of suicide attempts and suicidal ideation that is more commonly found with early-onset than with typical-onset bipolar disorder. Therefore, it is important to utilize best practices in treatment when working with this population in childhood, adolescence, and adulthood because treatment for this condition, to manage symptoms and stabilize mood, is usually lifelong. Currently there is a significant amount of research being done to provide more information on the effectiveness of treatment through medication management and talk therapy (Miklowitz et al., 2007).

Autism Spectrum Disorders/Pervasive Developmental Disorders

Autism Spectrum Disorders (ASD), known as Pervasive Developmental Disorders in the DSM-IV-TR, are being diagnosed at a rate of 1 in 110 children (CDC, 2010). The category of ADD/PDD includes five diagnoses: Autistic Disorder, Asperger Disorder, Pervasive Developmental Disorder Not Otherwise Specified (PDD-NOS), Rett's Syndrome, and Childhood Disintegrative Disorder. The most commonly diagnosed among the five are Autistic Disorder, Asperger Disorder, and PDD-NOS and will therefore be the focus of this review.

Autistic Disorder is clinically marked by a speech delay during early childhood, difficulty with self-care, and, in some cases, cognitive impairments. These children are usually identified early, when caregivers notice a child is not speaking or has lost speech, lacks eye contact, and moves their fingers close to their eyes between the ages of 18 and 36 months (Filipek et al., 1999). Because their impairments are significantly marked, these individuals will likely benefit from early intervention therapies in order to build their skills. Asperger's Syndrome is clinically distinguished from Autistic Disorder by a lack of speech delay and the ability to cognitively perform at average or above-average levels. Children diagnosed with Asperger's typically receive a diagnosis several years later than their Autistic Disorder counterparts, mostly because the red flags involved in Autistic Disorder are not present in individuals with Asperger's (Fitzgerald & Corvin, 2001).

Individuals with ASD demonstrate clinically significant impairment in the areas of communication, socialization, and repetitive behaviors or interests. Within these three categories, there are ranges of abilities and challenges within the diagnoses. For example, in the area of communication, one individual diagnosed with ASD might not communicate verbally at all, whereas another may communicate verbally but may be unable to do so in a way that is either functional or effective. This tells clinicians that ASD is a broad category with a variety of manifestations in areas of impairment, indicating that one child with ASD will present differently than another.

Obsessive-Compulsive Disorder

Obsessive-Compulsive Disorder (OCD) occurs in about 1 of every 200 children and adolescents (Flament et al., 1990). Symptomology of OCD with children and adolescents can present in many ways but is marked by recurrent intense behaviors and compulsions that interfere with daily life. Examples of common obsessions and compulsions include unrealistic and irrational beliefs that are persistent, ritualistic behaviors like hoarding or hand washing and internal behaviors such as counting or checking.

The onset of OCD can start, at the earliest, in preschool, but it generally appears between the ages of 10 and 12 years old (March & Benton, 2007). A significant percentage of children and adolescents diagnosed with OCD have a first-degree relative also diagnosed with OCD, indicating that childhood OCD has a strong genetic component (APA, 2000). Children and teens with OCD usually present with observable behaviors, which helps caregivers and professionals during initial assessment and screening. These behaviors include disrupted routines, such as missing school due to needing to perform compulsive rituals; physical complaints; problems with social relationships and self-esteem; and anger management issues.

Most clinicians agree that cognitive-behavioral therapy is the best treatment when working with children and teens with OCD. In cases where severe to moderate symptoms are present, medication can be considered and is supported by the American Academy of Child and Adolescent Psychiatry (Pediatric OCD Treatment Study Team, 2004).

Learning Disorders

Learning disorders are common in children. In schools, children with learning disabilities constitute the largest single category of special needs children. Children with learning disabilities make up over half of all children with exceptional student education eligibility. The DSM-IV-TR lists four learning disorders: Reading Disorder, Mathematics Disorder, Disorder of Written Expression, and Learning Disorder Not Otherwise Specified (APA, 2000). Whereas other organizations use different terms for these disorders (i.e., dyslexia for a reading disability and dyscalculia for a math disability), the trend has been to use either the more descriptive DSM terms for a subject-specific disorder or to refer to significant academic challenges without co-occurring weaknesses in IQ as learning disabilities.

Recent years have seen a major paradigm shift in assessing children for learning disorders within schools. Emphasis had previously been placed on the mental health professional serving as the expert in standardized testing. The change now puts the mental health professional in the role of a team member who helps guide a process using an "experimental science of interventions guided by problem solving and response to intervention" (Ysseldyke, 2009). Response to intervention (RTI) is the most prominent intervention format used in schools to support and assess a child suspected of having learning disabilities. Carefully monitoring the nature of the child's response to a variety of evidence-based interventions permits a school team to understand how the child learns and what additional support may be needed. Critical to these new roles, the school-based mental health professional helps to guide the team in examining the data, verifying that interventions have been provided as intended, and asking what other sources of information may be needed to fully understand the child's learning.

Mental health professionals will recognize that an accompanying shift has taken place in how a child is formally assessed. In the past, when mental health professionals considered specific learning disabilities, they relied on the discrepancy model. A child was given an assessment of intellectual functioning and assessed across a number of academic skill areas. The presumption was that a child with normal intelligence would achieve at normal levels in academic skills. However, a significant discrepancy between intelligence and achievement could then be seen as the basis for specific learning disability (SLD) eligibility. This model rested on the assumption that the causes of academic failure resided within the child and merely needed to be confirmed. The new experimental model, relying on RTI and similar active and sensitive remedial strategies, suggests that the cause of a child's academic failure is a mismatch between the learner's needs and the way the child is taught.

For the purposes of this review, our focus will be on Non-Verbal Learning Disorder (NVLD) because most academic learning disabilities involve interventions from a special education team. In working with the NVLD population, mental health professionals can serve an integral role because the main deficit is in social skills. Some of the characteristics of children with NVLD include good vocabulary, excellent memory, difficulty making and keeping friends, poor abstract reasoning, and anxious or depressive symptoms (Levine, Parker, & Zuckerman, 1995). Social skills group intervention is the primary recommended treatment for individuals with NVLD, and these children are often placed with ASD counterparts who have similar struggles with social skills. It is important for mental health professionals to be able to help identify this population and distinguish it from the other special needs groups in order for them to get the appropriate treatment.

INSTRUMENTS FOR MEASURING ATTENTION DEFICIT AND HYPERACTIVITY DISORDER

ADHD Rating Scale-IV

Instrument name. The ADHD Rating Scale-IV was published in 1998 and is utilized for diagnosing and assessing treatment for children and adolescents. There are two questionnaires within the scale, a home and a school version.

Type of instrument. This rating scale is an 18-item questionnaire with questions linked directly to DSM-IV diagnostic criteria for ADHD. Questions ask the respondent to choose the best description of the child over the past 6 months in areas that specifically address hyperactivity-impulsivity and inattention.

Use and target audience. The questionnaire is for parents, family members, and teachers to assess behaviors in both home and school environments. Once the screening tool has been completed, it needs to be scored and interpreted by a b-level health care provider.

Multicultural. The home version of the screening tool is available in both English and Spanish and uses language that can be easily understood by individuals of diverse backgrounds. The school version is available in English only.

Ease and time of administration. Participants answering the questionnaire typically complete it in 10 to 15 minutes. Once the questionnaire has been completed, the participants, ideally both caregivers at home and at school, submit it to be scored.

Scoring procedure. The respondent is requested to answer each question based on a 4-point Likert scale. The responses correspond with the frequency of behaviors: "Never or Rarely" is 0, "Sometimes" is 1, "Often" is 2, and "Very Often" is 3. Raw scores are tallied and corresponding percentile scores assigned in the two categories of hyperactivity-impulsivity (HI) and inattention (IA) and then are totaled for final measurement. The scoring sheet reflects results for boys and girls between 5 and 17 years old. The scoring tables provide guidelines for placing the child into percentiles within a 2-year age range.

Reliability. Internationally, reliability for the questionnaire has been measured for internal consistency and test–retest reliability. Internal consistency for the screening tool yields a Cronbach's alpha between .71 and .84. The test–retest reliability scores differ from country to country with a range from .73 to .94 (Zhang, Faries, Vowles, & Michelson, 2005).

Validity. The results suggest adequate content validity for this scale.

Availability and source. The manual can be purchased through Guilford Press at www.guilford.com. The questionnaire alone is available for free online through multiple sources.

Comment. The scale is designed to be completed independently by the child's parent/family member and teacher. If more than three of the questions are not rated by the respondent, the questionnaire should not be scored or interpreted.

Vanderbilt ADHD Diagnostic Rating Scales

Instrument name. The Vanderbilt ADHD Diagnostic Teacher Rating Scale (VADTRS) was developed in 1998 and soon thereafter the Vanderbilt ADHD Diagnostic Parent Rating Scale (VADPRS) became available in 2003.

Type of instrument. The VADTRS is a 43-item questionnaire and the VADPRS is a 55-item questionnaire. The questionnaires ask respondents to rate the child according to age appropriateness. In both versions there are two sections: The first section contains specific questions about observable behaviors, and the second section has questions about performance academically and behaviorally in the classroom.

Use and target audience. The tool is designed for parents and teachers of children between 6 and 12 years old. Parents or family members should complete the VADPRS, and teachers or school personnel should complete the VADTRS. The questionnaires are written at a level slightly below third-grade reading.

Multicultural. This rating scale performs well in large, ethnically diverse populations and is available in English, Spanish, and German (Dulcan, 2009).

Ease and time of administration. The questionnaire takes approximately 20 minutes to complete and score. Its availability as a free resource and its ease of administering make it a useful tool for assessing the age group. Respondents are asked to respond to questions by rating their responses on 4-point (first section) and 5-point (second section) Likert scales.

Scoring procedure. The first section is scored with frequency measurements, in which 0 through 4 are assigned values from "Never" to "Very Often." The second section is scored from 1 to 5, where 1–2 is "Problematic," 3 is "Average," and 4–5 is "Above Average." Several different outcomes will be measured by scoring the scales, including identification of subtypes (inattentive, hyperactive/impulsive, combined) and screenings for comorbidities, including Oppositional-Defiant/Conduct Disorder and Anxiety/Depression.

Reliability. Internal consistency exists in both parent and teacher versions. Inter-rater reliability exists. Test–retest reliability is not reported.

Validity. Concurrent validity is high, at .79 for both versions (Wolraich et al., 2003).

Availability and source. Free resource, available at http://www.nichq.org/adhd_tools.html.

Comment. There is a resource toolkit available to assist in explaining the diagnosis to families and teachers, and follow-up tools to assess treatment and resources.

SNAP-IV Rating Scale-Revised (SNAP-IV)

Instrument name. The Swanson, Nolan, and Pelham Rating Scale-Revised (SNAP-IV) was revised in 1992 and 2003 from its original version in 1982 in order to be consistent with the new DSM-IV-TR and its diagnostic criteria for ADHD.

Type of instrument. The SNAP-IV-R is a 90-item questionnaire that asks respondents, teachers and parents specifically, to check one of four columns that best describe the child.

Use and target audience. The scale is designed to help professionals assess children (between ages of 6 and 18) based on parent and teacher responses to the questionnaire.

Multicultural. The questionnaire requires that respondents have at least a high school reading level. The tool is available in English.

Ease and time of administration. The questionnaire takes 10 minutes to complete and should be scored after receipt of both teacher and parent responses.

Scoring procedure. Respondents are asked to score questions on a 4-point Likert scale from "Not At All" to "Very Often" (0–4). The scores are obtained by adding up the scores for each question and dividing the sum by the number of items in that subset. The subsets measure Inattention, Hyperactivity-Impulsivity, and Combined types of ADHD. Scores in the top 5% are considered significant. The website indicates that software for electronic administration and scoring is coming soon.

Reliability. Both test–retest and internal consistency reliability measurements are adequate, with a range between .76 and .97, while inter-rater reliability is weaker, between .43 and .49 (Collett, Ohan, & Myers, 2003).

Validity. Predictive validity measurements have been made for the rating scale which indicate adequacy for parent respondents but poorer for teachers.

Availability and source. Free resource, available at www.adhd.net.

Comment. Questions asked and language used in this rating scale might be a barrier for less educated and culturally diverse populations. The tool also screens for comorbid diagnoses, including Oppositional Defiant Disorder, Depression, and Conduct Disorder.

INSTRUMENTS FOR MEASURING DEPRESSION AND BIPOLAR DISORDER

Kids Schedule for Affective Disorders and Schizophrenia in School-Age Children (K-SADS-PL)

Instrument name. The Kids Schedule for Affective Disorders and Schizophrenia in School-Age Children (K-SADS-PL) was developed in 1996 to assess the severity of symptoms of psychiatric disorders, including Major Depression, Dysthymia, Mania, Hypomania, Cyclothymia, Bipolar Disorders, and many more.

Type of instrument. The K-SADS-PL is a semi-structured interview that encourages the administrator to utilize language appropriate to the educational level of the parent, child, teacher, and others.

Use and target audience. The interview should be administered to the parents, child or adolescent, and others (such as teachers) relevant to children between 6 and 18 years old who are suspected of having psychiatric disorders in the categories of affective disorders, psychotic disorders, anxiety disorders, behavioral disorders and substance abuse, eating disorders, and tic disorders (Sorenson, Thomsen, & Bilenberg, 2007).

Multicultural. The screening tool is in 19 different languages, and each is available through different sources internationally (Hersen, Hilsenroth, & Segal, 2004).

Ease and time of administration. Administration of the K-SADS-PL takes between 90 and 120 minutes and consists of six sections: (1) Introductory Interview, (2) Diagnostic Screening Interview, (3) Supplemental Completion Checklist, (4) Diagnostic Supplements, (5) Summary Lifetime Diagnostic Checklist, and (6) Children's Global Assessment Scale (C-GAS). The respondents are interviewed individually using sections 1 through 4. Sections 5 and 6 are a synthesis of all the data to be completed by the clinician after conducting the interviews. Each section has a detailed explanation of purpose, ranging from rapport building to symptom rating scales. When assessing preadolescents, it is recommended to conduct the parent interview first. When assessing adolescents, interview the adolescents first.

Scoring procedure. Each section is scored differently, and the manual provides a detailed description of scoring instructions. When discrepancies exist among respondents, the clinician is urged to use his or her best judgment in making a final selection. Discrepancies often exist in less observable behaviors, such as experiencing feelings of guilt, hopelessness, interrupted sleep, hallucinations, and suicidal ideation.

Reliability. Inter-rater and test–retest reliability have been measured for the K-SADS-PL and demonstrate a range for different diagnoses. For example, Attention Deficit yields a 0.55 reliability score while Major Depression yields a 1.00 reliability score, which is why this tool is used primarily to diagnose depression (Ambrosini, 2000).

Validity. The K-SADS is reported to have adequate construct validity but weak predictive validity when compared with other diagnostic tools (Ambrosini, 2000).

Availability and source. Free resource, available at www.moodresearch.com/resources/scales/children/KSADS-PL.pdf.

Comment. Questions do not have to be recited verbatim; the interviewer is encouraged to adapt language to the developmental level of the child.

Center for Epidemiological Studies Depression Scale Modified for Children (CES-DC)

Instrument name. The Center for Epidemiological Studies Depression Scale Modified for Children (CES-DC) was developed in 1980 from the original adult scale by the same name. The inventory is designed to indicate levels of depressive symptoms in children and adolescents between the ages of 6 and 17 years old.

Type of instrument. The CES-DC is a 20-item self-report inventory of how an individual has felt or acted during the past week.

Use and target audience. As a self-report inventory, this tool is designed to be answered directly by children and adolescents between the ages of 6 and 17 years old.

Multicultural. The CES-DC is available in English, Spanish, and Japanese.

Ease and time of administration. The self-report inventory takes 5 minutes to complete and asks respondents to rate how often they have felt during the past week from "Not At All," "A Little," "Some," or "A Lot." The tool uses child-friendly language at a sixth-grade reading level.

Scoring procedure. It takes an estimated 10 minutes to score the CES-DC, with possible total scores ranging from 0 to 60. Most questions are scored between 0 and 3, from "Not At All" to "A Lot," with the exception of some positively phrased questions, which are scored oppositely. A score over 15 is indicative of significant levels of depression (Weissman, Orvaschel, & Padian, 1980).

Reliability. The internal consistency coefficient alpha for the CES-DC is measured at 0.84 and the reported test–retest reliability is weaker, at 0.51.

Validity. The reported concurrent validity for the CES-DC is moderate, at 0.44, when measured against the Children's Depression Inventory (Faulstich, Carey, Ruggiero, Enyart, & Gresham, 1986).

Availability and source. Free resource, available at www.brightfutures.org/mentalhealth/pdf/tools.html.

Comment. The CES-DC is designed to be a preliminary screening tool and should be followed up by more thorough assessment before diagnosis. The tool includes a comment indicating that more evaluating is required for individuals who screen positively on the CES-DC.

Mood and Feelings Questionnaire Child and Parent Versions (MFQ-C & MFQ-P)

Instrument name. The Mood and Feelings Questionnaire Child and Parent Versions (MFQ-C & MFQ-P) were created in 1987 in order to quickly and effectively evaluate core symptoms of depression.

Type of instrument. The MFQ is a self-report inventory designed for children, adolescents, and their parents with a 32-item version and short 10-item version.

Use and target audience. The child version of the MFQ is designed for children and adolescents ages 8 to 18 years old. The parent version of the MFQ asks the same questions to the parent about their child's or adolescent's behavior.

Multicultural. The inventory is currently available in English.

Ease and time of administration. The MFQ is administered between 5 and 10 minutes between the long and short versions. The short version was designed to be the most efficient depression rating scale. The tool asks respondents to answer questions about how the child has felt over the last 2 weeks; answer choices are "Not True," "Sometimes," or "True."

Scoring procedure. A clinician can score this assessment in approximately 10 minutes.

Reliability. Both the child and parent versions of the inventory yield high alpha rates of internal consistency, .95 for the MFQ-C and .96 for the MFQ-P (Wood, Kroll, Moore, & Harrington, 1995).

Validity. The MFQ was measured against other depression inventories and yielded moderate to high criterion validity (Daviss et al., 2006).

Availability and source. Free resource, available at devepi.duhs. duke.edu/mfq.html.

Comment. For clinical efficiency and initial screening, the short version of the MFQ is recommended in practice.

Young Mania Rating Scale (YMRS)

Instrument name. The Young Mania Rating Scale (YMRS) was developed in 1978 from a revision of the original tool used for adults being assessed for bipolar disorder. Consequently, the Parent Version of the Young Mania Rating Scale (P-YMRS) was created as a supplement to the YMRS.

Type of instrument. The YMRS and P-YMRS are 11-item clinician-administered interviews designed for children and adolescents and their parents or caregivers to assess the severity of manic symptoms.

Use and target audience. The rating scale is for children and adolescents between the ages of 5 and 17 years old.

Multicultural. The YMRS has been translated into Spanish and Turkish, although these versions are not as readily available as the English version (Lam, Michalak, & Swinson, 2005).

Ease and time of administration. The YMRS and P-YMRS can be administered within 10 to 20 minutes and asks respondents to report symptoms over the previous 48 hours. In addition to client response, the clinician is encouraged to make clinical judgments based on observation during the interview.

Scoring procedure. The score of the interview is determined by adding up the highest number circled on each question. Scores range between 0 and 60; a score of 20 or above is indicative of manic or hypomanic symptoms. Individuals with Bipolar diagnoses scored at 25 qualifying for mania (Bipolar I) and 20 for hypomania (Bipolar II, Bipolar NOS, and Cyclothymia) (Gracious, Youngstrom, Findling, & Calabrese, 2002).

Reliability. The English version of the YMRS shows a good internal consistency reliability of .91. The reports on both the Spanish and Turkish versions also indicate reliability and validity measures for the YMRS (Frazier et al., 2007; Serrano, Ezpeleta, Alda, Matali, & San, 2011).

Validity. The YMRS has an excellent diagnostic efficiency rating of .97 (Frazier et al., 2007).

Availability and source. Free resources; the YMRS is available at louisville.edu/depression/clinicials-corner/Young%20Mania%20 Rating%20Scale-Measure.pdf and the P-YMRS is available at www. healthyplace.com/images/stories/bipolar/p-ymrs.pdf.

Comment. On their own, the YMRS and P-YMRS are not intended to diagnose bipolar disorder in children.

General Behavior Inventory (GBI)

Instrument name. The General Behavior Inventory (GBI) was created in 1981 in order to help identify individuals who are at risk for bipolar disorder.

Type of instrument. The GBI is a 73-item, self-report instrument to describe mood and behavior of a child or adolescent on a 4-point scale.

Use and target audience. The assessment tool is completed by children or adolescents as young as 11 years old. An adapted screening tool, the Parent Version of the General Behavior Inventory (P-GBI), asks parents to rate children and adolescents aged 5 to 17 years old.

Multicultural. The GBI and P-GBI are available in English.

Ease and time of administration. Children and adolescents respond to the 73 questions based on a 4-point scale on how frequently they experience behaviors, from "Never or Hardly Ever" to "Very Often or Almost Constantly." There is no information reported on how long it takes respondents to complete this self-report instrument.

Scoring procedure. The scoring consists of tabulating the dimensions of dysthymia, hypomania, and biphasia. Individuals are identified as dysthymic if the score sum is above the 95th percentile and hypomanic if the score sum is above the 85th percentile.

Reliability. This rating scale has good reliability with an alpha coefficient .90 for its hypomanic and depression scales (Danielson, Youngstrom, Findling, & Calabrese, 2003; Depue et al., 1981; Youngstrom et al., 2004).

Validity. The GBI is reported to have strong criterion validity and excellent discriminative validity (Danielson et al., 2003; Depue et al., 1981; Youngstrom et al., 2001).

Availability and source. The GBI is a free resource, available at www.bipolarchild.com/survey/gbi.html. The P-GBI can be obtained by contacting the author, Eric Youngstrom, but has been more commonly used in research and not in clinical use.

Reymond's Child Depression Scale (RCDS-2) and Reynold's Adolescent Depression Scale (RADS-2)

Instrument name. Reynold's Child Depression Scale (RCDS-2) and Reynold's Adolescent Depression Scale (RADS-2) were first developed in 1989 and revised in 2002.

Type of instrument. The RCDS-2 and RADS-2 are self-report inventories with 30 items designed to elicit current symptoms of mood, affect, self-worth, and body issues. Questions for the RCDS-2 are typically read aloud, and the child is asked to respond on a 4- or 5-point Likert scale.

Use and target audience. The RCDS-2 is designed for children between the ages of 8 and 12. The RADS-2 is designed for adolescents from 11 to 20 years old.

Multicultural. The RCDS-2 is available in English and Spanish, whereas the RADS-2 is only available in English.

Ease and time of administration. These screening tools should take between 10 and 15 minutes to complete and use language between second- and third-grade reading levels. The children or adolescents are asked questions based on how they've been feeling for the past 2 weeks.

Scoring procedure. The scores of the RCDS-2 and RADS-2 yield clinical cut-offs for the severity of the screener's symptoms among normal, mild, moderate, or severe. Clinical cut-off scores are provided for administers of the instruments to help identify more severe cases.

Reliability. The RADS-2 has an internal consistency reliability of between .91 and .93, and the test–retest reliability is .87 (Reynolds & Mazza, 1998).

Validity. Validity has been consistently demonstrated since 1981. The RADS-2 has a strong level of criterion validity of .76 and a .62 phi coefficient, with high sensitivity and specificity ratings: 89% and 90%, respectively (Reynolds & Mazza, 1998).

Availability and source. The instruments are available for purchase by PAR, Inc. at www4.parinc.com.

Comment. The administrator of the tool is asked to use discretion when deciding whether to allow the child or adolescent to read the questionnaire and respond in written form, or for the clinical professional to read the questions aloud and have the subject respond verbally.

INSTRUMENTS FOR MEASURING AUTISM SPECTRUM DISORDERS

Modified Checklist for Autism in Toddlers (M-CHAT)

Instrument name. The Modified Checklist for Autism in Toddlers (M-CHAT) was developed in 1999 for clinical, research, and educational purposes.

Type of instrument. The M-CHAT is a 23-item clinician administered or a self-report questionnaire in which parents are asked to respond "yes" or "no" questions about "how your child usually is."

Use and target audience. This screening tool is validated for use with toddlers between the ages of 16 and 30 months.

Multicultural. The M-CHAT is available in approximately 27 languages, with more translations being developed. In some languages, for example, Spanish and Portuguese, there are distinct versions for Europe and South America, demonstrating a high level of cultural sensitivity.

Ease and time of administration. The M-CHAT can be administered in 5 to 10 minutes, depending on method of administration and parent's need for clarification.

Scoring procedure. The screening tool can be scored in less than 2 minutes, either by hand or using the available electronic scoring system. A child who fails three or more of the questions in total or two of the critical items (indicated in the scoring instructions) should be referred for a comprehensive medical and psychological evaluation.

Reliability. The M-CHAT's internal reliability is found to be adequate, with a Cronbach alpha ranging between 0.83 and 0.85 (Robins & Dumont-Mathieu, 2006).

Validity. The current cross-validation studies are showing increased rates of sensitivity and a decreased number of false positives.

Availability and source. The M-CHAT is a free resource, available at http://www2.gsu.edu/~psydlr/DianaLRobins/Official_M-CHAT_Website.html.

Comments. In 2008, the authors created the M-CHAT Follow-up Interview to reduce the rate of false positives and, therefore, unnecessary referrals for further evaluation.

Childhood Asperger Syndrome Test (CAST)

Instrument name. The Childhood Asperger Syndrome Test (CAST) was developed in 2002 to be utilized with the general, instead of clinical, population that is sensitive to identifying the diagnoses within Autism Spectrum Disorders.

Type of instrument. The CAST is a 37-item yes/no questionnaire, to be self-completed by parents of the child being screened, which addresses communication and social aspects of the child's development.

Use and target audience. The test questionnaire is designed for children between the ages of 4 and 11 years old.

Multicultural. The CAST is available in English, Spanish, and 12 other languages that are all downloadable from the same website.

Ease and time of administration. It typically takes parents between 5 and 10 minutes to complete the CAST.

Scoring procedure. A scoring key is provided along with the CAST and indicates which of the yes or no responses should be scored as a 1. The maximum achievable score is 31, and the current cut-off score of 15 or greater predicts a possible Autism Spectrum Disorder or other social-communication issue(s) (Williams et al., 2005).

Reliability. This is not available.

Validity. This is not available.

Availability and source. The CAST is a free resource, available at http://www.autismresearchcentre.com/tests/cast_test.asp.

Comments. At the end of the CAST, Questions 38 and 39, titled "Special Needs Section," ask parents to identify expressed concerns by others as well as additional diagnoses that might have already been given to the child.

Autism Treatment Evaluation Checklist (ATEC)

Instrument name. The Autism Treatment Evaluation Checklist (ATEC) was developed by the Autism Research Institute to evaluate the efficacy of treatments for autism.

Type of instrument. The ATEC is a 77-item questionnaire that asks parents, professionals, or both, to rate a subject according to his or her abilities in four different categories, with a choice of four ratings.

Use and target audience. The questionnaire was designed for parents, medical professionals, and researchers treating children between the ages of 5 and 12 years old.

Multicultural. The ATEC is available in English.

Ease and time of administration. The checklist takes approximately 10 to 15 minutes to complete and can be easily done electronically on the website (given below).

Scoring procedure. Scoring of the ATEC is done quickly through the electronic scoring system in place online. The scores can be sent via e-mail to three individuals of your choice.

Reliability. The ATEC has a high internal consistency reliability rating of .94 and is being investigated for test–retest reliability at Arizona State University (Autism Research Institute, 2005).

Validity. Current studies are being conducted and prepared for publication on the validity of the ATEC.

Availability and source. The ATEC is a free resource, available at http://www.autism.com/ind_atec_survey.asp.

Comments. Although the ATEC is primarily used for measuring treatment progress, it is and can be used as a preliminary diagnostic tool. In measuring treatment efficacy, the Autism Research Institute recommends completing 6 to 10 ATECs over a 2- to 3-month period for sufficient time to allow the interventions to take effect. The tool is also available in hard copy format from the website but would require hand scoring and obtaining scoring instructions from the authors.

Social Communication Questionnaire (SCQ)

Instrument name. The Social Communication Questionnaire (SCQ), previously the Autism Screening Questionnaire (ASQ) was developed in 2003 as a cost- and time-effective tool for identifying if a child should be referred for comprehensive diagnostic testing for Autism Spectrum Disorders.

Type of instrument. The SCQ is a 40-item yes/no questionnaire that is to be completed by a parent or caregiver of the identified subject.

Use and target audience. The questionnaire can be administered to anyone over the age of 4 years old, with a cognitive age of at least 2 years old.

Multicultural. The SCQ is available in English and Spanish versions.

Ease and time of administration. The questionnaire can be administered in less than 10 minutes, with the parent or caregiver answering questions without supervision. Two versions of the SCQ exist, both Current and Lifetime questionnaires based on the age of the child. The Current version of the SCQ asks respondents to answer all 40 items based on behaviors within the last 3 months. The Lifetime version of the SCQ requests parents or caregivers to answer the first 20 items based on current (within the past 3 months) behaviors, and the last 20 items based on behaviors of the subject between the ages of 4 and 5 years old.

Scoring procedure. The SCQ is automatically scored when answers are chosen; then the clinician adds the scores to find a total. The cut-off score recommended for further diagnostic testing is 15.

Reliability. The SCQ reports having reliability measures of .83 for Cronbach's alpha and .76 for test–retest (Chandler et al., 2007).

Validity. This questionnaire has shown good cross-cultural validation (Chandler et al., 2007).

Availability and source. The SCQ is available for purchase through Western Psychological Services, www.wpspublish.com.

Comments. This instrument is a useful tool when working with older children and adolescents, although for some parents or caregivers, it might be difficult to recall behaviors of their children when the children were between the ages of 4 and 5 years old.

Autism Diagnostic Observation Scale (ADOS)

Instrument name. The Autism Diagnostic Observation Scale (ADOS) is the gold standard in diagnosis of Autism Spectrum Disorders.

Type of instrument. The ADOS is a semi-structured standardized behavioral observation and coding instrument that is conducted through various social and communication interactions with the subject.

Use and target audience. The instrument can be conducted with any individual from toddlerhood to adulthood. Instrument modules are designed to fit the subject's communicative abilities and are not distributed by specific ages.

Multicultural. The ADOS is available in English and Spanish.

Ease and time of administration. The behavioral observation takes approximately 30 to 45 minutes to complete and involves different activities based on the module appropriate for the subject. The appropriate module is chosen by the clinician based on the subject's linguistic skills and chronological age. Modules 1 and 2 involve moving around the observation room with play, whereas Modules 3 and 4 are conversation based and can be administered at a table. As the clinician administers different activities from the module, observations are recorded and later coded to identify a diagnosis.

Scoring procedure. After administration of the ADOS, the clinician codes behavioral observations based on cut-offs and adds the scores to provide accurate diagnoses within the spectrum of autism.

Reliability. This is not available.

Validity. This is not available.

Availability and source. The ADOS is available for purchase through Western Psychological Services, www.wpspublish.com.

Comments. The ADOS is a diagnostic tool that can be utilized by practitioners who attend a 2-day clinical training workshop or purchase and watch the training DVD.

INSTRUMENTS FOR MEASURING
OBSESSIVE COMPULSIVE DISORDER

Yale-Brown Obsessive Compulsive Rating Scale (Y-BOCS-II) and Children's Yale-Brown Obsessive Compulsive Scale (CY-BOCS)

Instrument name. The Yale-Brown Obsessive Compulsive Rating Scale-Second Edition (Y-BOCS-II) was developed in 2006 as a revision of the original, developed in 1989. The Children's Yale-Brown Obsessive Compulsive Scale (CY-BOCS) was adapted from the Y-BOCS and published in 1997. The scales were developed as a method of distinguishing symptoms of Obsessive-Compulsive Disorder from Depression or other Anxiety Disorders.

Type of instrument. The Y-BOCS II and CY-BOCS are two-part instruments consisting of a self-report checklist and clinician-administered scaling instruments. The CY-BOCS is available in at least five different versions.

Use and target audience. The Y-BOCS-II is used for adolescents older than 14 years of age and designed to measure symptom severity. The CY-BOCS is used with children and adolescents between the ages of 6 and 14 years old.

Multicultural. This tool is currently available in English only.

Ease and time of administration. The versions of Y-BOCS-II keep to 10 items and take 5 to 10 minutes to complete. The CY-BOCS is estimated at taking 40 minutes to complete, but with several different versions available and different numbers of questions, the time to administer the scales differs.

Scoring procedure. Scoring of the Y-BOCS-II is done on a 5-point scale, among "Extreme Symptoms" and "No Symptoms." The clinician then totals the items and places the respondent in one of five categories: subclinical, mild, moderate, severe, or extreme. The versions of CY-BOCS also require the totaling of symptoms in order to indicate clinical significance of symptoms present.

Reliability. The Y-BOCS-II yields a range of reliability rates for each of its subscales as follows: internal consistency reliability of .63 to .91, inter-rater reliability of .83 to .98, and test–retest reliability of .75 to .90. The CY-BOCS reports having an internal consistency measurement of .87.

Validity. The Y-BOCS-II is moderately to strongly correlated in both convergent and discriminant validity measures. The CY-BOCS has a high correlation of .62.

Availability and source. The Y-BOCS-II may be obtained by contacting the first, third, fourth, or final author by contacting via e-mail at estroch@health.usf.edu, phone at (727) 767-8293, or by mail at the Department of Pediatrics, University of South Florida, 800 6th Street South, Box 7523, St. Petersburg, FL 33701. The versions of the CY-BOCS are available by contacting Lawrence Scahill, MSN, Ph.D., lawrence.scahill@yale.edu or Child Study Center, 230 South Frontage Road, P.O. Box 207900, New Haven, CT 06520-7900.

Comment. The tools have been widely used in research and measurement of treatment effectiveness.

Spence Children's Anxiety Scale (SCAS)

Instrument name. Spence Children's Anxiety Scale (SCAS) was developed in 1997 by four clinicians specializing in anxiety disorders.

Type of instrument. The scale consists of 44 items, reflecting 38 of the symptoms of anxiety with 6 fillers to reduce negative response bias. Children are asked to rate how often these things happen to them on a 4-point scale.

Use and target audience. This instrument is designed for children between the ages of 7 and 14. It can be used for help in identifying diagnostic symptoms as well as a good evaluation tool for treatment effectiveness.

Multicultural. The SCAS is available in English, Spanish, and 12 other languages.

Ease and time of administration. This scale can be administered in 5 to 10 minutes and scored in the same amount of time.

Scoring procedure. The instrument results and scoring can be calculated in two ways, one that yields a total score and the other an alternate calculation involving its subscales. Questions on the scale are divided into six subscales identified in the categories of different anxiety disorders, one of the subscales being Obsessive-Compulsive. Instructions for scoring using SPSS are detailed on the website, www.scaswebsite.com.

Reliability. The SCAS has internal consistency reliability measurements between .60 and .92 and test–retest reliability between .45 and .60.

Validity. This is not available.

Availability and source. Free resource, available at www.scaswebsite.com.

Comment. Aside from its use in assessing clients and assisting with diagnosis and treatment planning, the SCAS is also used for community screening and prevention in order to monitor the outcome of interventions used to mitigate symptoms of anxiety.

INSTRUMENTS FOR MEASURING LEARNING DISORDERS

Children's Nonverbal Learning Disabilities Scale (C-NLD)

Instrument name. The Children's Nonverbal Learning Disabilities Scale (C-NLD) was developed to help identify children with neuropsychological, academic, and social-emotional deficits.

Type of instrument. The C-NLD is a 15-item self-report questionnaire that asks subjects (parents) to answer on a 4-point scale for how often their child demonstrates behaviors ranging from "Never/Rarely," "Sometimes," "Often/Always" and "I Don't Know."

Use and target audience. The scale is designed for parents of children between the ages of 5 and 18 years old.

Multicultural. The C-NLD is available in English only.

Ease and time of administration. The scale takes approximately 5 to 10 minutes for parents to complete. Questions are specific to the categories of motor, visual-spatial, and interpersonal skills and provide clarification with examples for many of the questions.

Scoring procedure. The C-NLD provides a guideline for scoring instructions, which indicate referral to a medical professional if the parent reports "Sometimes" or "Often" on over half of the responses in each category.

Reliability. This is not available.

Validity. This is not available.

Availability and source. Free resource, available at http://www.nldontheweb.org/nldentrylevelreading/nldratingscale.html.

Wide Range Achievement Test 4 (WRAT4)

Instrument name. The Wide Range Achievement Test 4 (WRAT4).

Type of instrument. An assessment of basic academic skills with subtests in Sentence Completion, Reading, Spelling, and Mathematical Computation. This assessment is standardized and intended to be used individually but can also be used in groups of five or fewer.

Use and target audience. The WRAT4 is primarily used for school-age children but has been standardized for individuals from 5 to 94 years old.

Multicultural. The norms are based on a representative sample of over 3,000 individuals. According to the publisher, the normative sample was selected on a stratified national sample with proportionate representation controlled for age, gender, ethnicity, geographic region, and parental/obtained education as an index of socioeconomic status.

Ease and time of administration. The time varies with administration time for children 5 to 7 years of age of 15 to 25 minutes and for children over 8 years being 30 to 45 minutes. The test is very easy to administer with most subtests resembling test formats children will be familiar with from regular classroom tests. Testing should be conducted in the following order: Word Reading, Sentence Comprehension, Spelling, and Math Computation.

Scoring procedure. The manual is very comprehensive, offering administration, scoring, and interpretation information. The child typically generates correct answers on a response form. These are then scored with reference to the scoring key. A scoring key is provided.

Reliability. The publisher states that "alternate-form immediate retest reliability coefficients ranged from .78 to .89 for an age-based sample and from .86 to .90 for a grade-based sample." Median internal consistency reliability coefficients for subtests and the reading composite for an age-based sample range from .87 to .96.

Validity. The publisher provides a statement on how validity evidence is derived for the WRAT4 but does not provide data in support of this statement.

Availability and source. The WRAT4 is published by, and available from, Psychological Assessment Resources, 16204 N. Florida Avenue, Lutz, FL 33549. Phone (800) 899-8378. www.wpspublish.com.

Comments. The WRAT4 is not intended to be used for formal identification of learning or cognitive disorders. Rather, it is quick and simple assessment of basic academic skills. Two alternative forms of the WRAT4 are available. This may be useful for retesting a child who is receiving intensive instruction or other remediation.

Peabody Individual Achievement Test-Revised (PIAT-R/NU)

Instrument name. Peabody Individual Achievement Test-Revised [1998 Normative Update] (PIAT-R/NU).

Type of instrument. Individualized, standardized test of academic achievement with subtests for General Information, Reading Recognition, Reading Comprehension, Written Expression, Mathematics, and Spelling.

Use and target audience. The PIAN-R/NU is designed for children between the ages of 5 and 22 years old or in grades K–12.

Multicultural. The child must be proficient in English. Administrators are cautioned that this test may not be appropriate for children with limited English proficiency.

Ease and time of administration. It typically takes approximately 1 hour to complete the test. Except for the subtest Written Expression, all subtests are untimed.

Scoring procedure. A scoring key is provided and most subtests have correct answers on the scoring sheet. The format varies by subtest. After determining a ceiling level, the child is asked questions to which he or she offers a verbal reply. For some subtests, the child sees the stimulus item and points to one of four choices. Basal is reached by the highest five consecutive correct answers. This procedure limits the number of out-of-range questions that the child confronts.

Reliability. The publishers provide split-half reliability for the total test of .98 (median of all grades). Kuder–Richardson reliability coefficients by grade range from .98 to .99. Critics have noted that such high reliability measures would not have been obtained if all scores above the basal and below the ceiling had been considered during the norming process.

Validity. The publisher provides detailed information on both content and construct validity. Correlations between the Peabody Picture Vocabulary Test Revised and the PIAT-R are offered.

Availability and source. Pearson Clinical Assessment, 19500 Bulverde Road, San Antonio, TX 78259-3701. Phone (800) 627-7271, Clinicalcustomersupport@pearson.com.

Comments. The PIAT-R/NU is a useful assessment that tends to be easily tolerated by children who have a history of academic challenge. Questions presented on an easel format, with multiple pictorial representations for some subtests, tend to reduce test anxiety.

STRATEGY FOR UTILIZING ASSESSMENT RESULTS

Prior to working with special needs populations, it is essential for mental health professionals to assess a child's ability to successfully participate in treatment based on their level of cognitive functioning. If a child has a dual diagnosis that would prevent therapeutic interventions from being effective, for example, Mental Retardation, a referral to other professionals could benefit these clients. Therefore, the first step involved in the protocol for assessing children with special needs is to gather psychological reports and any other relevant history in order to rule out other diagnoses that could prevent successful treatment.

After this first step has been taken, the following strategy will assist the mental health professional through the process of initiating services for clients with the aforementioned conditions:

1. Gather essential background information from multiple environments, including but not limited to parent reports, school records, and any previous treatment or evaluations from professionals. Reviewing these records will be important to assess cognitive functioning, history of disciplinary issues, and other issues.
2. Conduct interviews and behavioral observations of child, family members, and teachers or other professionals involved with the child.

3. Administer selected inventory/assessment tool.
4. Interpret results of inventory/assessment tool.
5. Provide any appropriate referrals to medical specialists if needed (neurologist, psychiatrist, etc.).
6. Meet with parents to discuss interventions and provide psychoeducation.
7. Determine treatment recommendations and interventions.

CASE EXAMPLE: RYAN

Background Information and Reason for Testing

Max and Carol have been married 10 years and have two children: Ryan (9 years old) and Seth (3 years old). They have a very stable marriage. Max works as an accountant for the local power company, and Carol is a testing supervisor for a juice company. Both sons are well cared for. Ryan attended preschool from the age of 3, and Seth will begin preschool soon. Ryan was cared for at home by Carol's mother during working hours until he began preschool.

Ryan had a number of problems at home and preschool. He preferred to play by himself. He was very interested in cars and trucks from an early age. His play was somewhat atypical, however, in that he tended to not use the cars within the context of any imaginary play. Rather, he focused on the car and especially the parts of the car or truck. He learned academic content quickly and was an early reader. He loved to read about cars and trucks and Carol and Max got him every early reader book they could find to encourage his early reading. He now reads very well, which helps him across the board. Math is easy for him, and he can do most of the problems without writing out the steps.

The present issue relates to a classroom incident. Ryan's teacher announced that a fellow student would be absent for a few days because her mother had died from a brain hemorrhage. While the other children remained silent, Ryan said, "So what," and continued his work. The other children could not comprehend this uncaring response, and some began to call Ryan names until the teacher stopped them from doing so. Nevertheless, Ryan was confused and became upset. He then refused to go back to school for several days (because, he said, "the other kids are mean to me"), and his parents kept him home.

Prior to testing, the clinician was able to review the results from school records in which Ryan was administered the Wechsler Intelligence Scale for Children, Fourth Edition (WISC-IV) in which he scored at or above the normal range on a Full Scale score, Working Memory, Perceptual Reasoning, and Processing Speed. The report indicates that Ryan scored slightly below the mean on Verbal Comprehension (Step 1). During a clinical interview, Ryan was asked if he liked to play with other children. He replied that he did not except when they played with cars and they did so the way he wanted them to play. When asked if he had any friends, he mentions only his mother, father, and brother Seth. When asked what he liked to do for fun, he said, "play with cars" (Step 1).

When asked about the classroom incident, Ryan said the other children don't like him and that they "don't know how to do things right." As part of the interview, the clinician asked Ryan to show how someone would look if they were sad. He replied that he was not sure. When asked how he could ask someone to stop something without using words, he pushed on an imaginary brake and pushed the horn button on a pretend steering wheel. He did this without eye contact.

In an initial interview, the parents were asked to describe their concerns about Ryan. They noted his intense focus on cars and trucks. They report that he would read about them and play with a collection of toy cars and trucks for hours each day. He was especially interested in the cars with hatchbacks and cars and trucks with doors or hoods that opened. He would operate these for long periods of time. When playing, he first had to "get them right" by which he meant lining them up and putting them in an order that only he knew. If his parents attempted to initiate play without Ryan setting his toys in the correct sequence, they reported that they could expect a tantrum. When he was younger, the parents reported not being concerned about his intense interest. They reported that as Ryan began preschool, he would still play with cars and trucks but always alone. He resisted efforts to get him to play with other children. They had some brief success with facilitated play centered on cars and trucks with other boys, but as soon as an adult left the play setting, a problem would ensue. Eventually, Ryan was left to play alone most of the time. Prior to entering kindergarten, Ryan developed an interest in picture books and then reading, mostly about cars and trucks, and the parents reported that they hoped his social issues would become less prominent as he seemed to do well with learning tasks (Steps 1 and 2).

The parents were each asked to complete the Childhood Autism Spectrum Test (CAST), a 37-item checklist. For this purpose, a version was used that is labeled CAST (and not the full test title) so as not to influence parent scoring. Both parents provided scores (Mother 23, Father, 27) that were well above the cut-off of 15 of the 31 items used for scoring. In a follow-up interview, both parents noted that item 25 ("Does s/he often do or say things are tactless or socially inappropriate?") and item 14 ("Does s/he have an interest which takes up so much time that s/he does little else?") were indicative of their child's behavior. When asked when they first noticed intense interests and social impairments, both reported that it was obvious from the age of 2 or 3 years (Step 3).

In utilizing the results of the observation, school report, assessment tools, and the DSM-IV-TR diagnostic criteria for Asperger's Disorder (299.80), Ryan appears to meet the criteria. Under "Qualitative impairment in social interaction, as manifested by at least two of the following:" Ryan scores positive for item b, "failure to develop peer relations appropriate to development level" and item d "lack of social or emotional reciprocity." For the "Restricted repetitive and stereotyped patterns of behavior, interests, and activities as manifest by at least one of the following:" Ryan scores a positive on d, persistent preoccupation with parts of objects, and his play behavior at home in his early years and now continuing to the present are strongly suggestive of meeting the b criteria, "apparently inflexible adherence to specific, nonfunctional routines or rituals. The remaining criteria are all satisfied, leaving Asperger's Disorder as the most likely diagnosis for Ryan (Step 4).

Treatment Recommendations

In an effort to rule out any possible physical etiology, Ryan should receive a comprehensive medical and neurological examination (Step 5). The parents should become knowledgeable about Asperger's Disorder by reading books and viewing videos on the disorder as well as registering with the state-funded Autism Spectrum Disorders support agency (Step 6). The parents should seek Exceptional Student Educational Services from Ryan's current school, beginning with an eligibility assessment. While special services will benefit Ryan, he is likely to be remain in the same mainstream classroom with the provision of inclusion supports as needed. His teachers should understand that Ryan has Asperger's Disorder and that he is not being intentionally rude or uncaring toward the other children. Rather, he is struggling with a disorder that impairs his social understanding. The teachers can help by directly and clearing explaining social situations to Ryan and by telling him what the expected social behavior will be for various settings. This should be practiced in brief pull-out settings first and then refreshed with quick prompts once they have been learned.

In an effort to target Ryan's social impairments, he will benefit from weekly social-communication groups conducted by a speech-language pathologist or other clinician. The parents are urged to de-emphasize supports for the car interest. They can do this by reducing and then eliminating the number of toy cars they buy for him and moving him to books with other themes. They are advised to broaden his interests while being respectful of them. Such broadening could include helping Ryan consider the places he can go in cars, or the activities and people he can become involved with using a car as transportation. Finally, it will be helpful to conduct weekly counseling sessions with Ryan (Step 7). Here the focus can be on appreciating the perspectives of others, role-playing a variety of social situations, reviewing his weekly social successes and challenges, and, when he is slightly more mature, understanding that he has a disorder called Asperger's Disorder.

FUTURE IMPLICATIONS

Assessing children for special needs will continue to be an important element of practice for mental health professionals. The pressures on children and the diminished scope of natural supports will require that large numbers of children receive quality professional care. At least three major areas of change are readily identifiable in the future. First, technology will broaden the access to assessment tools and information about childhood disorders. Second, viewing child's problems as existing solely within the child will yield with increasing speed to recognizing the larger family context in which the child lives. Change efforts become more system focused with both the family and the child needing to understand how they can call for supports. Finally, anticipated changes in the DSM-V will alter how we consider these special needs.

Technology is making the dissemination of information about special needs ever more accessible. Although a small percentage of the population have little or no access to the Internet, most families and certainly professionals have access to the widest possible array of sources of information on any disorder or treatment. This certainly can add stress to the lives of families as they might rely on information found on the Internet with limited discernment and confront a host of unsupported claims for miracle therapies. But it does also allow them to access sound information that will help them make good choices for their children. Professionals must be prepared to take advantage of these capabilities. Posting information of promising and sound treatments is one way. Sharing training videos that will enable families to enhance their capacity is another. Due to the Internet, professionals now have immediate access to an ever-widening assortment of free or very low–cost assessment instruments. Consider the CAST, mentioned in relation to Aspergers Disorder, as just one example. Fortunately, many assessment developers have discovered that they can benefit from their work through sales of support or value-added materials while freely giving away the assessment. Hopefully, this trend will continue. Cutting-edge technology with direct assessment of young children by analyzing eye movements in response to social stimuli or EEG measures that may provide information about subtle anomalies in the architecture of the young child's brain may soon replace or, at minimum, supplement traditional assessment techniques in ASD and perhaps other disorders (Bosl, Tierney, Tager-Flusberg, & Nelson, 2011; Klin, Jones, Schultz, Volkmar, & Cohen, 2002).

The rules of the assessment profession will certainly change with increased understanding of the etiology and diagnostic classification of the Autism Spectrum Disorders (Wing, Gould, & Gillberg 2011). With the discovery of the role of the MECP2 gene in Rett syndrome, this disorder will no longer be included under the Pervasive Developmental Disorders. Other major changes are anticipated related to bipolar and anxiety disorders.

Perhaps the most important development is the accelerating trend away from seeing any learning or behavioral disorder in childhood as existing only within the child. This trend is clearly evident in school practice. Now, before most children with suspected learning disorders are considered for special education, they are provided active and evidence-based interventions within the context of their classrooms and homes. A process is instituted to ensure that they are receiving quality instruction and that different teaching techniques are implemented and carefully monitored and changes are made, all in an effort to preclude the need for special education. This is also part of a larger trend toward early intervention and prevention of disorders. Here, the role of mental health professionals will be enhanced as they have the opportunity to guide a problem-solving team to determine the optimal learning and social conditions for a child now facing challenges. Assessment in this future becomes a dynamic process rather than a static one based on test giving. In this dynamic process, the clinician seeks to understand not just how the child scores on assessments but how the social settings and contexts can be altered to promote optimal growth for the child.

TABLE 7.1   Matrix: Child and Assessment Strategies and Inventories

Instrument	Specific Family Applications	Cultural/ Language	Instructions/Use: T = Time to Take S = Time to Score I = items	Computerized: (a) Scoring (b) Report	Reliability (R) Validity (V)	Availability
ADHD						
ADHD Rating Scale	Children ages 5–17	English and Spanish. Different scoring for boys and girls (school version available only in English, home version available in both)	T = 10–15 min S = I = 18	N/A	R = .73–.94 test-retest .71–.84 Cronbach's alpha V = Adequate	Available for purchase at www.guilford.com, as well as other online retailers. $45–$50
Vanderbilt ADHD Diagnostic Parent Rating Scale (VADPRS) Vanderbilt ADHD Diagnostic Teacher Rating Scale (VADTRS)	Children ages 6–12	English, German, and Spanish	T = 10 min S = 10 min I = Parent: 55, Teacher: 43	N/A	R = .93 or higher ICC acceptable and consistent V = concurrent .79	Free resource: www.nichq. org
SNAP-IV-R	Children ages 6–18	English	T = 10 min S = I = 90	N/A (coming soon)	R = .79–.97 coefficient alpha Inter-rater .43–.49 Internal consistency .76–.96	Free resource: www.adhd. net

Depression & Bipolar

Instrument	Population / Use	Languages	Time / Items	a / b	Reliability / Validity	Resource
Schedule for Affective Disorders and Schizophrenia in School-Age Children (K-SADS-PL)	Children ages 6–18; parent and child interviews. Collect summary ratings from all sources (school, etc.)	English, Spanish, Israeli, Greek, Korean, Farsi	T = 90–120 min; S = varies; I = unstructured interview plus 136 items	a = No; b = No	R = .63–.90; V = Predictive weak; construct adequate. V = Predictive good for parent poorer for teacher	Free resource: University of Pittsburgh http://www.wpic.pitt.edu/ksads/default.htm
Mood Feelings Questionnaire	Children ages 12–18	English	T = 5–10 min; S = 10 min; Items = 32 (short version10)	a = No; b = No	R = IC: .95 (child) .96 (parent); V = Moderate to high criterion (Daviss et al., 2006)	Free resource: Duke University http://devepi.duhs.duke.edu/mfq.html
Center for Epidemiological Studies - Depression Scale Modified for Children (CES-DC)	Children 6–17	English, Spanish, Japanese	T = 5 min; S = 10 min; I = 20	a = Yes; b = Yes	R = Test–retest .51 Internal consistency coefficient alpha .84; V = concurrent validity moderate .44 between Children's Depression Inventory	Free resource: Georgetown University http://www.brightfutures.org/mentalhealth/pdf/tools.html

TABLE 7.1 (Continued) Matrix: Child and Assessment Strategies and Inventories

Instrument	Specific Family Applications	Cultural/Language	Instructions/Use: T = Time to Take S = Time to Score I = items	Computerized: (a) Scoring (b) Report	Reliability (R) Validity (V)	Availability
Young Mania Rating Scale (YMRS) & Parent Version of the Young Mania Rating Scale (P-YMRS)	Children ages 5–17; clinician, parent, and teacher reports	English, Spanish, and Turkish	T = 15–30 min (YMRS); 5 min (P-YMRS) S = 10 min (YMRS); 5 min (P-YMRS) I = 11	N/A	R = Internal consistency .91 V = Diagnostic efficiency .97	Free resources: http://www.atlantapsychiatry.com/forms/ymrs.pdf http://www.bpkids.org/site/PageServer?pagename = lrn_08_20_03
General Behavior Inventory (GBI) & Parent Version, General Behavior Inventory (P-GBI)	GBI: Children 11 and older P-GBI: Parents of children ages 5–17	English	I = 73	N/A	R = alpha coefficient of .90 V = strong criterion validity & excellent discriminative validity	Free resources: GBI: available by contacting Dr. Richard A. Depue, RAD5@Cornell.edu P-GBI: Available by contacting Dr. Eric A. Youngstrom eay@cwru.edu
Reynold's Child Depression Scale-2 (RCDS-2) and Reynolds Adolescent Depression Scale (RADS-2)	Children ages 8–12; adolescents ages 13–18	RCDS: English & Spanish RADS: English	T = 10–15 min S = 5 min I = 30	N/A	R = Internal consistency .91–.93 Test–retest reliability .87 V = Strong criterion validity of .76	Available for purchase with Psychological Publications (800) 345-8378 or www.tjta.com

ASD/PDD

Name	Population	Languages	Time	a/b	Reliability/Validity	Resource
Modified Checklist for Autism in Toddlers (M-CHAT)	Children 16–30 months old	Available in 27 languages	T = 5–10 min, S = Less than 2 min, I = 23	a = Yes, b = No	R = Internal consistency: Cronbach's alpha .83–.85, V = Validation studies are ongoing	Free resource: http://www2.gsu.edu/~psydlr/DianaLRobins/Official_M-CHAT_Website.html
Childhood Asperger Syndrome Test (CAST)	Children ages 4–11; parent report	English, Spanish, and 12 other languages	T = 5–10 min, S = 5–10 min, I = 38	N/A	N/A	Free resource: http://www.autismresearchcentre.com/tests/cast_test.asp
Autism Treatment Evaluation Checklist (ATEC): Internet Scoring Program	Children ages 5–12; parent and clinician report	English	T = 10–15 min, S = Less than 5 min, I = 77	a = Yes, b = Yes	R = Internal consistency .94	Free resource: http://www.autism.com/ind_atec_survey.asp
Social Communication Questionnaire (SCQ)	Individuals over the age of 4	English, Spanish	T = Less than 10 min, S = Less than 2 min, I = 40	N/A	R = Cronbach alpha .83, Test-retest .76, V = Good cross-cultural validation	Available for purchase: Western Psychological Services www.wpspublish.com
Autism Diagnostic Observation Scale (ADOS)	Toddlers to adults	English and Spanish	T = 30–45 min, S = N/A, I = Varies by module 9–13 activities	a = Yes, b = Yes	N/A	Available for purchase: Western Psychological Services www.wpspublish.com

OCD

TABLE 7.1 (*Continued*) Matrix: Child and Assessment Strategies and Inventories

Instrument	Specific Family Applications	Cultural/ Language	Instructions/Use: T = Time to Take S = Time to Score I = items	Computerized: (a) Scoring (b) Report	Reliability (R) Validity (V)	Availability
Spence Children's Anxiety Scale	Children ages 7–14	English, Chinese, Swedish, Dutch, Norwegian, Catalan, Czech, Portuguese, Italian, Arabic, Greek, German, Japanese, Spanish	T = 5–10 min S = 10 min I = 44	a = Yes b = No	R = IC: .60–.92 TRT = .45–.60	Free Resource: Spence Children's Anxiety Scale www.scaswebsite.com
Children's Yale-Brown Obsessive Compulsive Scale (CY-BOCS) and Yale-Brown Obsessive Compulsive Rating Scale-Second Edition (Y-BOCS-II)	CY-BOCS: Children ages 6–14 Y-BOCS: Adolescents older than 14	English	Y-BOCS-II T = 5–10 min S = 5–10 min I = 10 CY-BOCS Various versions	Y-BOCS II a = Yes b = Yes CY-BOCS a = No b = No	Y-BOCS-II R = Internal consistency .63–.91 Inter-rater reliability .83–.98 Test–retest: .75–.90 V = Convergent and discriminant moderately to strongly correlated CYBOCS	CY-BOCS: Lawrence Scahill, MSN, Ph.D., lawrence.scahill@yale.edu, Child Study Center, 230 South Frontage Road, P.O. Box 207900, New Haven, CT 06520-7900 Y-BOCS-II: Eric Stroch at e-mail estroch@health.usf.edu, phone (727) 767-8293, or via mail at the Department of Pediatrics, University of South Florida, 800 6th Street South, Box 7523, St. Petersburg, FL 33701

LD

Test	Population	Language	Time/Subscales/Items	a/b	R/V	Availability
Children's Nonverbal Learning Disabilities Scale (C-NLD)	Children ages 5–18; parent report	English	T = 5–10 min S = 5 min I = 15	N/A	R = Internal consistency: .87, Intraclass correlations: .66–.91 V = High correlation: .62	Free Resource: http://www.nldontheweb.org/nldentrylevelreading/nldratingscale.html
Wide Range Achievement Test 4 (WRAT4)	Individuals ages 5–94	English	Varies by age T = 15–45 min S = 15 min I = varies by age	N/A	No data	Available for purchase: Psychological Assessment Resources, 16204 N. Florida Avenue, Lutz, FL 33549. Phone 800 899-8378. www.wpspublish.com
Peabody Individual Achievement Test-Revised (PIAT-R/NU)	Children ages 5–18; adults 18–22 years old	English	T = 60 min I = 482 (including subsets) S = N/A	a = Yes b = Yes	R = .78–.89 test–retest reliability .87–.86 internal consistency reliability V = N/A	Available for purchase: Pearson Clinical Assessment, 19500 Bulverde Road, San Antonio, TX 78259-3701. Phone (800) 627-7271 Clincialcustomersupport@pearson.com

REFERENCES

Ambrosini, P.J. (2000) Historical development and present status of the schedule for affective disorders and schizophrenia for school-age children. *Journal of the American Academy of Child & Adolescent Psychiatry, 29*, 49–58.

American Academy of Pediatrics, Subcommittee on ADHD and Committee on Quality Improvement. (2001). Clinical practice guideline: Treatment of the school-aged child with attention-deficit/hyperactivity disorder. *Pediatrics, 108*, 1033–1044.

American Psychiatric Association. (2000). *Diagnostic and statistical manual of mental disorders* (4th ed., text revision). Washington, DC: Author.

Autism Research Institute. (2005). Autism Treatment Evaluation Checklist ATEC Report. Retrieved from http://www.autism.com/ind_atec_report.asp

Birmaher, B., Axelson, D., Strober, M., Gill, M. K., Valeri, S., Chiappetta, L., et al. (2006). Clinical course of children and adolescents with bipolar spectrum disorders. *Archive of General Psychiatry, 63*, 175–183.

Birmaher, B., Brent, D. A., & Benson, R. S. (1998). Summary of the practice of parameters for the assessment and treatment of children and adolescents with depressive disorders. *Journal of the American Academy of Child & Adolescent Psychiatry, 37*, 1234–1238.

Bosl, W., Tierney, A., Tager-Flusberg, H., & Nelson, C. (2011). EEG complexity as a biomarker for Autism Spectrum Disorder risk. *BMC Medicine, 9*. doi:10.1186/1741-7015-9-18

Center for Disease Control & Prevention. (2010). Autism spectrum disorders: Data and statistics. Retrieved from http://www.cdc.gov/ncbddd/autism/data.html

Chandler, S., Charman, T., Baird, G., Simonoff, E., Loucas, T., Meldrum, D., et al. (2007). Validation of the social communication questionnaire in a population cohort of children with Autism Spectrum Disorders. *Journal of the American Academy of Child & Adolescent Psychiatry, 47*, 1324–1332.

Collett, B. R., Ohan, J, L., & Myers, K. M. (2003). Ten-year review of rating scales. V: Scales assessing Attention-Deficit/Hyperactivity Disorder. *Journal of the American Academy of Child & Adolescent Psychiatry, 42*, 1015–1037.

Danielson, C. K., Youngstrom, E. A., Findling, R. L., & Calabrese, J. R. (2003). Discriminative validity of the General Behavior Inventory using youth report. *Journal of Abnormal Child Psychology, 31*, 29–39.

Daviss, W. B., Birmaher, B., Melhem, N. A., Axelzon, D. A., Michaels, S. M., & Brent, D. A. (2006). Criterion validity of the Mood and Feelings Questionnaire for depressive episodes in clinic and non-clinic subjects. *Journal of Child Psychology and Psychiatry, 47,* 927–934. doi:10.1111/j.1469-7610.2006.01646.x

Depue, R. A., Slater, J. F., Wolfstetter-Kausch, H., Klein, D. N., Goplerud, E., & Farr, D. A. (1981). A behavioral paradigm for identifying persons at risk for bipolar depressive disorder: A conceptual framework and five validation studies. *Journal of Abnormal Psychology, 90,* 381–437.

Dulcan, M. K. (2010). *Dulcan's textbook of child and adolescent psychiatry.* Arlington, VA: American Psychiatric Publishing.

Faulstich, M. E., Carey, M. P., Ruggiero, L., Enyart, P., Gresham, F. (1986). Assessment of depression in childhood and adolescence: An evaluation of the Center for Epidemiological Studies Depression Scale for Children. *American Journal of Psychiatry, 14,* 1024–1027.

Filipek, P. A., Accardo, P. J., Baranek, G. T., Cook, E. H., Jr., Dawson, G., Gordon, B., et al. (1999). The screening and diagnosis of Autism Spectrum Disorders. *Journal of Autism and Developmental Disorders, 29,* 439–484.

Fitzgerald, M., & Corvin, A. (2001). Diagnosis and differential diagnosis of Asperger syndrome. *Advances in Psychiatric Treatment, 7,* 310–318.

Flament, M. F., Koby, E., Rapoport, J. L., Berg, C. J., Zahn, T., Cox, C., Denckla, M., & Lenane, M. (1990). Childhood obsessive-compulsive disorder: A prospective follow-up study. *Journal of Child Psychology and Psychiatry, 31,* 363–380.

Frazier, T. W., Demeter, C. A., Youngstrom, E. A., Calabrese, J. R., Stansbrey, R. J., NcNamara, R. K., et al. (2007). Evaluation and comparison of psychometric instruments for pediatric bipolar spectrum disorders for four age groups. *Journal of Adolescent and Child Psychopharmacology, 17,* 853–867.

Gracious, B. L., Youngstrom, E. A., Findling, R. L., & Calabrese, J. R. (2002). Discriminative validity of a parent version of the Young Mania Rating Scale. *Journal of the American Academy of Child & Adolescent Psychiatry, 41,* 1350–1359.

Hersen, M., Hilsenroth, M. J., & Segal, D. L. (2004). *Comprehensive handbook of psychological assessment.* Hoboken, NJ: John Wiley & Sons, Inc.

Klein, Dougherty, &Olino (2005). Toward guidelines for evidence-based assessment of depression in children and adolescents. *Journal of Clinical Child and Adolescent Psychology, 34,* 412–432.

Klin, A., Jones, W., Schultz, R., Volkmar, F., & Cohen, D. (2002). Visual fixation patterns during viewing of naturalistic social situations as predictors of social competence in individuals with autism. *Archives of General Psychiatry*, *59*, 809–816.

Lam, R. W., Michalak, E. E., Swinson, R. P. (2005). *Assessment scales in depression, mania and anxiety.* Boca Raton, FL: Taylor & Francis Group.

Levine, M. D., Parker, S., & Zuckerman, B. (1995). *Unpopular children: behavioral and developmental pediatrics: A handbook for primary care.* Boston: Little, Brown.

March, J., & Benton, C. (2007). *Talking back to OCD.* New York: Guilford Press.

March, J., Silva, S., Petrycki, S., Curry, J., Wells, K., Fairbank, J., et al. (2004). Treatment for Adolescents with Depression Study (TADS) team. Fluoxetine, cognitive-behavioral therapy and their combination for adolescents with depression: Treatment for Adolescents with Depression Study (TADS) randomized controlled trial. *Journal of the American Medical Association, 292,* 1231–1242.

Merikangas, K. R., He, J., Burstein, M., Swanson, S. A., Avenevoli, S., Cui, L., et al. (2010). Lifetime prevalence of mental disorders in U.S. adolescents: Results from the National Comorbidity Study-Adolescent Supplement (NCS-A). *Journal of the American Academy of Child & Adolescent Psychiatry, 49,* 980–989.

Miklowitz, D. J., Otto, M. W., Frank, E., Reilly-Harrington, N. A., Wisniewski, S. R., Kogan, J. N., et al. (2007). Psychosocial treatments for bipolar depression: a 1-year randomized trial from the Systematic Treatment Enhancement Program (STEP). *Archive General Psychiatry, 64,* 419–426.

National Institute on Mental Health. (2009). National survey tracks rates of common mental disorders among American youth. Retrieved from http://www. Nimh.nih.gov/science-news/2009/national-survey-tracks-rates-of-common-mental-disorders-among-american-youth.shtml

Ozonoff, S., et al. (2005). Evidence-based assessment of ASD in children and adolescents. *Journal of Child & Adolescent Psychology, 34,* 523–540. doi:10.1207/s15374424jccp3403_8

Pediatric OCD Treatment Study (POTS) Team. (2004). Cognitive-behavior therapy, sertraline, and their combination for children and adolescents with Obsessive-Compulsive Disorder: The Pediatric OCD Treatment Study (POTS) randomized controlled trial. *Journal of the American Medical Academy, 292,* 1969–1976.

Reynolds, W. M. & Mazza, J. J. (1998). Reliability and validity of the Reynolds Adolescent Depression Scale with young adolescents. *Journal of School Psychology, 36,* 353–376.

Robins, D. L., & Dumont-Mathieu, T. M. (2006). Early screening for Autism Spectrum Disorders: Update on the Modified Checklist for Autism in Toddlers and other measures. *Developmental and Behavioral Pediatrics, 27,* 111–119. doi:0196-206X/06/2702-0111

Serrano, E., Ezpeleta, L., Alda, J. A., Matali, J. L., & San, L. (2011). Psychometric properties of the YMRS for the identification of mania symptoms in Spanish children and adolescents with Attention Deficit/Hyperactivity Disorder. *Psychopathology, 44,* 125–132. doi:10.1159/000320893

Sorenson, M. J., Thomsen, P. H., & Bilenberg, N. (2007). Parent and child acceptability and staff evaluation of K-SADS-PL, a pilot study. *European Child & Adolescent Psychiatry, 16,* 293–297.

Sprafkin, J., Gadow, K. D., & Nolan, E. E. (2001). The utility of a DSM-IV-referenced screening instrument for Attention-Deficit/Hyperactivity Disorder. *Journal of Emotional and Behavioral Disorders, 9,* 182–191. doi:10.1177/106342660100900304

Weissman, M. M., Orvaschel, H., & Padian, N. (1980). Children's symptom and social functioning self-report scales: Comparison of mother's and children's reports. *Journal of Nervous Mental Disorders, 168,* 736–740.

Weissman, M. M., Wolk, S., Goldstein, R. B., Moreau, D., Adams, P., Greenwald, S., et al. (1999). Depressed adolescents grown up. *Journal of the American Medical Association, 281,* 1701–1713.

Williams, F. S., Allison, C., Bolton, P., Baron-Cohen, S., & Brayne, C. (2005). The CAST (Childhood Asperger Syndrome Test): test accuracy. *Autism.* 45–68.

Wing, L., Gould, J., & Gillberg, C. (2011). Autism Spectrum Disorders in the DSM-V: Better or worse than the DSM-IV? *Research in Developmental Disabilities, 32,* 768–773.

Wolriach, M. L., Lambert, W., Doffing, M. A., Bickman, L., Simmons, T., & Worley, K. (2003). Psychometric properties of the Vanderbilt ADHD Diagnostic Parent Rating Scale in a referred population. *Journal of Pediatric Psychology, 28,* 559–568.

Wood, A., Kroll, L., Moore, A., & Harrington, R. (1995). Properties of the Mood and Feelings Questionnaire in adolescent psychiatric outpatients: A research note. *Journal of Child Psychology and Psychiatry, 36,* 327–334.

Youngstrom, E. A., Findling, R. L., Calabrese, J. R., Gracious, B. L., Demeter, C., Bedoya, D. D., et al. (2004). Comparing the diagnostic accuracy of six potential screening instruments for bipolar disorder in youths aged 5 to 17 years. *Journal of the American Academy of Child & Adolescent Psychiatry, 43,* 847–858. doi:10.1097/01. chi.0000125091.35109.1e

Ysseldyke, J. (2009). When politics trumps science: Generalizations from a career of research on assessment, decision making, and public policy. *Communique, 38,* 6–8.

Zhang, S., Faries, D. E., Vowles, M., & Michelson, D. (2005). ADHD Rating Scale IV: Psychometric properties from a multinational study as a clinician-administered instrument. *International Journal of Methods in Psychiatric Research, 14,* 186–201. doi:10.1002/mpr.7

CHAPTER 8

Parent–Child and Family Assessment Strategy and Inventories

Lynelle C. Yingling

Just as efficient manufacturing requires managers to analyze system process assessment data (Deming, 1993), effective family therapy requires the therapist to analyze family system functioning assessment data (Satir, 1972). As team assessment and team decision making work well in industry, collaborative family assessment and collaborative goal setting work well in family therapy. The foundation for both environments is a systemic perspective. Perhaps systemic assessment can be explained effectively using a metaphor. When a horse trainer assesses the ability of a horse to run a fast race, he does not use a linear assessment technique of simply looking at the horse's feet. He uses a systemic or holistic assessment approach of looking at the horse's feet, muscle tone, joints, bone density, confirmation, lung capacity, heart rate, and so forth, along with the horse's will to run. Most important, he systemically examines how all of these attributes work together or work against each other to produce the overall assessment. Even then, a Seabiscuit can be overlooked if the assessor is not tuned in to the heart. Family systems assessment requires a shift in paradigm to a unique multidimensional dynamic perspective. Functioning congruently in this new paradigm requires letting go of old linear assumptions and trusting one's ability to remain upright while "skating on the ice without holding on to the rail." Thus, the first challenge of family assessment is to "let go of the rail" and experience a new dimension of balance.

Minuchin, Nichols, and Lee (2007) eloquently describe the developmental process of the field of family therapy. The early days of exploring the concept of systemic thinking required observation of family inter-action patterns to understand the problems. Then the focus shifted to techniques to change interaction patterns to solve the problems. The extreme focus on changing family interaction patterns overlooked the power of the individual. Then the focus on the individual overlooked the family systems basics. Now the field is in a developmental opportunity to look at the can of worms (Satir, 1972) constructively, by including many perspectives on understanding how the family dynamics impact the behavior of the individual, how the individual develops resilience to negative change, and how the professional can intervene in a way that facilitates the health of all members of the family system. Minuchin et al. (2007) describe family assessment this way: "The art of assessment is to discover what stands in the way of a family reaching its goals, and joining with them in a vision of how to get from where they are to where they want to be" (p. 9).

The development of the GARF (Yingling, Miller, McDonald, & Galewaler, 1998) was an attempt to be inclusive of different perspectives on observation of family dynamics and define core elements we could all agree on. The goal was then to connect those observations (family assessment variables) with specific behavioral symptoms. This process would then lead to development of intervention techniques based on a broader concept of family systems. Refinement of that effort is evidenced by recent psychometric improvements of assessment models and tools (Denton, Nakonezny, & Burwell, 2010; Olson, 2011). Over several years the FACES instrument has been reviewed and improved. The FACES IV recent validation publication (Olson, 2011) indicates continuous improvement in our understanding of family assessment.

Once the mind-set has changed to seeing the overall system as the client, the family therapist faces several challenges for effective family functioning assessment. Assessment data come from self-report of family members or observational report of an outside professional (therapist or researcher). Self-report data have several limitations:

- Each family member reports his or her unique perspective, which will differ from other members' perspectives. How to blend the perspectives effectively into a valid whole becomes the challenge to the therapist or researcher.
- Putting honest beliefs about family relationships on paper is threatening to some family members' sense of safety in the fam-ily. In a family system trying to hide a serious problem, courage to report the truth is very difficult to muster. Consequently, dis-tortion of the family functioning can occur in self-reports, espe-cially the family systems that most need accurate assessment.

- The victim of an abusive family system may be too young to express verbally and believably what is happening. Metaphorical expression through stories and drawings is open to misinterpretation and yet is often the only information available for courts to use in protecting children.

Observational data from the therapist or research observer is also subject to contamination in the following ways:

- Training is always limited by the personal biases of the instructors. If the instructor has not made the paradigm shift, the systemic thinking process will not be clear to the trainee. The therapist will then be vulnerable to focusing on linear solutions and overlooking the contribution of the system to perpetuating the problem.
- Working with families challenges the therapist's ability to keep clear boundaries by separating the client family's issues from the therapist's own family-of-origin issues. Family functioning biases from the therapist's childhood are difficult to keep filtered out of the client family assessment process.
- New ideas in the professional field often cloud the thinking of the family therapist. The current trend in the psychiatric community to diagnose everyone (even children) as bipolar tends to shape the assessment process as chemically driven. Because psychiatrists have more prestige than do family therapists, the latter are likely to succumb to the pressure of the psychiatrist to define the problem as chemically driven rather than as sustained by family functioning.

Even if the family therapist can accept the limitations of self-report and observational data, the *who*, *what*, and *how* of collecting data are still a challenge. One dilemma consists of deciding which subsystem data represent the "true" family system functioning and whether the information is valid if not all subsystem data are available. Another dilemma in measuring family functioning is determining which variables of family functioning to measure because various theoretical models use different variables. The Global Assessment of Relational Functioning (GARF) in the DSM-IV Appendix (American Psychiatric Association, 1994, pp. 758–759) was developed as a collaborative effort of the primary family assessment researchers of the time (Group for the Advancement of Psychiatry Committee on the Family, 1996). The three global variables agreed on were (a) problem solving, (b) organization, and (c) emotional climate.

Also, many pragmatic challenges to collecting data exist; for example, should family members complete forms at the office before an appointment (privacy is necessary for honest answers and sufficient time for all members to complete), or should the form be mailed out to clients in advance or placed on websites for client access? Should data be collected before the first session and following the last, or periodically throughout therapy (difficult to achieve consistently)?

After collecting self-report data, interpreting it also has challenges:

- Who is included in the family member's definition of family, and how clear is that on the self-report questionnaire?
- How does the therapist or researcher interpret differing scores of family members? How can one come up with a single global score without averaging everyone's scores? Does averaging the scores from various family members' perspectives distort the results?
- At what age can the therapist expect children to read and cognitively understand the questions so that the responses are reliable?
- How does the therapist overcome language barriers to ensure reliable results?

With all the limitations of family assessment data, these data are still important to the family therapist in making intervention decisions. The following sections of this chapter will describe several family systems instruments and models available for assessing clients. Next it describes an assessment strategy for utilizing these instruments with parents and children. Finally, a case example illustrates this strategy in clinical practice.

SELF-REPORT ASSESSMENTS FOR FAMILY MEMBERS AGE 10 AND OLDER

Systemic Assessment of the Family Environment (SAFE)

Instrument name. The Systemic Assessment of the Family Environment is referred to as the SAFE. It was developed by Yingling while teaching, directing a clinic, and supervising dissertation research in a doctoral program. The need for a brief inventory to assess three generational subsystems of the family system using a single instrument for clinical and research purposes prompted the development of the SAFE. The instrument was utilized in two clinic settings and research projects before its publication in 1998 in the *GARF Assessment Sourcebook* (Yingling et al., 1998).

Type of instrument. The SAFE is a self-report paper-and-pencil instrument for all family members age 10 and older.

Variables measured. Organizational structure and interactional processes are measured. These variables were identified as global constructs in family systems theory, which was generally included in other family assessment instruments. At the same time that the SAFE was defined, the GARF (American Psychiatric Association, 1994) was defined by Lyman Wynne's DSM task force as an observational tool using very similar constructs. The two models were then used simultaneously in a doctoral clinic and later in a free-standing family therapy institute by Yingling.

Use and target audience. Scoring flexibility permits the SAFE to be used for families with or without children by separating the completion and scoring of relationship dynamics by family subsystems: A = parent/spouse/partner to parent/spouse/partner; B = parent to child; and C = parent/spouse/partner to grandparent. Directions are clear for couples who have not been married and for stepfamilies. The wording of items is adapted for each of three respondent formats: child, parent, and grandparent.

Multicultural. All three formats (child, parent, and grandparent) have been translated into Spanish by linguist Todd Smith. It has also been translated and published in French (Favez, 2010). The constructs are global enough to be useful in various cultural settings.

Ease and time of administration. The 21-item semantic differential one-page paper-and-pencil instrument requires approximately 5 minutes for most clients to complete, making it very user friendly as a clinic intake tool. Directions are self-explanatory, even for most children.

Scoring procedure. Weighted scores for each blank on the semantic differential line are provided on a separate sheet and can be copied onto a transparency overlay for quick scoring. A paper-and-pencil scoring grid on a separate page creates a plotted outcome for each of the three generational relationships (parent–parent, parent–child, and parent–grandparent), as well as the overall averaged family system. Outcomes fall within one of four quadrants based on the intersection of interactional and organizational scores: competent, discordant, disoriented, or chaotic. Recommended interventions based on family therapy theory are implied by the quadrant results according to subsystem. Competent families may need only an opportunity to tell their story to manage an unusually heavy outside stressor, discordant families need communication skills training, and disoriented families need structural interventions. Chaotic families may need strategic interventions to realign structure before learning to communicate so that they can sustain an effective structure and create a safe environment in which family members can grow.

Reliability. Clinical use of the SAFE indicates highly reliable results with moderate- to low-functioning families who have enough safety to be honest in reporting. Children in low-functioning families do not always have the necessary level of safety.

Validity. One dissertation study (Scoville, 1999) tested the construct validity using Pearson correlations of the SAFE subscales with other accepted subsystem instruments. The SAFE Parent–Child Nuclear Family subscale score had a negative correlation of $r = -.74$ when correlated with the Beavers SFI score (the SFI scoring has higher numbers for lower functioning). Correlation of the SAFE Marital subscale with the ENRICH Marital Satisfaction scores yielded a coefficient of .82. No correlation was evident between the SAFE Family-of-Origin scores and the PAFS. Research on the SAFE is limited, although a variety of research projects around the world using the SAFE are in process.

Availability and source. The instrument and instructions are published in the *GARF Assessment Sourcebook* (Yingling et al., 1998). A more recent development of the stepfamily version is available at www. SystemsMediation.com under "Resources."

Comment. Through 20 years of use in private practice as well as in clinic settings, Yingling and several trainees have found the SAFE a valuable and efficient assessment tool to use with all clients. Some family mediators have found it especially helpful as a screening tool for planning mediation strategy. Initial concern about the need to reverse random items to increase reliability has not been confirmed by clinical observation. Despite the positive items loaded on the left side of the semantic differential scale, persons completing the questionnaire tend to spread out answers appropriately. Marking all responses on the same extreme rating is an immediate indication of untrue responses; the reason for this is then explored in therapy. The completed instrument is extremely efficient because it creates an immediate profile of three levels of the family system. The therapist does not need to score the instrument to see implications for therapeutic intervention. Immediate indications of power struggles in the marriage and contamination from extended family are especially helpful in determining effective therapeutic interventions.

GARF Self-Assessment for Families

Instrument name. The GARF Self-Assessment for Families was developed by Yingling based on the descriptors included in the Global Assessment of Relational Functioning clinical rating observational scale in the DSM-IV Appendix (American Psychiatric Association, 1994; Group for the Advancement of Psychiatry Committee on the Family, 1996; Kaslow, 1996; Yingling et al., 1998). The GARF clinical rating scale was developed by a DSM-IV task force under the leadership of Dr.

Lyman Wynne. A collaborative effort of family assessment researchers in the field produced the GARF, with possible results of calming the "range war" engaged in by the second generation of family therapists.

Type of instrument. This one-page, paper-and-pencil instrument lists all the descriptors included in the observational model of the GARF in the DSM-IV with a requested rating of 1 to 10 for each descriptor. The descriptors are grouped under the three variables with an "other" blank to allow family members to contribute their own thoughts to the family functioning concept. Self-scoring instructions are included on the single page.

Variables measured. The three variables measured by the GARF Self-Assessment are (a) problem solving/interactional skills for making this family work well, (b) the way in which this family is organized and structured, and (c) how members of this family feel about being a part of the family.

Use and target audience. All family members with basic reading and simple math skills (generally age 10 and above) can complete and score the instrument. It can be completed by any family subsystem members available, although more perspectives provide a more accurate picture of the family system. A primary use has been to train therapists in understanding and using the GARF clinical rating model. Dr. Dudley Chewning has developed a version of the GARF for assessing organizational team functioning (see www.SystemsMediation.com).

Multicultural. The instrument is available in English and Spanish at www.systemsmediation.com, as translated by linguist Jordan Smith.

Ease and time of administration. Completing and scoring the instrument generally requires approximately 5 minutes. Therapist plotting of family scores on the profile chart generally requires less than 5 minutes.

Scoring procedure. Simple scoring procedures are included on the one-page instrument. Points under the three variables are totaled and averaged by the family member or the therapist/researcher. A GARF Profile Chart is included on a second page, which plots the averaged scores of each variable for each family member in a comparison chart. This chart is quickly completed by the therapist and shared with family members to evoke discussion of how various members perceive the strengths and weaknesses of family functioning.

Reliability. No published or reported reliability testing is available for the self-report instrument. For data on the GARF clinical rating model, see Chapter 5 of this book; Dausch, Miklowitz, and Richards (1996); Yingling et al. (1998).

Validity. No published or reported validity testing is available for the self-report instrument. Personal use indicates moderate to high clinical utility and validity. For data on the GARF clinical rating model, see Chapter 5 of this book; Dausch et al. (1996); Denton et al. (2010); Wilkins and White (2001); Yingling et al. (1998).

Availability and source. The self-report is available at www.SystemsMediation.com.

Comment. This instrument works well for periodic assessment of family functioning by all family members to help set and measure change goals. Parenting coordinators and court-ordered family therapists find this instrument useful for assessing change in functioning. An unexpected use of the instrument has been to train therapists to become familiar with the GARF clinical rating model.

Family Adaptability and Cohesion Evaluation Scales (FACES IV)

Instrument name. FACES was originally developed in 1978 through the dissertation work of Portner and Bell under the supervision of David Olson at the University of Minnesota. Several revisions have occurred as the instrument has been widely used in family functioning research. FACES II was recommended by the authors as most useful for research purposes and FACES III for clinical use until FACES IV was tested and released in final format in 2008 (Olson, 2008).

Type of instrument. The FACES III is a 42-item, paper-and-pencil self-report instrument. Family members are asked to rate each item using a 5-point Likert scale with 1 (Strongly Disagree), 2 (Generally Disagree), 3 (Undecided), 4 (Generally Agree), and 5 (Strongly Agree).

Variables measured. Family cohesion and adaptability (now identified as flexibility) are the two measured variables. FACES IV has six scales with seven items each. Two balanced scales with higher linear scores reflecting healthy families assess balanced cohesion and balanced flexibility, similar to FACES II. There are four unbalanced scales with two each for cohesion (disengaged and enmeshed) and flexibility (rigid and chaotic) in which higher linear scores are problematic. It is highly recommended that the Family Communication and Family Satisfaction instruments be used with the FACES IV.

Use and target audience. This paper-and-pen instrument can be completed by all family members throughout the life cycle over age 12.

Multicultural. The instrument is available only in English. Questions have been raised about the cultural bias interpretations of the cohesion scale in past versions, although research supports use with Mexican–American families (Olson, Russell, & Sprenkle, 1989).

Ease and time of administration. Family member completion requires approximately 15 minutes. Scoring done by the Excel file should be relatively fast, as the file is set up to enter raw scores directly from the instrument and the computer then calculates the score.

Scoring procedure. Though hand-scoring is possible with the manual guide, an Excel file is available to automate the two types of curvilinear scores possible: dimension scores primarily for clinical work or descriptive research and ratio scores for more sophisticated research only. Dimension scores use a formula to convert raw scores to percentile scores, which are then plotted on a Circumplex model chart or the FACES IV Profile chart. The balanced scores for cohesion and flexibility are adjusted up or down based on the average of the two unbalanced scores for cohesion and for flexibility. The ratio score is created by a formula, which gives a cohesion ratio, flexibility ratio, and total Circumplex ratio score used for research.

Reliability. Internal consistency is reported for each of the six scales: Enmeshed = .77, Disengaged = .87, Balanced Cohesion = .89, Chaotic = .86, Balanced Flexibility = .84, and Rigid = .82 (Olson, 2011).

Validity. Face validity and discriminate validity have been reported as very good in early reports (Olson, 1986). Later research challenges to construct validity (Green, Harris, Forte, & Robinson, 1991) led to a change in scoring of the FACES III from curvilinear to linear and the development and testing of FACES IV (Franklin, Streeter, & Springer, 2001). The available FACES IV studies report that the confirmatory factor analysis of FACES IV with the SFI, FAD, and Family Satisfaction Scale supports the validity of the Balanced Cohesion and the Balanced Flexibility scales, as well as the Unbalanced Disengaged and Chaotic scales. However, the support for the validity of the Rigid and Enmeshed scales was weak (Olson, 2011).

Availability and source. Available from Life Innovations, Inc., c/o FACES IV, P.O. Box 190, Minneapolis, MN 55440-0190; 800-331-1661; cs@facesiv.com; www.facesiv.com.

Comment. Research challenging the long-standing FACES III validity in the early 1990s and a decade of testing FACES IV highlights the difficulty in creating a self-report instrument that accurately captures the dynamics of a family system. One possible outcome is for family therapists to focus on the basics of family functioning, reassessing original assumptions (Green et al., 1991). This challenge to thinking that the journey is complete will hopefully keep family therapists and researchers looking for constant improvement to the family functioning assessment process.

Beavers Self-Report Family Inventory (SFI)

Instrument name. The Self-Report Family Inventory (SFI) was developed by Robert Beavers and Robert Hampson following extensive research with the Beavers Systems Model Clinical Rating Scale on which it is based (Beavers & Hampson, 1990). Intent was to allow clinical constructs to drive the self-report instrument development.

Type of instrument. The 36-item self-report questionnaire uses a Likert scale response from 1 (Yes: Fits Our Family Very Well) to 5 (No: Does Not Fit Our Family). Items 35 and 36 are global ratings of Competence and Style.

Variables measured. The two major constructs of the clinical model are Health/Competence and Style. Attempts at measuring style reliably in self-report format have not been very successful; the Cohesion scale is used as an estimate of style. Primary factors measured in the SFI are Health/Competence as a global score and Conflict, Leadership, and Emotional Expressiveness as subscores.

Use and target audience. All family members age 11 and older complete the questionnaire.

Multicultural. Research using the clinical rating scale with Caucasian, African–American, and Mexican–American families indicates some style differences but no significant differences based on ethnicity (Hampson, Beavers, & Hulgus, 1990). The SFI is available in Spanish, Italian, German, Rumanian, San Carlos Spanish, Japanese, Chinese, Greek, Portuguese, and French, as well as English.

Ease and time of administration. Instructions are straightforward and require approximately 10 to 15 minutes to complete. An inexperienced rater will likely require 10 to 15 minutes for scoring each instrument.

Scoring procedure. Scoring is rather complex, with reversed numbers using mathematical formulas to obtain individualized item scores. A scoring grid is provided, along with a chart for equating the self-report score to the observational score. The score for Competence can then be plotted with the Style score on the "pair of pants" graph, which divides competence into a 10-point continuum with five categories: severely dysfunctional, borderline, midrange, adequate, and optimal.

Reliability. Reported Cronbach's alphas are between .84 and .93, with test–retest reliabilities of .85 or better.

Validity. Validity is supported by canonical correlations of .62 or better on the SFI and clinical rating of Competence (Hampson, Prince, & Beavers, 1999), as well as high correlations of .77 to .92 with factors in the FAD and FACES III instruments.

Availability and source. The SFI is published in the book *Successful Families: Assessment and Intervention* (Beavers & Hampson, 1990) and is printed in Walsh (2003). The SFI manual and scales are available from Robert B. Hampson, Ph.D., Psychology Department, P.O. Box 0442, Southern Methodist University, Dallas, TX 75275-0442;

rhampson@smu.edu. Use of the SFI is available without charge in exchange for a copy of the final study results.

Comment. The clinically based foundation for the SFI has the advantage of leading directly to clinical interventions for the highly trained and experienced family therapist. However, the scoring and theoretical interpretations are challenging for inexperienced clinicians and require specialized training.

McMaster Family Assessment Device (FAD)

Instrument name. The FAD developed from ongoing work on the clinical McMaster Model of Family Functioning (Epstein, Bishop, & Levin, 1978), and was first published in its current form in 1983 (Epstein, Baldwin, & Bishop, 1983). Development of the model continued at McGill University for a decade before moving to McMaster University in the late 1970s; in the 1980s, it moved to the Brown University Family Research Program. Beginning with an all-inclusive approach to item development with elimination of what did not support psychometric properties, the lack of theoretical foundation and supporting research have been criticized (L'Abate & Bagarozzi, 1993). A 1990 updated research report (Kabacoff, Miller, Bishop, Epstein, & Keitner, 1990) addressed some of the criticisms by providing a comprehensive report of data. For more recent challenges to the validity of the instrument in measuring proposed constructs with the current scoring, see Ridenour, Daley, and Reich (1999, 2000); Miller, Ryan, Keitner, Bishop, and Epstein (2000).

Type of instrument. The 60-item paper-and-pencil questionnaire is to be completed by all family members age 12 and above. Responses are on a 4-point Likert scale from Strongly Agree, Agree, and Disagree to Strongly Disagree.

Variables measured. The FAD includes a general functioning scale for Overall Health Pathology and six dimensional scales: Problem Solving, Communication, Roles, Affective Responsiveness, Affective Involvement, and Behavior Control. The scales are detailed in Walsh (2003). Ridenour and colleagues' (2000) construct validity challenge proposes that the FAD actually measures two constructs: Collaboration and Commitment. These two constructs appear to be similar to the SAFE and GARF constructs of Interactional Processes and Organizational Structure.

Use and target audience. The FAD was designed as a clinical screening tool for family functioning. The intent was "to identify problem areas in the most simple and efficient fashion possible" (Epstein et al., 1983, p. 171).

Multicultural. The FAD has been used in many countries and has versions in at least 16 different languages, including Afrikaans, Chinese, Croatian, Danish, Dutch, French, Greek, Hebrew, Hungarian, Italian, Japanese, Portuguese, Russian, Swedish, and Spanish.

Ease and time of administration. The questionnaire takes approximately 15 to 20 minutes to complete. Scoring for each questionnaire requires approximately 15 minutes.

Scoring procedure. A separate two-page scoring sheet that converts negative items and groups responses into the seven scales is provided. Scales are first summed and then divided by the number of completed answers in that scale to obtain an averaged score for each scale. Computerized scoring is available.

Reliability. Six of the seven scales have reported internal reliability correlations above .70. The Roles scale has a reported alpha of .69 in psychiatric and medical samples but a lower .57 correlation in non-clinical samples. Consequently, use of the Roles scale in non-clinical samples is questionable (Kabacoff et al., 1990).

Validity. Factor analyses results seem comparable to other similar instruments in accounting for variance. The General Functioning scale was reported as highly correlated with other items, supporting it as a single index of family functioning (Kabacoff et al., 1990).

Availability and source. A detailed description of the model is published in Walsh (2003). Comprehensive information is available in *Evaluating and Treating Families: The McMaster Approach* (Ryan et al., 2005).

Comment. The McMaster model authors contend that two basic findings from the original 1969 study are still valid: (a) family functioning variables (organizational, structural, and transactional patterns) are more powerful than intrapsychic variables in determining family member behavior; and (b) emotional health of a child is closely related to the emotional relationship between the child's parents (Walsh, 2003). Keeping these two principles in mind will be helpful as family therapy professionals continue to evolve the self-report family assessment process into clinically useful resources, as well as reliable research instruments.

SELF-REPORT ASSESSMENTS FOR FAMILY MEMBERS UNDER AGE 10

Self-report family assessment instruments provide family members a way to communicate how the family system is working for them when they may not be able to conceptualize and verbally communicate that information directly and quickly to the family therapist. Developing reliable and valid instruments is quite a challenge, as indicated from the development of the preceding instruments. However, those described instruments are designed for children approximately age 10 and above. How does a therapist hear the voice of the child younger than age 10? The younger the child is, the more the child functions on an intuitive metaphorical level. Consequently, instruments for children must be based on their communication styles.

SAFE Cartoons

Instrument name. The SAFE Cartoons instrument was adapted from the Systemic Assessment of the Family Environment (SAFE), described earlier.

Type of instrument. This single-page set of four cartoons is flexibly used with verbal instructions to children.

Variables measured. The assessment tool uses four cartoon drawings of family interactions involving parents and children but omitting grandparents: (a) father, mother, brother, and sister all holding hands and smiling with the children connected between the parents; (b) father and mother fighting with brother and sister watching helplessly; (c) mother, father, sister, and brother smiling (sister and brother are much larger in size than mother and father); and (d) mother and father watching helplessly as brother and sister fight while standing in front of the parents. These four pictures equate to the competent, discordant, disoriented, and chaotic quadrants in the scoring grid of the SAFE instrument.

Use and target audience. The SAFE Cartoons were developed for use with children age 10 and under to elicit communication about stressors in family functioning that are affecting the child.

Multicultural. The cartoons used are generic as to skin color, although specific racial characteristics have not been developed to relate to various cultures. Conversation with the child can be adjusted to account for cultural factors.

Ease and time of administration. This can be less than 5 minutes or expanded to the extent to which the child will continue to describe family functioning.

Scoring procedure. Children are handed a copy of the cartoon page and asked to tell the therapist which picture reminds them most of their family and why. If only one cartoon is selected, the therapist may ask if the family ever looks like any other of the cartoons and, if so, when. Comments from the child are recorded on the sheet by the therapist for the case file.

Reliability. This is not available.

Validity. This is not available.

Availability and source. The cartoon drawings are available in the *GARF Assessment Sourcebook* (Yingling et al., 1998) and www. SystemsMediation.com.

Comment. This tool has proven valuable in eliciting information about family functioning. Children will often comment that children are or are not bigger than the parents in this family (disoriented family). They will also talk about the parents fighting and how helpless they feel (discordant family). Insisting that the family is always the competent cartoon is a clue that something may be hidden in this family, resulting in the children feeling unsafe to be truthful.

GARF Self-Report for Families

Instrument name. The GARF Self-Report for Families was developed by Dr. Alice McDonald.

Type of instrument. Selection of the most representative fairy tale provides a "quantitative" global rating similar to that of the GARF. However, the instrument is used primarily to elicit discussion about stressors and strengths in the family from the child's perspective.

Variables measured. Five brief descriptions of somewhat modified but familiar fairy tales are printed: (a) The Three Bears, (b) Little Red Riding Hood, (c) Cinderella, (d) Hansel and Gretel, and (e) The Ugly Duckling. Descriptions are written to parallel the descriptors of the five levels of the GARF.

Use and target audience. Children ages 8 to 12 make up the targeted group, depending on reading level.

Multicultural. The fairy tales used are rather universal, although the language available at this time is limited to English.

Ease and time of administration. Depending on the reading level, the child will likely take 10 to 15 minutes to read through the fairy tales. Discussion time with the therapist varies.

Scoring procedure. Directions are for children to read through each story and decide which fairy tale is most like the family they live in right now; the selected story equates to one of the five quintiles in the GARF. If children are too young to read, the story can be read to them. To gain more specific information from older children who read well, the therapist can ask children to underline any descriptors in any of the five stories that remind them of their family.

Reliability. This is not available.

Validity. This is not available.

Availability and source. The instrument is available in the *GARF Assessment Sourcebook* (Yingling et al., 1998) and at www. SystemsMediation.com.

Comment. The underlined characteristics provide a great opportunity to discuss with the therapist their family problems on a metaphorical fairy tale level which feels safer for the child.

Kinetic Family Drawing Test

Instrument name. The Kinetic Family Drawing Test (KFD).

Type of instrument. This is a projective drawing measure of family functioning.

Use and target audience. This instrument is used primarily with children and adolescents, although all family members can participate.

Multicultural. The KFD has no cultural limits.

Ease and time of administration. Completion of the drawing generally requires less than 20 minutes.

Scoring procedure. The projective technique has very subjective interpretations and is perhaps more useful as a clinical tool to talk about feelings in the picture.

Reliability. Interscorer agreement is reported as .87 to .95.

Validity. Low and variable reports exist.

Availability and source. This instrument is distributed by Western Psychological Services, Inc.

Comment. The KFD (see Chapter 3 for a full description) has been used to provide the greatest control of the child in communicating family functioning, although interpretation is subjectively controlled by the therapist or researcher.

Family Genogram

Over the years the genogram has proved its value in assessing family dynamics. The detailed description and illustration of the genogram is provided in Chapter 2. Because of its value in elucidating parent–child dynamics, it is briefly reviewed here.

Instrument name. Bowen's model of transgenerational family therapy gave rise to the use of the genogram. McGoldrick developed functional guidelines for using the genogram, and Gerson developed the computerized software for drawing and labeling (McGoldrick & Gerson, 1985). DeMaria, Weeks, and Hof (1999) have expanded specific techniques.

Type of instrument. This is a graphic resource for collecting and interpreting three-generational family functioning information.

Variables measured. Basic family structure information is recorded for at least three generations: birth dates, marriages, divorces, children born/adopted, deaths, close/distant/conflictual/cut-off relationships, addictive and abusive patterns, and educational/career expectations. Asking individual family members with whom among those listed on the genogram they talk identifies resources to help solve problems as well as communication barriers within the nuclear family.

Use and target audience. The genogram can be flexibly used to assess historically any issue identified as a focus for therapy.

Multicultural. Cultural themes are especially well suited to explore with the genogram.

Ease and time of administration. Time varies, depending on number and extent of themes explored.

Scoring procedure. This author always writes the genogram on an easel so that family members see the data and can collaboratively define healthy or unhealthy patterns. The genogram page is stored in the client file and put in sight for each following therapy session.

Reliability. This is not available.

Validity. This is not available.

Availability and source. Guidelines are available in McGoldrick and Gerson (1985) and DeMaria et al. (1999).

Comment. The genogram visually helps ensure family connection and objectify data, providing a safer environment for the family to talk about problems or recognition of the need for change in the system. Genogram expansion can also be used as an assignment outside therapy for exploring patterns of interaction and identifying resources for problem solving.

CONSIDERATIONS IN UTILIZING FAMILY ASSESSMENT INSTRUMENTS

Psychotherapy incorporates a broad spectrum of theories from which to choose. Effective family assessment requires a full commitment to family systems theory and, even within this theory, many different viewpoints abound. Because theory is the continuing thread from assessment, hypothesis formulation, and revising intervention planning–implementation, a clear understanding of one's theoretical foundation is critical for good results. Instruments discussed in this chapter are based on family systems theories that generally include assumptions about functional family structure (parental hierarchy, egalitarian marital relationships, and differentiated adult–adult family-of-origin relationships); effective communication (honest and open disclosure, listening and understanding, and effective problem solving); and a general environment of safety and support, which nurtures individual development within the family.

Working Out Logistics of Collecting Information

The setting for therapy defines some parameters for family assessment. Operating in a clinic with plenty of waiting room and administrative staff allows for incorporating a wider array of assessment strategies; family members need private space to answer paper-and-pencil questionnaires honestly. Having a therapy team behind the mirror also expands opportunities for using clinical rating scales, perhaps reducing the number of self-report instruments needed. Working in a training facility is a "resort" setting that includes clinic space and administration, therapy teams, live and group supervision, and a research focus. Family assessment is and should be a major component of family therapy training facilities. The budget for operating a facility can limit the use of purchased instruments. However, all instruments discussed in this chapter are available at minimal or no cost except for duplication of materials and purchase of books or manuals to use in interpretation. Creating a computerized record-keeping system with research analysis of family assessment data is a great asset in improving services. However, a solo practitioner can benefit from incorporating at least some of the instruments and strategies discussed in this chapter as part of the intake process.

Confidentiality Complications for Release of Information

When a therapist is working with families involved in the court process, the therapist's clinical files sometimes become the target of subpoena. Without a release of information signed by all adult family members, the therapist must have a court order, statutory authorization, or threat of safety in compliance with state laws to release family information in the file. Protection of children's records is more unclear. Divorced parents have access to therapy records of their children unless prohibited by court order. Therapists can resist release of records, based on threat of harm, but the process is legally complicated. Collaborative work between family therapy and family law professional organizations is needed to clarify and protect family therapy files legally (including family assessment documents) while allowing disclosure when a threat of family (including spousal) violence exists. Greater understanding of HIPAA regulations will help clarify which documents are included in therapy records versus notes and which confidentiality procedures apply.

STRATEGY FOR UTILIZING FAMILY
SELF-REPORT INSTRUMENTS

Requesting clients to complete assessment instruments without a clear use in therapy or specifically authorized research is unethical. Consequently, assessment instruments must be brief and clinically useful. In a training facility, assessment data are especially useful in supervision to connect the theoretical base in assessment and intervention. In independent practice, assessment data should be utilized in creating treatment plans and should be shared with family members.

A suggested protocol for utilizing family assessment in the course of therapy includes these steps:

1. The family therapist should plan an intake procedure that includes some standardized method of self-report family functioning (this author uses the SAFE) and an assessment of family violence (a brief violence scale, clinical observations, or both).
2. With Internet resources, the family therapist can post all the intake forms on his or her website for clients to download, think through carefully, complete on their schedule and in privacy, and bring to the office at the first meeting. Information can also be returned to the family therapist in advance of the first meeting. Assessment becomes intervention as it frames the thinking of the clients before they ever see the family therapist.
3. Clients must first provide the family therapist with a written informed consent before turning in any written family functioning assessments.
4. Assessment continues throughout therapy, with regular documentation of family functioning in the GARF completed by the therapist.
5. Dynamic assessment guides the therapy process by the therapist's using clinical observations, the family genogram, and children's instruments to plan interventions and share data for goal setting with the client family.

CASE EXAMPLE

The following family story illustrates how family assessment tools can guide the process of therapy to a successful improvement in family functioning.

This family was referred to the author's office to help resolve parental access conflicts blocking the finalization of divorce, which had been ongoing for 2 years; this was the second time the parents had separated and filed for divorce. The mother was now requesting supervised access for the father to the 6-year-old son, with accusations of family violence. (This was investigated and found to be unfounded during the second divorce filing; the father had no attorney on the first filing charges, and the mother obtained a protective order against him. She had set him up to violate the order and then charged him with violation, resulting in his being on probation.)

During the first attempt at divorce, a social study had been conducted that recommended joint managing conservatorship (custody), with the father establishing primary residence because of the mother's history of psychological disturbance. The mother had revealed to the father that she was molested by her father, but had never been in therapy to resolve the trauma. She was completing her Master's degree in counseling when ordered into the program. The father admitted that he had historically had a problem with alcohol and was currently living with his parents because of financial difficulties resulting from the alcohol problems. The social study on the second divorce filing was almost finished when they came into therapy.

Family Assessment Process

The consent forms (Step 3), SAFE (Step 3), and a family violence abbreviated questionnaire based on the Conflict Tactics Scale (Step 3) were completed from Internet access (Step 2) before the first therapy session and brought to the first session. During the first session, the SAFE cartoons (Step 5) were discussed with the son in a private interview. The genogram (Step 5) was used during the first session with all three family members present. In addition to structural information, family-of-origin rules about divorce and conflict management were identified on the genogram. The son added his own family drawings on the bottom of the easel page, including parents, grandparents, and two of his mother's children from a prior marriage who did not have primary residence with her. At the conclusion of the session, the therapist assigned the GARF score on the GARF Profile Chart (Step 4). Observational data were revealed during the session and by outside faxes.

Assessment Results and Utility

Because of the history of domestic violence charges, screening for family violence was the first goal of assessment (Step 1). The family violence questionnaire showed very consistent reporting from both parents: significant physical conflict had occurred during their living together, with each accusing the other of being the primary perpetrator; however, the physical assaults had stopped since the separation 2 years ago. The SAFE final item under the marital relationship assessment provided more confidence in safety (Step 5). The father reported extreme control and submission in the relationship, but the mother reported a neutral response. If the accused abuser had reported "both work together equally" and the supposed victim had reported "one controls and the other submits," the therapist would have been more inclined to investigate safety further.

Surprisingly, the mother scored the marital relationship midrange on all items of the semantic differential. The father scored the marital relationship on the low side, with one exception to the lowest score. Both scored the relationship between themselves and the son as somewhat positive but not perfect, although the mother indicated more power struggles than did the father. The father scored his relationship with his own parents as generally good; the mother scored her relationship with her parents as generally bad. It appeared that the mother perceived the relationship with the father as better than the relationship with her parents, despite how bad the marriage was. The son's first response to the SAFE cartoon was to select the competent family as his family. Later he reported that his parents did sometimes fight like the discordant family.

The genogram (Step 5) revealed that the mother had a prior marriage in which two children had chosen to live with their father and see her infrequently. Although molestation was not revealed in the joint session, the mother indicated that conflict was handled by her mother submitting to her father's controlling behavior. The father's family-of-origin family resolved conflicts by talking things through, although his father traveled extensively; his mother, the primary caretaker, did not work outside the home.

Clinical observation (Step 5) was very revealing in this family. The mother had said that she could not be in the same room with the father, but attorneys did not back that up. She seemed quite comfortable in the same room but insisted that she leave the office first and be given at least 5 minutes before the father left. This action appeared to be more of an attempt to convince the therapist of safety fears than actual fears for safety. Outside the sessions, the mother repeatedly faxed accusations of the father physically abusing the son and her calling Child Protective Services (CPS) (i.e., the son had a bruise on his knee after spending the weekend with his father, or the son said he bumped the end of the bed when getting up to go to the bathroom, assuring his mother that his father was neglectful). The son's reaction with both parents in the room was obvious anxiety and no talking at all. After his private interview with the therapist, he was able to share openly with his parents that he needed for them to stop fighting, be best friends, give him sweet dreams, and not let him watch scary movies.

At the conclusion of each of the six sessions with this family, the therapist recorded the GARF scores (Step 4). Scores progressed as follows:

- Interactional changed from 20 at the first session and 25 at the third session a month later to 30 at the final session 6 weeks later.
- Organizational changed from 30 at the first session and 35 at the third session to 40 at the final session.
- Emotional Climate changed from 10 at the first session and 30 at the third session to 35 at the final session.
- The son's openness with the parents seemed to have a big impact on them. Although many contaminations kept the functioning level low, the emotional climate did seem to level out with the organization and interaction functioning.

Outcome for the Family

Although family functioning remained low, the parents were able to reach significant agreements in the later sessions, which relieved some of mother's anxiety regarding an abusive father. Guidelines for ensuring no drinking or illegal drugs when either parent was with the child were agreed to. Parenting guidelines regarding bedtime, parental exchange, and mutual support of the son's activities helped structure this family for more effective divorced co-parenting. Parents worked out a plan for the father to take possession of his personal property, which had been stored in the mother's house for 2 years and had possibly been stolen during a burglary. This concrete action seemed to free them up to move forward with the divorce. Further litigation was avoided and both parents believed that their son could have "sweet dreams."

CONCLUDING NOTE

Formalized self-report family assessment has developed over the past generation. The current "young adult" phase seems focused on proving or disproving theory—challenging the parent generation's knowledge and needing to contribute something new. The challenge will hopefully lead toward greater understanding in the long run. However, the challenge to the FACES instrument has taken over a decade to be somewhat resolved. Similar challenges are now facing the FAD. Hopefully this debate will

TABLE 8.1   Matrix: Parent–Child and Family Assessment Strategies and Inventories

Assessment Instrument	Specific Couple and Family Applications	Cultural/ Language	Instructions/Use: T = Time to Take S = Time to Score I = Items (# of)	Computerized: (a) Scoring (b) Report	Reliability (R) Validity (V)	Availability
Systemic Assessment of the Family Environment (SAFE)	All family members age 10 and older; provides four typologies of systemic functioning: competent, discordant, disoriented, chaotic	English, Spanish, French	T = 5 min S = 5 min or less I = 21	N/A	R = N/A V = .74 & .82	Yingling et al., *GARF Assessment Sourcebook*; www.SystemsMediation.com
GARF Self-Assessment for Families	All family members age 10 and older; provides scores in three variables: organizational structure, interactional processes, and emotional climate	English, Spanish	T = 5 min S = 5 min I = 16	N/A	R = N/A V = N/A	www.SystemsMediation.com
Family Adaptability and Cohesion Evaluation Scales (FACES-IV)	All family members age 12 and older; provides scores in two variables: cohesion and adaptability; six scales with two balanced and four unbalanced	English	T = 15 min S = 15 min or less if using Excel scoring file I = 42	N/A	R = .77, .87, .89, .86, .84, & .82 internal consistency of scales V = Four scales highly supported and two weak scales	Manual available from Life Innovations, Inc., c/o FACES IV, P.O. Box 190, Minneapolis, MN 55440-0190; 800-331-1661; cs@facesiv.com; www.facesiv.com

Beavers Self-Report Family Inventory (SFI)	All family members ages 11 and older; provides scores in two variables: health/competence overall and style with three subscales	English, Spanish, Italian, German, Rumanian, San Carlos Spanish, Japanese, Chinese, Greek, Portuguese & French	T = 10–15 min S = 10–15 min I = 36	N/A	R = .84 & .93 internal consistency; .85 test-retest V = .62	Robert B. Hampson, Ph.D., Psychology Dept., P.O. Box 0442, Southern Methodist University, Dallas, Texas 75275-0442; rhampson@smu.edu. Use of the SFI is available without charge in exchange for a copy of the final study results.
McMaster Family Assessment Device (FAD)	All family members age 12 and older; provides scores in seven variables: general functioning plus problem solving, communication, roles, affective responsiveness, affective involvement, and behavior control	English + 15 other languages completed with others in process	T = 15–20 min S = 15 min I = 60	a = Scoring available b = Printout of scores with subscales	R = .57–.70 internal consistency V = N/A	Ryan et al., *Evaluating and Treating Families: The McMaster Approach* (comprehensive guide)
GARF Self-Report for Families	Children ages 8–12 if adequate reading level; provides a global rating in one of five functioning quintiles	English	T = 10–15 min S = N/A I = 5	N/A	N/A	Yingling et al., *GARF Assessment Sourcebook*; www. SystemsMediation. com

TABLE 8.1 (*Continued*) Matrix: Parent–Child and Family Assessment Strategies and Inventories

Assessment Instrument	Specific Couple and Family Applications	Cultural/ Language	Instructions/Use: T = Time to Take S = Time to Score I = Items (# of)	Computerized: (a) Scoring (b) Report	Reliability (R) Validity (V)	Availability
SAFE Cartoons	Children age 10 and younger; provides a global rating in one of four typologies	Administer in any language	T = 5 min or less S = N/A I = 4	N/A	N/A	Yingling et al., *GARF Assessment Sourcebook*; www. SystemsMediation. com
Family Genogram	All members; structural and interactional data	Administer in any language	T = 10–30 min S = N/A I = N/A	N/A	N/A	McGoldrick, M., & Gerson, R., *Genograms in Family Assessment*; DeMaria, R., Weeks, G., & Hof, L., *Focused Genograms*
Kinetic Family Drawing (KFD)	Self-report/ children, adolescents, and parents; to assess family relationships and interaction	Administer in any language	T = 20 min S = Variable time to score/ interpret I = N/A	N/A	R = .87–.95 interscorer agreement V = Not reported	Journal article; Western Psychological Services

not take so long to find the good in the challenge. (See Franklin, Cody, & Jordan, 2003, for an excellent review of family assessment instrument research issues.) Perhaps the real benefit of using self-report family assessment instruments is in reframing the family members' thinking from linear to systemic before therapy begins.

Chewning (2001) suggests that effectively researching systemic change in family therapy may require a change in research procedures. Traditional statistical techniques need to be enhanced by using statistical process control (SPC) techniques used in industry (Wheeler & Chambers, 1992). Control charts are used to determine whether a system is stable before a measurement of change can be valid based on the normal variation range of the system. How much chaos can a family system experience—and how often—in order to continue to be a successful people making operation? The principles of systemic assessment are the same in any setting. Perhaps future research in family assessment can incorporate what industry statisticians have learned to improve the process.

REFERENCES

American Psychiatric Association. (1994). *Diagnostic and statistical manual of mental disorders* (4th ed.). Washington, DC: Author.

Beavers, W. R., & Hampson, R. B. (1990). *Successful families: Assessment and intervention.* New York: Norton.

Chewning, D. G. (2001). Using data to illustrate systemic improvement. *Journal of the Texas Association for Marriage and Family Therapy, 6,* 57–66.

Dausch, B. M., Miklowitz, D. J., & Richards, J. A. (1996). Global Assessment of Relational Functioning Scale: II. Reliability and validity in a sample of families of bipolar patients. *Family Process, 35,* 175–189.

DeMaria, R., Weeks, G., & Hof, L. (1999). *Focused genograms: Intergenerational assessment of individuals, couples, and families.* Philadelphia: Brunner/Mazel.

Deming, W. E. (1993). *The new economics for industry, government, education.* Cambridge, MA: MIT Center for Advanced Engineering Study.

Denton, W. H., Nakonezny, P. A., & Burwell, S. R. (2010). Reliability and validity of the Global Assessment of Relational Functioning (GARF) in a psychiatric family therapy clinic. *Journal of Marital and Family Therapy, 36*(3), 376–387.

Epstein, N. B., Baldwin, L. M., & Bishop, D. S. (1983). The McMaster Family Assessment Device. *Journal of Marital and Family Therapy, 9*(2), 171–180.

Epstein, N. B., Bishop, D. S., & Levin, S. (1978). The McMaster Model of Family Functioning. *Journal of Marriage and Family Counseling, 4*, 19–31.

Favez, N. (2010). *L'examen clinique de la famille: Modèles et instruments d'évaluation* [Clinical examination of the family: Models and assessment tools]. Wavre, Belgium: Editions Mardaga. www.mardaga.be

Franklin, C., Cody, P. A., & Jordan, C. (2003). Validity and reliability in family assessment. In A. Roberts & K. Yeager (Eds.), *Desk reference of evidence-based research in health care and human services.* New York: Oxford University Press.

Franklin, C., Streeter, C. L., & Springer, D. W. (2001). Validity of the FACES IV family assessment measure. *Research on Social Work Practice, 11*(5), 576–596.

Green, R. G., Harris, R. N., Jr., Forte, J. A., & Robinson, M. (1991). The wives data and FACES IV: Making things appear simple. *Family Process, 30*, 79–83.

Group for the Advancement of Psychiatry Committee on the Family. (1996). Global assessment of relational functioning scale (GARF): I. Background and rationale. *Family Process, 35*, 155–172.

Hampson, R. B., & Beavers, W. R. (1996). Measuring family therapy outcome in a clinical setting: Families that do better or do worse in therapy. *Family Process, 35*, 347–361.

Hampson, R. B., Beavers, W. R., & Hulgus, Y. (1990). Cross-ethnic family differences: Interactional assessment of white, black, and Mexican–American families. *Journal of Marital and Family Therapy, 16*(3), 307–319.

Hampson, R. B., Prince, C. C., & Beavers, W. R. (1999). Marital therapy: Qualities of couples who fare better or worse in treatment. *Journal of Marital and Family Therapy, 25*(4), 411–424.

Kabacoff, R. I., Miller, I. W., Bishop, D. S., Epstein, N. B., & Keitner, G. I. (1990). A psychometric study of the McMaster Family Assessment Device in psychiatric, medical, and nonclinical samples. *Journal of Family Psychology, 3*, 431–439.

Kaslow, F. W. (Ed.). (1996). *Handbook of relational diagnosis and dysfunctional family patterns.* New York: Wiley.

L'Abate, L., & Bagarozzi, D. A. (1993). *Sourcebook of marriage and family evaluation.* New York: Brunner/Mazel.

McGoldrick, M., & Gerson, R. (1985). *Genograms in family assessment.* New York: Norton.

Miller, I. W., Ryan, C. E., Keitner, G. I., Bishop, D. S., & Epstein, N. A. (2000). Commentary: Factor analyses of the Family Assessment Device by Ridenour, Daley, & Reich. *Family Process, 39*, 141–144.

Minuchin, S., Nichols, M. P., & Lee, W.-Y. (2007). *Assessing families and couples: From symptom to system.* Boston: Pearson Education.

Olson, D. H. (1986). Circumplex model VII: Validation studies and FACES III. *Family Process, 25,* 337–351.

Olson, D. H. (2008). *FACES IV manual.* Minneapolis, MN: Life Innovations.

Olson, D. H. (2011). FACES IV and the Circumplex model: Validation study. *Journal of Marital and Family Therapy, 3*(1), 64–80.

Olson, D. H., Russell, C. S., & Sprenkle, D. H. (Eds.). (1989). *Circumplex model: Systemic assessment and treatment of families.* New York: Haworth Press.

Ridenour, R. A., Daley, J. G., & Reich, W. (1999). Factor analysis of the Family Assessment Device. *Family Process, 38,* 497–510.

Ridenour, R. A., Daley, J. G., & Reich, W. (2000). Further evidence that the Family Assessment Device should be reorganized: Response to Miller and colleagues. *Family Process, 39,* 375–380.

Ryan, C. D., Epstein, N. B., Keitner, G. I., Miller, I. W., & Bishop, D. S. (2005). *Evaluating and treating families: The McMaster approach.* Philadelphia: Brunner-Routledge.

Satir, V. (1972). *Peoplemaking.* Palo Alto, CA: Science and Behavior Books.

Scoville, A. F. (1999). *Obesity and family functioning patterns of the marital, nuclear, and extended family systems.* Unpublished doctoral dissertation, Texas A&M University, Commerce.

Walsh, F. (2003). *Normal family processes* (3rd ed.). New York: Guilford Press.

Wheeler, D. J., & Chambers, D. S. (1992). *Understanding statistical process control* (2nd ed.). Knoxville, TN: SPC Press.

Wilkins, L. P., & White, M. B. (2001). Interrater reliability and concurrent validity of the Global Assessment of Relational Functioning (GARF) scale using a card sort method: A pilot study. *Family Therapy, 28*(3), 157–170.

Yingling, L. C., Miller, W. E., Jr., McDonald, A. L., & Galewaler, S. T. (1998). GARF *assessment sourcebook: Using the DSM-IV Global Assessment of Relational Functioning.* New York: Brunner-Routledge.

CHAPTER **9**

Child Custody and Divorce Assessment Strategy and Inventories

M. Sylvia Fernandez and Sloane E. Veshinski

With the rising rates of divorce, trial and family courts are frequently called on to set guidelines for custody and child visitation in these cases. Research suggests that high levels of parental conflict, diminished parental competence in child management behaviors, and decreased parental effectiveness increase stress in children as well as predict maladjustment (Famularo, Fenton, & Kinscherff, 1993; Jaffe, Wolfe, & Wilson, 1990; McGill, Deutsch, & Zibbell, 1999). Mental health clinicians are often asked to assist the courts in making appropriate decisions. Child custody evaluations are necessary when one or both parents are unable or unwilling to work out the issue of custody between themselves or when there is high conflict between the parents. To this end, clinicians conduct assessments of the family, including administering psychological tests; gather data about parent and child strengths and weaknesses and areas of conflict; and identify family support systems. In making recommendations, the well-being of the child or children is the priority. Clinicians seek to ensure that the child will be placed in an environment in which he or she is and feels safe in the care of the parents while preserving the positive aspects of the parent–child relationship (Garrity & Barris, 1994).

In the past 10–15 years, family courts have had to address changes that have evolved in how we define and view families. The rates of marriage and remarriage have resulted in varying constellations of families, from stepfamilies to blended families. The adult who has primary caregiving responsibility is shifting from biological parent to grandparents for a variety of reasons in some households, thus changing definitions of *parent.* The growing economic challenges of raising children and maintaining a family has strained family relationships which have sometimes resulted in divorce or separation (which often results in divorce). The practice of child custody evaluations has changed in the types of tests used, the revisions of tests, and the development of tests specifically for child custody evaluations (Quinell & Bow, 2001).

This chapter will focus on assessing the post-divorce parental relationship, the child's or children's relationship with each parent, and overall family functioning after divorce. The outcome of testing and assessment will be to make recommendations for child custody and visitation, as well as to determine the parents' ability to work together in the best interest of the child or children. The assessment instruments described here are best used in combination and not as stand-alone instruments because of the limitations of what each is designed to measure. Multiple qualitative and quantitative data sources provide the best information to make appropriate recommendations. The chapter begins by describing common issues and challenges surrounding divorce and custody. Next, it describes several assessment instruments. Then, it provides an assessment for utilizing these measures in clinical practice. Finally, it illustrates this strategy with an extended case example.

ISSUES AND CHALLENGES OF ASSESSING CHILD CUSTODY AND DIVORCE

When a couple with a child or children decides to divorce, subsequent decisions and arrangements have to be made with regard to custody and visitation. In the event of a need to adjudicate these arrangements, psychological tests and assessments are typically administered to determine each parent's mental and emotional health as well as that of the child or children involved. Multiple issues must be considered while attending to the presenting challenges when administering tests and conducting assessments to facilitate custody and visitation recommendations and decisions.

The multiple issues to be considered comprise the family context, family relationships, and family culture. The family context includes family demographics (i.e., the current ages of the children involved), socioeconomic status, and living conditions such as each parent's ability to provide for the child or children. Also, safe and appropriate living arrangements, educational level of parents, and family-of-origin issues such as the involvement of grandparents in the child's or children's lives and available family support systems, need to be considered. Identifying family relationships refers to family status (i.e., blended family, single parent–led family, gay/lesbian parental dyad, or grandparents functioning as parents). Delineating the family culture aids in ascertaining several features, such as individual members' perceptions of the family, identified parental systems (matriarchal or patriarchal), parental and gender roles, parenting styles (authoritative, authoritarian, permissive), and parenting skills.

Presenting challenges to testing and assessment may include the following:

- Presence of domestic violence, whether physical, emotional, sexual, or economic, and who the perpetrator(s) and victim(s) might be
- Presence and type of substance abuse, whether "recreational," daily, binge, or in recovery, and the type of substance abused, such as alcohol or other CNS (central nervous system) depressants, stimulants, hallucinogens, or designer drugs
- Presence of any active court actions, such as restraining orders, dependency actions, or misdemeanor or felony charges
- Motivational issues, that is, who is requesting the testing or assessment, or the effects of assessment outcome on the family constellation, and the win–lose mentality toward the assessment process
- Parental Alienation Syndrome (PAS) or other diagnosed pathologies of either or both parents and/or child or children

Issues for the clinician performing the testing and assessment include adherence to the professional code of ethics with regard to custody evaluations. The American Association for Marriage and Family Therapy (2001) states in its Code of Ethics, Section 3.14,

> To avoid conflicts of interest, marriage and family therapists who treat minors or adults involved in custody or visitation actions may not also perform forensic evaluations for custody, residence, or visitation of the minor. The marriage and family therapist who treats the minor may provide the court or mental health professional performing the evaluation with information about the minor from the marriage and family therapist's perspective as a treating marriage and family therapist, so long as the marriage and family therapist does not violate confidentiality.

> The American Counseling Association (2005) states in its Code of Ethics, Section A.7,

> When a counselor agrees to provide counseling services to two or more persons who have a relationship, the counselor clarifies at the outset which person or persons are clients and the nature of the relationships the counselor will have with each involved person. If it becomes apparent that the counselor may be called upon to perform potentially conflicting roles, the counselor will clarify, adjust, or withdraw from roles appropriately.

Besides keeping distinct the role and function of clinician and of the assessor/evaluator who makes the recommendation regarding custody and visitation, the psychological tests administered must also be used within the guidelines for the test and the assessor/evaluator must have the requisite training and skills to administer the test and interpret the results. Some of the instruments discussed in this chapter can be administered by a non-clinician; however, most require scoring and/or interpretation of the resulting scores by a trained master's-level clinician. It is incumbent on the assessor/evaluator to practice ethically. If an assessment is required of a family in which physical, emotional, or sexual abuse may be present, compounded by substance abuse or mental illness, a general clinician is well advised to refer the family to someone who specializes in this area for this assessment.

INSTRUMENTS

A Comprehensive Custody Evaluation Standard System (ACCESS)

Instrument name. A Comprehensive Custody Evaluation Standard System (ACCESS) developed by Barry Bricklin and Gail Elliot was published in 2002.

Type of instrument. ACCESS, a sequenced evaluation system to assist family courts in determining the primary custodial parent, consists of questionnaires, structured interviews, an observation system, and standardized tests. Two basic measurements used by ACCESS are the Bricklin Perceptual Scales (BPS) and the Perception-of-Relationships Test (PORT), both of which are described later in this section. Before making a final judgment and a custody plan, it is recommended that a Critical Target form be completed. This form is a subjective summary of 40 prescribed sources of information which also provides data for the development of a custody plan. The Custody Evaluation Kit provides three parent self-reports, three structured child interviews, and five structured interviews to be used with teachers, physicians, mental health professionals, and any other informant. The Family Interaction Observation system is used to determine parenting through interactions using games and puzzles.

Use and target audience. This system may be used with children 3 years and older.

Multicultural. Not reported.

Ease and time of administration. The ACCESS is fairly complex and time consuming because of the use of multiple other instruments and a recommendation for cross-validation with additional measures.

Scoring procedure. This is dependent on the combination of tests that are used.

Reliability. Not reported.

Validity. Not reported.

Availability and source. This system is available from Village Publishing.

Comment—using with families. This is a broad system for conducting child custody evaluations. It offers the evaluator a range of instruments that may be used in a variety of combinations. While the system is not psychometrically sound it is a valuable tool for assessment (*Mental Measurements Yearbook*, 2010).

Ackerman-Schoendorf Scales for Parent Evaluation of Custody (ASPECT)

Instrument name. The Ackerman-Schoendorf Scales for Parent Evaluation of Custody (ASPECT), developed by Marc Ackerman and Kathleen Schoendorf, was published in 1992.

Type of instrument. ASPECT evaluates parents' fitness for custody by quantifying characteristics pertinent to effective custodial parenting for the purpose of making custody recommendations (Ackerman, 2005). The ASPECT includes a Parent Questionnaire and unstructured interview to determine a Parental Custody Index (PCI). Comprising 57 open-ended questions, the Parent Questionnaire assesses the parent's psychological and family history; motivations for seeking custody; identification of strengths and weaknesses as a parent of self and the other parent; each parent's ideal custody and visitation arrangements; child-rearing philosophy, caregiving practices, and discipline techniques of each parent; current and future child care arrangements; and sources of regular social contact available to the child. The unstructured interview provides observational data on parent's appearance and expressions of emotion, and it allows for obtaining other information not provided on the questionnaire, such as parent's understanding of the effect of divorce on the child, prior arrests or abuse (physical, sexual, or substance), or indicators of psychopathology. An unstructured interview is also conducted with the child (or children) to ascertain the child's feelings about each parent, the evaluation process, and potential outcomes of the custody dispute. The Short Form has 41 items and may be administered by any mental health clinician.

Use and target audience. This instrument is designed for use with parents engaged in a child custody dispute and should be used as part of a battery of tests.

Multicultural. The normative sample is homogeneous and predominately Euro–American.

Ease and time of administration. Each parent is asked to individually complete a Parent Questionnaire and participate in an unstructured individual interview. Administration time will vary.

Scoring procedure. The ASPECT-PCI yields three scores: Observational, which assesses parent's self-presentation; Social, which assesses suitability of the social environment provided by the parent; and Cognitive-Emotional, which assesses the parent's cognitive and emotional capability to provide effective parenting.

Reliability. Reported internal reliability coefficients range from .50 to .76, and inter-rater reliability coefficients range from .92 to .96.

Validity. Is not yet established.

Availability and source. ASPECT may be obtained from Western Psychological Services and is available in two forms.

Comment—using with families. The ASPECT is an attempt to quantify aspects of parental effectiveness and interpret test results. Used in concert with other tests and sources of information (psychological tests, home visits, court records) ASPECT is a clinical tool that provides multidimensional information to determining and making custody recommendations (*Mental Measurements Yearbook*, 2010). This instrument is not intended for use with non-parent relatives, same-sex couples, cohabitating partners, or grandparents.

Behavior Assessment System for Children (BASC-2)

Instrument name. Behavior Assessment System for Children, Second Edition (BASC-2) was developed by Cecil R. Reynolds and Randy W. Kamphaus in 1992 and revised in 2004.

Type of instrument. BASC-2 is a multimethod, multidimensional system designed to assess behaviors observed by others and self-perceptions of individuals age 2 to 25. The BASC-2 consists of five subtests intended to gather information about children or adolescents from a variety of sources, such as Teacher Rating Scale (TRS), Parent Rating Scale (PRS), Student Observation System (SOS), Self-Report of Personality (SRP), and Structured Developmental History (SDH; Hamilton Fish Institute, 2003). The TRS, PRS, and SRP have strong psychometric properties. The BASC-2 measures both positive/adaptive behaviors and negative/maladaptive behaviors.

Use and target audience. Those completing the instrument are asked to read each statement on the questionnaire and mark the response that best describes how the child has acted over the previous 6 months. This instrument is used to assess individuals between the ages of 2 and 25 for emotional and behavioral disorders and design treatment interventions.

Multicultural. The norming sample included African–American, Asian–American, Euro–American, Hispanic, and Native American children from across the United States. The parent version is also available in Spanish.

Ease and time of administration. The BASC-2's five subtests may be used singly or in any combination. The instrument can be administered individually or in a group and takes about 15 to 35 minutes to complete.

Scoring procedure. The questionnaire has a built-in scoring system: the score is computed by summing up the number of circled items in each row. The total for each scale is found by summing the numbers in each column. The scores are Activities of Daily Living, Adaptability, Adaptive Skills, Aggression, Anger Control, Anxiety, Attention Problems, Attitude to School, Attitude to Teachers, Atypicality, Behavior Symptoms Index, Behavioral Symptoms Index, Bullying, Conduct Problems, Depression, Developmental Social Disorders, Ego Strength, Emotional Self-control, Emotional Symptoms Index, Executive Functioning, Externalizing Problems, Functional Communication, Hyperactivity, Inattention/Hyperactivity Attention Problems, Inattention/Hyperactivity, Internalizing Problems, Interpersonal Relations, Leadership, Learning Problems, Locus of Control, Mania, Negative Emotionality, Personal Adjustment, Relations with Parents, Resiliency, School Problems, Self-esteem, Self-reliance, Sensation Seeking, Sense of Inadequacy, Social Skills, Social Stress, Somatization, Study Skills, Test Anxiety, and Withdrawal. Computer scoring is also available. Although no specialized training is required for administration, individuals need to have at least a master's degree to interpret the results of the questionnaire.

Reliability. Internal consistency ranges between .80 and .95. Test–retest reliability ranges from .64 to .93. Inter-rater reliability ranges from .53 to .77. These range reports are inclusive of all eight versions.

Validity. Criterion validity ranged from .64 to .85. Concurrent validity ranged from .65 to .84.

Availability and source. Pearson offers 11 versions of the instruments, each of which is age specific.

Comment—using with families. The BASC-2 provides a multidimensional view of the child or adolescent from multiple informants using multiple methods. This instrument is most effective with children and adolescents when used as part of an assessment battery with preschool children. The derived information of personality and behavior can lead to educational and therapeutic interventions to facilitate coping with the divorce and/or for working with problems that have arisen as a result of the divorce (*Mental Measurements Yearbook*, 2010).

Bricklin Perceptual Scales (BPS)

Instrument name. Bricklin Perceptual Scales (BPS), developed by Barry Bricklin, was published in 2002.

Type of instrument. BPS is a structured tool designed to assess children's perceptions or emotional comprehension of each parent's actions in situations categorized as Competency, Supportiveness, Follow-up Consistency, and Admirable Character Traits.

Use and target audience. The BPS is designed for children 6 years and older.

Multicultural. Not reported

Ease and time of administration. The BPS is administered verbally to children, and the child rates each parent on 32 parenting functions in category specific situations. It takes about 40 minutes to complete.

Scoring procedure. The responses can be verbal or nonverbal. In response to a question, the child is required to punch through a card through a line that reveals each parent's score on the four categories.

Reliability. These data are not reported.

Validity. These data are not reported.

Availability and source. This tool is available from Village Publishing.

Comment—using with families. This is a tool that should be used only by those with extensive clinical practice and is highly subjective (*Mental Measurements Yearbook*, 2003).

Burks Behavior Rating Scales, Second Edition (BBRS-2)

Instrument name. Burks Behavior Rating Scales, Second Edition (BBRS-2), developed by Harold F. Burks in 1977 and revised in 2006 with Christian Gruber, is designed to measure behavior patterns in children and adolescents.

Type of instrument. The BBRS-2 is a 100-item rating scale designed for use with children or adolescents from 4 to 18 years of age who have been referred for school behavior and adjustment problems. There is a Teacher form and a Parent form.

Use and target audience. A parent or teacher rates on a 5-point Likert scale how often a behavior is seen in the child.

Multicultural. The normative sample was represented by gender, age, ethnicity, and region consistent with the 2005 U.S. Census.

Ease and time of administration. The instrument, written at the fifth-grade reading level, is completed in 15 to 20 minutes individually by raters, teachers, or parents, who have daily contact with the child. It is recommended that interpretations be made by or with a master's-level clinician.

Scoring procedure. The hand or computer scored instrument yields seven scores: Disruptive Behavior, Attention and Impulse Control Problems, Emotional Problems, Social Withdrawal, Ability Deficits, Physical Deficits, and Weak Self-confidence.

Reliability. Internal consistency reliability was reported to range from .84 to .89. Test–retest reliability ranged from .80 to .90. Inter-rater reliability ranged from .69 for parents and .62 for teachers.

Validity. Concurrent validity ranged from .42 to .78 with the Child Behavior Checklist/Teacher's report form, the Behavior Evaluation form, and the Conner's Rating Scales-Revised.

Availability and source. Both versions of the BBRS-2 are available from Western Psychological Services, which grants permission to use the instrument.

Comment—using with families. The BBRS-2 is a useful screening tool for rating behaviors and is age and developmentally specific. This instrument delineates problem behaviors and indicates special needs a child may have at home and/or school that, in turn, provide information for determining appropriate placement with parents(s) who can best meet the child rearing demands (*Mental Measurements Yearbook*, 2010).

Child Behavior Checklist (CBCL)

Instrument name. The Child Behavior Checklist (CBCL), authored by Thomas M. Achenbach and most recently published in 1980 and revised in 1994, is an instrument with 140 Likert-scale items. It is designed to record, in a standardized format, children's competencies and problems as reported by their parents, parent surrogates, or both.

Type of instrument. The items are divided into two sections. Section 1 consists of 20 competency items regarding the child's participation in a variety of activities, peer interaction, and school functioning. Section 2 consists of 120 items on behavior or emotional problems during the preceding 6 months. The CBCL measures aggression, hyperactivity, bullying, conduct problems, defiance, and violence. There are two versions: a 140-item children's version for ages 4 to 18 and a 100-item preschool version for ages 2 to 3. Teacher Report Forms, Youth Self-Reports, Direct Observation Forms, and Semi-structured Clinical Interview for Children are also available (Achenbach & Brown, 1991).

Use and target audience. The CBCL is a tool used by parents or parent surrogates to rate problem behaviors and competencies of children between the ages of 2 and 18. It can also be used to measure behavioral adjustment or a child's change in behavior over time or following a treatment.

Multicultural. The instrument was normed on 1,753 children, including those of African–American, Euro–American, and Hispanic ethnic descent, from 40 states and across socioeconomic levels. The CBCL is also available in Spanish.

Ease and time of administration. This instrument can be self-administered or administered through an interview with parents individually or in a group and takes about 15 minutes to complete. The responses are based on the child's current behavior or the behavior within the preceding 6 months for the children's version and preceding 2 months for the preschool version.

Scoring procedure. The 113 items yield subtests and scores that can be obtained through hand-scoring or computer scoring. There are three competence scales (Activities, Social, and School); a Total Competence scale score; eight Syndrome scales (Aggressive Behavior, Attention Problems, Delinquent Behaviors, Social Problems, Somatic Complaints, Thought Problems, Anxious–Depressed, and Withdrawn); an Internalizing Problem scale score; an Externalizing Problem scale score; and a Total Problem scale score.

Reliability. The reported range of the test–retest reliability is between .95 and 1.00. The reported range of the inter-rater reliability is between .93 and .96, and the reported range of internal consistency is between .78 and .97 (Achenbach, 1991a).

Validity. Criterion validity was assessed and found to be acceptable.

Availability and source. The instrument is available from the Achenbach System of Empirically Based Assessment Research Center for Children, Youth, and Families, which grants permission for use by master's-level clinicians.

Comment—using with families. Instrument completer's responses provide comprehensive descriptions of the child's behavior that clinicians can use to distinguish between typical and disturbed behaviors. Description of the child's emotional and behavioral functioning at home and school post-divorce allows for assessing differences in and level of functioning of the child's coping ability when he or she is with either parent. These data could additionally lead to a referral for therapeutic intervention (*Mental Measurements Yearbook*, 2003).

Child-Rearing Practices Report (CRPR)

Instrument name. The 91-item Child-Rearing Practices Report (CRPR), developed by J. H. Block, is designed to identify child-rearing attitudes and values (Block, 1972).

Type of instrument. The CRPR consists of two forms. The first is for parents to rate the phrases that describe their child-rearing practices. The second form is for adolescents and young adults to rate phrases that describe their parent(s).

Use and target audience. The report may be completed by the parent to describe his or her child-rearing behavior or by the adolescent or young adult child to describe the child-rearing orientations of his or her parents.

Multicultural. This test has been normed for use in Russian, Hungarian, Chinese, and French languages.

Ease and time of administration. The instrument employs a Q-sort technique. The time of completion is approximately 30 to 40 minutes.

Scoring procedure. This 91-item self-report instrument measures a number of constructs, including Control, Control by Anxiety, Control by Guilt, Inconsistency, Investment in the Child, Protectiveness, Supervision, and Enjoyment of the Child.

Reliability. Test–retest reliability scores range from .61 to .71.

Validity. This has not been reported.

Availability and source. Both forms are available from Block.

Comment—using with families. Information gained from the results of this tool can be used to assist families in discussing parenting and child-rearing practices, from the parents' as well as the children's perspectives. Because this test is geared for adolescents and young adult children, testing results can assist parents in re-establishing patterns of parenting as children move into different developmental levels. It can assist adolescents in addressing levels of maturity, independence, and collaboration with their parents with regard to issues such as discipline. For custody and visitation assessment, the CRPR identifies the differences and similarities between parents in their child-rearing attitudes and behavior. The differences become areas for negotiations and/or change in parenting patterns as a result of the alterations in living arrangements and custody. Additionally, recommendations for therapy may also be made based on the information obtained (*Mental Measurements Yearbook*, 2003).

Millon Pre-Adolescent Clinical Inventory (M-PACI)

Instrument name. The 97-item Millon Pre-Adolescent Clinical Inventory (M-PACI), developed by Theodore Millon, Robert Tringone, Carrie Millon, and Seth Grossman and published in 2005, is a multidimensional self-report personality inventory designed to identify, predict, and understand a range of common psychological disorders found in 9- to 12-year-olds.

Type of instrument. The M-PACI is used as an initial evaluation for troubled adolescents to confirm diagnostic hypotheses and in planning individualized treatment programs.

Use and target audience. The M-PACI is used for assessment specifically with troubled adolescents, 9 to 12 years of age.

Multicultural. The representation in the normative sample reasonably approximates the U.S. population in gender and ethnicity.

Ease and time of administration. The true/false items, written at the third-grade level, take approximately 15 to 20 minutes to complete. The inventory can be administered individually or in a group in paper-and-pencil or online format.

Scoring procedure. Three options available for scoring are MICROTEST Q Assessment System software, mail-in scoring, and hand-scoring. The 16 scales of the M-PACI are organized in three categories: (1) Emerging Personality Patterns: Confident, Outgoing, Conforming, Submissive, Inhibited, Unruly, and Unstable; (2) Current clinical signs: Anxiety/Fears, Attention Deficits, Obsessions/Compulsions, Conduct Problems, Disruptive Behaviors, Depressive Moods; and Reality Distortions; and (3) Response validity indicators: Invalidity and Response Negativity. Report formats in profile or interpretive are available.

Reliability. Cronbach's alpha reliabilities presented in the manual ranges from .63 to .84.

Validity. Concurrent validity coefficients range from .65 to .75 with the Behavior Assessment System for Children, Self-Report of Personality, Children's Depression Inventory, and the Revised Children's Manifest Anxiety Scale.

Availability and source. The M-PACI is available in paper-and-pencil format or online from Pearson.

Comment—using with families. The M-PACI is most effective with adolescents experiencing a level of significant problems or concerns so as to determine treatment options. The mental health needs and self-perceptions of a troubled adolescent in the family raises co-parenting issues and the "role" the troubled adolescent plays in the functioning, or lack thereof, of the family (*Mental Measurements Yearbook*, 2010).

Millon Adolescent Clinical Inventory (MACI)

Instrument name. The 160-item Millon Adolescent Clinical Inventory (MACI), developed by Theodore Millon, Carrie Millon, Roger Davis, and Seth Grossman and published in 1993, is a self-report personality inventory designed to assess adolescent personality characteristics, concerns, and clinical syndromes.

Type of instrument. The MACI is used as an initial evaluation of troubled adolescents to confirm diagnostic hypotheses, in planning individualized treatment programs, and in measuring treatment progress.

Use and target audience. The MACI is used for assessment specifically with "disturbed" adolescents, 13 to 19 years of age, in outpatient, inpatient, or residential treatment settings.

Multicultural. The minority representation in the normative samples ranged from 16% to 28%. The audiocassette version of the MACI is available in Spanish.

Ease and time of administration. Through a series of questions, the clinician assesses an adolescent's personality along with self-reported concerns. The true/false items are written at the sixth-grade level; it takes approximately 25 to 30 minutes to complete and can be administered individually or in a group.

Scoring procedure. Four options available for scoring are MICROTEST Q Assessment System software, mail-in scoring, hand-scoring, and optical scan scoring. The MACI has 27 content scales and four response bias scales. The Content scales are 12 Personality Patterns scales (Introversive, Inhibited, Doleful, Submissive, Dramatizing, Egotistic, Unruly, Forceful, Conforming, Oppositional, Self-Demeaning, and Borderline Tendency), 8 Expressed Concerns scales (Identity Diffusion, Self-Devaluation, Body Disapproval, Sexual Discomfort, Peer Insecurity, Social Insensitivity, Family Discord, and Childhood Abuse), and 7 Clinical Syndromes scales (Eating Dysfunctions, Substance Abuse Proneness, Delinquent Predisposition, Impulsive Propensity, Anxious Feelings, Depressive Affect, and Suicidal Tendency). The Response Bias scales are four modifying indices (Reliability, Disclosure, Desirability, and Debasement; *Mental Measurements Yearbook*, 2003).

Reliability. Cronbach's alpha reliabilities range from .73 to .91, with most of the internal consistencies in the 0.80s (Retzlaff, Sheehan, & Lorr, 1990). Test–retest reliabilities range from .57 to .92.

Validity. Responses to the MACI were favorably intercorrelated with the Beck Depression Inventory, Beck Anxiety Inventory, and Eating Disorder Inventory.

Availability and source. The MACI is available in paper-and-pencil format, audiocassette, or online from Pearson.

Comment—using with families. The MACI is most effective with adolescents experiencing a level of significant problems or concerns so as to determine treatment options and measure treatment progress. The mental health needs of a troubled adolescent in the family raise co-parenting issues, contradictory hidden parental messages, issues of loyalty in the family system, and the "role" the troubled adolescent plays in the functioning, or lack thereof, of the family (*Mental Measurements Yearbook*, 2003).

Parent Awareness Skills Survey (PASS)

Instrument name. The Parent Awareness Skills Survey (PASS), developed by Barry Bricklin, Ph.D., in 1990 and revised in 2002, identifies strengths and weaknesses of a parent's response to 18 typical child care situations.

Type of instrument. The PASS is a semi-structured interview that presents parents with 18 child care problems or dilemmas in six categories and asks how they would respond to each situation. The instrument reflects parent awareness skills of effective parenting regardless of the age of the children and specifics of their particular situation.

Use and target audience. This survey for parents of children ages 2 through 15 assesses parental awareness of their communication methods with their child and how attuned they are to the unique manner in which their child is able to respond and profit from that communication. The PASS is used for conducting custody evaluations.

Multicultural. The survey is easily understood by parents of diverse educational and cultural status.

Ease and time of administration. Individually and orally administered to each parent, it may take between 30 to 60 minutes depending on the experience of the clinician with the PASS. The parent is presented with 18 different situations and asked to tell what he or she would do in each situation. After responses have been recorded, probing questions are asked to determine the issues the parents believe they should think about before and after their choice of response.

Scoring procedure. Scores reflect parents' responses at three levels: (a) spontaneous level is the unprompted and uninterrupted initial response; (b) Probe Level I asks two gentle, nonleading questions; and (c) Probe Level II asks two direct questions. Each level allows respondents to improve their score. PASS responses are scored with a 0 for no awareness, a 1 for minimal awareness, or a 2 for pronounced awareness in each of the six areas at each of the three levels. The six areas are Awareness of Critical Issues, Awareness of Adequate Solutions, Awareness of Communicating in Understandable Terms, Awareness of Acknowledging Feelings, Awareness of the Importance of Relevant Aspects of a Child's Past History, and Awareness of Feedback Data. The scoring is subjective to the clinician's skill and knowledge in psychology and child development.

Reliability. Not reported.

Validity. Not reported.

Availability and source. The PASS Comprehensive Starting Kit is available from Village Publishing.

Comment—using with families. The PASS provides information on the parent's awareness of child-related critical issues and adequate solutions or interventions to these issues. The PASS also provides information about the level of parent's awareness of his or her communications to the child in understandable terms to them, the importance of acknowledging the child's feelings, the relevance of the child's past history, and the need to attend to the child's feedback to the parents' response. The derived data are used to determine relative strengths and weaknesses of each parent, their conscious efforts in employing good parenting, and the influence of parental behavior on the child to facilitate custody decision making. The basic assumption of the instrument is that parenting effectiveness is a function of parent's awareness of the appropriate skills. The PASS is a good screening tool and is best used in combination with other instruments (*Mental Measurements Yearbook*, 2003).

Parent–Child Relationship Inventory (PCRI)

Instrument name. The Parent–Child Relationship Inventory (PCRI), developed by Gerard Anthony and published in 1994, provides a qualitative evaluation of parent–child interactions.

Type of instrument. The PCRI is a 78-item self-report questionnaire that measures parents' dispositions/attitudes and behaviors about parenting and their children. Items are clustered in Content scales: Parental Support, Satisfaction with Parenting, Involvement, Communication, Limit Setting, Autonomy, and Role Orientation.

Use and target audience. The PCRI is used in evaluating parents and their children (ages 3 to 15). Separate norms are provided for mothers and fathers.

Multicultural. It is reported that the normative sample was less diverse than the U.S. population.

Ease and time of administration. The PCRI, written at the fourth-grade level, can be administered individually or in a group and takes about 15 minutes to complete.

Scoring procedure. The PCRI may be hand-scored, computer scored through purchase of software, or scored through a fax or mail-in service provided by Western Psychological Services.

Reliability. Internal consistency reliability of .82 and test–retest reliability of .81 is reported for the PCRI with internal and test–retest reliabilities ranged from .70 to .88 among the various scales.

Validity. This has not been reported.

Availability and source. The PCRI is available from Western Psychological Services.

Comment—using with families. Gerard (1994) indicated that the PCRI was developed to assess parents' attitudes toward parenting as well as toward their children. The evaluation of parental attitudes and skills, family interaction, the presence of abuse, and the identification of areas of difficulty between parents and their children provides information about conscious parenting and competence, and the quality of the familial relationship (*Mental Measurements Yearbook*, 2003).

Parenting Stress Index (PSI)

Instrument name. The Parenting Stress Index (PSI), a 120-item instrument developed by Richard Abidin, Ph.D., in 1983 is in its third edition (1995).

Type of instrument. The Parenting Stress Index (PSI), 3rd edition, is designed to identify stressful parent–child systems in order to provide interventions directed at reducing the stress. A screening tool for stress in the parent–child relationship, the PSI identifies dysfunctional parenting and predicts potential for parental behavior problems and child adjustment difficulties within the family system. It is used for early identification and prevention of family problems and helpful in planning intervention and treatment, assessing child abuse, and in evaluations for child custody.

Use and target audience. Although intended primarily for parents of the preschool child, the PSI can also be used with parents whose children are 12 years old or younger.

Multicultural. The PSI has been validated in cross-cultural research with individuals of Chinese, European, Italian, Portuguese, Latin American Hispanic, and French–Canadian descent.

Ease and time of administration. Parents take about 20 to 30 minutes to complete the paper-and-pencil PSI, which is written at the fifth-grade reading level. A 36-item Short Form, which takes 10 to 15 minutes to complete, is also available.

Scoring procedure. A total stress score and two scale scores, Child Domain and Parent Domain, each of which identifies sources of stress within the family, are available for the standard form. The Short Form only provides a total stress score. Scoring time for this tool varies based on whether it is hand-scored or if the PSI software is utilized.

Reliability. Reliability is reported to be strong with .95 for the total score, .90 for the child domain, and .93 for the parent domain.

Validity. Validity is reported to be strong.

Availability and source. Both forms can be administered in pencil-and-paper format or online using the PSI software system, which automatically scores item responses and generates a report available from Psychological Assessment Resources.

Comment—using with families. The PSI identifies three major sources of stress: child characteristics, parent characteristics, and situational/demographic life stress. Child variables include distract-ibility/hyperactivity; adaptability; reinforces parent; demandingness; mood; and acceptability. Parent variables include: competence; isola-tion; attachment; health; role restriction; depression; and spouse. Life stress factors include: interrupted infantile apnea; spina bifida; cra-niofacial birth defects; insulin-dependent diabetes; divorce; marriage; pregnancy; income increased; debt; moves; promotions; alcohol or drug problem; death of close family friend; new job; school; legal problems; and others. The identification of the sources of conflict, parents' ability to cope with these, and child–parent adjustment will facilitate assess-ing placement of the child in the least stressful environment and with the more appropriate parent while making recommendations for coun-seling/therapy or stress management education (*Mental Measurements Yearbook*, 2003).

Parental Bonding Instrument (PBI)

Instrument name. The 25-item Parental Bonding Instrument (PBI), developed by Gordon Parker, Hilary Tupling, and L. B. Brown, mea-sures parent–child relationships as perceived by the child.

Type of instrument. The instrument is retrospective, meaning the individual completes the instrument based on how he remembers his parents during his development until about no more than age 16. The measurement uses two scales: Care (12 items) and Overprotection (13 items). The adult responds to the items on a 4-point scale (Parker, Tupling, & Brown, 1979).

Use and target audience. Although targeted at children over 16 years old, preteens may also complete the instrument for how they remember their biological parents during their childhood up to the first 16 years.

Multicultural. Not reported.

Ease and time of administration. The instrument is completed for mothers and fathers separately and may take 2 to 5 minutes each.

Scoring procedure. The PBI is scored on a Likert scale with several items reverse scored; scoring takes approximately 5 to 7 minutes.

Reliability. The PBI is reported to have good internal consis-tency with split-half reliability coefficients of .88 for Care and .74 for Overprotection, and test–retest reliability correlations of .76 for Care and .63 for Overprotection.

Validity. The PBI is reported to have satisfactory construct and con-vergent validity.

Availability and source. The PBI is not copyrighted and can be freely used by clinicians and researchers.

Comment—using with families. The PBI can be useful in working with families to measure parental attitudes and behaviors as perceived by the child of any age. In child custody evaluations, the information gained from the PBI identifies the parent who the child perceives cares about him or her, who sets boundaries, who fosters his or her growth and development, and toward whom he or she feels most connected (*Mental Measurements Yearbook*, 2003).

Parental Nurturance Scale (PNS)

Instrument name. The 24-item Parental Nurturance Scale (PNS), developed by John R. Buri, is designed to measure parental approval, acceptance, and affirmation of the child from the perspective of the child.

Type of instrument. This instrument has 24 statements to which the child responds on a 5-point scale on how the statement applies to him or her and the gender-specific parent.

Use and target audience. The PNS can be used with a child of any age.

Multicultural. Not reported.

Ease and time of administration. Identical forms are used for mothers and fathers with only gender references changed.

Scoring procedure. Individual scores from each item are summed and half the items are reverse scored.

Reliability. Reported internal consistency has alphas of .95 for mothers and .93 for fathers. Test–retest reliabilities of .92 for mothers and .94 for fathers have been reported (Buri, 1989).

Validity. The PNS has good concurrent validity, with significant positive correlations with self-esteem for mother's and father's PNS (Fischer & Corcoran, 1994).

Availability and source. The PNS is available from Sage Publications.

Comment—using with families. The PNS is a valuable tool in that it provides the child's perception of parental nurturance, acceptance, and affirmation. The child's ability to verbalize this is seen as a positive factor when considering self-esteem and feelings of being loved and appreciated by each parent for assessment of the parent–child relationship in determining custody and visitation. The child's input about preferences for living with and/or visiting parents is tempered by this perception (*Mental Measurements Yearbook*, 2003).

Perception-of-Relationships Test (PORT)

Instrument name. The Perception-of-Relationships Test (PORT) is a seven-item projective test focused on drawings of self and family.

Type of instrument. This projective test is designed to measure the extent to which children feel or seek closeness with each parent and the impact of these relationships. The children are required to draw themselves and their parents and to draw an animal in the preferred parent's house and its dreams about its parents.

Use and target audience. This test can be used with children 3 years and older to assess children's perception of the nature of their relationship with their parents. This assessment allows for maximization of these relationships.

Multicultural. Not reported.

Ease and time of administration. PORT is administered individually and is well standardized and objectively scored. It takes about 30 minutes to complete.

Scoring procedure. A Parent of Choice is determined from each drawing, and the parent with the highest number of preferences is the identified Parent of Choice for the child. Scoring is subjective.

Reliability. Test–retest reliability is reported to be satisfactory.

Validity. Not reported.

Availability and source. This test is available from Village Publishing.

Comment—using with families. This test allows the evaluator to determine the degree to which a child seeks interaction with a given parent and the degree to which the child is able to work out a style of relating to each parent. Custody arrangements can then be made that provides the maximum benefits of these relationships (*Mental Measurements Yearbook*, 2010).

Relationship Conflict Inventory (RCI)

Instrument name. The 120-item Relationship Conflict Inventory (RCI), developed in 1989 by Arthur M. Bodin, is designed to evaluate relationship conflict and to measure progress and outcome of relationship therapy. The instrument was revised in 1996; the 2002 version has 121 items with an additional process item on meta-communication (Bodin, 2003).

Type of instrument. The RCI has 35 process items, which address "how" something is being discussed; 27 are on verbal conflict and 8 on physical conflict. Eighty-five content items address what is being discussed in terms of frequency, distress level, and causal attribution. This tool identifies process and content of relationship conflict.

Use and target audience. The instrument was designed for use with couples seeking a divorce and in conflict due to problematic communication (Bodin, 1996).

Multicultural. This has not been reported.

Ease and time of administration. The RCI, written at the sixth-grade reading level, typically takes 20 to 30 minutes to complete. A shortened version eliminates the content section, reducing it to 35 items with completion time of 15 to 20 minutes.

Scoring procedure. The subscales of the instrument report on Process Conflict and Content Conflict. Process Conflict focuses on Verbal Conflict (Communication Difficulties, Arguments, Painful/Deteriorating Relationship, Distancing, Intimidation, and Separation) and Physical Conflict (Physical Coercion/Intimidation, Indirect Aggression, three levels of Physical Abuse, and Use of Weapons). Content Conflict is channeled into nine clusters: Activities, Change, Characteristics, Communication, Habits, Preferences, Relationships, Responsibilities, and Values.

Reliability. This is currently being assessed.

Validity. This is currently being assessed.

Availability and source. The RCI is available from Bodin.

Comment—using with families. The RCI can be used with couples to assist them in identifying the content and process of conflict and adjusting styles of communication that lead to physical and verbal conflict. Results will assist couples in creating interventions that allow them to communicate in a more effective manner; identify areas of verbal and physical escalation, prior to their occurring; and increase positive communication to decrease and/or eliminate incidents of verbal and/or physical escalation. The focused overview of the relationship conflict provides information regarding parents' ability to acknowledge their differences, how they account for these differences in areas such as child rearing, and if they choose to argue about or seek accommodation for these differences. This information sets the stage for calm negotiations and mutual understanding and agreement regarding child custody and visitation in the best interest of the child (*Mental Measurements Yearbook*, 2003).

State–Trait Anger Expression Inventory (STAXI-2)

Instrument name. The State–Trait Anger Expression Inventory-2 (STAXI-2). developed by Charles Spielberger in 1988 and revised and expanded in 1999, is a 57-item self-report, for adolescents and adults, that measures the experience, expression, and control of anger.

Type of instrument. The experience of anger is understood in the context of state (subjective feelings) and trait (predisposition); the intensity and expression of anger may be focused outward or directed inward and includes degree of anger control.

Use and target audience. The STAXI-2 is designed for individuals age 16 years and older in which they provide self-ratings on how they feel right now, how they generally feel, and how they generally react when angry.

Multicultural. Whereas ethnicity is not reported, gender and age diversity is included in the normative sample.

Ease and time of administration. The STAXI-2 can be administered and scored by non-clinical personnel; however, it should only be interpreted by qualified clinicians with formal assessment training. STAXI-2 can be administered individually or in a group, and although this is not a timed test, it is typically completed in 12 to 15 minutes.

Scoring procedure. The 57 items of STAXI-2 are distributed across six scales: State Anger, Trait Anger, Anger Expression-Out, Anger Expression-In, Anger Control-Out, and Anger Control-In. All items are rated on a 4-point scale assessing frequency and intensity of angry feelings. STAXI-2 is hand-scored or optical scored, with subscale totals entered on a grid.

Reliability. The internal consistency reliability for the STAXI-2 scales ranges from .73 to .95.

Validity. There is concurrent validity of the STAXI-2 with Eysenck Personality Questionnaire psychoticism and neuroticism subscales, Buss–Durkee Hostility Inventory, and MMPI Hostility and Overt Hostility Scales.

Availability and source. STAXI-2 is available in two forms from Psychological Assessment Resources, Inc.

Comment—using with families. When used as a component of a battery of tests, STAXI-2 has been effective with couples experiencing marital difficulties, planning or in the process of divorce, or working to resolve issues in a conflictual marital situation. The STAXI-2 is also useful in determining how parents' anger at each other may affect their ability to deal with issues related to co-parenting and decision making in the best interests of the child or children. When it is administered to teenage children, their anger toward their parents for the divorce provides a context for their input with regard to custody and visitation (*Mental Measurements Yearbook*, 2010).

Teacher Report Form (TRF)

Instrument name. The 118-item Teacher Report Form (TRF) was developed by Thomas M. Achenbach in 1991 to obtain teachers' reports of children's academic performance, adaptive functioning, and behavioral/emotional problems.

Type of instrument. On a 3-point scale, teachers rate children's academic performance in each academic subject on a 5-point Likert scale. Teachers use a 7-point Likert scale to rate adaptive functioning in order to compare the child to typical students with regard to how hard he is working, how appropriately he is behaving, how much he is learning, and how happy he appears to be.

Use and target audience. The TRF was designed for use with children ranging from 6 to 18 years old.

Multicultural. The norming group included children of African–American, Euro–American, and Hispanic ethnic descent across socioeconomic levels from around the United States.

Ease and time of administration. Administered individually by a master's-level clinician, this instrument takes about 15 to 20 minutes to complete.

Scoring procedure. This instrument yields 17 subscales and scores that can be scored manually or by computer. The scoring system includes T scores and raw scores for two broad-band dimensions of child problem behavior: Externalizing and Internalizing. In addition, the scoring method includes T scores and raw scores for several narrow-band scales describing Delinquency and Aggression, Attention Problems, Withdrawal, Anxiety/Depression, Somatic Complaints, Social Problems, Thought Problems, and Sex Problems.

Reliability. Achenbach (1991b) reported the test–retest reliability to be .62 to .96, the inter-rater reliability to be .60, and the range of internal consistency to be .72 to .95.

Validity. Criterion validity was assessed and found to be acceptable.

Availability and source. This instrument can be obtained by permission from Achenbach System of Empirically Based Assessment.

Comment—using with families. Child academic achievement is a main area of concern for parents. This tool can assist parents and teachers in identifying areas of strength and weakness in a child's ability to learn. The TRF identifies children's academic performance, adaptive functioning, and behavioral/emotional problems that may be related to adjustment to changes necessitated by divorce (*Mental Measurements Yearbook*, 2003).

ASSESSMENT STRATEGY

The American Psychological Association, in 1994, developed guidelines for child custody evaluations that stressed the need for multiple methods of data collection and cautious interpretation of assessment data (Ackerman & Ackerman, 1997). When assessments or evaluations are conducted, systematic orientation and procedure are important to ensure consistent, comprehensive, and accurate data gathering. The following steps identify the essential information needed and from whom, the qualitative and quantitative data desired and data gathering methods, and how and when this assessment plan will be operationalized. The subsequent case example illustrates the use of the identified procedure.

1. Collect biopsychosocial data that include client's perception of current legal situation; educational, medical (physical and emotional), criminal, and employment history; past and present substance use and/or abuse; family constellation; support systems; and religious/spiritual orientation.
2. Review collateral data, such as divorce agreement, court orders, school records, and/or mediation agreements.
3. Collect and/or review clinical data to include prior and current individual, couples, and family counseling/therapy.
4. Interview the whole family and individual members.
5. Administer selected inventory/testing tools.
6. Interpret the results of the inventory.
7. Identify recommendations and interventions.
8. Provide feedback to the couple and/or family as appropriate.
9. Submit report and/or recommendations to the court.

CASE EXAMPLE

Background Information and Reason for Testing

John and Jane had been married for 16 years when John was transferred by his employer to another state across the country. John and Jane mutually agreed that Jane would stay where they presently were because their children, John Jr. (age 13), Madison (age 11), and Killian (age 6), were well established in their respective schools and it would be less disruptive to them. Six months after John relocated, he contacted Jane to ask for a divorce because he had met someone else; during this same period, he had only returned once to see his family. He also asked that the children be allowed to visit him during the summer and Christmas holidays. Jane, angry about the divorce, was denying John's request for visitation. As a result of their inability to come to an agreement about custody and visitation, the Family Court judge requested a child custody evaluation.

Individual and Testing Summary

In the initial interview and collection of biopsychosocial data for John, he verbalized understanding the reason for the interview was to determine custody and visitation privileges for him and his former spouse. He further indicated that he wanted a quick and fair resolution so that the children were not adversely affected by the divorce. John reported that he held an MBA in finance, was in good health, had no substance abuse or criminal history, and had worked for the same corporation for 15 years. His job relocation had resulted in his living less than 5 miles from his parents and allowed him to attend church with them weekly (Step 1). At the onset of this interview, John produced copies of the recently finalized divorce agreement and court motions that led up to this evaluation. Mediation was found to be unsuccessful because of John's and Jane's inability to come to an agreement. In this clinical interview, John verbalized that his experience in mediation with Jane was a negative one because she would not accept any recommendation he made with regard to the custody and visitation of the children. As a result of this conflict, neither party was able to come to an agreement about custody and visitation, which necessitated a referral by the court for evaluation (Step 2). John indicated no current or past history of individual, couples, or family therapy. When this was questioned, John indicated that their relationship was strong at the time he relocated, and it was only after the relocation that the issues between him and Jane surfaced. He was unable to fly home to take part in couples/family counseling, and he reported that Jane was opposed to counseling of any kind (Step 3). Furthermore, John indicated that, although he would like to be the primary residential parent of his children, he understood that they had attachments in their present home and school; he wanted to spend time with his children, while not overly disrupting their lives. He indicated that he was open to the idea of shared parental responsibility, as long as he was able to keep his children in his life. John also indicated that he had been timely with child support and was not currently in arrears (Step 4). John was administered the Parent–Child Relationship Inventory (PCRI) and the Ackerman-Schoendorf Scales for Parent Evaluation of Custody (ASPECT). He completed the instruments within the time guidelines and in full. On the PCRI, John's strengths were his positive satisfaction with parenting and adequate support with his parenting. It appeared that he had some discomfort with allowing his daughter's autonomy appropriate to their ages. On the ASPECT, all of his scores appeared to indicate that John is a fit and loving parent who appears to have some frustrations with Jane, his former wife, but is able to put those feelings aside in his children's best interests. He presented as having fair negotiating skills, specific to the co-parenting relationship. There were no overt signs of pathology or abusive behavior that would affect his ability to parent his three minor children. John presented with an acceptable level of knowledge specific to behavioral redirection, the effects of divorce on children, and key aspects of the co-parenting relationship, including flexibility and compromise. He presented with appropriate dress and demeanor and was cooperative throughout the process (Step 6 and Step 7).

In the initial interview and collection of biopsychosocial data for Jane, she acknowledged that the interview was to determine custody and visitation for her and John. Jane had 2 years of college education, was in good health, and reported no substance abuse or criminal history. She had held clerical jobs up through the first 3 years of her marriage until her oldest son was born; since then she had been a stay-at-home mother (Step 1). Jane provided copies of the divorce agreement and court motions that led up to the order for this evaluation, which was a consequence of the inability of John and her to come to an agreement (Step 2). Jane indicated no current or past experience with therapy of any kind (Step 3). During the clinical interview, she indicated that she needed to retain primary custody of her children because she has always been there for them and provided stability in their lives (Step 4). Jane was administered the Parent–Child Relationship Inventory (PCRI) and the Ackerman-Schoendorf Scales for Parent Evaluation of Custody (ASPECT). She completed the instruments in full within the time guidelines. On the PCRI, Jane's scores indicated an emphasis on discipline and setting limits, which appeared to be major characteristics. She also felt supported in her parenting. Her discipline and limit setting may have indicated a punishment orientation attitude. On the ASPECT, Jane's scores indicated her strong stand on behavioral redirection (punishment), although there was an indication of fairness and sensitivity to her children's developmental level and needs. Her assessment indicated an ability to co-parent with her former spouse, in the children's best interests, as well as a level of flexibility and ability to negotiate. Jane verbalized an acceptable level of knowledge specific to the divorce process and its effects on her minor children. She was also able to verbalize a need for consistency in the children's lives, which included "some" time with their father. Jane was appropriate in both her dress and demeanor during the assessment process (Step 6 and Step 7).

In the initial interview and collection of biopsychosocial data for the three children, John Jr., Madison, and Killian indicated a level of sadness over their parents' separation. All of the children indicated that they attended school regularly and received good grades and denied use of drugs and alcohol and arrest history. John Jr. added that he missed his father particularly because his father had attended all of his softball games. Madison said that even though she loved her father, she felt more comfortable living with her mother but wanted to visit her father. Killian stated that she loved both her parents the same. All three children were administered the Parental Nurturance Scale (PNS) and John Jr. and Madison were administered the Parental Bonding Instrument (PBI). Killian was not administered this instrument because of her young age.

John Jr.'s scores on the PNS indicated that he felt more nurturance and acceptance from his father than his mother. Scores were different by 18 points. Madison's scores indicated that she felt more acceptance and nurturance from her mother, although only 10 points separated the scores, which was significant in this case. Killian's scores indicated an equal feeling of nurturance and acceptance by both parents, although her level of understanding of the testing instrument is unclear because of her young age. John Jr.'s results on the PBI indicated that he felt cared for by both of his parents and not as overprotected as his younger sister had indicated (maybe because of his age and opportunities to explore different levels of freedom from his parents). Madison's scores indicated that she felt highly cared for and a high level of overprotection. Again, the ages of these children and the developmental milestones they were approaching appropriate to their genders may have played a role in these results.

The outcomes of the structured and unstructured assessments pointed toward a family in which both parents had focused on and loved their children, despite their own inability to make a decision about the children's best interests with regard to custody and visitation. John Jr. had expressed a strong desire to spend time with his father, as well as wanting to complete school in his current neighborhood middle school. Madison clearly indicated a desire to live with her mother and visit her father; Killian appeared to be too young to make a clear decision about each parent, although her statement about loving both parents demonstrated that good parenting had taken place in the home, with no issues of alienation on the part of either parent. Based on the test results and clinical interviews, it appeared that both parents took an active interest in the care and well-being of their children, but with different styles of parenting. This implied that neither parent was better than the other; they were simply different in their styles of discipline, communication, and boundary setting. In spite of the parents' interpersonal issues, which led to the divorce, and Jane's apparent anger over the situation, a clear plan of custody and visitation appeared to be one with which both parents could be happy.

Treatment and Custody Recommendations

To help John with his daughters, formal or informal education about child development and parenting approaches around the issue of independence of his children would be helpful, despite his scores indicating he was an effective parent; he shared the perspective that more information is always helpful (Step 7). It was recommended that Jane get individual therapy to manage her anger and deal with the loss she felt. It was also recommended that Jane arrange for family therapy for her and the children to discuss and process the changes in the home as a result of the divorce. John was also invited to take part in the family therapy, when in town or through Skype, in an effort to increase a positive co-parenting relationship as well as showing the children a "united front" in that both of their parents are there for them, despite the divorce and geographic distance. All of the children presented as well adjusted to the situation and did not appear to be in need of individual therapy at the time.

With regard to custody recommendations, shared parental responsibility was the most desired and appropriate course to take. The three children should remain in the family home with their mother for the remainder of their education. Because the father lived on the opposite coast, it was recommended that John Jr. spend the Christmas holiday and entire summer with his father. It was recommended that Madison and Killian spend the Christmas holiday (alternate years) and 3 weeks in the summer with their father. Spring break for all three children would be spent with the father (on alternate years), with the father having the first year's visit. Due to their ages, it was also recommended that this visitation schedule be revisited in 3 years. Telephone contact was highly recommended for all children, and John and Jane should continue to communicate openly with each other in regard to the medical, educational, and spiritual needs of their children.

Feedback of Results

The clinician met with John and Jane individually to discuss the results of the assessments (Step 8). Then the clinician met with them together to allow John and Jane an opportunity to share any information and for the clinician to identify to the parents the issues specific to each child individually and the parenting needs of the children collectively. Recommendations to be made to the Family Court judge were shared with both parents. Both Jane and John were in agreement with the report findings and the recommendations. Both shared relief that a resolution was reached that appeared to be in all family members' best interests.

TABLE 9.1   Matrix: Child Custody and Divorce Assessment Strategies and Inventories

Assessment Instrument	Specific Couple and Family Applications	Cultural/ Language	Instructions/Use: T = Time to Take S = Time to Score I = Items (# of)	Computerized: (a) Scoring (b) Report	Reliability (R) Validity (V)	Availability
A Comprehensive Custody Evaluation Standard System (ACCESS)	Children, parents, teachers, and physicians; multimethod sequenced evaluation system	English	T = Time consuming S = Dependent on types of scores used I = Varies by test	a = Yes depending on tests selected b = Yes depending on tests selected	R = Not available V = Not available	Village Publishing
Ackerman-Schoendorf Scales for Parent Evaluation of Custody (ASPECT)	Parents; multimethod for evaluating parents' fitness for custody	English	T = Time varies S = Dependent of types of scores used I = Varies by test	a = No b = No	R = .50–.76 internal reliability; .92–.96 inter-rater reliability V = Not reported	Western Psychological Services
Behavior Assessment System for Children, Second Edition (BASC-2)	Children self-perception and parents and parent surrogates observations; assesses and identifies children and adolescents' positive/adaptive behaviors and negative/ maladaptive behaviors	English, Spanish (parent version)	T = 15–35 min S = 15–35 min manually I = 5 separate subtests, each with varying number of items	a = Yes b = Yes	R = .80–.95 internal consistency; .64–.93 test– retest; .53–.77 inter-rater V = .64–.85 criterion validity	Pearson
Bricklin Perceptual Scales	Children; assess children's perceptions or emotional comprehension of each parent's action	English	T = 40 min S = Not reported I = 32	a = No b = No	R = Not reported V = Not reported	Village Publishing

Instrument	Description	Language	Administration	a / b	Reliability/Validity	Publisher
Burks Behavior Rating Scale, Second Edition (BBRS-2)	Parents and teachers; identifies problem behavior patterns in children and adolescents	English	T = 15–20 min S = 15–20 min I = 100	a = Yes b = Yes	R = .84–.89 internal consistency; .80–.90 test–retest reliability; .62–.69 inter-rater reliability; V = .42–.78 concurrent validity	Western Psychological Services
Child Behavior Checklist (CBCL)	Parents and parent surrogates; records children's competencies and problems	English, Spanish	T = 15 min S = 15 min I = 140 (ages 4–18), 100 (ages 2–3)	a = Yes b = Yes	R = .95–1.00 test–retest; .93–.96 inter-rater; .78–.97 internal consistency; V = Criterion validity acceptable	Achenbach System of Empirically Based Assessment Research Center for Children
Child-Rearing Practices Report (CRPR)	Parents and child; identifies child-rearing attitudes and values	English, Russian, Hungarian, Chinese, French	T = 30–40 min S = Not available I = 91	a = Not available b = Not available	R = Test–retest reliability scores at .61–.71; V = Not available	J. H. Block (author)
Millon Pre-Adolescent Clinical Inventory (M-PACI)	Children; self-report personality inventory to identify, predict, and understand psychological disorders	English	T = 15–20 min S = Not available I = 97	a = Yes b = Yes	R = .63–.84; V = .65–.75 concurrent validity	Pearson
Millon Adolescent Clinical Inventory (MACI)	Disturbed adolescents; self-report personality inventory designed specifically to assess adolescent personality characteristics and clinical syndromes	English, Spanish (audiocassette version)	T = 25–30 min S = 20–30 min manually I = 160	a = Yes b = Yes	R = .73–.91 internal consistency; .57–.92 test–retest; V = Favorably concurrent validity	NCS Assessments

TABLE 9.1 (Continued) Matrix: Child Custody and Divorce Assessment Strategies and Inventories

Assessment Instrument	Specific Couple and Family Applications	Cultural/Language	Instructions/Use: T = Time to Take S = Time to Score I = Items (# of)	Computerized: (a) Scoring (b) Report	Reliability (R) Validity (V)	Availability
Parent Awareness Skills Survey (PASS)	Parents; reflects parents' awareness of effective parenting	English	T = 30–60 min, including questioning S = 30–60 min I = 18 situations	a = No b = No	R = Not reported V = Not reported	Village Publishing
Parent-Child Relationship Inventory (PCRI)	Parents; provides a qualitative evaluation of parent–child interactions	English	T = 15 min S = Differs based on method I = 78	a = Yes b = Yes	R = .82 internal consistency; .81 test-retest reliability V = Not reported	Western Psychological Services
Parenting Stress Index (PSI)	Parents; identifies stressful parent–child systems	English	T = 20–30 min (long form); 10–15 min (short form) S = varies I = 120 (long form); 36 (short form)	a = Yes b = Yes	R = .95 total score; .90 child domain, .93 parent domain V = Reported strong	Psychological Assessment Resources
Parental Bonding Instrument (PBI)	Any age child; measures parent–child relationships as perceived by the child	English	T = 2–5 min each S = 5–7 min I = 25	a = No b = No	R = .74–.88 internal consistency; .63–.76 test-retest reliability V = Satisfactory construct and convergent validity	Not copyrighted

Instrument	Description	Language	Administration	a/b	Reliability/Validity	Publisher
Parental Nurturance Scale (PNS)	Any age child; measures parental approval, acceptance, and affirmation of their children from the perspective of the child	English	T = 5–10 min S = 5 min I = 24	a = No b = No	R = Alphas of .95 for mothers and .93 for fathers V = Good concurrent validity	Sage Publications
Perception-of-Relationships Test (PORT)	Children; measures the extent to which a child feels or seeks closeness with each parent and the impact of these relationships	English	T = 30 min S = Subjective I = 7 item projective	a = No b = No	R = Test retest satisfacoty V = Not reported	Village Publishing
Relationship Conflict Inventory (RCI)	Couples seeking a divorce; evaluates relationship conflict and to measure progress and outcome of relationship therapy	English	T = 20–30 min (long form); 15 = 20 min (short form) S = Not reported I = 120 (long form); 35 (short form)	a = No b = No	R = Not available V = Not available	Author: Arthur M. Bodin
State-Trait Anger Expression Inventory, Second Edition (STAXI-2)	Adolescents and adults; measures the experience, expression and control of anger	English	T = 12–15 min S = Depends on method I = 57	a = Yes b = Yes	R = .73–.95 internal consistency reliability V = Concurrent validity	Psychological Assessment Resources
Teacher Report Form (TRF)	Teacher; reports of children's academic performance, adaptive functioning, and behavioral/emotional problems	English	T = 15–20 min S = 15–20 min I = 118	a = Yes b = Yes	R = .62–.96 test-retest; .60 inter-rater; .72–.95 internal consistency V = Criterion validity acceptable	Achenbach System of Empirically Based Assessment

CONCLUDING COMMENTS

This chapter has described the use of psychological assessment methods and clinical interviews to evaluate the post-divorce parental relationship, the child's or children's relationship with each parent, and overall family functioning post-divorce, as well as to determine the parents' ability to work together in the best interest of the child or children with the purpose of making recommendations for child custody and visitation. In this chapter, 18 instruments were discussed and a protocol for using these instruments in clinical practice was provided and illustrated by a case example. The following matrix summarizes the key attributes of these tools and their use with families has been provided (see Table 9.1).

REFERENCES

Achenbach, T. M. (1991a). *Integrative guide to the 1991 CBCL/4-18, YSR, and TRF profiles*. Burlington, VT: University of Vermont, Department of Psychology.

Achenbach, T. M. (1991b). *Manual of the Teacher's Report Form and 1991 Profile*. Burlington, VT: University of Vermont, Department of Psychiatry.

Achenbach, T. M., & Brown, J. S. (1991). *Bibliography of published studies using the Child Behavior Checklist and related materials: 1991 edition*. Burlington, VT: University of Vermont, Department of Psychiatry.

Ackerman, M. J. (2005). The Ackerman-Schoendorf Scales for Parent Evaluation of Custody (ASPECT): A review of research and update. *Journal of Child Custody, 2*(1), 179–193. doi:10.1300/J190v02n01_10

Ackerman, M. J., & Ackerman, M. C. (1997). Child custody evaluation practices: A survey of experienced professionals (revisited). *Professional Psychology: Research and Practices, 28*(2), 137–145.

American Association for Marriage and Family Therapy. (2001, July 1). *Code of ethics*. Retrieved February 14, 2011, from http://www.aamft.org/imis15/content/legal_ethics/code_of_ethics.aspx

American Counseling Association. (2005). *Code of ethics*. Retrieved February 14, 2011, from http://www.counseling.org/Resources/CodeOfEthics/TP/Home/CT2.aspx

Block, J. (1972). Generational continuity and discontinuity in the understanding of societal rejection. *Journal of Personality and Social Psychology, 22,* 333–345.

Bodin, A. M. (1996). Relationship conflict—verbal and physical: Conceptualizing an inventory for assessing process and content. In F. W. Kaslow (Ed.), *Handbook of relational diagnosis and dysfunctional family patterns* (pp. 371–393). New York: Wiley & Sons.

Bodin, A. M. (2003). *Relationship Conflict Inventory.* Retrieved August 29, 2011, from http://www.familyandmarriage.com/rci.html

Buri, J. R. (1989). Self-esteem and appraisals of parental behavior. *Journal of Adolescent Behavior, 4,* 33–49.

Famularo, R., Fenton, R., & Kinscherff, R. (1993). Child maltreatment and the development of posttraumatic stress disorder. *AJDC, 147,* 755–760.

Fischer, J., & Corcoran, K. (1994). *Measures for clinical practice* (2nd ed.). New York: The Free Press.

Garrity, C., & Barris, M. (1994). *Caught in the middle: Protecting the children of high conflict divorce.* New York: Lexington Books.

Gerard, A. (1994). *Parent–child relational inventory (PCRI).* Los Angeles: Western Psychological Services.

Hamilton Fish Institute. (2003). Behavior assessment system for children. Retrieved August 29, 2011, from http://www.hamfish.org/

Jaffe, P., Wolfe, D., & Wilson, S. (1990). *Children of battered women.* Newbury Park, CA: Sage.

McGill, J. C., Deutsch, R. M., & Zibbell, R. A. (1999). Visitation and domestic violence: A clinical model of family assessment and access planning. *Family and Conciliation Courts Review, 37*(3), 315–334.

Mental Measurements Yearbook. (2003). Retrieved July 20, 2003, from http://0-web5.silverplatter.com.novacat.nova.edu

Mental Measurements Yearbook. (2010). Retrieved February 22, 2011, http://web.ebscohost.com.barry.edu/ehost/search/advanced?hid=11&sid=b74bebdb-d55a-4986-a069-d79f652f106b%40sessionmgr14&vid=1

Parker, G., Tupling, H., & Brown, L. B. (1979). A parental bonding instrument. *British Journal of Medical Psychology, 52,* 1–10.

Quinell, F. A., & Bow, J. N. (2001). Psychological tests used in child custody evaluations. *Behavioral Sciences and the Law, 19,* 491–501.

Retzlaff, P., Sheehan, E., & Lorr, M. (1990). MCMI-II scoring: Weighted and unweighted algorithms. *Journal of Personality Assessment, 55,* 219–223.

CHAPTER 10

Child Abuse Assessment Strategy and Inventories

Erna Olafson and Lisa Connelly

We were asked to introduce this new edition with an update about changes in this field. Among the most significant has been the death of the original first author of this chapter, William N. Friedrich. Bill was one of the pioneers in the assessment and treatment of all forms of child maltreatment, especially child sexual abuse, and he is greatly missed.

Perhaps the largest change since the first edition of this chapter appeared has been the shift from a focus on child maltreatment in these assessments to a more general one about exposure to trauma and adversity in childhood and adolescence, including but not limited to child maltreatment. We now have convincing data about the widespread exposure of children and adolescents to a range of potentially traumatic experiences in their families, communities, and schools (Finkelhor, Turner, Ormrod, & Hamby, 2009, 2010). Because children's exposure to these external events may affect the behaviors and symptoms youth develop, and because parents or caregivers are often ignorant about children's exposure to potentially traumatic events, youth self-report surveys or questionnaires are seen as increasingly essential.

In addition, in the past decade, the federally funded National Child Traumatic Stress Network (NCTSN), comprising 130 centers throughout the United States, has been very active in developing and testing new measures to assess children and families about their trauma and adversity histories and their trauma-linked symptoms and behaviors. A list of these new measures, with brief descriptions of them, can be accessed at the National Child Traumatic Stress Network's online measures review database (http://www.nctsnet.org/resources/online-research/measures-review).

In the evaluation of children and families for trauma, adversity, or maltreatment exposure and their effects, assessment questions will vary, depending on whether the assessor is conducting a psychological evaluation for diagnosis and treatment or whether he or she is doing a forensic assessment. Patient privilege will also differ markedly between clinical and forensic evaluations. Informed consent, confidentiality, and privilege must be clarified in writing at the outset before interviewing or testing begins, with informed patient or caretaker consent documented in standardized forms that include client signatures. Psychological assessments for forensic purposes should be clearly distinguished from those for treatment purposes.

When child abuse or domestic violence have been alleged, there are many circumstances in which clinical psychological assessments performed as part of treatment may end up in court. Parents may separate during or after treatment, sue for custody and visitation, and subpoena prior treatment and psychological testing records. Criminal prosecutions may also ensue. In cases where extrafamilial child abuse is alleged, families or victims may subsequently sue for damages.

For these reasons, all treatment and psychological testing records should be created and maintained as if they will be scrutinized in a court of law. Unforeseen legal involvements are more likely when domestic violence and child abuse are at issue than when psychologists test youngsters for attention deficit hyperactivity disorder, separation anxiety, or other childhood problems.

ASSESSMENT COMPLEXITIES

Acts Versus Diagnoses

The terms *domestic violence, child sexual abuse,* and *child physical abuse* cover a wide range of interpersonal behaviors. These are acts, not diagnoses (Olafson & Boat, 2000). Indeed, both victims and perpetrators may show few or no symptoms when assessed. The symptom patterns of victims are determined by many factors, including the severity and duration of the stressor or trauma, the degree of subsequent interpersonal support, and the age of the victim (Kolko & Swenson, 2002; Putnam, 2003; Trickett, Noll, Reiffman, & Putnam, 2001). Many child sexual abusers and batterers appear to be psychologically normal when interviewed and tested (Kolko & Swenson, 2002; Olafson, 1999; Salter, 2003).

Symptom Discontinuity

In addition, symptom patterns change as children develop (Olafson & Boat, 2000; Trickett, Noll, & Putnam, 2011). Following abuse or trauma, a child who appears to be asymptomatic at Time A may have a constellation of symptoms at Time B (Putnam, 2003). Psychologists who conduct assessments should be alert to this "sleeper effect," because at least one study has shown that sexually abused children who had the fewest initial symptoms evidenced the most marked deterioration over time (Gomez-Schwartz, Horowitz, & Cardarelli, 1990).

Developmentally Appropriate Criteria

Traumatized children are not Vietnam veterans. The Posttraumatic Stress Disorder (PTSD) diagnosis was constructed based on the symptom patterns observed in combat veterans returning from Vietnam. Other categories of trauma survivors—battered women, abused children, rape victims, and others—were then shoehorned into this construct (American Psychiatric Association [APA], 1980, 1994, 2000; American Academy of Child and Adolescent Psychiatry, 1998). This shoehorning may be more suitable for survivors of adult traumas such as rape than it is for children. The American Psychiatric Association's diagnostic manual, the DSM-IV and DSM-IV-TR (APA, 1994, 2000), has added notations about some ways in which children's posttraumatic symptom pattern expressions differ from adult responses. Many instruments developed to assess PTSD in children make the effort to be consistent with the DSM-IV-TR construct for PTSD and simply adapt the language of their questions slightly for children's reading level. This adult-based lens may well lead to distortions and omissions when researchers study traumatized children. Instruments that look freshly at children's responses to abuse and trauma instead of applying the lens of the adult PTSD construct are only recently being developed, for example, the Pediatric Emotional Distress Scale or the Trauma Symptom Checklist for Children, both reviewed in this chapter.

Single Versus Multiple Traumas in Adults and Children

Type I—single event—traumas are associated with different symptom patterns than Type II—multiple event—traumas. Posttraumatic Stress Disorder as described in the DSM-IV-TR applies most clearly to Type I traumas. The efforts to include a category for Complex Posttraumatic Stress Disorder in adults—the symptom constellation that is associated with chronic, severe trauma and maltreatment— have been so far unsuccessful (Cook et al., 2005; Pelcovitz et al., 1997). National committees within the National Child Traumatic Stress Network (NCTSN) continue to study the diagnosis of Complex PTSD for adults and a new diagnosis for polyvictimized children, Developmental Trauma Disorder (DTD). DTD assesses the impact of chronic, severe trauma across multiple developmental domains, and it integrates developmental and neurobiological components into the construct in order to assess children accurately. A multi-site study to assess this diagnosis for inclusion in the upcoming DSM-V is currently under way (Busuttil, 2009; Moran, 2007; van der Kolk, 2005).

How are traumatized children different from traumatized adults? Judith Herman wrote, "Repeated trauma in adult life erodes the structure of the personality already formed, but repeated trauma in childhood forms and deforms the personality" (Herman, 1992, p. 96). Trauma and abuse exert more powerful effects on the developing brains and bodies of children than on adults (Margolin & Vickerman, 2007). Childhood maltreatment occurs during sensitive developmental periods for children, such as during the experience-dependent maturation of the central nervous system, so that chronically traumatized children have smaller brains and lower IQs by the time they start school than do non-abused comparison groups (De Bellis et al., 1999; De Bellis et al., 2002; De Bellis & Kuchibhatla, 2006). One study has shown that children exposed to domestic violence have 8 points fewer IQ points than nonexposed children; a suppression greater than that found in children chronically exposed to lead (Koenen, Moffitt, Caspi, Taylor, & Purcell, 2003). Abuse and trauma in childhood also affect fundamental developmental processes such as attachment, socialization with others, emotional regulation, impulse control, and the integration of the self (Putnam, 2003, 2006). Chronic trauma has the most powerful impact on these psychobiological developmental processes in children age 7 and younger. Early intervention has been shown to reverse some of these neurobiological effects, so that preschoolers exposed to domestic violence who were treated with Child Parent Psychotherapy showed statistically significant increases in IQ points (Lieberman, Briscoe-Smith, Ghosh Ippen, & Van Horn, 2006).

Misdiagnoses

Because our understanding of children's posttraumatic responses is relatively recent and still very incomplete, many clinicians misdiagnose the posttraumatic symptom patterns they are seeing. Complete trauma and maltreatment history taking must be part of every psychological assessment, especially when Bipolar Disorder or Attention Deficit Hyperactivity Disorder form part of the differential diagnosis. The longitudinal study by Frank W. Putnam, M.D., and colleagues of sexually abused girls and matched controls found rates of apparent ADHD in the sexually abused girls of over 30%, whereas the mean for the non-abused controls was less than 10% (Putnam & Trickett, 1997). Prescribing drugs to a traumatized child for an Attention Deficit Disorder from which the child does not suffer, while missing the child's trauma history and symptoms, is not good clinical practice. The recent "epidemic" of childhood Bipolar Disorder diagnoses has erupted with only minimal attention paid to the frequent occurrence of bipolar-like symptoms in traumatized children. Children whose alleged manic symptoms include, for example, symptoms known to follow trauma and maltreatment, such as emotional dysregulation, impulse control disorders, or hypersexuality, should be questioned about maltreatment histories before these children are subjected to powerful medication regimens (Friedrich, 2002).

Limits of Instrumentation

We have no instruments to assess some of the most damaging sequelae of childhood maltreatment. Attachment is studied formally in laboratory settings using the Strange Situation but less formally in clinical settings, and observations comprise the most useful data points for children (Friedrich, 2002). Research continues on an adult measure, the Adult Attachment Interview (Bakermans-Kranenburg & van IJzendoorn, 2009). Self-report measures for youth have also been developed but do not yet have full reliability and validity data available (www.nctsn. org). Many psychological batteries depend heavily on patient self-report inventories that contain validity scales to assess reporting attitudes. Individual, ethnic, cultural, developmental, and gendered reporting styles influence parent and child reports. When abuse and trauma are at issue, validity is especially challenging to assess. For example, children, especially those traumatized children whose posttraumatic symptoms include numbing and avoidance, are often poor reporters of their own internal states and symptoms (Friedrich, 2002; Olafson, 1999). Parent reports tend to focus on children's externalizing symptoms while under-reporting children's internalizing symptoms such as anxiety and depression (Stover & Berkowitz, 2005). Even non-traumatized children minimize undesirable response patterns such as anger. Traumatized adults who have PTSD or dissociative symptoms may appear to be "faking bad" on standard measures, or their test results may erroneously indicate that they suffer from thought disorders (Briere, 1997; Carlson,

1997). Adults with PTSD symptoms may over-report their children's PTSD symptoms (Laor, Wolmer, & Cohen, 2001). Secondary motives may also affect reporting accuracy, as when clients are suing in civil court for damages, or when custody and visitation are at stake.

Comorbidity

Much childhood maltreatment does not produce posttraumatic symptoms but predisposes victims to depression, anxiety, conduct disorders, substance abuse, or somatic symptoms such as gastric disturbances, gynecological concerns, and headaches (Noll, 2008; Noll, Trickett, Harris, & Putnam, 2009; Sickel, Noll, Moore, Putnam, & Trickett, 2002). Depression in both adults and children is 2 to 3 times more likely when there is a history of child abuse and neglect than when there is no such history. For adult women, a history of child abuse is the single best predictor for drug and alcohol abuse. More than half of all abused children have significant school problems, and child abuse and neglect victims are more than twice as likely as non-victims to be unemployed as adults (Putnam, 2003). Childhood abuse, neglect, and exposure to other adversities, such as a mentally ill or imprisoned caregiver, are termed Adverse Childhood Experiences (ACEs). The Kaiser Permanente/Centers for Disease Control ACE studies have shown that those who experienced four or more ACEs during childhood were far more likely to engage in unhealthy behaviors throughout the life span and to experience violence or revictimization, severe mental illness, disease, disability, and premature mortality (Anda, Butchart, Felitti, & Brown, 2010; Edwards et al., 2005; Felitti et al., 1998). Adults who have experienced six or more ACEs die on average 20 years earlier than those with no ACEs (Brown et al., 2009; http://www.cdc.gov/ace/index.htm).

The emotional health of parents and their capacity for supportive caretaking following trauma are crucial protective factors for children following abuse and trauma. Mothers have been studied more than fathers have, and it has been found that maternal support is the single factor most predictive of good outcomes for child victims (Friedrich, 2002; Reece, 2000).

ASSESSMENT LIMITATIONS

This chapter does not address the neuropsychological symptoms suffered by many child maltreatment victims. If a batterer has beaten a pregnant woman's abdomen, shaken her or her child, or beaten the mother or child on the face or head, a complete neuropsychological assessment referral for these victims is recommended (Valera & Barenbaum, 2003). In many cases, impulsive and aggressive males and females would benefit from neuropsychological assessments to determine if targeted psychopharmacological interventions might be of assistance to counter the effects of possible brain damage from child abuse or adult affrays.

Adaptations of standard psychological inventories for adults that include the MMPI-2, MCMI-III, Rorschach (Exner System), WISC III, and WAIS III are not addressed in this chapter. Instruments that assess adult posttraumatic symptoms, such as the Trauma Symptom Inventory (TSI) are also not included, although evaluation of parents may be essential for treatment success. (Readers are referred to Briere, 1997; Foa, Keane, & Friedman, 2009; Friedrich, 2002; Olafson, 1999; Wilson & Keane, 1997.) Every competent evaluator should become aware of the limitations and the distorted diagnostic picture that may emerge when only standard instruments are applied to trauma survivors such as combat veterans and child sexual abuse victims.

SELECTION OF INSTRUMENTS

With the exception of general screening measures, the instruments reviewed in this chapter were chosen because they have shown promise or validity in the assessment of children and their parents where maltreatment or trauma exposure are issues. Parent and caregiver measures allow the examiner to assess the child's current functioning with particular focus on problems with dysregulation, for example, dissociation, PTSD, sexual behavior problems, and the quality of the parent's relationship with their child. Child-completed measures primarily assess problems with emotional and behavioral regulation. For a full discussion of posttraumatic stress disorder measures, see Foa et al. (2009). For a more complete list of trauma exposure screening measures and caregiver or child symptom inventories, go to the National Child Traumatic Stress Network's online measures review database (http://www.nctsnet. org/resources/online-research/measures-review). Included among the many measures listed and reviewed there are a number of promising instruments in the emerging field of infant and toddler mental health and additional structured interviews and instruments assessing Child and Adolescent PTSD, Grief Responses, Parental Support, and Stress Indexes for Adolescents and Adults.

ASSESSMENT INSTRUMENTS

Parent, Caregiver, and Teacher Report Measures

Child Behavior Checklist (CBCL) PTSD Subscale
Child Sexual Behavior Inventory (CSBI)
Child Dissociative Checklist (CDC)
Pediatric Emotional Distress Scale (PEDS)
Child Abuse Potential Inventory (CAPI)
Parent Child Conflict Tactics Scale (CTSPC)

Child Self-Report Measures

Trauma Symptom Checklist for Children (TSCC)
Trauma Symptom Checklist for Young Children (TSCYC)
Children's PTSD Reaction Index (CPTS-RI)
Children's Impact of Traumatic Events Scale Revised (CITES-R)
Impact of Events Scale (IES)
Adolescent Dissociative Experiences Scale (A-DES)
Childhood Trust Events Survey (CTES) and Childhood Trust Events
Survey-Adolescent (CTES-A)

PARENT, CAREGIVER, AND TEACHER
REPORT MEASURES

Child Behavior Checklist (CBCL) PTSD Subscale

The full Child Behavior Checklist is covered elsewhere in this edited volume (Chapter 9). The family of CBCL-related instruments is informative and useful in studies of traumatized and maltreated children. There have been two attempts to develop PTSD-related subscales from the CBCL (Levendosky, Huth-Bocks, Semel, & Shapiro, 2002; Wolfe, Gentile, Michienzi, Sas, & Wolfe, 1991). Levendosky and colleagues (2002) found no correlations between their version of the scale and a standard PTSD scale. However, Dehon and Scheeringa (2006) modified the subscale for preschoolers and studied 62 traumatized children aged 23 months through 6 years of age. Mothers were interviewed about the child's PTSD symptoms and then filled out the CBCL. The PTSD subscale correlated highly ($r = .66$) with the number of PTSD symptoms described during interviews, with a cutoff score of 9 having the best sensitivity and specificity for classifying children who met diagnostic criteria for PTSD (Dehon & Scheeringa, 2006).

Parental rejection of the child will be reflected in CBCL results. For example, elevated CBCL scores by parents, relative to teachers, are closely related to parental endorsement of such items as "My child knows how to bug me," and "I will feel better when this child is out of the room" (Friedrich, Lysne, Sim, & Shamos, 2004).

Child Sexual Behavior Inventory (CSBI)

Instrument name. The Child Sexual Behavior Inventory (CSBI) was developed by William N. Friedrich, Ph.D., with the assistance of numerous colleagues (Friedrich, 1997). This measure has been used in an increasing number of studies examining normative and disturbed sexual behavior in children.

Type of instrument. The CSBI is a 38-item measure developed for use with 2- to 12-year-old children. Either parent can complete it although the norms are based on maternal report. An additional four items designed to assess more aggressive and intrusive sexual behavior are described elsewhere (Friedrich, 2002). Clinical use with teachers, day care providers, and other relatives has also been reported in the literature. Training is required for administration and scoring.

Use and target audience. CSBI is intended for children living in a home setting, ages 2 to 12 years, and assesses a variety of sexual behaviors exhibited over the past 6 months falling into such face-valid factors as boundary problems, self-stimulation, gender-related behaviors, sexual intrusiveness, and sexual knowledge.

Multicultural. The CSBI has been translated into several Western European languages and has also been used in epidemiological studies of sexual behavior in several Eastern European countries, including Latvia, Moldova, Macedonia, and Lithuania (Sebre et al., 2004).

Ease and time of administration. The CSBI requires from 5 to 10 minutes to complete; parents should have the opportunity for clarification of individual items.

Scoring procedure. CSBI is hand-scored and provides three summary scores, including total sexual behavior, developmentally related sexual behavior, and sexual abuse specific items. Developmentally related sexual behaviors are those behaviors that are reported by at least 20% of the normative sample for that age and gender. Sexual abuse specific items are those behaviors that significantly discriminated abused from non-abused children for specific age and gender subgroups after controlling for age, gender, maternal education, and family income. A number of very unusual behaviors, which typically are exhibited primarily by sexually abused children, are not included in the SASI because of their rarity but, when present, certainly raise concern.

Reliability, validity, availability, and source. The CSBI has very adequate test–retest reliability, and parents typically correlate with each other. It has demonstrated utility in identifying sexually abused children. Studies of normative sexual behavior in Sweden, the Netherlands, and the United States show considerable similarities among the more unusual behaviors. The CSBI is available from Psychological Assessment Resources, Odessa, Florida.

Comment. The CSBI is the only normed, validated, and published measure of sexual behavior in children. Parents of sexually abused children tend to either minimize or maximize their child's sexual behavior more so than do parents of non-abused children, and reviewing each behavior with parents can be useful to determine the validity of their reports. Although high scores raise concern about possible sexual abuse, they may also reflect response bias, exposure to pornography or overt family sexuality, or some mixture of externalizing behavior problems with sexual provocativeness.

Child Dissociative Checklist (CDC)

Instrument name. The Child Dissociative Checklist (CDC) was developed by Frank W. Putnam, M.D., and his associates in the 1980s (Putnam, Helmers, & Trickettt, 1993; Putnam & Peterson, 1994). Over the course of its development, the CDC has progressed through three major versions. The current version (V3.0-2/90) is a 20-item instrument. It is designed to be both a clinical screening tool and a research tool for dissociative disorders but is not intended for use as a diagnostic instrument.

Type of instrument. The Child Dissociative Checklist is a 20-item parent/adult report measure using a 3-point scale response format (i.e., 2 = Very True, 1 = Somewhat or Sometimes True, and 0 = Not True). The CDC lists behaviors that describe children, and reporters are asked to circle the corresponding number (i.e., 2, 1, or 0) for each item that describes their child "now" or "within the past 12 months." However, clinicians are free to specify another time frame, when, for example, the instrument is administered periodically to assess treatment progress.

Use and target audience. The CDC is designed for children ages 5 to 14. The CDC should be completed by a parent, caretaker, teacher, therapist, or inpatient staff member who is very familiar with the child's behavior and is in frequent contact with the child.

Multicultural. Putnam (1997) reports, "We know less about the effects of gender and culture on CDC scores. I am certain that these factors influence reported scores in some cases, and probably more so for children than for adults" (p. 252). The CDC has been translated into Spanish and Italian. Translations are available by request at http://www.ohiocando4kids.org/Dissociation.

Ease and time of administration. The CDC is a brief, 20-item observer report measure that takes 5 to 10 minutes to administer and score.

Scoring procedure. The CDC score is the sum of all of the item scores and can range from 0 to 40 on Version 3.0. Developmental, cultural, and individual variables must be taken into account when interpreting a CDC score. CDC scores tend to decrease with age, suggesting that young children experience slightly more dissociation than do older children. However, in the most extreme cases of dissociation, maturation does not affect scores. Generally, a score of 12 or higher is considered an indication of pathological dissociation warranting further evaluation. Children who do not have a trauma or maltreatment history generally have very low scores on the CDC, just above a score of 2. Maltreated children have higher scores, a mean of 6.0. The mean for children with dissociative disorders is about 20.

Reliability. The CDC has been shown to be a reliable instrument in several studies. The CDC shows moderate to good 1-year test–retest stability ($r = .65$) and internal consistency (Cronbach's alpha = .86).

Validity. The validity of the CDC has primarily been assessed on its ability to discriminate among groups. Several studies have found that sexually abused children score significantly higher on the CDC than non-abused comparison children, and the CDC is generally able to discriminate between children with pathological dissociation and those without. In one study of four test samples, the CDC discriminated between normal control girls, sexually abused girls, children with Dissociative Disorder NOS, and children with Dissociative Identity Disorder (Putnam et al., 1993). Good convergent and discriminant validity have been indicated. The more serious the abuse history (e.g., combined physical and sexual abuse, multiple perpetrators), the higher the CDC score (Putnam, Helmers, Horowitz, & Trickett, 1994).

Availability and source. The CDC is a public domain document freely available for reproduction, distribution, and use. Readers who wish to make changes to it are asked to change the name to reduce confusion. The CDC is available by request at http://www.ohiocando4kids.org/Dissociation and in the appendices of Putnam (1997).

Comment. The complex disorders associated with severe and prolonged childhood trauma and maltreatment include pathological dissociation; indeed, dissociative disorders are rarely seen among those who have no victimization histories (Putnam, 1997). This easily administered, freely available, valid, and reliable instrument fills a need for screening children as young as 5 years old for the presence of pathological dissociation. High scores alert clinicians and evaluators to undertake structured clinical interviews for formal diagnosis. Many CDC items can be confounded with attention deficit disorders, so that interviews with parents are necessary to determine if endorsed items are suggestive of dissociation or are related to ADHD (Friedrich, 2002). The two diagnoses are not mutually exclusive. The CDC's sensitivity to dose exposure adds to its usefulness with children. Because the CDC is freely available and easily administered, it is widely used in clinical and research settings.

Pediatric Emotional Distress Scale (PEDS)

Instrument name. The Pediatric Emotional Distress Scale (PEDS) was published in 1999 by Conway Saylor, Ph.D., and colleagues. It is not a measure of Posttraumatic Stress Disorder as defined in the DSM-IV, a diagnosis derived from work with traumatized adults and then adapted for use with children. Instead, the items on this scale were chosen based on behaviors that have been identified as occurring to young children who have experienced or are experiencing trauma.

Type of instrument. The PEDS consists of 21 items (17 general behavior and 4 event-specific) rated by the parent or guardian to measure the behavioral problems of children ages 2 through 10 years old after trauma. The scale consists of three subscales: Anxious/Withdrawn, Fearful, and Acting Out. In addition, there are items that ask about posttraumatic behaviors by children such as games, stories, and play about the trauma.

Use and target audience. Children 2 through 10 years old who have been traumatized by homelessness, sexual abuse, natural disasters, and other negative experiences.

Multicultural. The PEDS is among the few instruments in which psychometric properties have been examined for homeless children. As a recently developed instrument, the PEDS has not been tested widely among diverse cultural groups. The PEDS is not intended for use alone as a diagnostic or forensic instrument, but as a screening measure that forms part of a more complete assessment.

Ease and time of administration. The PEDS takes 5 to 10 minutes to administer and score. The PEDS appears to be a sensitive measure of stress in children, and its brevity provides an advantage in assessments during high-stress situations.

Scoring procedure. The higher the scores are, the greater the child's distress is.

Reliability. The overall alpha coefficient for the first 17 items was .85. Test–retest reliability at 6 weeks ranged from .55 to .61. Inter-rater reliability between fathers and mothers ranged from .65 for the PEDS total and ranged from .47 to .64 for subscales.

Validity. Parental evaluations correlated with total scores. Further work on discriminant validity is needed. The scale shows good sensitivity and specificity for traumatized children compared with non-clinical samples of non-traumatized children. The scale shows good sensitivity to the stressors experienced by homeless children, for example. Although the PEDS assesses behavior problems that are common among traumatized children, many of these same behaviors also occur among clinical samples of children who have not been traumatized, and further studies are needed to assess the discriminant validity of this measure on traumatized versus non-traumatized clinical samples (Ohan, Myers, & Collett, 2002). Years of education affected maternal scores, with less educated mothers endorsing fewer items at a high level.

Availability and source. A copy of this brief scale is printed in Saylor, C. F., Swenson, C. C., Reynolds, S. S., & Taylor, M. (1999). The Pediatric Emotional Distress Scale: A brief screening measure for young children exposed to traumatic events. *Journal of Clinical Child Psychology, 28,* 70–81. Before using the scale, contact Conway Saylor for consent and further clinical information.

Comment. This brief and promising instrument fills a need by screening the responses of preschool children to trauma, but it is still in the early stages of development and validation, and further work on discriminant validity is expected. This instrument has the advantage of not trying to fit stressed and traumatized children's symptom patterns into diagnostic categories developed during research with adults. The scale was constructed in consultation with investigators who had studied the effects of disasters on children, and then the scale was reviewed by doctoral-level clinical psychologists for appropriateness. Because the symptoms of fearfulness, anxiety, withdrawal, and acting out observed in traumatized children are also commonly seen in non-traumatized clinical samples, discriminant validity studies may not usefully separate these two populations. Nevertheless, anxiety or acting out associated with abuse and trauma histories in children will require different treatment approaches than non-trauma-based anxiety or acting out in children. Complete abuse and trauma histories should always be obtained as part of differential diagnostic work for these presenting symptoms in young children.

Parenting Stress Index (PSI)

The Parenting Stress Index is covered in Chapter 9 of this volume and is widely used in trauma and maltreatment assessments.

Child Abuse Potential Inventory (CAPI)

Instrument name. The Child Abuse Potential Inventory (CAPI) was developed by Joel Milner (Milner, 1986).

Type of instrument. The CAPI was developed with the goal that it could be employed by protective services workers to screen for physical child abuse. Because of its use in the field, another goal was that it be relatively simple. The initial item pool represented the existing empirical and theoretical literature on maltreatment.

Use and target audience. The CAPI is intended to be used primarily as a screening tool for the detection of physical child abuse. Although specifically designed to be employed by protective services workers, it is also used as a psychological test.

Multicultural. The CAPI has norms not only for the United States but also for Spain. It has been translated into a number of other languages, and research in other cultures has indicated that the underlying constructs of the CAPI are present in other cultures. However, this is an under-researched area of the CAPI.

Ease and time of administration. There is no time limit for completing the test, and given the circumstances of its use, some parents approach this task in a very deliberate manner. Typically, it takes from 12 to 20 minutes to complete.

Scoring procedures. These scales can be hand-scored or computer scored. The primary clinical scale is a 77-item physical child abuse scale. This abuse scale can be divided into six factor scales: Distress, Rigidity, Unhappiness, Problems With Child and Self, Problems With Family, and Problems With Others. In addition, the CAPI contains three validity scales: lie scale, random response scale, and inconsistency scale. The validity scales are used in various combinations to produce three response distortion indices: faking good index, faking bad index, and random response index.

Reliability, validity, availability, and source. The CAPI manual (Milner, 1986) reports an impressive body of research supporting the internal consistency and temporal stability of the CAPI. In addition, the CAPI correlates with the Parenting Stress Index ($r = .62$) as well as relevant personality factors derived from the Edwards Personal Preference Schedule, the 16 personality factor questionnaire, and the MMPI. CAPI abuse classification rates in the literature are typically in the range of 80% to 90% when severe abuse parents are compared to non-abusing parents. The measure, manual, and scoring information are available from PSYTEC, Inc., DeKalb, Illinois.

Comment. Both the PSI and the CAPI assess relevant and similar dimensions of the parent–child relationship. The advantage of the CAPI is that it also assesses for physical abuse potential. Consequently, if physical abuse is ever an issue, it is preferable to administer the CAPI rather than the PSI. Otherwise for treatment purposes, the PSI-SF is usually sufficient to determine the degree to which parents are in need of support and how accurately they view their child. Because of its general nature, the CAPI cannot be used to differentiate between neglect and abuse.

Parent-Child Conflict Tactic Scale (CTSPC)

Instrument name. The Parent-Child Conflict Tactic Scale (CTSPC) was developed by Murray Straus and colleagues (1998), many of them at the Family Research Laboratory at the University of New Hampshire. This scale is one of several conflict tactic scales (CTS) developed by Straus and colleagues.

Type of instrument. The CTSPC is a brief measure that is practical for epidemiological research on child maltreatment and for clinical screening by professionals. It contains 22 items that assess nonviolent discipline, psychological aggression, and physical assault. In addition, five neglect items can also be included as well as supplemental questions regarding weekly discipline and sexual maltreatment experienced by the parent.

Use and target audience. The CTSPC is intended for the parents of children living in their home, typically ages 6 to 17, although the authors report that the prevalence and chronicity of corporal punishment decline rapidly from about the age of 5 on, and consequently using it with younger children is appropriate.

Multicultural. The CTSPC research reveals no clear differences between Euro–American and either African–American or Hispanic–American parents, although research on severe assaults has typically found higher rates for the two minority groups.

Ease and time of administration. The CTSPC requires 6 to 8 minutes to complete, and parents should have the opportunity for clarification of items.

Scoring procedure. The three core CTSPC scales contain 22 items. Fourteen supplemental questions that assess neglect, weekly discipline, and sexual maltreatment of the parent and the child can be added to the CTSPC core scales. The standard instructions for the CTSPC ask the parent to describe what happened in the previous year although this time period can be altered depending on the individual. The parent is asked to describe his or her practices with a specific child and can rate the frequency of discipline strategies on a 6-point scale, with additional information on whether or not the parent has used this strategy, has used this strategy in the past but not in the past year, or has never used this strategy. The CTSPC subscales include nonviolent discipline, psychological aggression, minor assault (corporal punishment), severe assault (physical maltreatment), and very severe assault (severe physical maltreatment).

Reliability, validity, availability, and source. The internal consistency of the CTSPC varies widely depending on the frequency of item endorsement, with very low coefficients for neglect and severe physical assault but acceptable coefficients for the other subscales. Given the recency of its development, research is only now developing regarding its discriminant and construct validity. A measure is available either from the Family Research Laboratory or from Straus et al. (1998). The CTSPC is a good companion to either the PSI-SF or the CAPI in that it allows the parent to more specifically indicate discipline strategies. Parents presenting to a clinical program vary in terms of their defensiveness on all self-report measures, and given the face validity of the items, outright denial is certainly likely. However, when used in the context of a clinical interview, or as part of an ongoing therapy process, the openness of the parent is usually appropriate and can help make them aware of the need for changes.

CHILD SELF-REPORT MEASURES

Trauma Symptom Checklist for Children (TSCC)

Instrument name. The Trauma Symptom Checklist for Children (TSCC) was developed by John Briere (1996) and has been used extensively and translated into a number of languages. The TSCC has been used in a growing body of clinical research of both disturbed and non-disturbed children.

Type of instrument. The TSCC was designed to be used for 8- to 15-year-old children. It contains 54 items that are answered on a 4-point response format (i.e., Never, Sometimes, Oftentimes, and Almost All the Time). The TSCC can be used with both the full version and an abbreviated version that does not include the sexual concern items. No specific training in clinical psychology or related fields is required for administration and scoring of this measure, but it should be interpreted by professionals with training in psychometrics. It can be either hand-scored or computer scored.

Use and target audience. The TSCC is intended for children ages 8 to 15 and assesses a broad range of trauma-related symptoms, including anxiety, depression, anger, posttraumatic symptoms, dissociation, and sexual concerns. Both dissociation and sexual concerns include two subscales. These are dissociation-obvious and dissociation-fantasy, and sexual concerns-preoccupation and sexual concerns-distress, respectively.

Multicultural. The TSCC has been used in numerous countries and has been translated into a large number of languages. Translations are available at www.parinc.com.

Ease and time of administration. The TSCC typically takes about 18 minutes to complete. The administrator should be available to clarify items, particularly those included in the sexual concerns subscale.

Scoring procedure. The TSCC can be either hand or computer scored, and in addition to the clinical scales mentioned above, it also includes two validity scales pertaining to under-response and hyper-response.

Reliability, validity, availability, and source. The TSCC has very adequate test–retest reliability and its validity continues to be demonstrated in a number of studies. It is available from Psychological Assessment Resources, Odessa, Florida, at 1-800-331-TEST, or www.parinc.com.

Comment. The TSCC is the only self-report measure available for this age range of children that includes not only PTSD-related symptoms but also sexual concerns. Both of these in combination are among the most relevant dimensions to assess sexually abused children (Kendall-Tackett, Williams, and Finkelhor, 1993). Unlike many other posttrauma measures, the TSCC also assesses levels of anxiety, depression, and anger, all three of which are very common posttraumatic reactions. However, other anxiety and depression measures such as the BDI, the CDI, and the MASC, appear to provide a finer-grained assessment of these dimensions (Friedrich, 2002). The utility of the TSCC can be maximized if after administration of the test, the evaluator reinterviews the child by anchoring endorsed PTS items to specific events (Friedrich, 2002). One disadvantage of the TSCC, or any self-report measure, is that it is filled out by the child, and both traumatized and non-traumatized children may be poor reporters of their own internal states. Poor reporting may be due partly to the fact that young children and children from certain cultures lack the language to express feelings accurately. In addition, traumatized children often minimize and deny their distress. For this reason, the CITES-R, which offers a semi-structured interview format that may be more effective in helping children disclose internal states, should be considered as a supplement for those traumatized children who produce flat-line TSCC profiles (Friedrich, 2002). The CITES-R is stronger than the TSCC in assessing the avoidant aspects of children's PTSD, and the TSCC is stronger than the CITES-R on most other scales (Crouch, Smith, Ezzell, & Saunders, 1999). Neither scale thoroughly assesses the sexually avoidant pattern known to occur in many sexual assault victims (Friedrich, 2002).

Trauma Symptom Checklist for Young Children (TSCYC)

Instrument name. The Trauma Symptom Checklist for Young Children (TSCYC) was developed and initially tested by John N. Briere and colleagues (Briere et al., 2001) as a caregiver or parent-report measure to supplement Briere's earlier Trauma Symptom Checklist for Children (1996). The TSCYC assesses the same broad range of trauma-related symptoms as the TSCC but for a different age range (3 to 12 rather than 8 to 16). For children aged 8 to 12, administration of both scales allows comparison of caregiver and child responses and may yield more useful clinical information than the use of either instrument alone (Lanktree et al., 2008).

Type of instrument. The TSCYC is a 90-item, caregiver report measure intended to assess both acute and chronic posttraumatic symptoms in children ages 3 to 12. As with the TSCC, items are answered on a 4-point response format: Never, Sometimes, Lots of Times, and Almost All of the Time. An abbreviated version is available. No training is required for administration, but the TSCYC must be interpreted by professionals trained in psychometrics.

Use and target audience. The TSCYC is intended for parent/caregiver report of children ages 3 to 12 to assess a range of trauma-related symptoms. Unlike many caregiver measures, it contains two reporter validity scales for under-reporting and over-reporting (Response Level and Atypical Response) as well as an item that assesses average waking hours per week the reporting caregiver spends with the child on a scale from 1 (0–1 hours) to 7 (over 60 hours). The TSCYC contains eight clinical scales: Posttraumatic Stress Intrusion (PPS-I), Posttraumatic Stress Avoidance (PTS-AV), Posttraumatic Stress Arousal (PTS-A), Sexual Concerns (SC), Dissociation (DIS), Anxiety (ANX), Depression (DEP), and Anger/Aggression (ANG). There is also a summary score for Posttraumatic Stress Total (TOT).

Multicultural. The TSCYC has been translated into a number of languages. Translations are available at www.parinc.com.

Ease and time of administration. The TSCYC can be administered in 15 to 20 minutes.

Scoring procedure. The TSCYC can be easily hand-scored, but a computer program is also available. There are separate norms for males and females and for children in three age groups (3–4, 5–9, and 10–12).

Reliability and validity. Validity and reliability were studied in a multi-site sample of 219 children who had been sexually abused, physically abused, or exposed to domestic violence (Briere et al., 2001). The individual clinical scales showed good to excellent reliability, with *Alpha* internal consistency ranging from .81 for Sexual

Concerns to .93 for PTSD-Total. The average *alpha* was .87. As for construct validity, Briere and colleagues (2001) write, "The TSCYC scales most associated with different types of childhood abuse were those measuring posttraumatic stress, followed by sexual concerns and dissociation," but there was an unexpected lack of association between anxiety, depression, and anger and abuse history even though these scales had good face validity (p. 1009). The authors suggest that dysphoric mood may broadly discriminate between abused and non-abused children without varying as a function of type of abuse, a hypothesis to be tested in future analyses of the TSCYC in a sample that contains both abused and non-abused children. A comparative study of the TSCC and TSCYC (Lanktree et al., 2008) has found moderate convergence with respect to both scales, especially for anxiety, depression, anger, dissociation, and sexual concerns. However, two PTS subscales failed to correlate with the TSCC PTS scales; the Avoidance subscale correlated with no TSCC scale, and the PTS Arousal scale correlated with TSCC Anxiety rather than with the PTS scale on the TSCC. The authors conclude that the TSCYC and the TSCC display moderate convergent and discriminant validity with respect to one another.

Availability. The TSCYC is available from Psychological Assessment Resources, Odessa, FL at (800)-331-TEST, or www.parinc.com.

Comment. The advantage of both the TSCC and the TSCYC is that they assess not only single incident traumas using the formal PTSD construct, but also a number of symptom domains more consistent with the emerging proposed diagnosis for chronically maltreated children, Developmental Trauma Disorder. As a caregiver report measure, the TSCYC enables assessment of these pervasive maltreatment responses for children as young as three. In addition, caregiver reports for children aged 8 to 12 may well serve as a corrective to the under-reporting characteristic of many children on self-report measures. Because of the ease with which it can be administered and the gaps it fills among existing instrumentation, the TSCYC is widely used by National Child Traumatic Stress Network centers and by many clinicians throughout the United States, and further work on its validity and multicultural applications is under way.

Children's PTSD-Reaction Index (CPTS-RI)

Instrument name. The Children's PTSD-Reaction Index (CPTS-RI) was developed by Robert Pynoos and his associates at UCLA in 1987 and has been widely used in the United States, Europe, and Asia. It has been selected as one of the instruments by which the federally funded NCTSN collects data on traumatized youth among its 35 centers.

Type of instrument. The CPTS-RI is a clinician-administered scale, but it can also be used as a self-report measure. Training is required for administration and scoring.

Use and target audience. It is intended for children aged 7 to 18 to assess symptoms following exposure to trauma. The Child Version is worded for ages 7 to 12; the Parent Version mirrors the Child Version for ages 7 to 12; and the Adolescent Version contains minor changes in wording from the Child Version designed for youth aged 13 to 18.

Multicultural. The PTSD-Reaction Index has been translated into several languages and has been used in Armenia, Kuwait, Cambodia, and the United States.

Ease and time of administration. All three instruments are designed as self-report measures, which makes them easier to administer than other children's PTSD measures such as the Children's PTSD Inventory, the CPTSDI (Saigh, 2002) or the Clinician-Administered PTSD Scale for Children, the CAPS-C (Nader et al., 2002). All three versions of the CPTS-RI contain 27 questions in the traumatic exposure section. For PTSD symptoms, the Child Version contains 20 questions, the Parent Version 21, and the Adolescent Version 22 questions. The instruments can also be administered verbally to individuals or groups.

Scoring procedure. Scores are hand tallied. Scores of 12 to 24 = mild PTSD, 25 to 39 = moderate, 40 to 59 = severe, and higher than 60 very severe PTSD.

Reliability. Internal consistency for the child version is .69 to .80, inter-rater reliability for the adolescent version .88; and test–retest reliability for adolescents over one week .93.

Validity. Children with greater exposure to traumas had higher scores (Thaber & Vostanis, 1999). Both sensitivity and specificity for PTSD diagnosis are moderate or good. The CPTS-RI factors overlap with but do not exactly measure PTSD symptoms as constructed in the DSM-IV. However, because PTSD in children differs from the DSM-IV's largely adult-based construct (AACAP, 1998) these differences may not signal diminished validity.

Availability and source. The CPTS-RI is not commercially available, but it may be obtained from Robert Pynoos, M.D., at UCLA or Kathleen Nader, DSW, in Cedar Park, Texas. A recently released administration and scoring CD for use by NCTSN sites and others (2003) is available through Robert Pynoos, M.D., Trauma Psychiatry Service, UCLA, 300 UCLA Medical Plaza, Los Angeles, CA 90024-6968.

Comment. Among the new instruments designed to measure PTSD symptoms in children, the CPTS-RI has several advantages. More extensively researched than some of the other new child instruments, it does not require clinician administration. It has been shown to be suitable for children with different kinds of trauma, of different ages, and from varied cultures. It is among the best studied of contemporary instruments for posttraumatic stress disorder as defined in the DSM-IV-TR. As the regional centers of the National Child Traumatic Stress Network apply this instrument to collect their data on a variety of traumatized youth, from domestically violent homes to homeless shelters to residential treatment homes, its utility may increase. One disadvantage is that this instrument is not designed to measure complex posttraumatic stress disorder, that is, the pervasive effects of long-term exposure to severe trauma and abuse that many children experience in their homes, schools, and neighborhoods (Herman, 1992; Pelcovitz et al., 1997). In addition, like other PTSD child measures, the CPTS-RI assesses traumatized children using a construct first identified in adults and then adapted for children, rather than building the construct afresh by studying traumatized children (AACAP, 1998).

The Children's Impact of Traumatic Events Scale-Revised (CITES-R)

Instrument name. The Children's Impact of Traumatic Events Scale-Revised (CITES-R) was published in 1991 by Vicky Veitch Wolfe, Carole Gentile, and others, and is a 78-item questionnaire to which child sexual abuse victims answer Very True, Somewhat True, or Not True with respect to their thoughts and feelings about the abuse (Wolfe et al., 1991). Although the CITES-R is designed as a clinician-administered structured interview, older children with good reading ability may complete it as a self-report measure. It is most useful as a semi-structured interview, however, and may serve as a useful transition from assessment into treatment (Friedrich, 2002). It is designed to assess PTS symptoms, eroticism, perceptions of support following disclosure, and abuse attributions such as blame. The CITES-R has 11 scales. It has no normative data. There exists also a reworded version of the scale designed for youths who have witnessed domestic violence (CITES-FVF; Ohan et al., 2002). There is no manual available.

Type of instrument. The CITES-R is a structured interview instrument, although it can be used with older children as a self-report measure.

Use and target audience. The CITES-R is for sexual abuse victims aged 8 to 16. It fills a gap by inquiring not only about trauma-related symptoms but also about factors that mediate the development of symptoms, such as abuse-related attributions by victims (blame, responsibility, power/control) and victims' perceptions of social reactions of others following disclosure (Crouch et al., 1999).

Multicultural. The CITES-R has been used with White and African–American U.S. populations.

Ease and time of administration. The CITES-R takes 20 to 40 minutes to administer as a structured interview and 5 to 10 minutes to score. There are no normative data available.

Scoring procedure. The scale is hand-scored. No computerized version is available. There are four rationally derived scales: PTSD, Eroticism, Social Reactions, and Attributions. These scales are further subdivided, so that a total of 11 subscales are available.

Reliability. Subscales range in internal consistency from .56 to .91. Dangerous World and Personal Vulnerability have poor internal consistency, and the others range from moderate to excellent.

Validity. Validity of subscales ranged from very poor to moderate. In general, the most robust scales are for Intrusive Thoughts, Avoidance, Hyperarousal, and Sexual Anxiety. The scales titled Dangerous World, Social Support, and Empowerment have been found to be less robust and should be interpreted with caution (Chaffin & Schultz, 2001). Three of the four scales have been found to show improvement in symptoms during treatment, but subscales in the abuse attributions scale did not change in the expected direction (Chaffin & Shultz, 2001).

Availability and source. The CITES-R and the CITES-FVF are available from Vicki Veitch Wolfe, Children's Hospital of Western Ontario, 800 Commissioners Road East, London, Ontario, Canada, N6A 5C2 or go to http://www.uwo.ca.

Comment. The CITES-R measures constructs not assessed by other scales, so that clinicians should consider adding it to pretreatment assessments for sexually abused children or children who have witnessed domestic violence. Because it is best used as a semi-structured interview, the CITES-R may enable clinicians to obtain responses from traumatized children that they would not provide on self-report measures such as the TSCC. However, the lack of a manual, or normative data, and of consistently good psychometrics across various scales and subscales limit the usefulness of this scale. Clinicians should be familiar with the major publications about this scale, such as those by Chaffin and his colleagues (2001) and by Crouch and colleagues (1999) to assess test results in light of their findings about the robustness of the CITES-R scales and subscales.

Impact of Events Scale (IES)

Instrument name. The Impact of Events Scale (IES) was published in 1979 by Mardi Horowitz, Nancy Wilner, and William Alvarez. It was designed to measure the psychological impact of trauma or stress on adults. It has since been used with children and adolescents as young as 8 years old. The IES was created prior to the inclusion of PTSD in the American Psychiatric Association's diagnostic manuals: PTSD first appeared in DSM-III in 1980.

Type of instrument. The IES is a 15-item, self-report measure. Seven of the items measure intrusion, eight measure avoidance, and when combined, they provide a total subjective stress score. Respondents are asked to rank each item on a 4-point scale according to how often each has occurred in the past 7 days. The scale assesses the frequency with which experiences of "intrusions," "avoidance," and emotional numbing related to traumatic/stressful events were experienced in the last week.

Use and target audience. The scale can be used with adults and with children and adolescents 8 to 18 years old. Because of its brevity, it can easily be administered in the immediate aftermath of mass catastrophes as well as individual traumas. However, like many PTSD measures developed on adults and adapted for children, the IES has not undergone adequate developmental modification. Questions are merely reworded rather than changed to reflect child-specific posttraumatic symptoms and behaviors

Multicultural. The IES has been translated into many languages and has been applied to adolescents from various cultures. The IES has helped to demonstrate that reactions to trauma are consistent across cultures. It has discriminated between traumatized and non-traumatized youth in Britain, Cambodia, among refugee populations in Asia and in the West, and among French children exposed to disasters. It has been translated into many languages.

Ease and time of administration. The IES takes 10 minutes to administer and score.

Scoring procedure. A total score is calculated by summing all 15 item responses.

Reliability. Both the intrusion and avoidance scales have displayed acceptable reliability (alpha of .79 and .82, respectively), and a split-half reliability for the whole scale of .86 (Horowitz, Wilner, & Alvarez, 1979). The factor structure is not clear, and one possible subscale, Numbing, has only 2 items. There is no normative base available.

Validity. The IES has also displayed the ability to discriminate a variety of traumatized groups from non-traumatized groups (see Briere, 1997 for review) including Britain, Cambodia, the United States, and France. The IES can be used for repeated measurement over time, and its sensitivity to change allows for monitoring clients' progress in therapy.

Availability and source. Horowitz, M., Milner, M., & Alvarez, W. (1979). Impact of Events Scale: A measure of subjective stress. *Psychosomatic Medicine, 41,* 209–218.

Comment. As one of the earliest trauma-specific measures developed, the IES has been useful, especially as a quick and dirty screening measure that can be administered even during the chaotic days following mass disasters. It has been very widely translated and used since its first appearance a generation ago, and in its original form, is better used as a screening device than as a full PTSD assessment tool. A recent revision, the IES-R (Weiss, 2002; Weiss & Marmar, 1997), has been developed for adults, but normative data for children are not yet available.

The IES was developed as an instrument before PTSD had been constructed and does not reflect full PTSD criteria (Horowitz et al., 1979). Designed to measure the impact of a single trauma rather than the chronic severe trauma and maltreatment experienced by many children being assessed, it has nevertheless been very widely used with children and adults in the generation since its creation, and widely translated. It has been moderately good at distinguishing traumatized from non-traumatized people in a variety of cultures. The lack of developmental adaptation limits its applicability to children and adolescents.

Adolescent Dissociative Experiences Scale (A-DES)

Instrument name. When compared to parents of younger children, parents of teenagers are less familiar with the details of their children's lives. Because of this, and because adolescents are better self-reporters of behavior than younger children, the utility of the CDC during adolescence is limited. The Adolescent Dissociative Experiences Scale (A-DES) was the product of a collaborative effort among a number of individuals organized by Judith Armstrong, Eve Bernstein Carlson, and Frank Putnam to come up with a self-report scale for teenagers to screen for pathological dissociation (Armstrong, Carlson, Libero, & Smith, 1997).

Type of instrument. The A-DES is a 30-item self-report screening tool for serious dissociative and posttraumatic disorders. Items are neutrally worded and are generally worded in the present tense. The questions ask about different kinds of experiences that happen to people. The answer response format is a 0 to 10 scale, anchored at the ends with Never (0) and Always (10). Adolescents circle the corresponding number based on how often the experiences happen to them when they have not had drugs or alcohol.

Use and target audience. The A-DES is a self-report measure for adolescents ages 11 to 20.

Multicultural. The A-DES has been translated into many languages, and they are available by request at http://www.ohiocando4kids.org/ Dissociation.

Ease and time of administration. The A-DES is a brief 30-item adolescent self-report measure. It takes about 10 minutes to administer and score.

Scoring procedure. The A-DES is scored by summing item scores and dividing by 30 (number of items). The overall score ranges from 0 to 10. A mean score of 4 or above signifies pathological dissociation. As a rule of thumb, the A-DES score is approximately the Dissociative Experiences Scale (DES), an adult measure of dissociation (Putnam, 1997), score divided by 10. The A-DES-T is a taxometric subscale of the A-DES measuring pathological dissociation. It is scored by adding item scores and dividing by 8 (number of items). Scores of 4 or higher are considered indicative of significant dissociation deserving further clinical evaluation. The A-DES-T may also be used as a shortened version of the A-DES.

Reliability. Psychometric data on the A-DES indicate excellent reliability (Cronbach's alpha = .93; split-half = .92).

Validity. The A-DES differentiated abused and non-abused psychiatric patients and dissociative adolescents who were diagnosed independently of the A-DES scored significantly higher on the A-DES than other inpatients.

Availability and source. The A-DES is a public domain document freely available for reproduction, distribution, and use. (Readers who wish to make changes to it are asked to change the name to reduce confusion.) The complete 30-item A-DES is available by request at http://www.ohiocando4kids.org/Dissociation and in the appendix of Putnam, F. W. (1997). *Dissociation in children and adolescents: A developmental perspective.* New York: Guilford Press.

Comment. Because of its face validity, the A-DES depends on the willingness of youth to report unusual feelings and internal states. It is not to be used for diagnosis but as a screening measure to be followed by a full clinical interview to assess the presence or absence of dissociation. However, adolescents who engage in daydreaming or fantasy games such as Dungeons and Dragons may score high on this scale. In addition, as an adaptation of an adult interview, some of its components are not appropriate for adolescents. However, despite these caveats, the A-DES is a useful instrument to screen for dissociation among adolescents (Ohan et al., 2002).

The Childhood Trust Events Survey (CTES) and the Childhood Trust Events Survey–Adolescent (CTES-A)

Instrument name. The Childhood Trust Events Survey (CTES) and the Childhood Trust Events Survey–Adolescent (CTES-A).

Type of measure. The Childhood Trust Events Survey (CTES) and the Childhood Trust Events Survey–Adolescent (CTES-A) are not formal instruments but are, instead, trauma, stressor, and adversity history questionnaires. Both measures were developed by members of the National Child Traumatic Stress Network Trauma Treatment Training Center at Cincinnati Children's Hospital, to supplement existing trauma history surveys by including chronic adversities that do not meet formal definitions for trauma but that nevertheless have pervasive impact on the developing child. Some items were derived from the Traumatic Events Screening Inventory for Children (TESI-CI) and the UCLA PTSD Index (Pynoos, Rodriguez, Steinberg, Stuber, & Frederick, 1998; Ribbe, 1996). In addition, the CTES surveys are the only child history surveys that include all of the questions contained in the pathbreaking Adverse Childhood Experiences (ACES) studies by Felitti and colleagues (Felitti et al., 1998) at San Diego's Kaiser Permanente and the Centers for Disease Control and Prevention.

Use and target audience. The CTES is a youth, self-report survey for children from 8 to 18 that asks about trauma and adverse experiences exposure in 26 yes/no questions. It can be filled out by the child or administered by a clinician who reads the questions to the child and fills out the form. There are caregiver versions available for both the CTES and the CTES-A for caregivers to provide information they have about the child's trauma and adversity history.

Comment. The CTES-A was created especially for use with polyvictimized adolescents, especially those in juvenile justice and residential treatment centers. It contains 30 yes/no questions and space available to provide details about the experiences and circle the age ranges when traumas and adversities occurred.

Multicultural. There is a Spanish version of the CTES.

Ease and time of administration. The CTES and CTES-A can be administered in 15 to 20 minutes.

Scoring procedure. Although it may be useful to tabulate the number of ACEs for clinical purposes, there is no clinical cutoff or scoring system. Go to the Centers for Disease Control and Prevention's ACE Study webpage (http://www.cdc.gov/ace/index.htm) for research papers about the impact of multiple ACES on mental and physical health throughout the life span.

Reliability and validity. Because this is a trauma and adversity history questionnaire, there are no reliability or validity data available.

Availability and source. Both measures are available at http://www.ohiocando4kids.org/Childhood_Trauma.

Comment. The CTES and CTES-A are being used in many juvenile justice facilities and mental health agencies in Ohio.

DEPRESSION MEASURES

Children and adults who have been victimized by abuse and violence are far more likely than non-victims to suffer from major depression or dysthymia (Kolko & Swenson, 2002; Putnam, 2003). A history of child physical or sexual abuse appears also to alter major depression's clinical presentation and be associated with earlier onset and less responsiveness to standard depression treatments with SSRIs, but depressive symptoms linked to a history of child abuse do respond to cognitive-behavioral therapies (Putnam, 2003). When boys are sexually abused, their symptom presentation during childhood and into adulthood is more severe than that of sexually abused girls (Gold, Lucenko, Elhai, Swingle, & Sellers, 1999). The Beck Depression Inventory and the Children's Depression Inventory are covered elsewhere in this volume.

ANXIETY MEASURES

The Multidimensional Anxiety Scale for Children (MASC) is an appropriate ancillary measure to the Trauma Symptom Checklist for Children, which also assesses anxiety, although the anxiety scale from the TSCC is not as inclusive. Affective distress is common in maltreated children, and the MASC provides a much more detailed assessment of anxiety, should there be any indication of this disorder based on the CBCL or the TSCC. The MASC is fully covered elsewhere in this volume.

STRATEGY FOR UTILIZING CHILDHOOD ABUSE AND TRAUMA INSTRUMENTS

Because trauma, maltreatment, and abuse vary greatly in their content and their effects, no single protocol is recommended. This chapter has given information about 13 instruments without covering all that are available in this rapidly developing and exciting field of inquiry. To complete an assessment, select the tests based on the assessment question— for example, is trauma suspected? If so, was the trauma a one-time event or repeated over time? Were there multiple traumas and stressors? Are there concerns about anxiety or depression? Was the child maltreated by a family member or by a stranger? Was there sexual assault, so that possible sexualized behaviors need to be assessed? The following are general guidelines that are then applied to a single case for illustrative purposes.

Select psychological tests appropriate to this child. Include self-report measures, if the child is old enough, and parent or caretaker report measures, as well as teacher report measures if possible and appropriate.

Depending on the circumstances for this evaluation, review confidentiality and privilege parameters with the child, caretakers, and others, if applicable.

Administer and score the tests.

Collect additional information on the child's history, circumstances, and family situation through interview, observation, clinical records, court or social workers or victim advocates if applicable.

Review and share the findings and your report with the child and with the child's caretakers.

Make recommendations for the family or other interested parties as indicated by your test findings and your interviewers.

CASE EXAMPLE
William N. Friedrich, Ph.D., ABPP, LP

Abby is a 10-year-old girl who was referred because she sexually touched Calvin, a 4-year-old boy, in a day care setting. In her 3 months in this day care, she had inserted herself into a parental role and frequently helped out with serving snacks, getting children packed up when parents arrived, and helping two younger children with toileting. One of these was Calvin, the 4-year-old boy who reported being sexually touched during toileting.

Abby was adopted at the age of 4. She lived with her adoptive parents and had a 17-year-old sister, the biological daughter of her parents. Her post-adoption adjustment was characterized as uneventful, and she had never been identified as having behavioral problems. For example, her grades in school were typically above average. Her pre-adoptive experiences included neglect and physical abuse; sexual abuse has never been confirmed although it has been expected, given her rearing circumstances.

Betsy, the adoptive mother, was interviewed, and she reported that Abby had exhibited a 9- to 12-month history of greater sexual interest and genital touching after the adoption, but this had faded before she entered kindergarten. More recently, she had started talking about boyfriends, and Betsy felt that Abby had a longstanding problem of being overly friendly with adult males. However, this has never presented itself as a problem. She also wondered if the interest in boyfriends paralleled her 17-year-old daughter's having a boyfriend.

Betsy also reported that she and her husband were in marital therapy and most likely would be separating. Her return to full-time employment was in response to this likelihood and was why Abby was now in after school day care. She agreed that Abby had a very helpful side to her and thought this varied directly with her anxiety.

Betsy wondered whether Abby was adversely affected by the upsurge in family tension over the previous 6 months. She also was concerned about Calvin, the 4-year-old boy, whom she knew from having observed him at the day care. Betsy described a number of incidents suggesting that he was an aggressive and provocative child. It was her opinion that Abby was in a vulnerable position with him and regretted that the two had been together unsupervised in the bathroom.

At the end of this first meeting, Betsy completed the Child Behavior Checklist, the Parenting Stress Index-Short Form, the Child Sexual Behavior Inventory, and the Parent-Child Conflict Tactics Scale. She signed a release form to have Abby's teacher complete a Teacher Report form, which was modified to include three additional sexual items: plays with sex parts in public, sex play with peers, and sex problems (Friedrich, 1997). Betsy also agreed to ask the day care provider to complete a CBCL and CSBI on Abby.

Abby was very subdued on my first meeting her and exhibited some separation anxiety in the waiting area, which persisted into the first few minutes of the interview. She had little recollection of her preadoptive life although she had been told that she was hospitalized once as a baby for not gaining weight. She said she likes school and wants to be a teacher when she grows up. She identified her best friend as a 7-year-old girl in the neighborhood.

She was highly uncomfortable speaking about the incident with Calvin and flushed and squirmed in the chair during this portion of the interview. She agreed that she had touched Calvin's penis three times and volunteered that he had asked her to touch him the first time and that his penis "grew bigger when I touched it." He asked to see her "privates" but she only showed them to him "once." She felt "funny" when this happened but was able to elaborate after looking over a feelings poster that she had felt "scared," "excited," "ashamed," and "anxious." She knew it was "wrong" and assured the interviewer that it would never happen again because "Calvin can use the bathroom himself." She completed the MASC, CDI, and TSCC after having agreed to my request that she read each item carefully and answer "honestly."

Parent and Caregiver Reports. Betsy's responses to the Child Behavior Checklist suggested social competence scores within normal limits, including Social, a subscale measuring relationships with friends. Two clinical elevations were noted, one on Anxious/

Depression (T = 66) and also on Withdrawal (T = 65). She endorsed such items as "cries," "nervous," "fearful," "guilty," and "self-conscious" for Anxious/Depressed and "secretive," "shy," and "withdrawn" for Withdrawal. She endorsed four items on the Child Sexual Behavior Inventory. These were "stands too close to others," "overly friendly with men they don't know well," "touches another child's sex parts," and "interested in the opposite sex." This translated into T scores of 67 on total sexual behavior, 71 on developmentally related sexual behavior, and 60 on sexual abuse specific items. On the Parenting Stress Index-Short Form, she answered validly and nondefensively, with her defensive responding score at the 45th percentile. Scores range from 15% on Parental Distress, 51% on Parent-Child Dysfunctional Interaction, and 44% on Difficult Child. This results in a total Stress Score at the 40th percentile. Finally, she reported primarily positive parenting strategies on the Conflict Tactic Scale, for example, use of time out, positive reinforcement, but also admitted to occasional shouting and slapping on the hand.

Further support for the accuracy of Betsy's perceptions of Abby comes from the Achenbach Teacher Report Form completed by Abby's fifth-grade teacher. Adaptive Functioning scores were in the normal range. Clinical scales were also in the normal range with the exception of a mild elevation on Withdrawn (T = 63). The teacher did not endorse any of the three sexual behavior items.

The day care provider had only known Abby for 3 months. Consequently, she was less sure of many items on Social Competence. However, she did not report any clinical problems. On the Child Sexual Behavior Inventory, she endorsed two of the four items Betsy had, that is, "stands too close to others" and "touches another child's sexual parts." This translated into a Total Sexual Behavior of T = 52, T = 45 for Developmentally Related Sexual Behavior, and T = 45 for Sexual Abuse Specific Items. At the bottom of the measure she wrote that had she rated Calvin, she would have endorsed 15 to 20 items. This comment suggested that Calvin was far more sexually focused than was Abby.

Child Report. Abby did report a clinically significant elevation (T = 67) on Social Anxiety from the MASC, with a secondary elevation on Humiliation/Rejection, a subscale from that domain. A sample item from Humiliation/Rejection is "I'm afraid other people will think I'm stupid." However, she did not report significant level of Physical Symptoms or Harm Avoidance, and her MASC total score was T = 57.

On the Child Depression Inventory, she was clinically elevated on Negative Self-Esteem (T = 68; e.g., "I do not like myself") and Interpersonal Problems (T = 67; e.g., "I am bad many times"). On the Trauma Symptom Checklist for Children, she answered validly and most T scores were in the 52 to 58 range with the exception of Sexual Concerns (T = 72) and the related subscale, Sexual Distress (T = 87).

Summary. In summary, parent and caregiver ratings of Abby's general behavior suggests a girl who feels less sure with peers and responds with some withdrawal. She also tends to be more anxious and emotional than average. Some of her sexual behaviors are more specific to the incident with Calvin, but others suggest a needy girl whose interpersonal boundaries need shoring up. Her adoptive mother does not report Abby to be overly challenging to parent; she describes her in a generally positive tone, and she generally employs very appropriate discipline techniques.

It is not very common, but always heartening, to see overlap between parent and child reports. Abby reported a significant level of peer insecurity and feelings of badness. When questioned, the Negative Self-Esteem items from the Child Depression Inventory were related to her behavior with Calvin and suggest some elevation in shame. In addition, her report of elevated Sexual Concerns is appropriate to the situation and reflects a girl who is not denying her vulnerability in this domain. The fact that other trauma-related scales from the TSCC were not elevated is also a positive and in keeping with her report that she remembers very little of her life prior to her adoption.

Recommendations. The test data allow us to suggest that Abby's preference for caretaking and befriending younger children put her in a vulnerable situation with a provocative and sexualized boy. Her adoptive parents' potential separation and divorce most likely add to her behavioral reactivity. Treatment suggestions include a greater focus on developing peer relations via play dates (Frankel & Wetmore, 1996), helping Abby see herself more accurately and with less shame, and increasing overall positive parent–child interactions (Hembree-Kigin & McNeil, 1995). In addition, Betsy and her husband were requested to work even harder on providing reassurances to Abby about her continued well-being despite their problems.

CONCLUSION AND RECOMMENDATIONS

The evaluation of traumatized or maltreated children is made complex by several factors. First, these evaluations often have forensic implications. Second, the evaluation target can be very elusive, not only because of "sleeper effects" but also because there is no one psychological diagnosis or syndrome type associated with trauma, adversity, and maltreatment. Third, maltreated children being evaluated are often quite guarded about what they reveal and frequently are less capable of accurately talking about their feelings than children from non-abusive households. Fourth, maltreatment often occurs in deleterious contexts that have their own pernicious effects on the developing child. For example, it is very difficult to sort out the effects of poverty versus the effects of physical abuse, and to attempt to do so is contraindicated. Rather, the evaluator needs to know the child's context and spell it out clearly as part of the evaluation. Fifth, psychologists trained in traditional assessment need to learn an entirely new set of assessment strategies for abused or traumatized children than are typically taught in graduate school and used in clinical practice. Finally, evaluators need to know how PTSD may superficially overlap with many other diagnoses that can be less precise in describing the child's functioning, such as attention, mood, or anxiety disorders.

The assessment of the abused child should include objective measures that assess the more common symptoms associated with maltreatment. In addition, maltreatment occurs in a context, and the assessment of the parent's potential for further abuse (if the parent was the abuser), or parental perceptions of the child, is as important as the input parents provide on behavior rating scales. This chapter has compiled some of the most commonly used and valid tools in this area.

It is also very important to remember that psychological assessment in abuse and trauma cases may be initiated as a clinical activity but that legal issues are also operative and the evaluator may need to testify, even when the case did not start out as a forensic case.

THE USE AND MISUSE OF TESTS

Child Custody Evaluations

This is one arena where maltreatment allegations are often raised. Psychologists asked to conduct these evaluations need to keep in mind that these evaluations can be profoundly difficult to accomplish. Prejudices about the psychological features of parents involved in custody disputes need to be set aside, and any competent assessment must include testing on both parents. The overwhelming majority (85%–90%) of divorcing parents with minor children settle custody without a dispute that requires professional evaluation. Custody disputes indicate that there is something wrong, and it is simplistic to reflexively believe that both parents have character disorders and are simply using the children as bargaining chips.

There is research indicating that in many custody disputes, one parent may be concerned about the safety and well-being of children in the other household (Brown, Frederico, Hewitt, & Sheehan, 2000). Throughout the marriage, the protective parent may have buffered the children from intermittent psychotic episodes, drinking binges, battering, emotional abuse, or child physical or sexual abuse by the other parent. When this parent finally gives up on the marriage, he or she may well learn that the courts do not buffer the children as this parent once did.

Physical abuse, partner battering, and child sexual abuse are crimes to be investigated and adjudicated rather than evaluated and mediated in domestic relations courts. Psychologists are not detectives; they must be aware of their roles and the limitations of their scope of practice when these issues arise.

CAUTIONS AGAINST OVERLY SIMPLISTIC INTERPRETATION

Psychological tests cannot be used to definitively determine (a) if a child has been abused, (b) if a parent will abuse again, (c) if abuse is the sole cause of the child's symptoms, or (d) if a parent is a batterer or a sexual perpetrator. Many abused children are asymptomatic, and the impacts can be extremely variable. Many batterers and sexual abusers appear psychologically normal when evaluated.

Group data are used to establish norms for the measures that are suggested in this chapter, but each case must be interpreted in the context of the child's history and culture. For example, an abused child who scores low on a test of sexual behavior may or may not have a sexual abuse history. The same is true if a child scores high on this same measure. In addition, the child who scores low may score low for a number of reasons. For example, the child (a) may truly not have sexual behavior problems, (b) may have sexual behavior problems but has a parent who does not report them because this parent is protective of a spouse, (c) may have sexual behavior problems but has a parent who does not report them because this parent is a poor observer, or (4) may have sexual behavior problems that are more subtle and likely to cause future problems but do not show up in terms of current overt behavior.

Similar problems occur with PTSD. Follow-up interviewing as well as an appreciation of the child's context is critical to determining if a child has PTSD after scoring either low or high on a structured PTSD protocol. Some children deny some PTSD symptoms simply because they are so bothered by any reminders that they deny all symptoms related to the event in question.

PARENT–CHILD RELATIONSHIP

The parent–child relationship is critical to the child's short- and long-term adjustment. Our assessment framework does not specifically assess parent–child attachment because measures to do so still lack convincing normative data. However, the CTSCP and the PSI can be used to evaluate the strength and quality of a parent's relationship with a child and thus indirectly speak to the security of attachment. Reports of overly harsh parenting, whether emotional or physical, certainly imply insecure attachment, because attachment is compromised in over 95% of cases where maltreatment is present (Cicchetti & Toth, 1995).

ASSESSMENT AND TREATMENT PLANNING

Assessment results must be relevant to therapy to justify the use of screening measures and tests. The first step is to view assessment and treatment as seamlessly connected. Assessment measures should prepare the child for therapy by outlining which issues are important. These same measures can be transported into therapy and used as a basis for early sessions, at least with some children. For example, cognitive distortions expressed on the CITES-R can lead to CBT-based interventions such as Trauma-Focused Cognitive Behavioral Therapy (TF-CBT; Cohen, Mannarino, & Deblinger, 2006).

Therapists can also benefit from input from the evaluator regarding the child's ability to be open and nondefensive. Severe abuse that is not accompanied by the child reporting distress on at least some of the TSCC subscales, for example, raises concerns about the child's perceptions of how safe it is to be open about emotions. There can be other reasons for a child's lack of self-disclosure, such as cultural constraints or dissociation, but lack of permission to talk about the abuse is one strong possibility that needs to be clarified early in the treatment process.

Finally, the field of therapy for maltreated children moves forward if we learn what works. As therapists implement the most strongly evidence-based therapy for traumatized children and their caregivers, Parent-Child Interaction Therapy (PCIT; McNeil & Hembree-Kigin, 2010), we strongly encourage therapists to re-administer measures at intervals throughout therapy, at the conclusion of therapy, and after time has elapsed after treatment, in order to learn which children seem to get better and which do not and in this way inform their practice.

TABLE 10.1   Matrix: Child Abuse and Family Assessment Strategies and Inventories

Assessment Instrument	Specific Applications	Cultural/Language	Instructions/Use: T = Time to Take S = Time to Score I = Items (# of)	Computerized: (a) Scoring (b) Report	Reliability (R) Validity (V)	Availability
Child Behavior Checklist (CBCL)	For children living in the home, ages 18 months to 18 years, to assess a broad range of internalizing and externalizing symptoms	Translated into over 30 languages, including several versions of Spanish, and are used throughout the world	T = 10–17 min S = 10 min I = 100 or 113	(a) yes (b) yes	R = Excellent test-retest (0.75–0.97); good interparent agreement V = Very good construct	Dr. Achenbach at the Center for Children, Youth and Families at the University of Vermont in Burlington 05401, or via their website at www.aseba.org.
Child Sexual Behavior Inventory (CSBI)	For children 2–12, assesses sexual behaviors exhibited over the past six months	Dutch, English, French German, Latvian, Lithuanian, Moldovan Polish, Spanish, Swedish	T = 5–10 min S = 5 min I = 38	(a) no (b) no	R = Excellent test-retest (0.85) Cronbach's alpha = 0.72–0.92 V = Good convergent and divergent	Available from PAR Odessa, Florida. It can be obtained either through 1-800-331-TEST or their website, www.parinc.com.
Child Dissociative Checklist (CDC)	For children 5–14, designed to be both a clinical screening tool and a research tool	Spanish, Italian	T = 5–10 min S = 5–10 min I = 20	(a) no (b) no	R = moderate to good 1-year test-retest stability (r = 0.65) Cronbach's alpha = 0.86 V = Good CONV and DIVG	Public domain document freely available for reproducing, distribution and use, available by request at http:// www. ohiocando4kids. org/Dissociation

TABLE 10.1 (Continued) Matrix: Child Abuse and Family Assessment Strategies and Inventories

Assessment Instrument	Specific Applications	Cultural/Language	Instructions/Use: T = Time to Take S = Time to Score I = Items (# of)	Computerized: (a) Scoring (b) Report	Reliability (R) Validity (V)	Availability
Pediatric Emotional Distress Scale (PEDS)	2–10 year olds who have been traumatized by homelessness, sexual abuse, natural disasters, and other negative experiences	Has been examined for homeless children, has not yet been tested on a wide variety of cultural groups	T = 5–10 min S = 5–10 min I = 21		R = IC: 0.85 total IR: 0.65 total TR: 0.56 total	Journal article
Child Abuse Potential Inventory (CAPI) (3rd ed.)	Intended to be used as a screening tool for the detection of physical child abuse. It is also used as a psychological test.	Norms for the US and Spain. Translated into other languages. Research finds the constructs are present in other cultures.	T = 12–20 min S = 20 min I = 77	(a) yes (b) no	R = Split half = 0.96, alpha = 0.93; test-retest 0.71–0.92 V = Excellent divergent and construct	Available from PSYTEC, Inc., PO Box 564, DeKalb, Illinois, 60115
Parent Child Conflict Tactics Scale (CTSPC)	For parents of children living in the home, 6–17, assess nonviolent discipline, psychological aggression, and physical assault	Research reveals no clear differences between Euro-American and either African-American or Hispanic-American parents	T = 6–8 min S = 8 min I = 22 to 36	(a) no (b) no	R = Cronbach's alpha = 0.58–0.68; test-retest = 0.80 V = Moderate to excellent construct validity	Family Research Laboratory or from the journal article

Instrument	Description	Notes	Time/Items	(a)(b)	Reliability/Validity	Availability
Trauma Symptom Checklist for Children (TSCC)	Children ages 8–15, assesses a broad range of trauma-related symptoms.	Used in many countries & available in many languages	T = 18 min S = 8 min I = 54	(a) yes (b) yes	R = IC: 0.89 total TR: N/R V = CONV: 0.75–0.82 subscales DISC: sexually abused/non-abused	Psychological Assessment Resources, Odessa, Florida, at 1-800-331-TEST, or www.parinc.com
Trauma Symptom Checklist for Children Young (TSCYC)	Children ages 3–12, caretaker report	Used in many countries & available in many languages	T = 15 min S = 8 min I = 90	(a) yes (b) yes	Excellent reliability, with *Alpha* internal consistency ranging from .81 for Sexual Concerns to .93 for PTSD-Total. The average alpha was .87. As for construct validity	Psychological Assessment Resources, Odessa, Florida, at 1-800-331-TEST, or www.parinc.com.
Children's PTSD Reaction Index (CPTS-RI)	Intended for children ages 7–18 to assess symptoms following exposure to trauma	Translated into several languages and has been used in Armenia, Kuwait, Cambodia, and the United States	T = 20–45 min S = 20–45 min I = 27 (traumatic exposure section, 20 (child), 21 (parent), 22 (adolescent) PTSD symptoms section	(a) no (b) no	R = IC: 0.69–0.80 IR: 0.88 total TR: 0.93 over 1 week V = CONV: 0.29–0.91	Not commercially available, but it may be obtained from Robert Pynoos, MD at UCLA or Kathleen Nader, DSW, in Cedar Park, Texas.

TABLE 10.1 *(Continued)* Matrix: Child Abuse and Family Assessment Strategies and Inventories

Assessment Instrument	Specific Applications	Cultural/Language	Instructions/Use: T = Time to Take S = Time to Score I = Items (# of)	Computerized: (a) Scoring (b) Report	Reliability (R) Validity (V)	Availability
Children's Impact of Traumatic Events Scale Revised (CITES-R)	Sex abuse victims 6–18, assesses PTS symptoms, eroticism, perceptions of support following disclosure, and abuse attributions	White and African-American United States populations	T = 20–40 min S = 5–10 min I = 78	(a) no (b) no	R = IC: 0.56–0.91 V = vary poor to moderate	No manual, Vicki Veitch Wolfe, Children's Hosptial of Western Ontario, 800 Commissioners Rd E., London, Ontario, Canada, N6A 5C2 or http:// www.uwo.ca
Impact of Events Scale (IES)	Used with adults and children 8–18, can be used for immediate aftermath of mass catastrophes as well as individual traumas	The IES has been translated into many languages and has been applied to adolescents from various cultures	T = 10 min S = 10 min I = 15	(a) no (b) no	R = alpha of .79 and .82, and a split-half reliability of .86 V = discriminates traumatized groups from non-traumatized groups	Journal article
Adolescent Dissociative Experiences Scale (A-DES)	Ages 11–20, screening tool for serious dissociative and posttraumatic disorders	The A-DES has been translated into many languages and they are available by request at http://www. ohiocando4kids. org/Dissociation	T = 10–15 min S = 10 min I = 30	(a) no (b) no	R = Cronbach's alpha = 0.93; split-half = 0.92 V = face validity	Public domain document freely available for reproducing, distribution and use, available by request at http://www. ohiocando4kids. org/Dissociation

REFERENCES

American Academy of Child and Adolescent Psychiatry. (1998). Practice parameters for the assessment of children and adolescents with posttraumatic stress disorder. *Journal of the American Academy of Child and Adolescent Psychiatry, 37*(Suppl. 10), 4–26.

American Psychiatric Association. (1980). *Diagnostic and statistical manual of mental disorders* (3rd ed.). Washington, DC: Author.

American Psychiatric Association. (1994). *Diagnostic and statistical manual of mental disorders* (4th ed.). Washington, DC: Author.

American Psychiatric Association. (2000). *Diagnostic and statistical manual of mental disorders* (4th ed., text revision). Washington, DC: Author.

Anda, R. F., Butchart, A., Felitti, V. J., & Brown, D. W. (2010). Building a framework for global surveillance of the public health implications of adverse childhood experiences. *American Journal of Preventive Medicine, 39*(1), 93–98.

Armstrong, J. G., Putnam, F. W., Carlson, E. B., Libero, D. Z., & Smith, S. R. (1997). Development and validation of a measure of adolescent dissociation: The Adolescent Dissociative Experiences Scale. *Journal of Nervous Mental Disorders, 185,* 491–497.

Bakermans-Kranenburg, M., & van IJzendoorn, M. H. (2009). No reliable gender differences in attachment across the life-span. *Behavioral and Brain Sciences, 32,* 22–23.

Briere, J. (1996). *Trauma Symptom Checklist for Children (TSCC), Professional manual.* Odessa, FL: Psychological Assessment Resources.

Briere, J. (1997). *Psychological assessment of adult posttraumatic states.* Washington, DC: American Psychological Association.

Briere, J., Johnson, K., Bissada, A., Damon, L., Crouch, J., Gil, E., et al. (2001). The Trauma Symptom Checklist for Young Children (TSCYC): Reliability and association with abuse exposure in a multi-site study. *Child Abuse & Neglect, 25,* 1001–1014.

Brown, D. W., Anda, R. F., Tiemeier, H., Felitti, V. J., Edwards, V. J., Croft, J. B., et al. (2009). Adverse childhood experiences and the risk of premature mortality. *American Journal of Preventive Medicine, 37*(5), 389–396.

Brown, T., Frederico, M., Hewitt, L., & Sheehan, R. (2000). Revealing the existence of child abuse in the context of marital breakdown and custody and access disputes. *Child Abuse and Neglect, 24*(6), 849–859.

Busuttil, W. (2009). Complex post-traumatic stress disorder: A useful diagnostic framework? *Psychiatry, 8*(8), 310–314.

Carlson, E. B. (1997). *Trauma assessments: A clinician's guide.* New York: Guilford Press.

Chaffin, M., & Shultz, S. K. (2001). Psychometric evaluation of the children's impact of traumatic events scale-revised. *Child Abuse & Neglect*, 25(3), 401–412.

Cicchetti, D., & Toth, S. L. (1995). Child maltreatment and attachment organization: Implications for intervention. In S. Goldberg, R. Muir, & J. Kerr (Eds.), *Attachment theory: Social, developmental, and clinical perspectives* (pp. 279–308). Hillsdale, NJ: Analytic Press.

Cohen, J. A., Mannarino, A. P., & Deblinger, E. (2006). *Treating trauma and traumatic grief in children and adolescents*. New York: Guilford Press.

Cook, A., Spinazzola, J., Ford, J., Lanktree, C., Blaustein, M., Cloitre, M., et al. (2005). Complex trauma in children and adolescents. *Psychiatric Annals*, 35, 390–398.

Crouch, J. L., Smith, D. W., Ezzell, C. E., & Saunders, B. E. (1999). Measuring reactions to sexual trauma among children: Comparing the Children's Impact of Traumatic Events Scale and the Trauma Symptom Checklist for Children. *Child Maltreatment, 4*, 255–263.

De Bellis, M. D., Keshavan, M. S., Clark, D. B., Giedd, J. N., Boring, A. M., Frustaci, K., et al. (1999). Developmental traumatology, part II: Brain development. *Biological Psychiatry, 45*, 1259–1284.

De Bellis, M. D., Keshavan, M. S., Frustaci, K., Shifflett, H., Iyengar, S., Beers, S. R., et al. (2002). Superior temporal gyrus volumes in maltreated children and adolescents with PTSD. *Biological Psychiatry, 51*(7), 544–552.

De Bellis, M. D., & Kuchibhatla, M. (2006). Cerebellar volumes in pediatric maltreatment-related posttraumatic stress disorder. *Biological Psychiatry, 60*, 697–703.

Dehon, C., & Scheeringa, M. (2006). Screening for preschool PTSD with the Child Behavior Checklist. *Journal of Pediatric Psychology, 31*, 431–435.

Edwards, V. J., Anda, R. F., Dube, S. R., Dong, M., Chapman, D. F., & Felitti, V. J. (2005). The wide-ranging health consequences of adverse childhood experiences. In K. Kendall-Tackett & S. Giacomoni (Eds.), *Victimization of children and youth: Patterns of abuse, response strategies* (pp. 8-1–8-12). Kingston, NJ: Civic Research Institute.

Felitti, V. J., Anda, R. F., Nordenberg, D., Williamson, D. F., Spitz, A. M., Edwards, V., Koss, M. P., et al. (1998). The relationship of adult health status to childhood abuse and household dysfunction. *American Journal of Preventive Medicine, 14*, 245–258.

Finkelhor, D., Turner, H., Ormrod, R., & Hamby, S. L. (2009). Violence, abuse, and crime exposure in a national sample of children and youth. *Pediatrics, 124*, 1411–1423.

Finkelhor, D., Turner, H., Ormrod, R., & Hamby, S. L. (2010). Trends in childhood violence and abuse exposure: Evidence from two national surveys. *Archives of Pediatrics & Adolescent Medicine, 164*(3), 238–242.

Foa, E. B., Keane, T. M., & Friedman, M. J. (2009). *Effective treatments for PTSD: Practice guidelines from the International Society for Traumatic Stress Studies.* New York: Guilford Press.

Frankel, F., & Wetmore, B. (1996). *Good friends are hard to find: Helping your child find, make, and keep friends.* London: Perspective Publishing.

Friedrich, W. N. (1997). *Child Sexual Behavior Inventory.* Odessa, FL: Psychological Assessment Resources.

Friedrich, W. N. (2002). *Psychological assessment of sexually abused children and their families.* Thousand Oaks, CA: Sage.

Friedrich, W. N., Lysne, M., Sim, L., & Shamos, S. (2004). Assessing sexual abuse in high-risk adolescents with the Adolescent Clinical Sexual Behavior Inventory (ACSBI). *Child Maltreatment, 9*(3), 239–250.

Gold, S., Lucenko, B., Elhai, J., Swingle, J., & Sellers, A. (1999). A comparison of psychological/psychiatric symptomatology of women and men sexually abused as children. *Child Abuse & Neglect, 23,* 683–692.

Gomez-Schwartz, B., Horowitz, J. M., & Cardarelli, A. P. (1990). *Child sexual abuse: The initial effects.* Newbury Park, CA: Sage.

Hembree-Kigin, T. L. & McNeil, C. B. (1995). *Parent-child interaction therapy.* New York: Plenum.

Herman, J. L. (1992). *Trauma and recovery: The aftermath of violence— From domestic violence to political terror.* New York: Basic Books.

Horowitz, M. J., Wilner, N., & Alvarez, W. (1979). Impact of Event Scale: A measure of subjective stress. *Psychosomatic Medicine, 41,* 209–218.

Kendall-Tackett, K. A., Williams, L. M., & Finkelhor, D. (1993). Impact of sexual abuse on children: A review and synthesis of recent empirical studies. *Psychological Bulletin, 113,* 164–180.

Koenen, K. C., Moffitt, T. E., Caspi, A., Taylor, A., & Purcell, S. (2003). Domestic violence is associated with environmental suppression of IQ in young children. *Development and Psychopathology, 15,* 297–311.

Kolko, D. J., & Swenson, C. C. (2002). *Assessing and treating physically abused children and their families: A cognitive-behavioral approach.* Thousand Oaks, CA: Sage.

Lanktree, C. B., Gilbert, A. M., Briere, J., Taylor, N., Chen, K., Maida, C. A., et al. (2008). Multi-informant assessment of maltreated children: Convergent and discriminant validity of the TSCC and TSCYC. *Child Abuse & Neglect, 32,* 621–625.

Laor, N., Wolmer, L., & Cohen, D. J. (2001). Mothers' functioning and children's symptoms 5 years after a SCUD Missile attack. *American Journal of Psychiatry, 158,* 1020–1026.

Levendosky, A. A., Huth-Bocks, A. C., Semel, M. A., & Shapiro, D. L. (2002). Trauma symptoms in preschool-age children exposed to domestic violence. *Journal of Interpersonal Violence, 17,* 150–164.

Lieberman, A. F., Briscoe-Smith, A., Ghosh Ippen, C., & Van Horn, P. (2006). Violence in infancy and early childhood: Relationship-based treatment and evaluation. In A. F. Lieberman & R. DeMartino (Eds.), *Interventions for children exposed to violence* (pp. 65–84). New Brunswick, NJ: Johnson & Johnson Pediatric Institute.

Margolin, G., & Vickerman, K. A. (2007). Posttraumatic stress in children and adolescents exposed to family violence: I. Overview and issues. *Professional Psychology: Research and Practice, 38*(6), 613–619.

McNeil, C. B., & Hembree-Kigin, T. L. (Eds.). (2010). Parent-child interaction therapy (2nd ed.). New York: Springer.

Milner, J. S. (1986). *The Child Abuse Potential Inventory: Manual* (2nd ed.). DeKalb, IL: Psytec.

Moran, M. (2007). Developmental trauma merits DSM diagnosis, experts say. *Psychiatric News, 42*(3), 20.

Nader, K. O., Kriegler, J. A., Blake, D. D., Pynoos, R. S., Newman, E., & Weather, F. (2002). *The Clinician-Administered PTSD Scale, Child and Adolescent Version (CAPS-C).* Available from Kathleen Nader, DSW, 2809 Rathlin Drive, Suite 102, Cedar Park, TX 78613; or National Center for PTSD, White River Junction, VT (www.ncptsd.org).

Noll, J. G. (2008). Sexual abuse of children—Unique in its effect on development? *Child Abuse & Neglect, 32,* 603–605.

Noll, J. G., Trickett, P. K., Harris, W. W., & Putnam, F. W. (2009). The cumulative burden borne by offspring whose mothers were sexually abused as children. *Journal of Interpersonal Violence, 24*(3), 424–449.

Ohan, J. L., Myers, K., & Collett, B. R. (2002). Ten-year review of rating scales IV: Scales assessing trauma and its effects. *Journal of the American Academy of Child & Adolescent Psychiatry, 41*(12), 1401–1422.

Olafson, E. (1999). Using testing when family violence and child abuse are issues. In A. R. Nurse (Ed.), *Psychological testing with families* (pp. 230–256). New York: Wiley & Sons.

Olafson, E., & Boat, B. (2000). Long-term management of the sexually abused child: Considerations and challenges. In R. M. Reece (Ed.), *The treatment of child abuse* (pp. 14–35). Baltimore: Johns Hopkins University Press.

Child Abuse Assessment Strategy and Inventories   307

Pelcovitz, D., van der Kolk, B., Roth, S., Mandel, F., Kaplan, S., & Resick, P. (1997). Development of a criteria set and a structured interview for disorders of extreme stress (SIDESNOS). *Journal of Traumatic Stress, 10,* 3–16.

Putnam, F. W. (1997). *Dissociation in children and adolescents: A developmental perspective.* New York: Guilford Press.

Putnam, F. W. (2003). Ten-year research review update: Child sexual abuse. *Journal of the American Academy of Child and Adolescent Psychiatry, 42*(3), 269–278.

Putnam, F. W. (2006). The impact of trauma on child development. *Juvenile and Family Court Journal, 57*(1), 1–11.

Putnam, F. W., Helmers, K., Horowitz, L. A., & Trickett, P. K. (1994). Hypnotizability and dissociativity in sexually abused girls. *Child Abuse & Neglect, 19,* 645–655.

Putnam, F. W., Helmers, K., & Trickett, P. K. (1993). Development, reliability and validity of a child dissociation scale. *Child Abuse & Neglect, 17,* 645–655.

Putnam, F. W., & Peterson, G. (1994). Further validation of the child dissociative checklist. *Dissociation, 7,* 204–211.

Putnam, F. W., & Trickett, P. K. (1997). The psychobiological effects of sexual abuse: A longitudinal study. *Annals of New York Academy of Science, 821,* 150–159.

Pynoos, R., Rodriguez, N., Steinberg, A., Stuber, M., & Frederick, C. (1998). UCLA PTSD Index for DSM-IV. Unpublished manuscripts. UCLA Trauma Psychiatry Service.

Reece, R. M. (Ed.). (2000). *Treatment of child abuse: Common ground for mental health, medical, and legal practitioners.* Baltimore: Johns Hopkins University Press.

Ribbe, D. (1996). Psychometric review of Traumatic Event Screening Instrument for Children (TESI-C). In B. H. Stamm (Ed.), *Measurement of stress, trauma, and adaptation* (pp. 386–387). Lutherville, MD: Sidran Press.

Saigh, P. A. (2002). *The Children's Post Traumatic Stress Disorder-Inventory (CPTSD- I).* Available from Phillip A. Saigh, Ph.D., Department of Educational Psychology, Graduate Center, City University of New York, 365 Fifth Avenue, New York, NY 10016.

Salter, A. C. (2003). *Pedophiles, rapists, and other sex offenders: Who they are, how they operate, and how we can protect ourselves and our children.* New York: Basic Books.

Saylor, C. F., Swenson, C. C., Reynolds, S. S., & Taylor, M. (1999). The Pediatric Emotional Distress Scale: A brief screening measure for young children exposed to traumatic events. *Journal of Clinical Child Psychology, 28,* 70–81.

Sebre, S., Sprugevica, I., Novotni, A., Bonevski, D., Pakalniskiene, V., Popescu, D., et al. (2004). Cross-cultural comparisons of child-reported emotional and physical abuse: rates, risk factors and psychosocial symptoms. *Child Abuse & Neglect, 28*(1), 113–127.

Sickel, A. E., Noll, J. G., Moore, P. J., Putnam, F. W., & Trickett, P. K. (2002). The long-term physical health and healthcare utilization of women who were sexually abused as children. *Journal of Health Psychology, 7*(5), 583–597.

Stover, C. S., & Berkowitz, S. J. (2005). Assessing violence exposure and trauma symptoms in young children: A critical review of measures. *Journal of Traumatic Stress, 18*(6), 707–717.

Straus, M. A., Hamby, S. L., Finkelhor, D., Moore, D. W., & Runyan, D. (1998). Identification of child maltreatment with the Parent-Child Conflict Scales: Development of psychometric data for a national sample of American parents. *Child Abuse & Neglect, 22*, 249–270.

Thaber, A. A. M., & Vostanis, P. (1999). Post-traumatic stress reactions in children of war. *Journal of Child Psychology & Psychiatry, 40*, 385–391.

Trickett, P., Noll, J., & Putnam, F. (2011). The impact of sexual abuse on female development: Lessons from a multigenerational, longitudinal research study. *Development and Psychopathology, 23*, 453–476.

Trickett, P., Noll, J., Reiffman, A., & Putnam, F. (2001). Variants of intrafamilial sexual abuse experiences: Implications for short- and long-term development. *Developmental Psychopathology, 13*, 1001–1019.

Valera, E. M., & Berenbaum, H. (2003). Brain injury in battered women. *Journal of Consulting and Clinical Psychology, 71*, 797–804.

van der Kolk, B. (Guest Ed.). (2005). Child abuse and victimization. *Psychiatric Annals, 35*, 374–430.

Weiss, D. (2002). *The Impact of Events Scale-Revised*. Available from Daniel Weiss, Ph.D., Department of Psychiatry, University of California at San Francisco, CA 94143-0984.

Weiss, D. S., & Marmar, C. R. (1997). The Impact of Event Scale-Revised. In J. P. Wilson & T. M. Keane (Eds.), *Assessing psychological trauma and PTSD* (pp. 399–411). New York: Guilford Press.

Wilson, J. P., & Keane, T. M. (Eds.). (1997). *Assessing psychological trauma and PTSD*. New York: Guilford Press.

Wolfe, V. V., Gentile, C., Michienzi, T., Sas, L., & Wolfe, D. A. (1991). The Children's Impact of Traumatic Events Scale: A measure of post-sexual abuse PTSD symptoms. *Behavioral Assessment, 13*(4), 359–383.

CHAPTER 11

Family Assessment
Current and Future Prospects

Luciano L'Abate

Since the publication of the first edition of this volume, many changes have occurred in the field of couple and family assessment, both conceptually and practically. These changes have diminished the need to summarize in this chapter information now readily available elsewhere but not presented to readers a few years ago (L'Abate, 2004a).

In the original version of this chapter (L'Abate, 2004b), I criticized the whole enterprise of couple and family assessment as having inadequate links with theory or with theoretical models as well as inadequate links between theory, evaluation, and interventions. At that time, I suggested some possibly embryonic solutions to improve these links even though there was no sufficient conceptual and empirical evidence to support them. Since the publication of that commentary, however, those solutions have become fully operational and validated at conceptual, empirical, and practical levels of theory-construction, evaluation, and intervention. These solutions will compose the substance of this chapter.

CONCEPTUAL CHANGES

Conceptually, the notion of the traditional couple qua couple or family qua family, respectively, composed of two opposite gender adults or of two same-gender parents and two children, is no longer tenable. Only 25% of all domiciles in the United States are composed of that traditional system. The other 75% are composed of singles, remarried, not married but living together, same-sex couples, children living with grandparents, grandparents living with their adult children, adult children having gone back to live with their parents (the boomerang effect), or children alternating in living with divorced parents. When we add ethnic, educational, economic, and religious variables, the terms *couple* and *family* have lost their original meanings (Hofferth & Casper, 2007). Add varied compositions thereof and reach your own conclusion about whether to use terms like *couples* and *families*, unless we qualify what kind of couples or families we are addressing.

Therefore, after wrestling with whether I should use *family* (L'Abate, 1976, 1986), *personality* (L'Abate, 1994), *self* (L'Abate, 1997), or even *intimate relationships* (L'Abate, 2005), finally with the help of my Italian colleagues, I was able to settle on the term *Relational Competence Theory* (RCT; Cusinato & L'Abate, 2011; L'Abate, Cusinato, Maino, Colesso, & Scilletta, 2010). Competence means how effective we are in dealing with ourselves and with others, intimates and non-intimates.

This was the name I had been looking for from the outset (L'Abate, 1976). Simplicistically, I cannot record "personality" or "self" in a vacuum either as a structure with a camera or as a process with a videotape. However, I can record and videotape any short interactions between two or more people who are communally and agentically linked by blood, economic, and/or emotional ties. From those videotapes we can start to develop hypotheses about what kind of interaction we might be observing and ideally measuring, if (big IF) or (big OR) provided we have a theory about human relationships that applies to individuals, couples, and families. This would be admittedly an ambitious and grandiose undertaking where fearful fools like me have been trying to tread for years.

Instead of those structural labels, like couple, family, personality, or self, I chose to use four processual qualifications for what I called "intimate relationships" that are close, committed, interdependent, and prolonged. Non-intimate relationships are neither close nor committed, occasionally interdependent instrumentally but not communally, and from time to time prolonged instrumentally. Therefore, we are looking at how we relate with intimate and non-intimate others day in and day out. We do not live in a vacuum of relationships. As I have insisted for a long time (L'Abate, 1976, 1986), we live in a lasting context of both intimate and non-intimate relationships. It took quite a few years for psychologists to become aware of this focus (Mesquita, Barrett, & Smith, 2010).

This conceptual shift in focus has important practical implications for how we are going to evaluate as well as intervene with couples and families. For instance, are we going to have different theories for individuals, couples, and families? And, if we do, are we going to have different instruments to evaluate individuals, couples, and families? A specific focus that would be different for individuals rather than for couples and for couples rather than for families would lead to a veritable Tower of Babel conceptually as well as practically. The number of necessary instruments would reach unfathomed proportions. Have we reached this point? If different theories focus on individual personalities while different theories focus on couples, and different theories focus on families, the whole conceptual enterprise of evaluating couples and families would reach a bewildering hodgepodge of constructs and of instruments, without any relationship among themselves.

Could this conclusion represent the present status of couple and family evaluation (Williams, Edwards, Patterson, & Chamow, 2011)? Many tests for either individuals, or couples, or families seem to be published and validated without any underlying conceptual foundations except empirical ones. This proliferation of models, not to speak of evaluation instruments, has been visible in recent texts about family psychology (Liddle, Santisteban, Levant, & Bray, 2002; Pinsof & Lebow, 2005) among others. Theory-construction has been entirely overlooked or ignored at the pulpit and throne of empiricism at all costs. Theory be dammed (L'Abate, 2009d, 2011).

Could these conceptual and practical Towers of Babel be the outcome of not having an overarching theoretical framework? This is the question I posed myself decades ago when I started to develop what eventually emerged and transformed itself into a full-fledged RCT. A theory of human relationships cannot be just for individuals or just for couples or just for families but for all of us, because we all live in relationships with each other. Ambitious? Yes. Grandiose? Absolutely.

Validated? Partially, according to three levels of validation: (1) evidence *independent* of the theory, as shown, for instance, in a bibliography of secondary references related at face value (or face validity) with RCT (L'Abate, 2009a); (2) evidence derived from other sources but *related* to RCT (concurrent validity) as shown, for instance, in Model 7 about Being, Doing, and Having— modalities obtained from combining the six resource classes of exchange theory (Foa & Foa, 1974), or in Model 14, with three roles of the deadly Drama Triangle: Victim, Persecutor, and Rescuer (L'Abate, 2009b); and (3) evidence *directly derived* from specific models of RCT, as explained and expanded below (construct validity).

These considerations lead to a second conceptual change consisting in the construction of a hierarchical theoretical framework for RCT. This overall framework, originally stated in linear fashion (L'Abate, 1976, 1986, 1994, 1997, 2005, 2006; L'Abate & De Giacomo, 2003), was eventually transformed into a pyramidal structure, similar to the organizational chart of any educational, industrial, military, political, and religious enterprise. This structure has been expanded in numerous publications (Cusinato & L'Abate, 2011; L'Abate, 2008b; L'Abate & Cusinato, 2007; L'Abate et al., 2010).

A *real* theory needs to be stated in hierarchical fashion, like branches from a tree, just like evolution. Complexity in theory, as well as in complex organizations, is difficult if not impossible to be described according to a linear progression, one component after another, especially when these components are all interconnected, as in RCT and in most human organizations. Most models are either self-evident in their underlying dimensions or will be expanded below.

The seemingly abstract nature of the whole RCT has been reduced to a concrete structured interview (L'Abate, 2009e) as well as interactive practice exercises, such as Planned Parenting (L'Abate, 2011d).

Requirements of RCT

Note that the requirements for RCT apply to its 16 models as well as to its instruments produced to evaluate them, as is the case in most organizations, from the top to the bottom. There are at least four requirements that must be fulfilled by RCT: (1) *verifiability,* to the extent that all 16 models of the framework are liable to being empirically validated, because of the inherent interconnectedness of all the models, all models must be validated; that is, the validity of RCT is represented by the sum total of the validity of its 16 models, each model evaluated one at a time; (2) *applicability* to diverse populations of individuals, couples, and families differing along a dimension of functionality–dysfunctionality, including the DSM classification (L'Abate, 2006); (3) *redundancy*, in the sense that a given construct could be viewed (described, explained) from the viewpoint of different models, such as Model 4, the ability to love, could be described also with Being in Model 7, composed of importance and intimacy, interactions in Model 10, positive bestowal of importance to Self and intimate Others in Model 11, and Intimacy in Model 15; and (4) *fruitfulness*, that is, producing a vast group of followers and an even larger number of evaluators, to the extent that validation of some models was performed by Italian-speaking researchers using Italian-speaking participants of all ages, using, however, instruments correlated with established measures validated in the United States.

One important Model 15 on *intimacy* in this framework deals with hurt feelings defined as the sharing of joys as well as of hurt feelings and fears of being hurt (L'Abate, 2011a). Indeed, De Giacomo, L'Abate, Pennebaker, and Rumbaugh (2010) argued that the so-called unconscious is composed of hurt feelings that have been kept inside and that have not been expressed directly but might have been expressed indirectly or inappropriately, verbally, nonverbally, or in writing. If and when expressed, these feelings might have been followed by avoidance, abuse, punishments, and censures, as in the development of non-organic psychopathology (L'Abate, 2005). When offset by joys, these feelings would tend to dissipate, depending on the ratio of hurts and joys (Cusinato & L'Abate, 2011; L'Abate, 2011a; L'Abate et al., 2010).

PRACTICAL CHANGES

In addition to conceptual changes, a great many practical changes have occurred since 2004 that might transform the way couple and family assessment could occur in this century.

The Growing Influence of the Internet

There is no doubt that the Internet is fast becoming the most important innovation in this century, leading to the conclusion (L'Abate & Sweeney, 2011) that this century is characterized by the information processing paradigm, among many other competing paradigms. There is also no doubt that slowly but surely, the Internet will become the major channel of service delivery in this century in education, promotion of physical and mental health, sickness prevention, and psychotherapy, replacing face-to-face, talk-based interventions and rehabilitation. This innovation has occurred at the same time with other innovations (L'Abate, in press).

The Laboratory Method in Clinical Psychology

Even though this method took 40 years to eventually come out in mainstream psychological practices (L'Abate, 2008d), it relies on standard operating practices in evaluation and intervention by clinicians and researchers who combine practice with research, using evaluation of process and outcome on a pre–post-intervention basis (L'Abate, 2008e).

Growth of Self-Help in Health Promotion and Prevention

Self-help (Harwood & L'Abate, 2010) and low-cost approaches to promote physical and mental health (L'Abate, 2007b) document how many less-expensive alternatives or adjuncts are available to mental health professionals to administer to troubled people in need of help. These many alternatives seem apparently ignored at best or overlooked at worst by mainstream or "Main Street" psychotherapists (DeMaria, 2003). With all the prolific development of literally hundreds of paper-and-pencil, self-report tests, we are still unable to identify which individual, couple, or family could qualify for which self-help, promotional, preventive, or psychotherapeutic intervention. Perhaps this inadequacy in our blind quest for validated instruments can be corrected, as suggested below.

The practically universal assumption about face-to-face talk-based psychotherapy being the uniformly and still uncritically accepted medium of intervention needs to be challenged. Apparently, no other avenues of help are considered except face-to-face talk. Most psychotherapists, apparently, are either ignorant of other less-expensive approaches or are afraid to lose their participants to less expensive and probably more effective types of intervention (L'Abate, in press). Are there other explanations?

Self-help and low-cost approaches, together with the other innovations briefly reviewed here, imply that completely different training for mental health professionals should occur as soon as possible. For instance, I proposed an online training program for professionals who want to learn how to administer online structured, interactive practice exercises for individuals, couples, and families (L'Abate, 2008a, 2011c).

The Importance of Homework Assignments in Psychotherapy

The importance and cost-relevant advantages of administering homework assignments as a standard practical procedure for individuals, couples, and families is supported by a great deal of research by Kazantzis et al. (2005; L'Abate, L'Abate, & Maino, 2005) and by Kazantzis and L'Abate (2007). In fact, I have consistently proposed that psychological interventions in various mental health approaches should consist of homework assignments interspersed by occasional control sessions. Professionals should be consulted either face-to-face or online after participants have been administered interactive practice exercises or workbooks and monitored in their written homework assignments. Participants would consult a professional for feedback and evaluation about the value, relevance, and progress of homework assignments—just like the veterinarian does with my dog, my dentist does with my teeth, and my mechanic checks with my car (L'Abate, 2004d, 2007a, 2011c, in press).

Technology in Psychology, Psychiatry, and Neurology

It is doubtful whether expensive projective techniques like the Rorschach or the TAT will survive the onslaught of new, less expensive, more specific innovations and computer-related technical instruments—in time of administration, scoring, interpretation, reporting, and documenting—as those available at the present time (L'Abate & Kaiser, in press). The exponential growth of new technologies in psychology, psychiatry, and neurology will require training of skilled and semi-skilled technicians and paraprofessionals to administer and monitor a great many of these technologies under the direction and supervision of a full-fledged professional according a hierarchical personnel structure (L'Abate, 2002, p. 230; L'Abate & Sweeney, 2011).

Distance Writing as the Preferred Method of Evaluation and Intervention in the 21st Century

The outcome of all these innovations might be the death kernel for traditional face-to-face talk as we know it now, that is, talk occurring between a professional and a participant as the main if not sole means of communication and healing in the delivery of mental health services (L'Abate, 2008c, 2008f, 2009c; L'Abate & Sweeney, 2011). Distance writing will become the major channel of communication with face-to-face talk limited and reserved for specific instructions and rapport building in severe cases that cannot be dealt with otherwise. Think about how the present generation of children and youth are communicating today through texting and Skype. Now envision how they will communicate with mental health professionals in the not-too-distant future when they will need professional mental health help, especially if these resources are increasingly available online.

Even in the best controlled face-to-face, talk-based studies with long-term follow-up, success is always relative. For instance, Lock, LeGrange, Agras, Bryson, and Jo (2010), after a 12-month follow-up, found that "roughly a quarter of participants—22% of those assigned to family-based therapy and 25% of those assigned to adolescent-focused therapy—*never achieved remission* [italics mine]. Clearly treatment challenges remain" (p. 1031). These results imply that face-to-face talk-based treatments need to be augmented and bolstered by additional, hopefully cost-effective but different approaches, especially those involving another medium of information processing, whether individualized written homework assignments (L'Abate, 2011) or even nonverbal modalities (L'Abate, 2005, 2008f).

I have argued for a long time that face-to-face talk is not enough to change behavior for the better, especially with couples and families. With severe psychopathology we need to use synergistically a variety of treatment options, including medication (L'Abate, 1999, 2002, 2005; L'Abate et al., 2010). The more options we have, the more choices we can give to our participants.

A Monumental Undertaking: The Comprehensive
Soldier Fitness Program

Even though this incredibly vast program has been developed by the
U.S. Army, its practically universal scope with hundreds of thousands
of soldiers might well become the major influential blueprint for further
developments in mental health evaluations and interventions in this century (Cornum, Matthews, & Seligman, 2011), including "assessment (a)
s the linchpin" of the entire program. The global assessment tool validated to evaluate this program includes not only self-reports about one's
own emotional and personal characteristics but also reports about one's
family and even spirituality (Peterson, Park, & Castro, 2011).

   This program includes monitoring online, prevention online, and
follow-up through the ranks that serves as an important stepping stone
for most mental health professionals (Seligman & Fowler, 2011). Space
prevents me from reporting the details of this program in this chapter.
However, interested mental health professionals should consider reading
critically the whole issue of the *American Psychologist* (February 2011)
dedicated to this program because this program raises a great many
questions not yet considered, such as explaining the high number of sui-
cides, comparison of some programs with competing programs, and the
overwhelmingly enthusiastic tone of most articles, without real evidence
as to that program's long-term success.

CONNECTIONS BETWEEN THEORY
AND TEST INSTRUMENTS

In constructing RCT, I was continuously mindful from its outset of the
need to couple it with evaluation of its models with validated instruments
as well as with cost-effective interventions that can be tested in the laboratory as well as in primary, secondary, and tertiary prevention (Cusinato &
L'Abate, 2011; L'Abate, 2002, 2005; L'Abate et al., 2010). I was especially
mindful of the relationship between theory building and test construction to evaluate models composing the theory. Evaluation of RCT models,
therefore, went on contemporaneously with theory building: one model
after another (L'Abate, 2009d, 2011b; L'Abate et al., 2010).

   In the next section I will review briefly *relational* instruments that
were created and derived specifically from RCT models in their concurrent, criterion, and construct validities. The detailed results and original
test forms are available in L'Abate et al. (2010) while more recent, additional or revised forms and research results are available in Cusinato and
L'Abate (2011).

VALIDATED INSTRUMENTS TO EVALUATE RCT MODELS

Model 1: The Relational Answers Questionnaire (RAQ)

RAQ (Cusinato & L'Abate, 2011; L'Abate et al., 2010, Appendix A, pp. 265–267) was developed and validated through various versions over the years to evaluate an information professing model consisting of Emotionality (input), Rationality (throughput), Activity (output), Awareness (feedback), and Context (L'Abate, 1986, 1994, 1997, 2005). It consists of 10 items for each dimension of the model validated in six different studies employing hundreds of participants, both Italians and Croatians. The results of these studies tend to support the construct, criterion, and convergent validities of this instrument and, therefore, of the model underlying it.

Model 2: The Self-Presentation Questionnaire

This is a recent instrument created, developed, and validated by Cusinato, that will be published in Cusinato and L'Abate (2011) to evaluate how we present ourselves publically at first blush to make a good impression; this is called impression management. Its importance is relevant to Model 2 in how our public façade is consistent or inconsistent with how we behave in the privacy of our home (phenotypical level) and with how we perceive ourselves consciously or unconsciously (genotypical level). These levels and their consistencies and inconsistencies are determined, in great part, by generational and intergenerational determinants.

Models 3, 7, 11, 12, and 15: The EcoMap

Contrary to the other self-report, paper-and-pencil tests, this multimodel instrument is administered individually, face-to-face, and verbally to assess and evaluate quantitatively how individuals, couples, and families relate with themselves and each other in their immediate and distal contexts. Forms, instructions, and case examples of individuals, couples, and families are available in L'Abate et al. (2010, Appendix B., pp. 269–273). Additional and more recent evidence to support the significant research and clinical versatility of this instrument is available in Cusinato and L'Abate (2011).

Model 7: Modalities

Even though this model is based on resource exchange theory (Foà & Foà, 1974), the combination of its six resources into three modalities is original and not considered by Foa and Foa. However, I changed what they called *status* into *importance* (redundantly considered also in Model 11), their *love* into *intimacy* (redundantly considered also in Model 15) and combined them into a modality called Being or Presence, being emotionally and instrumentally available to Self and Intimate Others. Then I combined Information and Services into a modality called Doing or Performance, and Goods and Money were combined to compose a modality called Having or Production. Who controls Doing and Having has Power (Guinote & Vescio, 2010). Consequently, this model could be evaluated by using the instruments Foa and Foa developed to validate their six classes of resources combined according to the modalities of Model 7.

Model 8: Task for the Likeness Continuum

This model was originally formulated as a developmental–dialectic continuum rather than a dichotomy (L'Abate, 1976, p. 79), representing our identity (redundantly also our genotypical level in Model 2). This same/different dichotomy is still present in the literature on attraction and marital relationships. Instead, I suggested a curvilinear dimension with three degrees of symbiosis, sameness, and similarity and three degrees of differentness proper, oppositionality, and alienation. This model is basic to the growth of personality differentiation and of psychopathology, as well as being the foundation for Styles in Intimate Relationships (Model 9) and an arithmetical Model 10 of intimate interactions.

In a variety of studies with functional and dysfunctional participants of various ages, Cusinato and Colesso (2008) were able to demonstrate the inherent developmental curvilinearity of this model. Instructions for this task are available in L'Abate et al. (2010, Appendix C, pp. 275–278).

Model 11: Self–Other Profile Chart

This is unquestionably the oldest, most important, and most validated model of RCT. It consists of four relational propensities emerging from how a sense of importance is bestowed on Self and on Intimate Others. When importance is bestowed positively on Self and Others, a propensity called Selfulness emerges that is connected with adequate to superior functioning. When importance is bestowed positively on Self and negatively on Others, a propensity called Selfishness emerges that, in its extremes, according to Axis II of the DSM, leads to Cluster B personality disorders and eventually to murder. When importance is bestowed negatively on Self and positively on Others, a propensity called Selflessness emerges that, in its extremes, leads to Cluster C personality disorders and eventually to suicide. When importance is bestowed negatively on both Self and Others, a propensity called No-self emerges that leads to extremes in psychopathology (Axis I).

The Self–Other Profile Chart (SOPC) has been validated in 18 studies with university students as well as inmates and students scoring high or low on the Beck Depression Inventory (L'Abate et al., 2010, Appendix D, pp. 279–283). These studies tend to confirm the convergent, criterion, and construct validities of this instrument and, therefore, of Model 11. This model is also available as an interactive practice exercise for individuals, couples, and families, as discussed below (L'Abate, 2011d).

Model 13: General and Personal Priorities

Originally, in the 1980s, two instruments were created to evaluate this model: the Priorities Inventory and the Priorities Scale (L'Abate et al., 2010, pp. 195–198), providing some suggestive evidence for the validity of these two instruments and the provisional validity of this model. More recently, this model was evaluated with participants in remission from psychotic illness and matched with non-clinical participants using the EcoMap described above (L'Abate et al., 2010, pp. 196–197; Appendix E, pp. 285–287). Even though results tentatively support the validity of this model, its correlations with other models of RCT need to be evaluated, especially with Models 8 and 12, because the model predicts functional and dysfunctional priorities.

Model 15: Intimacy: Sharing of Joys and Hurts and Fears of Being Hurt

This model has been reviewed in detail in other publications (L'Abate, 2005, 2011a). After an initial study (Cusinato, Aceti, & L'Abate, 1998), this model did not generate sufficient evidence until L'Abate et al. (2010, pp. 226–227) reported on the results of eight studies that supported the convergent and construct validities of a paper-and-pencil, self-report scale, originally validated by Stevens and L'Abate (1989) and revised by Cusinato and his students (L'Abate & Cusinato, 1994). More importantly, it has been converted into two interactive practice exercises to administer to individuals, couples, and families (L'Abate, 2011a, 2011d).

Model 16: Negotiation

This model has been evaluated in three different studies—(1) with 120 non-clinical married couples, (2) with 100 married couples with children, and (3) with 373 couples before and after marriage (L'Abate et al., 2010, pp. 232–233)—using a variety of instruments already validated in the United States to measure the ability to negotiate. Results from these studies tend to support the construct, convergent, and criterion validities of this model.

EXPERIMENTAL NON-VALIDATED RCT INSTRUMENTS

Even though they are still at an experimental stage and, therefore, not yet validated, I constructed paper-and-pencil, self-report questionnaires that deal with the ecological systems of individuals, couples, and families, that is, settings (Model 3). These checklists attempt to go above and beyond personal characteristics, asking participants to rate activities performed at home or at work. Consequently, one questionnaire was constructed to evaluate perceived agentic contexts and actual physical settings, as in Model 3.

Ratings include constructive patterns through a checklist of behaviors necessary to discriminate levels of functionality in individuals, couples, and families (L'Abate, 2008c, pp. 344–345; 2008e, pp. 13–14). As the whole psychological profession seems unable to develop tests that measure specifically what treatment should be administered for which concern, issue, or problem, we might need to add measures of contexts and settings as perceived and reported by participants to arrive at discriminative criteria to identify which individuals, couples, or families are more likely to benefit from self-help interventions or from promotional, preventive, and psychotherapeutic interventions.

Furthermore, I constructed a list of destructive (i.e., Model 9, reactive or abusive) patterns in couple relationships that asks partners to define and give examples of those patterns, which oftentimes they are not aware of (L'Abate, 2008c, p. 350). Patterns with the highest frequencies and severities as rated by both partners can be administered face-to-face or in writing as homework assignments, according to a supplemental checklist (L'Abate, 2008c, pp. 351–352). With co-workers from Australia and Italy, we have also constructed, and are in the process of validating, a checklist to identify nonviolent, personality disordered women (L'Abate, van Eigen, & Rigamonti, 2011). Once validated, this checklist could be transformed into an interactive practice exercise.

Interventions

Psychological interventions need to be differentiated according to levels of prevention. At least three levels are necessary to view interventions according to a continuum rather than on an either–or view. Primary prevention includes universal approaches that deal with functional or semifunctional individuals, couples, families, such as self-help (Harwood & L'Abate, 2010) or promotion of physical and mental health (L'Abate, 2007b). Secondary approaches deal with identified, targeted, or at-risk populations such as adult children of alcoholics. Tertiary prevention, such as psychotherapy, is an expensive enterprise that can be reduced in costs if therapists were to rely more on written homework assignments, such as interactive practice exercises (L'Abate, 2011d).

In addition to self-report, paper-and-pencil questionnaires, and rating sheets, as well as the EcoMap described above, models of RCT can be evaluated through (1) 100% replicable enrichment programs in primary prevention (L'Abate & Weinstein, 1987; L'Abate & Young, 1987), (2) self-help workbooks in secondary prevention (L'Abate, 2004c; 2011c), and (3) therapeutic tasks in tertiary prevention (L'Abate, 2001, 2011a). All evaluative instruments, all enrichment programs, all workbooks or interactive practice exercises, and prescriptive therapeutic tasks are written; therefore, they are reproducible and replicable by anyone who can read and write.

Interactive Practice Exercises: Workbooks

The number of such workbooks available on the market has increased steadily in the past decade and there is no sign that this trend will abate (L'Abate, 2004b, 2004c, 2004d). I used to proclaim that these interactive practice exercises were cost effective (clearly 10% of what a face-to-face talk session will cost), versatile (for use as adjuncts or as sole interventions in primary, secondary, and tertiary prevention face to face or at a distance), and are mass-produced, making them available to wider populations than talk therapies are (L'Abate, 1999, 2002). However, I had to recant my claims once we found that in our private practice, workbooks increased significantly the number of sessions compared to control groups that did not receive those homework assignments (L'Abate, L'Abate, & Maino, 2005). These results, however, were contradicted by results obtained by Goldstein (L'Abate & Goldstein, 2007) with decompensating personality disorders women in a charity Buenos Aires hospital.

The first meta-analysis of workbooks found a medium estimated effect size of .44 (Smyth & L'Abate, 2001). Additional effect size analyses were conducted on studies conducted in the former Family Study Center over 30 years ago (L'Abate, 2004d). However, because these studies were conducted by my students under my direction and supervision, even though effect sizes were largely positive, replications by researchers not associated with me are crucial to establish the cost-effectiveness of these workbooks.

Workbooks can be classified according to four major domains:

- Media of intervention—talking, writing, and nonverbal. Writing and nonverbal tasks, such as sharing hurts (explained below).
- Function of evaluative instruments—instruments (used here in a generic sense to include a wide variety of approaches) that are not only diagnostic and predictive, as in the past and most, if not all, approaches presented in this book, but also and especially prescriptive. Illustrations below introduce a new kind of prescriptive test, matching interventions with evaluation, provided interventions take place in writing, and especially through workbooks.
- Theoretical derivation—some workbooks are theory independent but often derived from clinical practice or lore instead. Some are theory related, in the sense that some tenuous connections between the theory and its evaluative approach exist. Finally, some are theory derived or model derived, as will be discussed.
- Functional versus dysfunctional participants—workbooks can be classified also according to whether they can be administered to non-clinical populations for lifelong learning or whether they can be administered to clinical and severely disordered populations.

One important advance produced by these workbooks consists of transforming into interactive practice exercises inherently inert, relatively passive, single- or multiple-score tests, DSM symptom lists, and factor analyses of behaviors. In view of their connections between evaluation and interventions, workbooks developed from single test scores, like the Beck Depression Inventory, among many others, as well as multiple-dimension scores, like the MMPI-2, among many others, are worthy examples of how psychological tests can be transformed easily into prescriptive, interactive practice exercises.

For instance, given any array of behavioral items from any test or factor analysis, it is a simple step to convert those items into a workbook by asking respondents first to define each item (using a dictionary if needed) and then to give two examples to describe the item. Once this task is completed, respondents are asked to rank order items according to how these items apply to themselves. This rank order determines how subsequent assignments will be administered. The item ranked first becomes the first assignment, the second item becomes the next assignment, until all items considered relevant by the respondent are completed, usually no more than six. This format allows therapists to administer nomothetically the same number of assignments in research. However, because of the individualized nature of rank orders, these assignments become also idiographic, allowing research to occur with individualized treatment.

As in the case of evaluating the validity of RCT models according to three types of evidence, workbooks can also be classified according to whether they are (1) *independent* from any theory or at least independent from RCT but derived from theories or models unrelated to, or completely different from, RCT models; (2) *related* to RCT by their face value in covering topics similar to those included in RCT models; and (3) completely *derived* from RCT models.

An example of a theory-independent but prevention-related prescriptive test is found in the Family Profile Form (Kochalka & L'Abate, 1997) transformed into an interactive practice exercise. This is a specific instance of how an evaluative instrument can be linked with specific interactive exercises. There are others, such as those derived from single- or multiple-score tests. Another example of a theory-independent workbook (among others) is the one developed from the MMPI. A prescriptive test is the RAQ which is coupled with a negotiation workbook. Examples of theory-related workbooks are so many that it is difficult to choose an exemplary one. Most workbooks derived from DSM diagnoses would fit into this classification (L'Abate, 2011d).

Thus, through the use of prescriptive tests such as those described here and specifically matching workbooks with evaluation, the considerable gap that exists between evaluation and treatment can be bridged. This gap will continue to exist as long as talk is used as the sole medium of intervention.

CONCLUDING NOTE

I am ending this chapter by paraphrasing what I concluded in my previous version years ago (L'Abate, 2004a): "Unless professional associations and managed care companies require pre–post intervention evaluations unquestioningly as a standard operating procedure (as veterinarians do with pets), the field of couple/family evaluation will remain in the hands of a small section of dedicated professionals, such as those represented in this book. The majority of couple and family professionals, I am sorry to say, could not care less because there are no consequences to current professional practices still based on the artistic subjectivity of the professional, rather than basing one's evaluation on intersubjective and objective approaches above and beyond the personal (and very likely incomplete) opinion of a professional, including myself—note my claims about cost-effectiveness of workbooks" (L'Abate, in press).

The prognosis for the field of couple/family evaluation is easy to state. As long as face-to-face talk remains the sole medium of intervention, the status quo will prevail. By relying on writing and new technologies as additional media of intervention at a distance from participants, drastic changes may occur, requiring changes that many couple and family therapists may be afraid to undertake—the devil we have is better than the devil we do not know. These changes will require that many couple and family professionals retrain to join the 21st century rather than remain stuck in the previous one. Given the choice of practicing as an artist (Entin, 2007) or as a scientist, I prefer to practice as a professional scientist (L'Abate, 2007a, in press).

REFERENCES

Cornum, R., Matthews, M. D., & Seligman, M. E. P. (2011). Comprehensive soldier fitness: Building resilience in a challenging institutional context. *American Psychologist, 66,* 4–9.

Cusinato, M., Aceti, G., & L'Abate, L. (1998). Condivisione del dolore and intimità di coppia [Sharing of hurts and couple intimacy]. *Famiglia, Interdisciplinarità, Ricerca: Rivista di Studi Familiari, 2,* 31–49.

Cusinato, M., & Colesso, W. (2008). Validation of the continuum of likeness in intimate relationships. In L. L'Abate (Ed.), *Toward a science of clinical psychology: Laboratory evaluations and interventions* (pp. 337–352). New York: Nova Science Publishers.

Cusinato, M., & L'Abate, L. (Eds.). (2011). *Advances in relational competence theory: With special attention to alexithymia.* New York: Nova Science Publishers.

De Giacomo, P., L'Abate, L., Pennebaker, J. M., & Rumbaugh, D. M. (2010). From A to D: Amplifications and applications of Pennebaker's analogic to digital model in health promotion, prevention, and psychotherapy. *Clinical Psychology & Psychotherapy, 17,* 355–362.

DeMaria, R. (2003). Psychoeducation and enrichment: Considerations for couples and family therapy. In T. L. Sexton, G. R. Weeks, & M. S. Robbins (Eds.), *Handbook of family therapy* (pp. 411–430). New York: Brunner/Routledge.

Entin, A. D. (2009). Psychologist as an artist: Artist as psychologist. *The Family Psychologist, 25,* 4–7.

Foà, U. G., & Foà, E. B. (1974). *Societal structures of the mind.* Springfield, IL: Charles C Thomas.

Guinote, A., & Vescio, T. K. (Eds.). (2010). *The social psychology of power.* New York: Guilford Press.

Harwood, T. M., & L'Abate, L. (2010). *Self-help in mental health: A critical evaluation.* New York: Springer-Science.

Hofferth, S. L., & Casper, L. M. (Eds.). (2007). *Handbook of measurement issues in family research.* Mahwah, NJ: Erlbaum.

Kazantzis, N., Deane, F. P., Ronan, K. R., & L'Abate, L. (Eds.). (2005). *Using homework assignments in cognitive behavior therapy.* New York; Routledge.

Kazantzis, N., & L'Abate, L. (Eds.). (2007). *Handbook of homework assignments in psychotherapy: Theory, research, and prevention.* New York: Springer-Science.

Kochalka, J., & L'Abate, L. (1997). Linking evaluation with structured enrichment: The Family Profile Form. *American Journal of Family Therapy, 25,* 361–374.

L'Abate, L. (1976). *Understanding and helping the individual in the family.* New York: Grune & Stratton.

L'Abate, L. (1986). *Systematic family therapy.* New York: Brunner/Mazel.

L'Abate, L. (1994). *A theory of personality development.* New York: Wiley.

L'Abate, L. (1997). *The self in the family: Toward a classification of personality, criminality, and psychopathology.* New York: Wiley.

L'Abate, L. (1999). Taking the bull by the horns: Beyond talk in psychological interventions. *Family Journal: Therapy and Counseling for Couples and Families, 7,* 206–220.

L'Abate, L. (2001). Hugging, holding, huddling, and cuddling (3HC): A task prescription in couples and family therapy. *Journal of Clinical Activities, Assignments, & Handouts in Psychotherapy Practice, 1,* 5–18.

L'Abate, L. (2002). *Beyond psychotherapy: Programmed writing and structured computer-assisted interventions.* Westport, CT: Ablex.

L'Abate, L. (2004a). Commentary: Current and future prospects. In L. Sperry (Ed.), *Assessment of couples and families: Contemporary and cutting-edge strategies* (pp. 247–269). New York: Brunner/Routledge.

L'Abate, L. (2004b). *A guide to self-help workbooks for clinicians and researchers.* Binghamton, NY: Haworth.

L'Abate, L. (2004c). The role of workbooks in the delivery of mental health services in prevention, psychotherapy and rehabilitation In L. L'Abate (Ed.), *Using workbooks in mental health: Resources in prevention, psychotherapy, and rehabilitation for clinicians and researchers* (pp. 3–64). Binghamton, NY: Haworth.

L'Abate, L. (2004d). Systematically written homework assignments: The case for homework based treatment. In L. L'Abate (Ed.), *Using workbooks in mental health: Resources in prevention, psychotherapy, and rehabilitation for clinicians and researchers* (pp. 65–102). Binghamton, NY: Haworth.

L'Abate, L. (2005). *Personality in intimate relationships: Socialization and psychopathology.* New York: Springer-Science.

L'Abate, L. (2006). Toward a relational theory for psychiatric classification. *American Journal of Family Therapy, 34,* 1–15.

L'Abate, L. (2007a). Decisions we family psychologists need to make now for the near or distance future: Whether we like them or not. *The Family Psychologist, 23,* 17–21.

L'Abate, L. (Ed.). (2007b). *Low-cost interventions to promote physical and mental health: Theory, research, and practice.* New York: Springer.

L'Abate, L. (2008a). Appendix. Proposed curriculum for a diploma or graduate degree in "Structured Online Mental Health Interventions." In L. L'Abate (Ed.), *Toward a science of clinical psychology: Laboratory evaluations and interventions* (pp. 385–392). New York: Nova Science Publishers.

L'Abate, L. (2008b). Applications of relational competence theory to prevention and psychotherapy. In K. Jordan (Ed.), *The Quick Theory Reference Guide: A resource for expert and novice mental health professionals* (pp. 475–492). New York: Nova Science Publishers.

L'Abate, L. (2008c). A proposal for including distance writing in couple therapy. *Journal of Couple & Relationship Therapy, 7,* 337–362.

L'Abate, L. (Ed.). (2008d). *Toward a science of clinical psychology: Laboratory evaluations and interventions.* New York: Nova Science Publishers.

L'Abate, L. (2008e). What is the laboratory method in clinical psychology? In L. L'Abate (Ed.), *Toward a science of clinical psychology: Laboratory evaluations and interventions* (pp. 1–34). New York: Nova Science Publishers.

L'Abate, L. (2008f). Working at a distance from participants: Writing and nonverbal media. In L. L'Abate (Ed.), *Toward a science of clinical psychology: Laboratory evaluations and interventions* (pp. 355–383). New York: Nova Science Publishers.

L'Abate, L. (2009a). Bibliography: Selected secondary references for models of relational competence theory. In L. L'Abate, P. De Giacomo, M. Capitelli, & S. Longo (Eds.), *Science, mind, and creativity: The Bari symposium* (pp. 177–196). New York: Nova Science Publishers.

L'Abate, L. (2009b). The Drama Triangle: An attempt to resurrect a neglected pathogenic model in family therapy theory and practice. *American Journal of Family Therapy, 37,* 1–11.

L'Abate, L. (2009c). A historical and systematic perspective about distance writing and wellness. In J. F. Evans (Ed.), *Wellness & writing connections: Writing for better physical, mental, and spiritual health* (pp. 53–74). Ennumclaw, WA: Idyll Arbor.

L'Abate, L. (2009d). In search of a relational theory. *American Psychologist, 64,* 776–788.

L'Abate, L. (2009e). A theory-derived structured interview for intimate relationships. *The Family Psychologist, 25,* 12–14.

L'Abate, L. (2011a). *Hurt feelings in intimate relationships: Theory, research, and applications.* New York: Cambridge University Press.

L'Abate, L. (Ed.). (2011b). *Paradigms in theory construction.* New York: Springer-Science.

L'Abate, L. (2011c). Psychotherapy consists of homework assignments: A radical iconoclastic conviction. In H. Rosenthal (Ed.), *Favorite counseling and therapy homework techniques: Classic anniversary edition* (pp. 219–229). New York: Routledge.

L'Abate, L. (2011d). *Sourcebook of interactive practice exercises in mental health.* New York: Springer-Science.

L'Abate, L. (in press). *Clinical psychology and psychotherapy as a science.* New York: Springer-Science.

L'Abate, L., & Cusinato, M. (1994). A spiral model of intimacy. In S. M. Johnson & L. S. Greenberg (Eds.), *The heart of the matter: Perspectives on emotion in marital therapy* (pp. 108–123). New York: Brunner/Mazel.

L'Abate, L., & Cusinato, M. (2007). Linking theory with practice: Theory-derived interventions in prevention and psychotherapy. *The Family Journal: Counseling and Therapy with Couples and Families, 15,* 318–327.

L'Abate, L., Cusinato, M., Maino, E., Colesso, W., & Scilletta, C. (2010). *Relational competence theory: Research and mental health applications.* New York: Springer-Science.

L'Abate, L., & De Giacomo, P. (2003). *Improving intimate relationships: Integration of theoretical models with preventions and psychotherapy applications.* Westport, CT: Praeger.

L'Abate, L., & Goldstein, J. (2007). Workbooks for the promotion of mental health and life-long learning. In L. L'Abate (Ed.), *Low-cost approaches to promote physical and mental health* (pp. 285–302). New York: Springer-Science.

L'Abate, L., & Kaiser, D. A. (Eds.). (in press). *Handbook of technology in psychology, psychiatry, and neurology: Theory, research, and practice.* New York: Nova Science Publishers.

L'Abate, L., L'Abate, B. L., & Maino, E. (2005). A review of 25 years of part-time professional practice: Workbooks and length of psychotherapy. *American Journal of Family Therapy, 33,* 19–31.

L'Abate, L., & Sweeney, L. G. (Eds.). (2011). *Research on writing approaches in mental health*. Bingley, UK: Emerald Group Publishing.

L'Abate, L., van Eigen, A., & Rigamonti, S. (2011). A relational and cross-cultural perspective on non-violent externalizing personality disordered women. *American Journal of Family Therapy, 39,* 325–347.

L'Abate, L., & Weinstein, S. E. (1987). *Structured enrichment programs for couples and families*. New York: Brunner/Mazel.

L'Abate, L., & Young, L. (1987). *Casebook of structured enrichment programs for couples and families*. New York: Brunner/Mazel.

Liddle, H. A., Santisteban, S. A., Levant, R. F., & Bray, J. H. (Eds.). (2002). *Family psychology: Science-based interventions*. Washington, DC: American Psychological Association.

Lock, J., LeGrange, D., Agras, W. S., Bryson, S. W., & Jo, B. (2010). Randomized clinical trial comparing family-based treatment with adolescent-focused individual therapy for adolescents with anorexia nervosa. *Archives of General Psychiatry, 67,* 1025–1032.

Mesquita, B., Barrett, L. F., & Smith, E. R. (Eds.). (2010). *The mind in context*. New York: Guilford Press.

Peterson, C., Park, N., & Castro, C. A. (2011). Assessment for the U.S. Army comprehensive soldier fitness program: The global assessment tool. *American Psychologist, 66,* 10–18.

Pinsof, W. M., & Lebow, J. L. (Eds.). (2005). *Family psychology: The art of the science*. New York: Oxford University Press.

Seligman, M. E. P., & Fowler, R. D. (2011). Comprehensive soldier fitness and the future of psychology. *American Psychologist, 66,* 82–86.

Smyth, J. M. , & L'Abate, L. (2001). A meta-analytic evaluation of workbook effectiveness in physical and mental health. In L. L'Abate (Ed.), *Distance writing and computer-assisted interventions in psychiatry and mental heath* (pp. 77–90). Westport, CT: Ablex.

Stevens, F. E., & L'Abate, L. (1989). Validity and reliability of a theory-derived measure of intimacy. *American Journal of Family Therapy, 17,* 359–368.

Williams, L., Edwards, T. M., Patterson, J.-E., & Chamow, L. (2011). *Essential assessment skills for couple and family therapists*. New York: Guilford Press.

Index

71603745R00202

Made in the USA
San Bernardino, CA
16 March 2018